Interest in growth theory has reawakened since the middle of the 1980s, but it is some time since a comparative exercise has been carried out. This volume explores the catch-up and convergence evidence on European growth on a cross-sectional basis, armed not only with new theoretical ideas, but also with the empirical evidence since 1950 on which to draw. Individual chapters cover macroeconomic accounts, national accounts by industry, measures of fixed capital stocks, technology indicators, human capital, total factor productivity, and changes in trend rates of growth, and each assesses the pitfalls, benefits and implications of the methods used. The result is an authoritative quantitative account of the dimensions of European economic growth within an explicitly internationally comparative framework.

T0312112

**Quantitative aspects of
post-war European
economic growth**

Centre for Economic Policy Research

The Centre for Economic Policy Research is a network of over 300 Research Fellows, based primarily in European universities. The Centre coordinates its Fellows' research activities and communicates their results to the public and private sectors. CEPR is an entrepreneur, developing research initiatives with the producers, consumers and sponsors of research. Established in 1983, CEPR is a European economics research organization with uniquely wide-ranging scope and activities.

CEPR is a registered educational charity. Institutional (core) finance for the Centre is provided by major grants from the Economic and Social Research Council, under which an ESRC Resource Centre operates within CEPR; the Esmée Fairbairn Charitable Trust; the Bank of England; 18 other central banks and 42 companies. None of these organizations gives prior review to the Centre's publications, nor do they necessarily endorse the views expressed therein.

The Centre is pluralist and non-partisan, bringing economic research to bear on the analysis of medium- and long-run policy questions. CEPR research may include views on policy, but the Executive Committee of the Centre does not give prior review to its publications, and the Centre takes no institutional policy positions. The opinions expressed in this volume are those of the authors and not those of the Centre for Economic Policy Research.

Quantitative aspects of post-war European economic growth

Edited by

BART VAN ARK

and

NICHOLAS CRAFTS

 CAMBRIDGE
UNIVERSITY PRESS

CAMBRIDGE UNIVERSITY PRESS
Cambridge, New York, Melbourne, Madrid, Cape Town, Singapore, São Paulo

Cambridge University Press
The Edinburgh Building, Cambridge CB2 2RU, UK

Published in the United States of America by Cambridge University Press, New York

www.cambridge.org
Information on this title: www.cambridge.org/9780521496285

First published 1996
This digitally printed first paperback version 2006

A catalogue record for this publication is available from the British Library

Library of Congress Cataloguing in Publication data
Quantitative aspects of post-war European economic growth / edited by
Bart van Ark and Nicholas Crafts.
        p.   cm.
Includes index.
ISBN 0 521 49628 4 (hardback)
1. Europe – Economic conditions – 1945–
2. Europe – Economic policy.
3. Economic development.
I. Ark, Bart van.   II. Crafts, N. F. R.
HC240.Q36   1996   338.94′009′045–dc20   96–16149   CIP

ISBN-13 978-0-521-49628-5 hardback
ISBN-10 0-521-49628-4 hardback

ISBN-13 978-0-521-03293-3 paperback
ISBN-10 0-521-03293-8 paperback

Contents

Figures

Tables

Contributors

Javier Andrés *University of Valencia and Ministry of Finance, Madrid*
Bart van Ark *University of Groningen*
Stephen N. Broadberry *University of Warwick and CEPR*
Nicholas Crafts *London School of Economics and CEPR*
Rafael Doménech *University of Valencia and Ministry of Finance, Madrid*
Theo van de Klundert *Tilburg University*
Angus Maddison *University of Groningen*
Terence C. Mills *Loughborough University*
César Molinas *Ministry of Finance, Madrid*
Mary O'Mahony *NIESR, London*
Anton van Schaik *Tilburg University*
Bart Verspagen *Maastricht Economic Research Institute on Innovation and Technology*
Karin Wagner *Wissenschaftszentrum Berlin für Sozialforschung and Fachhochschule für Technik und Wirtschaft Berlin*

Preface

The work reported in this book is the outcome of a network of (mainly) European economists which operated during 1992/3 sponsored by the SPES programme of the European Commission, directed by Nicholas Crafts and Gianni Toniolo and administered by CEPR. The reawakening of economists' interest in growth since the mid-1980s has been one of the principal reasons for this project. At the same time it is now quite a while since the last exercise of a similar kind, the much used and respected collection edited by Boltho (*The European Economy: Growth and Crisis*, OUP, 1982).

Members of the network on European growth devoted a good deal of effort to exploring quantitative aspects of economic growth with a view to improving understanding of and facilitating access to the key raw materials of a database for studying post-war growth. In addition, the evidence on key topics such as convergence, investment in broad capital and trend growth was evaluated on a cross-sectional basis. This work is reported here and is accompanied by a complementary volume (Crafts and Toniolo, 1996) based on a series of case studies of post-war growth in individual counries written in such a way to give the reader a genuinely comparative picture.

The case studies volume also contains chapters on important aspects of the general experience of growth and an overview chapter which is intended to provide the context into which the country studies fit. This organization permitted the establishment of a common format for the country studies and facilitated exchange of ideas and mutual criticism of initial drafts with the result that the chapters are more comparable than would otherwise have been the case.

The authors in both volumes were able to revisit the topic of post-war growth armed not only with some new theoretical ideas but also with the experience of the 1980s on which to draw. Moreover, the analysis has been based not only on applied economics but also on economic history.

Thus, while the overall project was greatly informed by insights from growth theory, the approach in the country studies emphasizes the presentation of chronological and institutional detail. The case study approach and the adoption of a longer-run perspective than is normal for economists allow insights to be obtained which do not emerge from standard cross-section regressions based on the post-1960 period.

Bart van Ark and Nicholas Crafts   1 September 1996

1 Catch-up, convergence and the sources of post-war European growth: introduction and overview

BART VAN ARK and NICHOLAS CRAFTS

1 Introduction

Since the mid-1980s there has been a great resurgence of interest in growth economics. There are perhaps two main reasons for this. First, Americans and Europeans have become worried about growth slowing down and about catching up and eventual overtaking in productivity terms by Asian rivals. Second, new theoretical ideas have enriched earlier models, in particular, by endogenizing technical progress and by serious analysis of the roles of imperfect competition and multiple equilibria in growth outcomes.

In this new research the question that has attracted the most attention has been the convergence controversy (Romer, 1994, p. 4). Does the growth process tend to involve reductions in the gaps in income levels between leaders and followers and, if so, what does this imply for the structure of growth models? The chapters in this work all concern issues related to this debate and, in particular, explore aspects of the catch-up process in post-war European growth. At the same time, in pursuing these issues, these essays also shed a good deal of light on the part played by the accumulation of various kinds of capital in promoting differences in productivity performance.

The objective of the volume is to provide authoritative estimates of the dimensions of economic growth in Europe in an explicitly internationally comparative framework together with an evaluation of some of the competing hypotheses in the recent growth literature. As such, it complements and is complemented by a sister collection of studies of the experience of individual European countries (Crafts and Toniolo, 1996).

Historical data can often be frustrating to work with and are full of pitfalls for the unwary. In this area, moreover, theory has to some extent run ahead of measurement. Some key variables in the new growth theories can at present be measured, at best, very crudely and decisive

1

tests of competing hypotheses are generally not possible. This introduction reviews the important issues and seeks to provide appropriate warnings without adopting a defeatist attitude (Section 3).

The other main task of this introductory essay is briefly to establish the theoretical and historical context for the detailed analysis which is contained in the rest of the book (Section 2). In doing so, we have deliberately started at a fairly basic level with a view to making the remainder of the papers reasonably accessible to the non-expert.

2　Basic ideas and an initial view of the historical record

As is well known, the post-war period comprises an initial phase when growth by historical standards was very rapid followed by much slower, but still historically respectable, growth since the early 1970s. It is also widely recognized that especially during the so-called 'Golden Age' of growth there was a pronounced tendency within Western Europe for countries which initially had relatively low income and productivity levels to grow more rapidly. By the early 1990s nine countries were within ± 8% of the median whereas in 1950 only two were (see Table 1.1).

Abramovitz (1986) in a deservedly famous paper drew attention to the importance of the catching-up of the leaders by the followers in the post-1945 growth process in the OECD countries. Exactly how to interpret the apparent inverse correlation between initial income levels and subsequent growth performance is a key issue to which we shall return several times and which echoes throughout the book.

Crafts and Toniolo (1996) provide a lengthy overview of this catching-up episode which points to a number of special features of the 1950s and 1960s which were conducive to catching up. In this volume, the chapters by Broadberry (Chapter 8) and van de Klundert and van Schaik (Chapter 10) demonstrate in different ways that the long-run growth record underlies the much greater and more widespread importance of catching-up in the Golden Age than before or since. The catch-up phenomenon is to be found not only at the national but also at the regional level (Crafts, 1995).

At the same time the evidence also points to relative success and failure by different economies in the catching-up process and is perhaps a reminder of Abramovitz's (1986) warning that catch-up is not an automatic process but depends on 'social capability' for growth. Thus the growth regression in van de Klundert and van Schaik (Chapter 10), having normalized for the initial productivity gap and the investment rate, finds that in the early post-war period German growth was exceptionally rapid and British growth unusually slow. Similar exercises

Table 1.1 GDP per person in 1990 international dollars

		1950 (European rank)	1973 (European rank)	1950–73 growth % (European rank)
1.	Switzerland	8,939 (1)	17,953 (1)	3.1 (12)
2.	UK	6,847 (2)	11,992 (7)	2.4 (16)
3.	Sweden	6,738 (3)	13,494 (2)	3.1 (12)
4.	Denmark	6,683 (4)	13,416 (3)	3.1 (12)
5.	Netherlands	5,850 (5)	12,763 (6)	3.4 (10)
6.	Belgium	5,346 (6)	11,905 (8)	3.5 (9)
7.	France	5,221 (7)	12,940 (5)	4.0 (8)
8.	Norway	4,969 (8)	10,229 (12)	3.2 (11)
9.	W. Germany	4,281 (9)	13,152 (4)	5.0 (4)
10.	Finland	4,131 (10)	10,768 (10)	4.2 (7)
11.	Austria	3,731 (11)	11,308 (9)	4.9 (5)
12.	Ireland	3,518 (12)	7,023 (15)	3.1 (12)
13.	Italy	3,425 (13)	10,409 (11)	4.9 (5)
14.	Spain	2,397 (14)	8,739 (13)	5.8 (2)
15.	Portugal	2,132 (15)	7,568 (14)	5.6 (3)
16.	Greece	1,558 (16)	6,229 (16)	6.2 (1)
	Japan	1,873	11,017	8.0
	USA	9,573	16,607	2.4

		1973 (European rank)	1992 (European rank)	1973–92 growth % (European rank)
1.	Switzerland	17,953 (1)	21,036 (1)	0.9 (16)
2.	Sweden	13,494 (2)	16,927 (8)	1.2 (15)
3.	Denmark	13,416 (3)	18,293 (3)	1.7 (9)
4.	W. Germany	13,152 (4)	19,351 (2)	2.1 (5)
5.	France	12,940 (5)	17,959 (4)	1.7 (9)
6.	Netherlands	12,763 (6)	16,898 (9)	1.5 (12)
7.	UK	11,992 (7)	15,738 (11)	1.5 (12)
8.	Belgium	11,905 (8)	17,165 (6)	1.9 (7)
9.	Austria	11,308 (9)	17,160 (7)	2.2 (3)
10.	Finland	10,768 (10)	14,646 (12)	1.6 (11)
11.	Italy	10,409 (11)	16,229 (10)	2.4 (2)
12.	Norway	10,229 (12)	17,543 (5)	2.9 (1)
13.	Spain	8,739 (13)	12,500 (13)	1.9 (7)
14.	Portugal	7,568 (14)	11,130 (14)	2.1 (5)
15.	Ireland	7,023 (15)	10,711 (15)	2.2 (3)
16.	Greece	6,229 (16)	8,238 (16)	1.5 (12)
	Japan	11,017	19,425	2.5
	USA	16,607	21,558	1.1

Source: Maddison (1995).

in Dowrick and Nguyen (1989) and Crafts (1992) confirm this result which also emerges from the regional data analysed in Crafts (1995).

Models based on traditional neoclassical growth theory specified the proximate sources of economic growth in terms of the growth of capital and labour and exogenous technological change. In the long run, growth was independent of the investment rate because capital accumulation was assumed to be subject to diminishing returns and sustained growth of output per head depended on (unexplained) technical progress. In strict versions of the Solow model we would expect long-run convergence of income levels and growth rates across all countries, given that factors of production are mobile, technology is universal and there are constant returns to scale. In such a world catching up would be based on higher investment in countries characterized initially by relatively low capital to labour ratios and relatively high returns to capital.

Empirical investigation of long-run growth performance led to the development of growth accounting – considered in more detail below – which was based on a more eclectic view of growth. Nevertheless this could be construed as, in essence, a much more sophisticated version of the Solow model in which differences in technological knowledge or social capability between countries were allowed. The classic studies by Denison (1967) and Maddison (1987) are in this tradition, as is the chapter by Maddison on this volume (Chapter 2). Here catching up would come in part at least from reductions in the total factor productivity gap between leader and followers though it might not completely eliminate gaps in income levels.

In Chapter 2 of this volume Maddison provides estimates using a similar, slightly modified growth accounting approach compared to his earlier work, which incorporate the latest data revisions. A summary is shown here in Table 1.2. The picture which results is very similar to that in his earlier work. In the Golden Age the three fast-growing European countries had very rapid total factor productivity (TFP) growth and relatively little is attributed to accumulation of physical and human capital. In turn, the much slower-growing UK (like the USA) has a similar capital accumulation record but much less rapid TFP growth. Table 1.2 also shows that the European experience in this respect is different from the more rapidly growing Japan. Although TFP growth in Japan was quite large during the period 1950–73, most of the Japanese growth came from accumulation of human and physical capital. In his earlier work Maddison (1991) gave a detailed comparison between the pre-1950 period and the Golden Age in which once again the chief source of the acceleration in growth was the large rise in TFP growth after 1950.

In every case a reduction in TFP growth dominates the slowdown in

Table 1.2 Sources of economic growth, 1950–92 (annual average percentage point contribution to growth rate)

	France	West Germany	Netherlands	UK	Japan	USA
1950–73						
(1) GDP	5.02	5.99	4.74	2.96	9.25	3.91
(2) Labour inputs	0.01	0.32[a]	−0.05	−0.11	1.89[b]	0.81
(3) Human capital	0.36	0.19	0.43	0.13	0.52	0.48
(4) Non-residential capital[c]	1.59	2.20	1.50	1.64	3.06	1.05
(5) Augmented factor inputs (2 + 3 + 4)	1.96	2.71	1.88	1.66	5.47	2.34
(6) Total factor productivity (1 minus 5)	3.06	3.28	2.86	1.30	3.78	1.57
(7) Four other explanatory items[d]	1.34	1.64	1.80	0.59	3.01	0.33
(8) Explained growth (5 + 7)	3.30	4.35	3.68	2.25	8.48	2.67
(9) Unexplained growth (1 minus 8)	1.72	1.64	1.06	0.71	0.77	1.24
1973–92						
(1) GDP	2.26	2.30	2.14	1.59	3.76	2.39
(2) Labour inputs	−0.32	−0.27	−0.05	−0.40	0.32	0.86
(3) Human capital	0.69	0.12	0.57	0.42	0.46	0.43
(4) Non-residential capital[c]	1.26	0.93	0.82	0.93	1.97	0.90
(5) Augmented factor inputs (2 + 3 + 4)	1.63	0.78	1.34	0.95	2.75	2.19
(6) Total factor productivity (1 minus 5)	0.63	1.52	0.80	0.64	1.01	0.20
(7) Four other explanatory items[d]	0.65	0.70	0.50	0.31	0.79	−0.05
(8) Explained growth (5 + 7)	2.28	1.48	1.84	1.26	3.34	2.14
(9) Unexplained growth (1 minus 8)	−0.02	0.82	0.30	0.33	0.42	0.25

Notes: [a] Including adjustment for labour dishoarding of 0.32 percentage point.
[b] Including adjustment for labour dishoarding of 0.88 percentage point.
[c] Including adjustment for age effect and (in case of Germany and Japan for 1950–73) capacity reactivation.
[d] Foreign trade effect, catch-up effect, structural effect and economies of scale.
Source: Derived from Maddison, Chapter 2, Table 2.26.

growth after 1973 (although the reduced growth rates of capital and labour inputs also play a part, in particular in Japan) while the gap in both TFP growth and GDP growth between the UK and the other European countries narrows markedly.

As in his earlier work, Maddison (see Chapter 2, Table 2.26) seeks to account for the observed change in GDP growth in great detail. He decomposes GDP growth along the lines of the preceding discussion, assessing the contribution of augmented factor inputs, but on top of that foreign trade, scale effects and structural change effects.

The historical literature provides several reasons why catching up of this kind may have been particularly strong in early post-war Europe and so much less important since the 1960s. These include an emphasis on the continuing importance of post-war reconstruction in the 1950s (Dumke, 1990), the suggestion that technology transfer became easier than previously (Nelson and Wright, 1992), the hypothesis that interest group obstacles to progress were reduced by war (Olson, 1982) and the possible beneficial impact of trade liberalization which would be consistent with the econometric results in Ben-David (1993) and Helliwell (1992). It would also appear that the pace of trade liberalization fell while the sclerotic tendencies feared by Olson reasserted themselves during the 1970s and 1980s. Also the European technology gap had been much reduced and together these factors may explain a good part of the growth slowdown.

In trying to explain where TFP growth comes from, recent growth economics has been concerned to construct models in which most or all 'technical progress' is endogenous and results from investment decisions which are themselves based on optimizing behaviour. Investment is in broad capital, i.e., it includes human as well as physical capital and perhaps considers both investment in knowledge as well as skills. In some models externalities to investment, notably through learning effects, are important. Good overviews are available in Sala-i-Martin (1990) and (less technical) in van de Klundert and Smulders (1992).

In these new growth models diminishing returns to (broad) capital are much less severe than in the traditional Solow model. This implies at a minimum that convergence to the steady state will be much slower and that increases in investment will have a longer-lasting impact on the growth rate. Also the assumptions on which traditional growth accounting relies are potentially undermined – for example, the capital income share of national income may no longer be an appropriate weight for capital in computing the rate of growth of total factor inputs. More fundamental is the possibility that accumulation of the reproducible factors of production embraced in broad capital may not be subject to diminishing returns in which case there is endogenous growth with no prediction of convergence of income levels or growth rates. Rebelo (1991) is a seminal article in this genre while Mankiw, Romer and Weil's influential (1992) model is of the Augmented-Solow variety in which there is human as well as physical capital but with diminishing returns to broad capital.

In models where growth is not endogenous, catching up can be expected and, *ceteris paribus*, growth will be faster the lower is the initial income level. In general, however, the world will be one of conditional convergence where the steady-state level of income may vary if technology is not completely transferable or if institutions and accumulation strategies differ. In models where growth is endogenous there may still be catching-up effects, for example, through the diffusion of technology to lower-investing follower countries, although such cases would not involve ultimate convergence of income levels.

Faced with a much wider range of growth models, with the availability of larger databases and with more sophisticated econometrics, many recent studies of the sources of growth have relied much more on estimation and less on the meticulous but *a priori* assumption approach of the traditional growth accounts. A good overview and exploration of the robustness of results obtained from investigation of the international cross-sectional experience since 1960 can be found in Levine and Renelt (1992). This is used by Crafts and Toniolo (1996) to explore the contribution which the new empirical growth economics can make to the analysis of speeding up and slowing down in European growth. A similar exercise could be performed using the results in Andrés *et al.* (Chapter 9).

Table 1.3 gives a flavour of the results which this new empirical work has produced. Here the regression estimated by Levine and Renelt (1992) to 'explain' post-war growth is used to estimate average European growth in different periods. The underlying equation for the growth of real GDP per head finds a positive relation with investment and education variables and a negative relationship with initial income per head and the share of government consumption in GDP. Thus it too can be thought of as in the conditional convergence tradition.

Traditional growth accounting, as in Maddison (1991) and in this volume, attributes the move to the rapid growth of the Golden Age and the subsequent slowdown predominantly to changes in TFP growth stemming from a variety of sources 'explained' and 'unexplained'. Table 1.3 tells the story a different way. It suggests that investment in broad capital was largely responsible for the acceleration in growth during the Golden Age while the post-1973 slowdown comes from the erosion of catch-up possibilities and the swelling of government

Table 1.3   Accounting for changes in European output head growth using a Levine–Renelt approach (percentage per year)

	1923–38	1950–73	1973–89
Constant	2.01	2.01	2.01
Initial GDP/head	−2.43	−2.49	−3.55
Investment/GDP	1.42	2.22	2.06
Secondary enrolment	0.16	0.68	0.79
Primary enrolment	1.90	1.99	1.79
Government consumption/GDP	−0.62	−0.87	−1.27
Estimated	2.44	3.54	1.83
Actual	2.12	3.84	2.14

Notes: Estimates are for the unweighted average of European countries in Maddison (1991), excluding Belgium and Switzerland.

Sources: The estimates are derived using equation (ii) in Levine and Renelt (1992) with population growth and irrelevant dummies ignored. The initial income variable was expressed as a percentage of the US level in each year and was then multiplied by 1960 US income per person. Basic sources of GDP, GDP per head, population and investment in non-residential capital stock from Maddison (1991, 1995) and OECD *Economic Outlook*, supplemented for inter-war investment by Maddison (1992) and for inter-war government consumption expenditure by den Bakker *et al.* (1990), Feinstein (1972), Hansen (1974), Hjerrpe (1989), Krantz and Nilsson (1975), Rossi *et al.* (1992), Sommariva and Tullio (1986) and Villa (1993). Primary and secondary enrolment from Mitchell (1992).

consumption. Table 1.3 would imply a larger role for the exhaustion of catch-up in the recent past than was assumed by Maddison; the difference between 1950–73 and 1973–89 in row 2 of the table of 1.06% per year compares with an average change in the catch-up effect for Maddison's four European countries of 0.13% (Chapter 2, Table 2.26).

These results must be regarded as at best illustrative of what new growth economics may eventually say about post-war European growth and this method of accounting for the sources of growth is also highly problematic. For example, results can be quite sensitive to the precise specification of the underlying regression equation and variables are often measured as crude proxies. It is noticeable that the equation explains the slowdown of European growth after 1973 pretty well but is less successful in anticipating the difference between the inter-war period and the Golden Age.

This is perhaps not surprising for two different reasons. First, catching up may be highly contingent on circumstances which are in any case not readily captured in regression equations of this kind, which can be thought of as raising TFP growth and which do not arise from investment in broad capital, though they do stem from enhanced social capability. This seems to be suggested in Abramovitz (1986). Second, and perhaps more important for present purposes, in the new growth economics theory has run a good way ahead of measurement. This applies in particular to human capital and social capability.

Human capital stock is typically proxied by measures of the education of the labour force and investment in human capital by school enrolment ratios. This leaves out of account both the quality/intensity of schooling and, crucially, on-the-job training. Better estimates are seriously needed given the great emphasis placed on human capital in recent growth models. Social capability is at best measured by measures which distinguish between the first and third world rather than reflecting the subtleties of institutional differences which underlie conditional convergence within the OECD. For example, there appear to be major differences in the post-war period between the UK and West Germany in capital markets, industrial relations and vocational training systems which contribute to differential success in catching up but are not reflected in standard regression studies (Bean and Crafts, 1996).

3   Key concepts and measurement issues

The empirical and quantitative study of economic growth has made great advances during the past century. The greater complexity of society and the desire of policy-makers and interest groups to influence some of the basic parameters in the economy increased the need for statistical indicators to monitor economic performance on a more systematic basis than before. In particular during the period following World War II the amount of economic statistics increased rapidly and their quality improved significantly.

All the papers in this volume have made a very extensive use of official statistics (either in an adjusted form or not) to analyse the topics mentioned above in a European context for the post-World War II period. Some of the chapters in this book (i.e. Chapters 6, 8, 10 and 11) go back to the period before the war, for which one had to rely to a larger extent on estimates provided by individual scholars.

Below we briefly review some of the key concepts and measurement issues which are raised in one or more of the contributions to this volume.

3.1   National accounts of sectoral accounts

The development of comprehensive national accounts, which cover output, expenditure and income simultaneously in a single accounting system, has been a major improvement over the scattered availability of primary statistics to monitor economic growth performance across countries in previous times.

Although the concept of national accounting goes back as far as the seventeenth century, the quality of national accounts and the number of countries they cover improved rapidly after World War II. Following the introduction of the first System of National Accounts (SNA) in 1952, the international comparability of the accounts greatly improved. At present the fourth revision of SNA (1993) is in the process of implementation by the vast majority of countries in the world. In particular OECD has done much in the past decades to improve the comparability of the accounts across its member states, and Eurostat helped to enforce the execution of common guidelines in constructing the national accounts across European Union countries.

Despite these major steps towards standardization of national accounts, one cannot yet speak of identical computation methods, not even among West European countries. The accounts are often vested in a long tradition of national statistical practices, which have determined the nature and organization of collecting primary statistics, such as production censuses, tax records or expenditure surveys, on which the national accounts are based. Various institutional constraints, such as national laws concerning the collection of these primary statistics, make it difficult to change such historically grown practices overnight.

The chapter by Maddison on national accounts (Chapter 2) identifies some of the problem areas one still faces in using national accounts for international comparisons. The most important ones are differences in weighting procedures and adjustments for inadequate coverage of unregistered economic activity. Van Ark's chapter (Chapter 3) on sectoral accounts points to differences in industrial classification schemes and statistical units (i.e. enterprises versus establishments) which affect the allocation of secondary activities to particular sectors.

However, the differences in growth rates for the countries investigated in this volume due to such inconsistencies should not be exaggerated. For the countries under consideration, Maddison suggests allowing a margin of uncertainty of around 0.2% when making comparisons of annual compound growth rates of real GDP across OECD countries since 1950.

As far as estimates of total GDP are concerned, one can rely nowadays on OECD (previously OEEC) *National Accounts Statistics* back to 1960 and in some cases even further back. For sectoral output OECD did not undertake substantive backward extrapolations of successive revisions, so that van Ark's chapter relies to a larger extent on national sources. Some national statistical offices have undertaken backward reconstruction of the national accounts themselves. However, the contribution of economists and economic historians is also indispensable to obtain an adequate picture of the quantitative growth record of these countries, in particular for the period before 1960. Although it is unlikely that further revisions will change the macro-picture for the post-war period very substantially, it could have bigger consequences for the sectoral growth rates, and in particular for the estimates of labour input.

Parallel to the development of national accounts within each country, and the improved comparability of the growth rates derived from it across countries, the comparability of levels of GDP and its subcategories has also been greatly improved. This is mainly thanks to the pioneering work of OEEC during the 1950s (Gilbert and Kravis, 1954; Gilbert and associates, 1958) and the work of Kravis and his associates who started the International Comparison Project (ICP) in the early 1970s (see, for example, Kravis, Heston and Summers, 1982). Purchasing power parities, which represent the number of currency units required to buy goods equivalent to what can be bought with, say, one US dollar, are now widely used to convert GDP to a common currency. PPPs are highly preferable as a conversion factor over exchange rates as the latter have become increasingly vulnerable to capital movements and currency trade. Moreover, in any case exchange rates do not represent the relative price levels of non-traded goods and services.

The chapter by Maddison in this volume provides an assessment of the reliability and range of purchasing power parities from successive ICP rounds. It appears that by merging national growth rates of GDP, with level estimates based on PPPs from various ICP rounds, a range of GDP per capita estimates emerges which differ up to 16% for the same years for countries such as Italy and the UK (see Table 2.3). When using, say, 1990 GDP levels in conjunction with growth rates to obtain level estimates, the errors in the comparisons could be as big as 25% for 1950.

It is clear from this brief discussion that the uncertainty about the comparative levels of GDP is still much bigger than that of the comparative growth rates. Nevertheless the two types of estimates are widely used in particular to test catch-up and convergence hypotheses. In this respect many scholars have made use of the Penn World Tables (see, for example, Summers and Heston (1988, 1991)) which covers a wider range of individual countries than Maddison does here. Although Summers and Heston have been careful in notifying readers of the degree of reliability of their estimates, many users have often not taken too much care of this.

For long-term analysis, one way to check the margin of error of historical estimates of GDP across countries is to carry out benchmark comparisons of income and output for earlier years. Recent work in this field (reported by van Ark in Chapter 3, and by Broadberry in Chapter 8) shows a great potential for new evidence in this field (see also below).

3.2   Growth accounting

For the study of comparative economic performance, figures on GDP are of course not sufficient. Following production theory, the fundamental questions for growth accountants are how much and what resources are needed to obtain a certain level of production and, even more important, how relative factor proportions change in the process of growth.

The earliest growth accounts only took into consideration the physical quantities of the two main factors of production, i.e. labour input and capital input. Usually the number of employees was taken to measure labour input, though estimates of total hours worked would have been more precise concerning the volume of labour input. Capital was mostly estimated as the stock of fixed assets either including or excluding residential buildings. After accounting for the contribution of these two factor inputs, weighted at the share of factor income in total income, the residual was often crudely interpreted as technological progress.

In the more sophisticated growth accounts, which originated from the pioneering work in this field in particular by Denison (1962), and are represented in this volume by Chapter 2 by Maddison, crude factor inputs have been augmented to account for differences in quality across countries. The most current measures which have been used to augment labour input are years of formal education and the sex–age mix of the labour force. Augmentation of physical capital input is a much more complicated and fundamental matter, and most growth accountants have proceeded with no, or virtually no, augmentation of capital for quality changes.

The chapters by van Ark (Chapter 3) and O'Mahony (Chapter 4), which both present estimates of the joint factor productivity performance at sectoral level, show that even for manufacturing where capital accounts for a relatively large share of factor inputs, the contribution of the crude physical stock to real output growth has been important but not exclusive. Furthermore, at present differences in physical capital stock explain much less of the remaining productivity gaps between advanced countries (or more specifically between European countries and the USA) compared to be beginning of the post-war period.

Following the specifications of the Solow model, growth accountants have usually assumed that the weights for each of the factor inputs equalled factor income shares. The chapters by Maddison (Chapter2), van Ark (Chapter 3) and O'Mahony (Chapter 4) all use coefficients for capital and labour which represent value added shares. Arguments from the new growth theory suggest that as the social return from capital accumulation exceeds that of its marginal product, capital's contribution will be understated by this method. However, recent econometric tests on the coefficients of these factors suggest that, when capital is augmented to include elements of human capital, the traditional Solow model performs relatively well (Mankiw *et al.*, 1992; Oulton and O'Mahony, 1994).

In our view, the real novelty of the new growth theory lies in directing the attention to more meso- and micro-oriented approaches to growth (as reflected in the chapters by Broadberry, O'Mahony and van Ark) which complement the more familiar macro-approach (as represented in the chapters by Maddison, Andrés *et al.* and van de Klundert and van Schaik), and in its emphasis on the need to measure the effects of technology spillovers on productivity growth. In relation to the latter, the chapter by Verspagen on technology indicators suggests that a proper measurement of technological changes may help to account for a significant part of the residual found by the traditional growth accountants.

Notwithstanding the achievements in tracing the origins of growth over the past decades, one major limitation of growth accounts remains that it does not capture the effects of the 'social capability' of a country to grow. The latter is a fairly vague and broad concept, which partly refers to personal attributes, but also to competitiveness, the degree of foreign investment and the infrastructure of political and economic institutions. Such factors are difficult to measure, let alone to put together in a weighted system of growth accounts.

A second limitation of the growth accounting approach is related to its failure to capture the reasons for growth and stagnation of the country (or countries) at the technology frontier. In his paper, Maddison most clearly emphasizes the 'mystery' of the strong fall in the contribution of the residual to GDP growth in the USA. Apparently growth accounts tell us more about how countries catch up with the leader than how they win or lose the leadership position itself.

3.3   *Broad capital and its contribution to growth*

One of the most hotly debated and controversial issues in the tradition of production theory has been the conceptualization of the contribution of capital to growth. This has also left its traces on the measurement of capital in empirical growth studies.

One line of debate concerned the actual measure of physical capital. In the past many scholars used investment flows as a proxy for capital for lack of anything better. Two chapters in this volume (Chapter 2 by Maddison and Chapter 4 by O'Mahony) discuss the estimation methods of physical capital stock. Most OECD countries nowadays have detailed stock estimates of their physical assets for at least several decades, usually estimated on the basis of the perpetual inventory method. This is a procedure by which investments are cumulated while assuming service lives, depreciation and retirement patterns and premature destruction due to wars. In practice there are large differences between the assumptions utilized in otherwise fairly similar countries, in particular concerning the lives of the assets. Although the latter may differ across countries to some extent because of a different composition of the stock or a different pace of technological change, it is most doubtful that the average life of equipment in, for example, the UK was 25 years compared to 14 years in Germany. Both Maddison and O'Mahony therefore standardized their capital stock estimates for asset lives and retirement patterns, at an aggregate and sectoral level respectively.

A more fundamental issue concerns the scope of the capital concept. Maddison and O'Mahony both use fixed non-residential gross capital stock as their point of departure, but others have preferred to include residential capital (including Maddison elsewhere) or even consumer durables (see, for example, Jorgenson (1990)). Of course the inclusion of these assets in the physical capital stock increases the effect of capital on growth.

More important from the perspective of the recent thinking about growth is the extension of capital from tangible to intangible assets, and in particular the introduction of human capital. Growth accountants have continued to use proxy measures of human capital, such as the average years of schooling of the labour force or secondary enrolment rates. However, the former adjusts insufficiently for the 'content' of the education, whereas the latter is an input rather than an output measure of human capital formation.

A range of studies by the National Institute of Economic and Social Research (NIESR) has shown the importance of comparing levels of educational attainment across countries, and more specifically, levels of vocational qualifications (for example, Daly *et al.* (1985) and Mason *et al.* (1994)). The chapter by Broadberry and Wagner (Chapter 6) provides a careful comparison of the nature of skills applied in the manufacturing production of Germany, the UK and the USA over the past century. It emphasizes the limited substitutability between a production strategy as applied in the USA geared towards standardized mass production using large portions of physical capital and managerial capabilities, and a strategy focused on craft production with a greater emphasis on shopfloor skills, as applied in Britain (before World War II) and Germany.

The second element of intangible capital, and which features most prominently in the most recent versions of new growth models (see, Romer, 1990), concerns knowledge which cannot be directly attributed to education. At present, 'knowledge capital' is still measured in an imperfect manner, either by input measures such as the expenditure on research and development, or by output measures such as patents, of which the actual 'technology content' is very difficult to determine, owing to different patenting practices over time and across countries.

Nevertheless the chapter by Verspagen (Chapter 5) applies a range of time-series and cross-country models to test the relation between the increase in knowledge capital (such as the stock of R&D or patents) and real GDP, which on the whole points towards a fairly strong relation. Verspagen also experimented with growth accounting techniques, using coefficients for R&D or patents derived from regression analysis, showing much larger effects of R&D on labour productivity growth in Germany and France than in the UK. This result coincides with the observation by Broadberry and Wagner that the 'mission-oriented' R&D strategy of the UK has been less successful than the 'diffusion-oriented' strategy of Germany.

We may conclude that the advances made in broadening the concept of capital and improving its measurement suggest a larger role for capital than has been assumed in the past on the basis of physical capital stock estimates. However, even after a further perfection of the estimates, which is necessary in the case of both education and knowledge capital, there will still be substantial scope for a residual representing catch-up and convergence factors due to more efficient use of factor inputs and institutions. What is perhaps more important is that in recent decades, i.e. since 1973, growth slowed down substantially more than the new capital measures would suggest, which again makes us look for other factors explaining the slowdown.

3.4 Sectoral productivity performance

Much of the growth analysis presented in this volume refers to productivity measures rather than GDP or per capita income. Productivity has a more direct link to the production function framework and to the concept of technological progress than GDP. Furthermore it makes it possible to disaggregate productivity measures to the sectoral or industry level.

Output per unit of labour input is the simplest and most straightforward productivity concept, and it involves less empirical difficulties to calculate than, for example, capital or total factor productivity. Labour productivity is particularly useful for long-term growth studies. In the short run, productivity measures can be volatile, in particular at a disaggregated level, as they are strongly affected by changes in capacity utilization and shifts in product composition due to competitive pressures. In the long run, labour productivity is directly related to income per head of the population, after adjusting the former measure for differences in labour participation rates and the number of hours each person works.

A major difficulty in international comparisons concerns the estimation of comparative levels of productivity. Although the ICP purchasing power parities can be used for converting total GDP to a common currency, these PPPs are expenditure PPPs and are therefore not the most appropriate ones for comparisons of output and productivity by industry. In Chapter 3, van Ark analyses the development of the industry of origin approach which originated from the work by Rostas (1948) and Paige and Bombach (1959), and which has recently been revived by a range of studies, among which those of the International Comparisons of Output and Productivity (ICOP) project at the University of Groningen.

The coverage of countries as well as sectors by the industry of origin approach is still relatively small. These estimates are particularly difficult for so-called 'comparison resistant' service industries. However, even for commodity sectors, such as agriculture and industry, there are fundamental problems. Most important among these are the theoretical need for separate PPPs for output and for intermediate inputs in order to obtain comparable estimates of output across countries.

Van Ark (Chapter 3) provides estimates of comparative labour productivity and joint factor productivity for agriculture, manufacturing and the residual sector of the economy for France, Germany, The Netherlands and the UK vis-à-vis the USA, which has been the world's productivity leader, for the post-World War II period. It appears that comparative productivity performance differs widely between sectors. Van Ark also shows that, on the whole, the commodity sectors (i.e. agriculture and manufacturing) of the European countries have performed less well compared to the USA than the residual sectors of the economy, which consisted mainly of services. However, even in the latter case the USA has mostly remained the productivity leader, although a significant catch-up can also be observed for these sectors.

In Chapter 8 Broadberry discusses comparative productivity performance for twelve countries for manufacturing and the total economy covering most of this century. In some cases Broadberry provides fresh estimates of historical benchmark comparisons of productivity across countries, for example between the UK and the USA for 1907 and between Germany and the UK for 1935–37, which in combination with some existing historical estimates provide an important tool to check the plausibility of estimates based on backward extrapolations of contemporary relative output estimates over long periods of time. As, at present, a large number of the estimates still rely on comparisons of rather small product samples for earlier benchmarks (in particular, based on Rostas (1948)), or on backward extrapolations of expenditure PPP-based estimates of sectoral productivity, further research on historical benchmark estimates should be one of the important research priorities in the reconstruction of the growth of Europe.

Chapter 7 by van Ark focuses on the comparative productivity performance in manufacturing of two East European nations, i.e. former Czechoslovakia and former East Germany, and two South European countries, Portugal and Spain. Van Ark's estimates show a significantly lower productivity performance of the two East European countries than has been suggested in earlier studies. His lower estimates are mainly due to the fact that these estimates are adjusted from a gross output basis to a value added basis. The latter allows for a significant amount of inefficient use of intermediate inputs in the production process of these countries.

The comparison with Spain and Portugal suggests that the two South European countries, but in particular Spain, have been much more successful than the East European countries in improving their productivity performance relative to Northwest Europe. The greater scope for diffusion of technology, international trade and the convergence of institutional arrangements has created a greater realization of the catch-up potential for follower countries in the southern periphery of Europe than in the eastern periphery.

3.5 Convergence

In the pure Solow or Augmented-Solow models of growth we would expect unconditional convergence, i.e., that countries actually move towards the same income and productivity levels in the steady state. In less strict versions of these models the notion would be one of conditional convergence where the steady state might differ, for example, on grounds of 'social capability'. As an unconditional convergence process takes place, we would expect in the cross-section of countries to observe both a negative relationship between the initial level of income per head and the subsequent rate of growth of income per head and also a reduction in the coefficient of variation of per capita income which would eventually tend to zero. Barro and Sala-i-Martin (1991) called these types of convergence β- and σ-convergence respectively. These tendencies would also be expected with conditional convergence but here the eventual steady-state levels of income will not be completely equalized.

In models which exhibit endogenous growth based on non-diminishing returns to reproducible factors of production and where long-run labour productivity growth does not depend on exogenous technical change, such as that of Rebelo (1991), there is no prediction of conditional convergence, and growth rates depend simply on the rate of accumulation of (broad) capital. Econometric investigation of the relationship between initial income levels and growth might then be thought to be a way of testing the hypothesis of endogenous growth and of inferring both the extent of diminishing returns and the likelihood of reductions in the dispersion of income levels.

An important paper by Durlauf and Johnson (1992) showed that such a view is too simplistic. A negative relationship between initial income level and growth (i) is at best necessary for σ-convergence not sufficient, (ii) can be spuriously induced by the control variables in a multiple equilibrium case and (iii) may simply be reflecting technological catching-up effects in a world where underlying growth is actually endogenous. In other words evidence of catch-up is not decisive evidence of eventual convergence.

Investigations of the figures for advanced countries constructed by Maddison (1991) have found both β- and σ-convergence during the Golden Age period, but such findings do not seem to apply to the whole period from 1870 covered by the data, as Broadberry (Chapter 8) notes. Against this background, several of the papers in this volume explore in detail the implications of post-1950 β-convergence which is, of course, reflected in Table 1.1.

Mankiw *et al.* (1992) suggested that the Augmented-Solow model, based on a well-behaved production function using both human and physical capital and exhibiting conditional convergence, provided a good approximation to recent experience of growth and, allowing for differences in savings rates and demographic pressures, a good explanation for international differences in income levels. In Chapter 9 of this volume this claim is scrutinized in great detail by Andrés, Doménech and Molinas with reference to the OECD countries during the period 1960–90. Their dataset includes all of Western Europe and they disaggregate by time period and country grouping. Andrés *et al.* find a good deal of support for the claims of Mankiw *et al.* and find that the main results are very robust. Nevertheless, they argue that the convergence process differs over time and between countries, convergence being more rapid among the rich OECD countries and during relatively fast growth periods.

In contrast to this Augmented-Solow-type analysis, in Chapter 10 van de Klundert and van Schaik consider the value of an endogenous growth model driven by physical investment of the type proposed by Scott (1989), which allows for catch-up in special circumstances only, and examine the evidence for advanced countries from 1870 to 1989. Their key findings are that catch-up is only found in 1950–73 but not in other periods and that growth is significantly related to the investment rate but the estimated equations usually have an insignificant constant. Their conclusions are that the Scott model is not refuted and that conditional convergence should not be taken to be a general phenomenon, even among the rich.

Two important points arise from van de Klundert and van Schaik's results. First, the inverse relationship between initial income level and subsequent growth found by econometric investigations of datasets from the post-war period may reflect the special circumstances of that period and should not be taken to apply universally. Second, even in a world of endogenous growth, there may be episodes of catching up, perhaps following technology shocks. Their estimates suggest the importance of the distinctions made by Durlauf and Johnson (1992).

Nevertheless, the results are not conclusive. In some regressions the constant is significant, indicating a possible exogenous component in growth. Also the suggestion of endogenous growth based on physical investment is inconsistent with evidence that suggests that profit's share of national income *is* a good approximation of the growth of capital to output growth (Oulton and O'Mahony, 1994). This would imply that there are diminishing returns to physical investment rather than constant returns as required by endogenous growth.

The results obtained by Verspagen (Chapter 5) throw further light on the catching-up experience in post-war Europe. His Figure 5.2, derived from his econometric estimates of the impact of patenting on growth, suggests that σ-convergence (and thus by implication β-convergence) was considerably accentuated by patenting, particularly during the 1960s. Verspagen concludes that there were 'catching up effects related to genuine convergence in technological competences'. He also concludes, however, that over the period 1963–88, in terms of R&D spending and technological specialization, relatively backward countries do not seem to converge towards the leaders.

This view stresses the role of reduction of technology gaps in post-war European catch-up growth while also recognizing that differing technological capabilities remain, i.e., the technology assumptions underlying the pure Solow or Augmented-Solow models are rejected. These results are in many ways similar to those obtained by Helliwell (1992) whose econometric study found strong convergence effects in technical progress in the OECD during 1963–89. Helliwell also found evidence that these were intensified by increasing openness to international trade, a point which is echoed in a number of the country studies in Crafts and Toniolo (1996).

Broadberry (Chapter 8) considers convergence in productivity in the long run both for the whole economy and for the manufacturing sector. A comparison of his Tables 8.3 and 8.4 is instructive. These tables show that levels and trends of productivity have often differed greatly between manufacturing and the whole economy and that in manufacturing it is likely that convergence should be seen as local rather than global. The data support the warning by Durlauf and Johnson (1992) that post-war catch-up growth in the OECD should not be taken as a full endorsement of the underlying assumptions of the Augmented-Solow model.

Broadberry also suggests that there is a danger of exaggerating the role of technology transfer in manufacturing in conditional convergence. In effect, he suggests that convergence in overall productivity levels also depended substantially on structural change and/or reduced productivity gaps in non-manufacturing. Details of these aspects of convergence are reviewed by van Ark (Chapter 3), whose conventional shift-share analysis finds, however, only a small role for structural change. This is a topic which deserves more research.

Broadberry's discussion of convergence in manufacturing centres on a view of persistent differences in investment and production strategies, notably that Europe was much less committed to mass production than North America even after World War II. In Chapter 6 the implications for human capital formation are worked out by Broadberry and Wagner. Their chief finding is a continuing emphasis on accumulating craft skills in Europe contrasting with a much greater American reliance on highly qualified management.

Overall, what do these studies teach us about convergence in post-war European growth? First, catching-up seems to be a strong feature of the Golden Age during which there are signs of apparent β- and σ-convergence. Second, in other periods tendencies to either β- and σ-convergence among European countries are at best weak. Third, catch-up in the Golden Age seems to involve reductions in, but not complete elimination of, technology gaps; this is especially true of the European periphery. Fourth, the experience of catch-up in post-war Europe is not decisive evidence in favour of the Augmented-Solow model or in favour of unconditional convergence.

3.6 Trend growth rates

The notion of a Golden Age followed by an epoch of much slower growth is obviously plausible but deserves to be given a sound econometric basis. Explicit comparison of trend growth rates in different periods can also say something about the role of reconstruction in early post-war growth which was highlighted in a famous contribution by Janossy (1969) who thought that the 'end of the economic miracle' in Europe would be a return to the previous trend growth path. In statistical terms the view of the long run held in various ways by, for example, Abramovitz, Janossy and Maddison is that the growth of productivity followed a segmented trend.

The appropriate procedure for estimating trend growth rates involves testing for the presence of a unit root, i.e., to distinguish between (trend stationary) series where the trend in terms of the log of output can be written as

$$y_t = \alpha + \gamma t + u_t \tag{1}$$

and those where the trend is of the type

$$y_t = y_{t-1} + \mu + e_t \tag{2}$$

In (2) note that $(y_t - y_{t-1})$ is a constant and the series is thus said to contain a unit root – in equation (2) the coefficient on y_{t-1} is, of course, equal to 1. This implies that

$$y_t = y_0 + \mu t + \sum_{i=1}^{t} e_t \tag{3}$$

As (3) reveals, in the second (difference stationary) case shocks have persistent effects because y_t now includes the sum of all the error terms. In terms of growth theory, the traditional Solow (or Augmented-Solow) model would have a trend of type (1) whereas an endogenous growth model such as that of Rebelo would have a trend of type (2).

There are therefore two reasons for testing for a unit root. First, if the series is of type (2), then ordinary least squares (OLS) estimation relying on (1) as a maintained hypothesis may give seriously misleading results, as is clearly set out in Mills (1992). Second, the tests may throw some light on the question of the endogeneity of growth. The standard Dickey–Fuller or Augmented Dickey–Fuller tests investigate a unit root null hypothesis against a trend stationary alternative. In the equation

$$y_t = \delta + \rho y_{t-1} + \phi t + e_t \tag{4}$$

(augmented if necessary by lagged changes in the dependent variable to eliminate serial correlation) the test is of $\rho = 1$ (the unit root null) against the trend stationary alternative $\rho < 1$. Given the suggestion of 'epochs in growth' entertained by economic historians, however, it is preferable to consider a segmented trend stationary alternative and not doing so may lead to inappropriate acceptance of the unit root null.

Crafts and Mills (Chapter 11) explore trend growth along these lines taking as a starting point the phases of growth set out by Maddison (1991). Given the low power of the standard tests in distinguishing a value for ρ near but below 1 from $\rho = 1$, they also employ a number of additional tests suggested in the recent literature. For European countries the results generally give support for much higher trend growth during the period 1951–73 than before or since and they also find that, in all cases, the unit root null hypothesis is rejected in favour of the segmented trend alternative. Tests generally reject the pure Janossy 'return to normal' hypothesis, thus indicating that the changed economic environment of the post-war period provided a boost to growth rates other than just through reconstruction. However, allowing break points in the post-war period to be determined endogenously, suggests that Janossy was right to emphasize the impact of reconstruction on catch-up in the first part of the Golden Age. In growth accounting terms, this would probably show up as a surge in total factor productivity with capital and labour enabled to work much more effectively.

4   Conclusions and agenda for future research

The big challenges in explaining post-war European growth are to understand precisely what were the special features of the economic environment which underpinned the Golden Age and why they could not be sustained for longer. Achieving these goals requires detailed information on growth performance and the proximate sources of growth together with investigation of the incentive structures facing both private agents and governments which sustained the growth path as an equilibrium. The chapters in this book add to knowledge of the former while the sister volume (Crafts and Toniolo, 1996) concentrates rather more on the latter.

Broadly speaking, the balance of the evidence in these essays tends to support a view of post-war Europe which stresses that broad capital is central to the growth process but which sees diminishing returns to investment in the long run, in the absence of technological change. Catching-up also seems to have involved, in part at least, post-war reconstruction, reductions of technology gaps and enhanced social capability.

A striking feature of early post-war Europe is the apparently very large role for TFP growth. A standard reaction from a modern growth economist might be to assume that with better measurement of broad capital this would tend to disappear and that the message from growth accounting is misleading. In this case, however, the traditional story may have a good deal to recommend it and in the fastest growth cases European catch-up in the 1950s and 1960s may have benefited very substantially from more efficient factor usage arising from reconstruction, trade liberalization and structural change.

Clearly, much more remains to be done to refine the measurement of growth performance in post-war Europe. Two aspects are particularly important: (i) better price data for use in international comparisons both of growth rates and relative levels of output and productivity; (ii) better estimates of factor inputs including labour and both physical and human components of the stock of broad capital.

Gordon (1992) highlighted a number of problems relating to differences in practices of central statistical offices in the context of rapid product improvement, particularly in computers. His suggestion that there may be serious biases in growth comparisons between Europe and the United States deserves detailed examination. In terms of productivity level comparisons, a key requirement remains to build up further historical information on purchasing power parity exchange rates; here again careful study of product quality differences is essential.

The services sector poses a particularly large challenge and has perhaps been unduly neglected relative to manufacturing. An interesting issue is whether productivity growth and, especially, quality improvement in services is commonly underestimated. For example, research into productivity improvement in public and professional services suggests the dangers of the common practice of proxying real output growth in this sector by employment growth (Millward, 1990). There is also much to be gained from more internationally comparative studies of service sector performance.

Historical measurement of conventional factor inputs still deserves further work. With regard to the physical capital stock, further research on asset lifetimes to improve the implementation of the perpetual inventory method of estimation is a high priority, as O'Mahony points out (Chapter 4). Labour force accounting should also be strengthened; perhaps most important is better information on comparisons of actual working hours which are a key ingredient in productivity comparisons.

Better estimates of human capital formation are a still more urgent need. In particular, we need to know more about the impact of vocational and on-the-job training and not to rely so heavily on data relating to schooling. The deficiencies of our current knowledge in this area are especially unfortunate, given the very strong emphasis on human capital in much of modern growth theory.

Finally, in terms of focal points for further analysis, three key themes stand out. First, there is the importance of thinking about structural breaks, not simply in terms of econometric analysis of trends but also in terms of recognizing that catch-up and convergence as seen in Europe in the 1950s and 1960s is an atypical experience. Second, there is the need to explore much further aspects of the conditionality of convergence, in particular, to take 'social capability' seriously in a growth context. Third, there is a high priority for comparative analysis of the post-war growth and productivity experience of Eastern and Western Europe based on a more accurate database than has hitherto been available.

NOTES

We are grateful to Angus Maddison for helpful comments, but he bears no responsibility for errors.

REFERENCES

Abramovitz, M. (1986), 'Catching Up, Forging Ahead, and Falling Behind', *Journal of Economic History*, **46**, 385–406.

den Bakker, G.P., T.A. Huitker and C.A. van Bochove (1990), 'The Dutch Economy, 1921–39: Revised Macroeconomic Data for the Interwar Period', *Review of Income and Wealth*, **36**, 187–206.

Barro, R. and X. Sala-i-Martin (1991), 'Convergence across States and Regions', *Brookings Papers on Economic Activity*, 107–82.

Bean, C. and N.F.R. Crafts (1996), 'British Economic Growth Since 1945: Relative Economic Decline … and Renaissance?', in N.F.R. Crafts and G. Toniolo (eds.), *Economic Growth in Europe since 1945*, Cambridge: Cambridge University Press, 131–72.

Ben-David, D. (1993), 'Equalizing Exchange: Trade Liberalization and Income Convergence', *Quarterly Journal of Economics*, **108**, 653–79.

Crafts, N.F.R. (1992), 'Productivity Growth Reconsidered', *Economic Policy*, **15**, 388–426.

Crafts, N.F.R. (1995), 'The Golden Age of Economic Growth, in Postwar Europe: Why did Northern Ireland Miss out?', *Irish Economic and Social History*, **22**, 5–25.

Crafts, N.F.R. and G. Toniolo (eds.), (1996), *Economic Growth in Europe since 1945*, Cambridge: Cambridge University Press.

Daly, A., D. Hitchens and K. Wagner (1985) 'Productivity, Machinery and Skills in a Sample of British and German Manufacturing Plants', *National Institute Economic Review*, 111, 48–61.

Denison, E.F. (1962), *The Sources of Economic Growth in the United States and the Alternatives before Us*, New York: Committee for Economic Development.

Denison, E.F. (1967), *Why Growth Rates Differ*, Washington, DC: Brookings.

Dowrick, S. and D.-T. Nguyen (1989), 'OECD Comparative Economic Growth, 1950–85: Catch-Up and Convergence', *American Economic Review*, 79, 1010–30.

Dumke, R.H. (1990), 'Reassessing the Wirtschaftswunder: Reconstruction and Postwar Growth in West Germany in an International Context', *Oxford Bulletin of Economics and Statistics*, 52, 451–90.

Durlauf, S.B. and P.A. Johnson (1992), 'Local versus Global Convergence across National Economies', NBER Working Paper No. 3996.

Feinstein, C.H. (1972), *National Income, Expenditure and Output of the UK, 1855–1965*, Cambridge: Cambridge University Press.

Gilbert, M. and I.B. Kravis (1954), *An International Comparison of National Products and the Purchasing Power of Currencies*, Paris: OEEC.

Gilbert, M. and associates (1958), *Comparative National Products and Price Levels*, Paris: OEEC.

Gordon, R.J. (1992), 'Measuring the Aggregate Price Level: Implications for Economic Performance and Policy', CEPR Discussion Paper No. 663.

Hansen, S.A. (1974), *Økonomisk Vækst i Danmark*, Copenhagen: Akademisk Forlag.

Helliwell, J.F. (1992), 'Trade and Technical Progress', NBER Working Paper No. 4226.

Hjerrpe, R. (1989), *The Finnish Economy, 1860–1985*, Helsinki: Bank of Finland.

Janossy, F. (1969), *The End of the Economic Miracle*, White Plains: IASP.

Jorgenson, D.W. (1990), 'Productivity and Economic Growth', in E.R. Berndt and J.E. Triplett (eds.), *Fifty Years of Economic Measurement*, Chicago: University of Chicago Press.

Krantz, O. and C.-A. Nilsson (1975), *Swedish National Product, 1861–1970*, Lund: CWK Gleerup.

Kravis, I.B., A. Heston and R. Summers (1982), *World Product and Income*, Baltimore: Johns Hopkins University Press.

Levine, R. and D. Renelt (1992), 'A Sensitivity Analysis of Cross-Country Growth Regressions', *American Economic Review*, 82, 942–63.

Maddison, A. (1987), 'Growth and Slowdown in Advanced Capitalist Economies', *Journal of Economic Literature*, 25, 649–98.

Maddison, A. (1991), *Dynamic Forces in Capitalist Development*, Oxford: Oxford University Press.

Maddison, A. (1992), 'A Long-Run Perspective on Saving', *Scandinavian Journal of Economics*, 94, 181–96.

Maddison, A. (1995), *Monitoring the World Economy 1820–1992*, Paris, OECD Development Centre.

Mankiw, N.G., D. Romer and D.N. Weil (1992), 'A Contribution to the Empirics of Economic Growth', *Quarterly Journal of Economics*, 107, 407–37.

Mason, G., B. van Ark and K. Wagner (1994), 'Productivity, Product Quality and Workforce Skills: Food Processing in Four European Countries', *National Institute Economic Review*, 147, 62–84.

Mills, T.C. (1992), 'An Economic Historians' Introduction to Modern Time Series Techniques in Econometrics', in S.N. Broadberry and N.F.R. Crafts (eds.), *Britain in the International Economy, 1870–1939*, Cambridge: Cambridge University Press, pp. 28–46.

Millward, R. (1990), 'Productivity in the UK Services Sector: Historical Trends 1856–1985 and Comparisons with the USA 1950–85', *Oxford Bulletin of Economics and Statistics*, **52**, 423-36.

Mitchell, B.R. (1992), *European Historical Statistics*, 3rd edn, Cambridge: Cambridge University Press.

Nelson, R.R. and G. Wright (1992), 'The Rise and Fall of American Technological Leadership', *Journal of Economic Literature*, **30**, 1931–64.

Olson, M. (1982), *The Rise and Decline of Nations*, New Haven: Yale University Press.

Oulton, N. and M. O'Mahony (1994), *Productivity and Growth: A Study of British Industry, 1954–86*, Cambridge: Cambridge University Press.

Paige, D. and G. Bombach (1959), *A Comparison of National Output and Productivity*, Paris: OEEC.

Rebelo, S. (1991), 'Long Run Policy Analysis and Long Run Economic Growth', *Journal of Political Economy*, **99**, 500–21.

Romer, P.M. (1990), 'Endogenous Technological Change', *Journal of Political Economy*, **98**, S71–102.

Romer, P.M. (1994), 'The Origins of Endogenous Growth', *Journal of Economic Perspectives*, **8**(1), 3–22.

Rossi, N., A. Sorgato and G. Toniolo (1992), 'Italian Historical Statistics: 1880–1990', University of Venice Department of Economics Working Paper 92–18.

Rostas, L. (1948), *Comparative Productivity in British and American Industry*, Cambridge: Cambridge University Press.

Sala-i-Martin, X. (1990), 'Lecture Notes on Economic Growth', NBER Working Papers Nos. 3563 and 3564.

Scott, M.F. (1989), *A New View of Economic Growth*, Oxford: Oxford University Press.

Sommariva, A. and G. Tullio (1986), *German Macroeconomic History, 1880–1979*, London: Macmillan.

Summers, R. and A. Heston (1988), 'A Set of International Comparisons of Real Product and Price Levels: Estimates for 130 Countries, 1950–1985', *Review of Income and Wealth*, **34**, 1–25.

Summers, R. and A. Heston (1991), 'The Penn World Table (Mark 5): An Expanded Set of International Comparisons, 1950–1988', *Quarterly Journal of Economics*, **106**, 327–68.

van de Klundert, T. and S. Smulders (1992), 'Reconstructing Growth Theory: A Survey', *De Economist*, **140**, 177–202.

Villa, P. (1993), *Une analyse macroeconomique de la France au xxe siècle*, Paris: CRNS Editions.

2 Macroeconomic accounts for European countries

ANGUS MADDISON

In order to understand the nature of economic growth, and to analyse the reasons for differences in levels of performance over time and between countries, it is extremely useful to have a standardized set of accounts for the countries under comparison. They are of fundamental importance not only for growth accountancy of the type practised by Denison, but also for econometricians and others who use such magnitudes in regression analysis.

This chapter provides (Section 1) measures of the overall (GDP) growth rate in constant national prices; (Section 2) a set of PPP converters to put the national estimates into a comparable price framework; (Section 3) a set of integrated demographic, labour input and labour productivity measures – which show both levels and growth rates; (Section 4) measures of the quality of the labour force, in particular its educational level (human capital); (Section 5) internationally comparable estimates of the growth and level of the physical (non-residential) capital stock; (Section 6) an attempt to put the major causal influences into an explanatory framework of growth accounts.

This chapter assesses the quality of the evidence for ten European countries, and uses the information to analyse the performance of these economies. For comparative purposes, I have also included Japan and the USA. Japan is a major economy which started at a lower level than the European countries in 1950, but has since grown faster. The USA has been the world economic leader in the twentieth century, but since 1950 has grown more slowly than Europe and Japan which have moved much closer to US levels of performance.

27

1 GDP growth

1.1 The quality of the evidence

(a) The standardized conceptual framework

The first attempts at national accounts date back to the seventeenth century (Petty, Gregory King, Vauban etc). Later writers who attempted ambitious international comparisons were Mulhall (1880s–90s) and Colin Clark (1940). The big step forward in producing comparable measures of output came from OEEC in 1948–60. The methods developed in UK and US wartime national accounting were systematized for international use in (1952) guidelines for a standardized national accounting system. Richard Stone (1956) provided guidelines for quantity and price indexes. Milton Gilbert in OEEC and Stone in Cambridge provided a technical assistance service to OEEC countries in developing their national accounts. There were several volumes of country studies (including Netherlands and France). OEEC (1954) provided the first comparative statistics of national product and expenditures which included figures back to 1938, and from 1947 onwards for all the countries included here, except Spain. These estimates were adjusted where necessary to the standardized system which countries did not necessarily follow in their own statistics.

The first two national accounts yearbooks of OEEC contained detailed notes on the kinds of adjustment made to the national figures to bring them in line with the standardized system. Detailed source notes of this kind are no longer published by OECD, but the individual country statistics now conform more closely to the standardized system which is undergoing its fourth revision. I used the OECD estimates for 1960 onwards for all countries except Ireland, where the authorities have recently made downward revisions to the growth estimates (see source notes to Appendix table A.1).

Thanks to the efforts of Simon Kuznets and others, the International Association for Research in Income and Wealth was set up in 1948 and served as a forum for official national accounts statisticians and academic researchers to discuss methodological problems. Kuznets stimulated scholars in many countries to push back their national accounts in time. For the countries considered here we now have such estimates for most of the twentieth century and part of the nineteenth.

The international comparability of West European GDP estimates has improved markedly in the past fifty years thanks to the work of OEEC in the 1950s and the pressures from Eurostat over the past 30 years to get EC countries to standardize their accounts.

There are variations in the techniques for measuring changes in output volume in the different countries, e.g. price deflation as opposed to physical indicators. The impact of these differences on the measurement of growth performance is difficult to assess, but there are two problems ((b) and (c) below) where the impact of differences can be more clearly appreciated.

(b) Differences in weighting procedures
The weighting base for constant price estimates is now more similar than it used to be. The Eurostat recommendation is to change the weighting system every five years. Thus the UK since 1970 has changed its weights every five years for years ending with 0 and 5 (CSO, 1985, p. 24). If UK indices were presented for a 20-year period in '1985' prices, they would in fact be made up by linking four successive five-year segments, each successive segment being weighted by the price structure of successive 'base' years. The '1985' appellation is simply a 'reference' point or numeraire.

The situation in Germany is similar to that in the UK (see Statistisches Bundesamt, 1992). The German accounts were revised in 1957, 1960, 1970, 1977, 1982, 1985 and 1991, and a retrospective series in '1985' prices was published in 1992 back to 1950. In Belgium, Ireland, and Sweden, the practice appears to be the same as in Germany and the UK. In France the benchmark is changed about every 10 years. For Portugal revisions are at longer intervals. For Spain I have used Prados's estimates to 1960, where his weighting was also for longer intervals.

In The Netherlands, a chaining procedure has been used since 1981, i.e. the weighting base is changed every year, using the Laspeyres formula for the volume index and the Paasche for the price index. The weights for the volume changes are taken from the previous year and those for prices are for the reporting year. Den Bakker (1991) shows how Dutch growth rates are affected for the 1921–39 period using ten different alternative index numbers. The growth of GDP volume over his period was 51.2% using the chain index, 59.5% using 1921 weights and 50.7% using 1939 weights. An official publication has linked the various estimates (six segments) back to 1900 (see notes to Appendix table A.1).

Hitherto, the Department of Commerce has published a revised series every five years showing the growth of US GDP going back more than sixty years. The official figures from 1929 onwards are estimated with a single set of (1987) prices throughout. However, Young (1993) has published two alternatives to the official index for 1959 onwards, one of which is like the standard EC procedure, and the other like the Dutch procedure. With the official (1987) weighted) index, GDP growth from 1959 to 1992 was 2.88% a year; with shifting five-year weighting, 3.16% a year; and, with the Dutch chain technique, 3.12% a year. As the Young (1993) estimates are close to European practice, I used them rather than the officially preferred measure for the USA.

(c)   Revisions to correct for inadequate coverage

Another important problem which affects the comparability of accounts, is that the coverage of economic activity may become inadequate, e.g. because of changes in the importance of the underground economy. In the course of time corrections are usually made to deal with this. In most of these countries these adjustments have been relatively minor, but more substantial adjustments have been made in Italy, The Netherlands, Portugal, Spain and Sweden. The problem has been most noticeable in Italy, where there have been four official benchmark revisions of the post-war national accounts, each involving a substantial upward revision in the level of output. The Italian authorities have not themselves linked all of these estimates as the adjustment procedure is complicated. The latest weighting base is 1985. I adjusted the estimates and linked the segments for 1861–1989 in Maddison (1991b) where the procedure is explained in detail. For Spain, Prados has used a similar technique to deal with successive upward revisions in GDP level (see country note in Appendix table A.1). Recently, the Portuguese authorities made a 14.2% upward adjustment in the accounts for 1990, which I also applied to earlier years. As we have just experienced a major round of such adjustments, this problem does not at present appear to be a serious obstacle to inter-country comparability.

(d)   Conclusion on comparability of growth measures

There have been several serious attempts to assess the comparability of the growth measures for OECD countries. McGibbon (1964), Beckerman (1966) and Denison (1967) were relatively sanguine about the comparability of post-war growth rates. Denison (1967) made downward adjustments for Belgian GDP growth of 0.23% a year and for France by 0.28% a year (see Maddison (1967) for a résumé of the discussion). In my view, it would be prudent to assume that there is still an element of non-comparability in the growth measures. Over the half century we are considering, differences in growth rates between these countries of less than 0.2% a year should probably not be regarded as significant.

1.2   Assessment of growth performance

Tables 2.1(a) and 2.1(b) show rates of growth of GDP for three long periods 1870–1913, 1913–50 and 1950–92 for our twelve countries. The annual figures for 1947–92 can be found in Appendix tables A.1, A.2 and A.4.

It is clear that the period after 1950 was exceptionally good for all the European countries (except Sweden) and for Japan. It is also obvious that performance in the 1913–50 period was poor by previous standards in all the European countries affected by war, but in the countries least touched by war (The Netherlands, Portugal and Sweden), the 1913–50 period was one of growth acceleration. US performance was poorer in 1913–50 than earlier, mainly because of the wasted decade 1929–38 when the country was in deep depression.

When we break down the 1950–92 period into two segments at 1973 (a generally accepted dividing line), we see that 1950–73 was truly a golden age for the European economies and Japan. They were all able to exploit opportunities for recovery and catch-up with the world leader, thanks to enlightened domestic policy, and a better international economic order. Since 1973, economic growth has slackened considerably in all the European countries (except Ireland) as well as in Japan and the USA. In the majority of cases, however, the 1973–92 growth rates have been better than those before 1950.

2   Real GDP levels

In order to assess and compare the economic performance of nations it is necessary to compare GDP *levels* as well as *growth* rates. If we could not compare levels, one would infer from Table 2.1(b) that in 1950–92, the economic performance of virtually all the other countries was superior to that of the USA. Thanks to our ability to compare levels, we know that such a proposition is only partially true, because US GDP per capita is higher than that of all the other countries. We also know that, in favourable circumstances, opportunities for growth may be better for countries trying to rise from low income levels than they are for the lead country. A major topic in growth economics is the problem of convergence, divergence and catch-up. Hence we need to compare growth levels.

As measures of individual country growth performance are in national prices, and would be virtually impossible to recalculate in international prices, the best option for historical comparisons is to merge estimates of levels in international prices for a benchmark year (see Table 2.3) with

Table 2.1(a)   Real GDP growth 1870–1992 (annual average compound growth rates)

	1870–1913	1913–50	1950–92	1950–73	1973–92
Belgium	2.0	1.0	3.2	4.1	2.1
France	1.5	1.1	3.8	5.0	2.3
Germany	2.8	1.1	4.3	6.0	2.3
Ireland	0.5	0.6	3.3	3.2	3.5
Italy	1.9	1.5	4.3	5.6	2.7
Netherlands	2.2	2.4	3.6	4.7	2.1
Portugal	1.3	2.2	4.4	5.7	2.7
Spain	1.7	1.0	4.9	6.8	2.5
Sweden	2.2	2.7	2.7	3.7	1.5
UK	1.9	1.3	2.4	3.0	1.6
European average	1.8	1.5	3.7	4.8	2.3
Japan	2.3	2.2	6.7	9.2	3.7
USA	3.9	2.8	3.3	3.9	2.5

Source: Appendix table A.1.

Table 2.1(b)   Per capita real GDP growth 1870–1992 (annual average compound growth rates)

	1870–1913	1913–50	1950–92	1950–73	1973–92
Belgium	1.0	0.7	2.8	3.5	1.9
France	1.3	1.1	3.0	4.0	1.7
Germany	1.6	0.3	3.7	5.0	2.1
Ireland	1.0	0.7	2.9	3.1	2.7
Italy	1.3	0.8	3.8	5.0	2.4
Netherlands	0.9	1.1	2.6	3.4	1.4
Portugal	0.5	1.2	4.0	5.7	2.1
Spain	1.2	0.2	4.0	5.8	1.9
Sweden	1.5	2.1	2.2	3.1	1.2
UK	1.0	0.8	2.0	2.5	1.4
European average	1.1	0.9	3.1	4.1	1.9
Japan	1.4	0.9	5.7	8.0	3.0
USA	1.8	1.6	2.0	2.4	1.4

Source: Appendix table A.4.

the available national time series (see Appendix table A.2). As relative price structures change over time it would be desirable to make these linked interspatial–intertemporal comparisons in separate segments, with independent benchmarks, e.g. for 1913, 1950, 1973, and 1990, but the only comprehensive benchmark coverage for these twelve countries is for 1985 and 1990, and I chose to base the estimates on the latter year.

The OEEC (see Gilbert and Kravis, 1954; Gilbert and Associates, 1958; Paige and Bombach, 1959) was a pioneer in estimating the purchasing power parities (PPPs) of currencies as a substitute for exchange rates. OEEC made the comparisons for both the expenditure and product accounts. Since 1980, Eurostat/OECD has carried out expenditure comparisons, so we have their PPP expenditure converters for 1990, 1985, 1980, as well as the Kravis *et al.* (1982) estimates for 1975.

Table 2.2(a) shows the PPP converters for GDP from successive rounds of the joint Eurostat/OECD/UN exercise which is called the 'International Comparison Project' (ICP). Eight of our European countries were covered in all these exercises, but Portugal missed out on ICP3, and Sweden on ICP3 and 4. Table 2.2(a) shows only the 'multilateral' Geary Khamis converters which until recently were the preferred option of OECD. In addition there are binary PPPs of the Paasche, Laspeyres and Fisher type. In earlier work (Maddison 1982 and 1991a). I used the Paasche PPP, which is equivalent to using US relative prices, and is more favourable to the follower countries than the Geary Khamis converter. In 1990, Eurostat/OECD used an EKS multilateral converter as their preferred option – this is also shown in Table 2.2(a); however, this measure is not available for earlier years. Table 2.2(b) shows the exchange rates for the benchmark years. These have been more volatile than the PPP converters.

2.1   The quality of the evidence

Table 2.3 shows the alternative estimates of the 1990 GDP per capita which can be derived from the four latest ICP rounds. Using the USA as a benchmark, we see in this table that the range of variation in the results of the successive exercises can be quite large. Thus, for Italy, ICP4 yielded a relative standing 20% higher than ICP3; for Belgium the results of ICP4 implied a real product per capita relative to the USA 19% higher than ICP5; for Germany, Ireland, Portugal and the UK, the range was over 17%. The lowest range was for Spain, Sweden and The Netherlands, but even there it was over 9%. The average range of variation in the levels recorded in the four ICP rounds was 17% for the European countries.

Table 2.2(a) 'International' dollar PPPs for GDP from successive ICP rounds (units of national currency per US dollar)

	GK ICP3 1975	GK ICP4 1980	GK ICP5 1985	GK ICP6 1990	EKS ICP6 1990
Belgium	41.60	36.60	44.60	38.362	39.432
France	4.69	5.24	7.27	6.450	6.614
Germany	2.81	2.37	2.48	2.052	2.091
Ireland	0.388	0.461	0.723	0.688	0.691
Italy	582.0	759.0	1,302.0	1,384.11	1,421.6
Netherlands	2.84	2.53	2.55	2.084	2.17
Portugal	n.a.	31.70	66.20	91.737	103.75
Spain	42.30	63.70	95.30	105.71	109.55
Sweden	n.a.	n.a.	8.15	8.979	9.341
UK	0.406	0.487	0.568	0.587	0.6023
Japan	271.0	240.00	222.00	185.27	195.45

Source: ICP3 from Kravis *et al.* (1982, p. 21); ICP4 from Ward (1985); ICP5 from OECD (1987); ICP6 EKS version from OECD (1992, pp. 30–1); Geary Khamis version from OECD (1993a, pp. 32–3) rebased with the USA as the reference country.

Table 2.2(b) Exchange rates

	1975	1980	1985	1990
Belgium	36.78	29.24	59.38	33.42
France	4.29	4.23	8.99	5.45
Germany	2.46	1.82	2.94	1.62
Ireland	0.452	0.487	0.946	0.605
Italy	652.85	856.45	1,909.44	1,198.10
Netherlands	2.53	1.99	3.32	1.82
Portugal	25.55	50.06	170.40	142.56
Spain	57.41	71.70	170.04	101.93
Sweden	4.15	4.23	8.60	5.92
UK	0.452	0.430	0.779	0.563
Japan	296.79	226.74	238.54	144.79

Source: OECD, *National Accounts 1960–1992*, Paris, 1994, pp. 154–5.

Table 2.3 Alternative estimates of the level of real GDP per capita in 1990 using Geary Khamis PPP converters from successive ICP rounds (USA = 100)

	ICP3	ICP4	ICP5	ICP6	Range of variation between: All rounds 3 to 6	Rounds 3 and 6
Belgium	77.10	80.65	67.97	76.86	1.19	1.00
France	80.53	82.95	72.15	81.30	1.15	1.01
Germany	82.02	83.53	72.61	85.45	1.18	1.04
Ireland	49.67	58.45	49.71	50.87	1.18	1.02
Italy[a]	62.91	75.18	66.46	72.95	1.20	1.16
Netherlands	72.31	77.76	70.85	75.79	1.10	1.05
Portugal	n.a.	41.92	41.89	48.87	1.17	n.a.
Spain	56.22	58.75	51.75	55.66	1.09	1.04
Sweden	n.a.	n.a.	71.06	80.92	1.14	n.a.
UK	64.41	75.60	70.22	74.55	1.17	1.16
Japan	82.89	85.16	79.48	84.83	1.07	1.02

Note: [a] Downward adjustment of 3% for reasons explained in Maddison (1991b).
Source: The PPP converters of the 1975, 1980, 1985 and 1990 ICP rounds were used to make a dollar conversion of GDP in national prices for these years. The estimates were updated in volume terms to 1990, and adjusted by the change in the GDP deflator for the numeraire country (the USA). They were divided by the population estimates for the relevant years and expressed a percentage of US GDP per capita.

There are some differences between the procedure in the different ICP rounds. ICP3 was carried out on a global basis; the Geary Khamis technique for calculating PPPs was affected by the price structures of all the 34 participating countries. In ICP4 and ICP5 the PPP calculations for EC countries were based only on the price structures of the 12 Member states (a constraint known as 'fixity'), whilst the estimates for Sweden, Japan and the USA were influenced by the price structures for all 24 OECD countries. In the 1990 exercise, Eurostat changed its officially preferred aggregation method from the Geary Khamis procedure to the EKS procedure, but the ICP also provided a Geary Khamis version of the results (which I use) which was not subject to the fixity rule. Hence ICP3 and ICP6 were methodologically much closer to each other than to ICP4 and ICP5, and the variance in the standing of countries in rounds 3 and 6 is a good deal lower than the variance between all four rounds (see Table 2.3).

Table 2.4   Levels of GDP per capita 1870–1992 (USA = 100.0 in year cited)

	1870	1913	1950	1973	1992
Belgium	107	78	56	72	80
France	80	65	55	78	83
Germany	78	72	45	79	90
Ireland	72	51	37	42	54
Italy	60	47	36	63	75
Netherlands	107	74	61	77	78
Portugal	44	26	22	46	52
Spain	56	42	25	53	58
Sweden	68	58	70	81	79
UK	133	95	72	72	73
European average	81	61	48	66	72
USA	100	100	100	100	100
Japan	30	25	20	66	90

Source: Appendix table A.5.

Unfortunately, with the exception of Blades and Roberts (1987), the authorities producing these international comparisons generally do not discuss or explain the discrepancies between the various rounds.

There is clearly a margin of uncertainty in these measures of relative performance levels. In my view, the last column of Table 2.3 gives some idea of the range of uncertainty about GDP levels. For most countries it is under 5%, but a good deal more for Italy and the UK. However, in extrapolating the 1990 benchmark backwards to 1950 with the national indicators of GDP in constant national prices one compounds the possible error in measuring 1990 levels, and the possible errors in measuring growth. Thus there may well be errors of up to a quarter in the measure of inter-country differences in levels of GDP per capita in 1950 in Appendix table A.4.

Apart from the ICP exercises to compare levels of expenditure between countries, there are also comparisons from the production side. The first comprehensive one was by Paige and Bombach (1959) for the UK and USA. Since then there have been a large number of comparisons for individual sectors but very few for the whole economy. These studies are therefore most useful for sectoral productivity analysis (see Chapter 3 by van Ark in this volume).

Table 2.5 Reconciliation of per capita GDP level and labour productivity level in 1992

	GDP per capita (USA = 100.0)	Labour productivity (USA = 100.0)	Labour input per head of population (USA = 100.0)	Percentage of population employed	Hours worked per person employed	Hours of labour input per head of population
Belgium	80	98	81[a]	37.9	1,586	601
France	83	102	82	39.3	1,542	606
Germany	90	95	95	44.9	1,563	702
Ireland	54	72[a]	(73)[a]	31.9[a]	(1,700)[a]	542[a]
Italy	75	85	(90)	(44.7)	(1,490)	666
Netherlands	78	99	79	43.8	1,338	587
Portugal	52	46[b]	(106)[b]	46.6	(1,700)[b]	810[b]
Spain	58	69	(83)	(32.3)	1,911	618
Sweden	79	79	99	48.3	1,515	732
UK	73	82	89	44.0	1,491	656
European average	72	83	88	41.4	1,582	652
Japan	90	69	131	51.8	1,874	970
USA	100	100	100	46.6	1,589	741

Note: [a] 1991; [b] 1990.
Source: Tables 2.4, 2.7, 2.9, 2.10, 2.13 and A.3.

3 Labour input and labour productivity

The relative standing of individual countries in terms of labour productivity may differ very considerably from their ranking in terms of GDP per capita.

Table 2.5 presents a confrontation of the two measures, and provides the major elements which explain the difference.

In terms of per capita GDP, the USA has a clear lead over all the other countries, but its labour input is higher than that in most European countries and its level of labour productivity is not clearly distinguishable from that of Belgium, France, Germany and The Netherlands. Japan has very high labour inputs compared with European countries – nearly 50% higher than the European average – so its standing is very much lower in labour productivity than in GDP per capita.

In the Golden Age, 1950–73, labour inputs generally declined in Europe, whereas they rose appreciably in Japan and the USA (Table

Table 2.6　Total labour force (000s)

	Belgium	France	Germany FR	Ireland	Italy	Japan
1938	3,633	19,490	19,914	1,329	20,217	32,906
1950	3,515	20,070	23,053	1,272	20,274	36,374
1960	3,573	20,055	26,351	1,118	21,914	45,426
1973	3,840	22,027	27,433	1,131	24,209	53,260
1987	4,115	24,109	29,386	1,319	28,260	60,840
1988	4,127	24,169	29,607	1,310	28,510	61,660
1989	4,144	24,297	29,799	1,292	28,521	62,700
1990	4,179	24,853	30,369	1,305	28,830	63,840
1991	4,210	25,019	30,682	1,334	28,927	65,050
1992	4,237	25,108	30,949	n.a.	28,944	65,780

	Netherlands	Portugal	Spain	Sweden	UK	USA
1938	3,517	2,902	10,191	3,329	22,927	55,350
1950	4,239	3,288	11,838	3,481	22,965	65,016
1960	4,686	3,424	12,930	3,679	24,777	73,126
1973	5,310	3,576	13,369	3,977	25,633	91,756
1987	6,486	4,567	14,675	4,421	27,979	122,122
1988	6,641	4,616	14,972	4,471	28,255	123,893
1989	6,713	4,677	15,160	4,527	28,427	126,077
1990	6,872	4,948	15,333	4,540	28,498	126,954
1991	7,011	5,069	15,382	4,516	28,296	126,867
1992	7,133	4,764	15,432	4,429	28,143	128,548

Source: 1987 onwards generally from OECD, *Labour Force Statistics 1972–92* Paris, 1994. For Italy I made an upward adjustment to the official figures to include undeclared people working illicitly. When the national accounts were revised upwards for the benchmark year 1982, the authorities estimated a total of 28 million jobs compared with 22.2 million people figuring in the labour force estimates, see ISTAT (1987, pp. 9 and 31). I adjusted the official figures upwards to allow for this underground employment. The adjustment coefficient for 1987–92 was 17.6%. 1938–73 generally from Maddison (1991a). This latter source does not include Ireland, Portugal and Spain. For the 1930s the source for these three countries was Dewhurst and Associates (1961, p. 837) and 1938 was estimated by interpolation from neighbouring years. 1950–73 for Ireland and Portugal are from OECD, *Labour Force Statistics*, various years, and from OECD (1979b). Spain 1950 and 1960 are from Mueller (1965); he made an upward adjustment for undercounting of females in agriculture and some services (the figures for 1950 before adjustment were 10,793, and 1960 11,817).

Table 2.7 Total employment (000s)

	Belgium	France	Germany FR	Ireland	Italy	Japan
1938	3,316	18,769	19,656	n.a.	19,287	32,290
1950	3,341	19,663	21,164	1,220	18,875	35,683
1960	3,456	19,709	26,063	1,055	21,059	44,670
1973	3,748	21,434	27,160	1,067	22,708	52,590
1987	3,649	21,577	27,157	1,087	24,925	59,110
1988	3,702	21,759	27,364	1,091	25,146	60,110
1989	3,760	22,012	27,761	1,090	25,156	61,280
1990	3,814	22,648	28,486	1,126	25,595	62,490
1991	3,819	22,671	28,993	1,125	25,807	63,690
1992	3,801	22,557	29,141	n.a.	25,652	64,360

	Netherlands	Portugal	Spain	Sweden	UK	USA
1938	3,169	n.a.	n.a.	3,159	20,818	44,917
1950	4,120	3,196	11,662	3,422	22,400	61,651
1960	4,630	3,347	12,800	3,616	24,225	69,195
1973	5,150	3,486	13,031	3,879	25,076	87,390
1987	5,864	4,248	11,726	4,337	25,074	114,697
1988	6,032	4,353	12,119	4,399	25,914	117,192
1989	6,155	4,445	12,597	4,466	26,684	119,550
1990	6,356	4,723	12,890	4,465	26,942	120,081
1991	6,522	4,865	12,917	4,383	26,054	118,441
1992	6,655	4,573	12,642	4,195	25,465	119,164

Source: The sources are the same as for Table 2.6. The difference between Table 2.6 and Table 2.7 is unemployment.

2.11). For 1973–92 labour inputs were generally more negative in Europe than in the Golden Age, there was less intensive use of the labour supply and unemployment rose to unprecedented levels for the post-war period. This was in sharp contrast to the USA where the growth of labour input accelerated.

Labour productivity growth was much faster after 1950 in Europe and Japan than in the USA. In all countries, labour productivity decelerated after 1973. In most cases this deceleration was very sharp, but least so in Ireland and the UK (see Tables 2.13 and 2.14).

There is clear evidence (Tables 2.15(a) and 2.15(b)) that the eleven countries all made progress in catching up with US productivity levels. The process of convergence was quite rapid in 1950–73 and slowed down generally thereafter, except in Belgium, Ireland and the UK.

Table 2.8 Alternative estimates of employment (national accounts version) (000s)

	Belgium	France	Germany	Ireland	Italy	Japan
1987	3,600	21,763	27,050	n.a.	22,878	62,084
1988	3,653	21,957	27,261	n.a.	23,088	63,119
1989	3,712	22,246	27,658	n.a.	23,123	64,358
1990	3,764	22,477	28,479	n.a.	23,327	65,717
1991	3,770	22,484	29,227	n.a.	23,516	67,065
1992	3,753	22,376	29,487	n.a.	23,276	67,833

	Netherlands	Portugal	Spain	Sweden	UK	USA
1987	4,911	3,646	11,808	4,383	25,083	108,469
1988	4,989	3,649	12,205	4,443	25,914	111,545
1989	5,084	3,687	12,624	4,508	26,684	114,184
1990	5,203	3,719	13,072	4,550	26,942	115,082
1991	5,279	n.a.	13,134	4,482	26,059	113,867
1992	5,323	n.a.	12,981	4,282	25,461	114,090

Alternative estimates as ratio of Table 2.6

	Belgium	France	Germany	Ireland	Italy	Japan
1987	0.987	1.009	0.996	n.a.	0.918	1.050
1988	0.987	1.009	0.996	n.a.	0.918	1.050
1989	0.987	1.011	0.996	n.a.	0.919	1.050
1990	0.987	0.992	1.000	n.a.	0.911	1.052
1991	0.987	0.992	1.008	n.a.	0.911	1.053
1992	0.987	0.992	1.012	n.a.	0.907	1.054

	Netherlands	Portugal	Spain	Sweden	UK	USA
1987	0.837	0.858	1.007	1.011	1.000	0.946
1988	0.827	0.838	1.007	1.010	1.000	0.952
1989	0.826	0.830	1.002	1.009	1.000	0.955
1990	0.819	0.787	1.014	1.019	1.000	0.958
1991	0.809	n.a.	1.017	1.023	1.000	0.961
1992	0.800	n.a.	1.027	1.021	1.000	0.957

Source: OECD, *National Accounts 1979–1992*, Vol. 2, Paris, 1994.

Table 2.9   Annual hours worked per person

	Belgium	France	Germany FR	Ireland	Italy	Japan
1938	2,267	1,848	2,316	2,230	1,927	2,391
1950	2,283	1,926	2,316	2,250	1,997	2,166
1960	2,174	1,919	2,081	[2,140]	2,059	2,095
1973	1,872	1,771	1,804	2,010	1,612	2,042
1990	1,638	1,539	1,566	[1,700]	1,500[a]	1,951
1991	1,607	1,540	1,551	[1,700]	1,495[a]	1,912
1992	1,586	1,542	1,563	n.a.	1,490[a]	1,874

	Netherlands	Portugal	Spain	Sweden	UK	USA
1938	2,244	n.a.	n.a.	2,204	2,267	2,062
1950	2,208	2,200	2,200	1,951	1,958	1,867
1960	2,051	n.a.	n.a.	1,823	1,913	1,795
1973	1,751	[1,900]	[2,150]	1,571	1,688	1,717
1990	1,347	[1,700]	1,941	1,508	1,537	1,594
1991	1,338	n.a.	1,931	1,501	1,511	1,584
1992	1,338[b]	n.a.	1,911	1,515	1,491	1,589

Notes: [a] The 1985 figure (1,531) was the latest available. I have assumed that the figure continued to fall thereafter at a slightly slower rate than in 1973–85.
[b] Hours assumed to be the same as in 1991.
Source: Belgium: annual hours actually worked (ouvriers inscrit, moyenne générale) from *Bulletin de Statistique*, Ministère des Affaires Economiques, Brussels, May 1993 for 1987 onwards, earlier years from Maddison (1991a, p. 256); France, *Comptes et Indicateurs Economiques, Rapport sur les Comptes de la Nation 1990*, INSEE, Paris, Table 03.21, for 1987 onwards, earlier years from Maddison (1991a); Germany from *Mitteilungen aus der Arbeitsmarkt und Berufsforschung*, Nürnberg, for 1960 onwards, earlier years from Maddison (1991a). Ireland 1938 and 1950 estimated from J.F. Dewhurst and Associates, *Europe's Needs and Resources*, Twentieth Century Fund, New York, 1961. Other years derived from ILO *Yearbooks of Labour Statistics*, various editions, and assuming weeks worked per year were 49 in 1950, 47.9 in 1973 and 46.2 in 1990. Italy monthly hours actually worked, multiplied by 12; figures are from *Rassegna di Statistiche del Lavoro*. The latest figures refer to 1985. Netherlands 1987 from J.C.M. Ḥesemans, 'Ontwikkeling van de arbeidsduur 1982–1987', *Supplement bij de Sociaal-Economische Maandstatistik*, 1988, no. 3, on hours of full and part-time workers, with weights for each category from the US Bureau of Labor Statistics; earlier years from Maddison (1991a); contractual hours for subsequent years from *Arbeidsrekeningen* with adjustment to actual hours from *Sociaal-economische Maandstatistiek*. Portugal 1950 as for Ireland. Later years derived roughly from ILO *Yearbooks of Labour Statistics*. Spain 1950 as for Ireland. Later years from OECD, *Employment Outlook*. Sweden 1990 onwards derived from source cited for total hours in Table 2.10, divided by employment figure in Table 2.8 (upper). 1938–73 from Maddison (1991a). UK from *New Earnings Surveys*, Dept. of Employment, London. Earlier years from Maddison (1991a). Japanese official figures from *Japan Statistical Yearbook* for regular workers, adjusted downwards 5% to allow for shorter hours of self-employed and temporary workers. USA from *Employment and Earnings*, various issues.

Table 2.10   Total hours worked (million)

	Belgium	France	Germany	Ireland	Italy	Japan
1938	7,517	34,685	45,523	n.a.	37,166	77,205
1950	7,628	37,871	49,016	2,745	37,693	77,289
1960	7,513	37,822	54,237	2,258	43,361	93,584
1973	7,016	37,960	48,991	2,145	36,605	107,389
1990	6,249	34,855	44,609	1,914	38,393[a]	121,918
1991	6,057	34,913	44,968	1,913	38,581[a]	121,775
1992	6,028	34,783	45,547	n.a.	38,221[a]	120,611

	Netherlands	Portugal	Spain	Sweden	UK	USA
1938	7,111	n.a.	n.a.	6,962	47,194	92,619
1950	9,097	7,031	25,656	6,676	43,859	115,102
1960	9,496	n.a.	n.a.	6,592	46,342	124,205
1973	9,018	6,623	28,017	6,094	42,328	150,049
1990	8,562	8,029	25,019	6,735	41,410	191,409
1991	8,726	n.a.	24,943	6,578	39,368	187,611
1992	8,904[b]	n.a.	24,159	6,355	37,968	189,352

Note: [a] and [b] See notes to Table 2.9.
Source: Figures derived from Tables 2.7 and 2.9, except for Sweden where total hours were taken from *Statistika Meddelanden, Nationalräkerschapen 1980–92*, N10SM9301, SCB, Stockholm (and earlier editions).

There is probably a margin of error of around 10% in the labour productivity measures for the 1990s, given the evidence of the last column of Table 2.3, and the problems of measuring labour input accurately, which are discussed in this section. For 1950, the range of error would be higher (probably up to a third). However, there are some countries where the estimates of labour input are more shaky than in others. I have indicated these cases by inserting parentheses in Table 2.5. The shakiest labour productivity measures are for Ireland, Italy, Portugal and Spain. I made an effort to correct the inadequate official figures for Italy. In the case of Ireland, Portugal and Spain I am not as familiar with the database, but for Spain there are clear grounds for believing that there is a substantial amount of underground employment which is not adequately caught in the official statistics. Its productivity level is therefore probably overstated in Table 2.13.

The rest of this section is largely devoted to an assessment of the quality of labour input statistics, which have been merged from different sources. A more detailed assessment of these problems and a proposed accounting framework for labour input statistics can be found in Maddison (1980). The summary results of the section are presented in Tables 2.11 to 2.16.

Table 2.11 Rate of growth of labour input and labour force (annual average compound growth rate)

	Labour input		Labour force	
	1950–73	1973–92	1950–73	1973–92
Belgium	−0.36	−0.80[a]	0.39	0.52
France	0.01	−0.46	0.41	0.69
Germany	−0.00	−0.38	0.76	0.64
Ireland	−1.07	−0.63[a]	−0.51	0.92[a]
Italy	−0.13	0.22	0.77	0.94
Netherlands	−0.07	−0.07	0.98	1.56
Portugal	−0.26	1.14[b]	0.37	1.52
Spain	0.38	−0.78	0.53	0.76
Sweden	−0.40	0.22	0.58	0.57
UK	−0.15	−0.57	0.47	0.49
European average	−0.21	−0.21	0.48	0.86
Japan	1.44	0.61	1.67	1.12
USA	1.16	1.23	1.51	1.79

Notes: [a] 1973–91.
[b] 1973–90.
Source: First two columns from Table 2.10; second two columns from Table 2.6.

Table 2.12 Unemployment rate (percentage of the labour force)

	1950	1960	1973	1992
Belgium	5.0	3.3	2.4	10.3
France	2.0	1.7	2.7	10.2
Germany	8.2	1.1	1.0	5.8
Ireland	4.1	5.6	5.7	15.7[a]
Italy	6.9	3.9	6.2	11.4
Netherlands	2.8	1.2	3.0	6.7
Portugal	2.8	2.2	2.5	4.0
Spain	1.5	1.0	2.5	18.1
Sweden	1.7	1.7	2.5	5.3
UK	2.5	2.2	2.2	9.5
European average	3.8	2.4	3.1	9.7
Japan	1.9	1.7	1.3	2.2
USA	5.2	5.4	4.8	7.3

Note: [a] 1991.
Source: Tables 2.6 and 2.7.

Table 2.13   Labour productivity (GDP per man-hour)
(1990 Geary Khamis dollars)

	Belgium	France	Germany FR	Ireland	Italy	Japan
1938	5.27	5.35	4.84	n.a.	3.78	2.19
1950	6.06	5.65	4.37	3.80	4.28	2.03
1960	8.26	9.03	8.65	5.48	6.70	3.90
1973	16.53	17.77	16.64	10.06	15.58	11.15
1990	26.81	28.93	26.49	20.36	23.95	18.80
1991	28.18	29.09	27.48	20.76	24.13	19.58
1992	28.55	29.62	27.55	n.a.	24.59	20.02
	Netherlands	Portugal	Spain	Sweden	UK	USA
1938	6.26	n.a.	n.a.	4.27	6.02	8.64
1950	6.50	2.58	2.60	7.08	7.86	12.66
1960	9.78	n.a.	n.a.	9.86	9.69	16.28
1973	19.02	9.86	10.86	18.02	15.92	23.45
1990	28.93	13.19	18.95	22.49	22.60	28.55
1991	28.99	n.a.	19.42	22.77	23.23	28.78
1992	28.80	n.a.	20.22	23.11	23.98	29.10

Source: Derived from Appendix table A.2 and Table 2.10.

Table 2.14   Rate of growth of labour productivity
(GDP per man-hour)
(annual average compound growth rates)

	1950–73	1973–92
Belgium	4.5	2.9
France	5.1	2.7
Germany	6.0	2.7
Ireland	4.3	4.1[a]
Italy	5.8	2.4
Netherlands	4.8	2.2
Portugal	6.0	1.7[b]
Spain	6.4	3.3
Sweden	4.1	1.3
UK	3.1	2.2
European average	5.0	2.6
Japan	7.7	3.1
USA	2.7	1.1

Note: [a] 1973–91.   [b] 1973–90.
Source: Table 2.13.

Table 2.15(a)   Relative levels of labour productivity
(US level = 100 in year specified)

	1950	1973	1992
Belgium	48	70	98
France	45	76	102
Germany	35	71	95
Ireland	30	43	71^a
Italy	34	66	85
Netherlands	51	81	99
Portugal	20	42	45^b
Spain	21	46	69
Sweden	56	77	79
UK	62	68	82
European average	40	64	83
Japan	16	48	69

Note: ^{a} 1991. ^{b} 1990.
Source: Table 2.13.

Table 2.15(b)   Rate of catch-up on US labour
productivity levels
(annual average compound growth rates)

	1950–73	1973–92
Belgium	1.7	1.8
France	2.3	1.6
Germany	3.1	1.4
Ireland	1.6	2.8^a
Italy	2.9	1.3
Netherlands	2.0	1.1
Portugal	3.3	0.4^b
Spain	3.5	2.2
Sweden	1.4	0.1
UK	0.4	1.0
European average	2.2	1.4
Japan	4.9	1.9

Note: ^{a} 1973–91. ^{b} 1973–90.
Source: Derived from Table 2.15(a), taking rates of
growth between the standing of the country relative to
the USA in the years in question.

Table 2.16   Structure of employment in 1950, 1973 and 1992 (percentage of total employment)

		Agriculture forestry and fishing	Mining, manufacturing, utilities and construction	Services
France	1950	28.3	34.9	36.8
	1973	10.9	38.5	50.6
	1992	5.1	28.1	66.8
Germany	1950	22.2	43.0	34.8
	1973	7.1	46.6	46.3
	1992	3.1	37.8	59.1
Japan	1950	48.3	22.6	29.1
	1973	13.4	37.2	49.4
	1992	6.4	34.6	59.0
Netherlands	1950	13.9	40.2	45.9
	1973	6.1	35.5	58.4
	1992	3.9	24.3	71.8
UK	1950	5.1	46.5	48.4
	1973	2.9	41.7	55.4
	1992	2.2	26.2	71.6
USA	1950	13.0	33.3	53.7
	1973	4.1	32.3	63.6
	1992	2.8	23.3	74.0

Source: Maddison (1991a, pp. 248–9), and OECD, *Labour Force Statistics 1972–1992*, Paris, 1994.

3.1   The quality of labour force and employment statistics

The OECD has had an annual publication since 1961, originally *Manpower Statistics* and now called *Labour Force Statistics*, which has an integrated approach to demographic and labour market accounts. The *Quarterly Labour Force Statistics* contains the most recent statistics for 15 countries but excludes Belgium, Ireland and The Netherlands. These are the main sources I used for labour force and employment. The OECD procedures are, in principle, based on ILO's guidelines for measuring economic activity, which in their turn are modelled largely on the procedures of the US Bureau of Labor Statistics. In the 1970s, the OECD set up a Committee on Employment and Unemployment Statistics, and made a special survey (1979) of the extent to which national statistics conformed to the 1976 ILO guidelines, particularly for the measurement of unemployment which had at that time become a major issue. There are also quinquennial studies on demographic trends which have appeared from 1956 onwards at more or less regular intervals. The 1979 edition, OECD, *Demographic Trends 1950–1990* covered both the demographic and labour force accounts.

Eurostat (the statistical office of the European Community) has also helped to strengthen the quality of European labour statistics by promoting and financing labour force sample surveys on lines pioneered by the US Bureau of Labor Statistics. These are a more reliable indicator of labour force participation than administrative records which were the old basis for European employment statistics. These new standardized labour force surveys have greatly strengthened the quality of employment estimates in France and The Netherlands.

The US Bureau of Labor Statistics provides a useful complement to the above sources. It makes regular estimates of civilian labour force and employment for 1959 onwards for six of the countries (France, Germany, Italy, The Netherlands, Sweden and the UK) covered here, and has often taken the initiative in adjusting national statistics to a standardized basis, e.g. for France and The Netherlands.

In the past, ILO has not published labour market accounts, but concentrated more on administrative sources (e.g. registered unemployment). The *ILO Yearbooks* (and the quarterly editions) do, however, provide some useful information on working hours.

In the 1980s, the OECD national accounts started to include figures on employment, which are intended to be comparable with the national accounts. There is more sectoral detail than in LFS, but these employment figures are supplied by the member countries without clearly defined OECD guidelines to standardize them, and they are different from those which appear in *Labour Force Statistics* (compare the figures in Tables 2.7 and 2.8). For Belgium, France, Germany, Sweden and the UK the differences are not really significant, but the differences are bigger for Japan and the USA and quite important for The Netherlands, Portugal and Spain. In the case of The Netherlands, the national accounts refer to man-years with an incomplete adjustment to correct for variations in working time. For Italy the national accounts (Table 2.8) estimate is a good deal lower than my own adjusted estimate in Table 2.7. However, it is bigger than the LFS figure, because an allowance is made for domestic and foreign workers who do not respond to the labour force survey.

The LFS series are to be preferred in growth accounts for the following reasons:

(a) LFS figures are available on a consistent basis back to 1950, whereas those in the national accounts are generally for a shorter period; for Ireland they are not available and there are gaps in what is available for The Netherlands and Spain.

(b) The LFS figures are part of a coherent set of accounts which also include information on labour force and unemployment. This is not the case with the figures in the national accounts.

(c) The LFS figures have a clear methodological foundation and have been developed with a view to international comparability. There is a substantial literature analysing and describing these problems. The figures on employment in the national accounts are not always clearly defined (e.g. how they treat part-time workers, the armed forces, double or multiple job-holders etc.). There is no explanation by OECD of why they differ from the LFS, and there has been no effort to ensure their international comparability (see Elfring (1988) on some of these problems).

3.2   Measurement of working hours

There has been a substantial reduction of hours worked over time, and there are sizeable variations between countries. Hours per person are lowest in The Netherlands and highest in Spain. Only three of our countries (France, Germany and Sweden) have official labour market accounts which estimate total working time in hours. The German estimates have been published on a regular basis since 1960, and show full detail on weekly hours of full- and part-time workers, time lost for sickness, overtime work, short-time working, absence due to strikes, weather conditions in the building industry etc. (see *Mitteilungen*, the quarterly publication of the German Labour Market Institute in Nuremberg, which has an annual article with full details). The Swedish national accounts are not so explicit but are comprehensive and exclude time not actually worked even if it is paid. Guidelines for labour market accounts were set out in Maddison (1980) with estimates for France, Germany and the UK which are similar to those in *Mitteilungen*. The French authorities now use this approach in their national accounts as they took over the procedures and adjustments developed by Roland Granier.

Construction of comprehensive accounts of working time requires merger of different types of information. The estimates for The Netherlands and the UK are based on a thorough search of sources for the different pieces of information. For Belgium and Italy I used official estimates of actual time worked, but the Italian estimates were discontinued after 1985. For Ireland, Portugal and Spain I made rough estimates from ILO sources on weekly working hours with a crude allowance for time off for holidays, sickness etc.

The OECD *Employment Outlook* has improved the working hours estimates which it publishes in its statistical annexe, but it has not attempted to establish comprehensive and comparable estimates on a regular basis.

4 Human capital

The sophisticated growth accounts developed by Denison (1967) adjusted the quality of labour inputs for variations in the age, sex and education of employed persons. OECD *Labour Force Statistics* gives an annual breakdown of labour force participation by age and sex and for early years, this information is contained in OECD (1979b). However, past analysis (Maddison, 1987, 1991a) suggests that the sex and age variations are relatively unimportant compared with the changes in levels of education, so they are ignored here.

Table 2.17 provides a measure of educational achievement in years of formal education (broken down by primary, secondary and higher) from census sources in recent decades. As these provide information for different age cohorts, it is possible to infer what average levels were several decades earlier or later. An exhaustive analysis of the census information (1960 and 1970 rounds) for all our countries is available in Kotwal (1975) and summary statistics of this type can be found in OECD (1974). In subsequent OECD publications these estimates of educational stocks were dropped but Table 2.17 gives estimates for 1950 and 1973, and an extrapolation for 1992 based on these sources for our twelve countries. Table 2.18 shows the growth of the educational stock and its impact on the quality of labour. Table 2.19 provides a comparative estimate of the level of the education stock as well as a 'human' capital–output ratio analogous with the more familiar 'physical' capital–output ratio. It is clear from Table 2.19 that the European countries, and Japan in particular, had large 'reserves' of human capital, i.e. they had levels of education which were high relative to their output performance at that time. Their situation in terms of physical capital was then much poorer.

Our measure of human capital is incomplete. For vocational training and adult education, quantitative indicators of a comparative kind are more difficult to obtain and it seems improbable that one can get a satisfactory comparative view of the situation in the countries under observation. Woodhall (1977) provided a comprehensive view of

Table 2.17   Average years of formal education experience of population aged 15–64 in 1950, 1973 and 1992

	Primary	Secondary	Higher	Total	Weighted total
1950					
Belgium	6.00	2.41	0.23	8.64	9.83
France	4.96	3.04	0.18	8.18	9.58
Germany	4.00	4.37	0.14	8.51	10.40
Ireland	6.00	2.77	0.28	9.05	10.44
Italy	3.67	1.13	0.12	4.92	5.49
Netherlands	6.00	1.17	0.24	7.62	8.12
Portugal	1.77	0.47	0.05	2.29	2.53
Spain	4.53	0.31	0.11	4.95	5.13
Sweden	6.00	2.27	0.16	8.43	9.50
UK	6.00	3.27	0.13	9.40	10.84
Japan	5.88	2.08	0.16	8.12	9.11
USA	5.61	3.40	0.45	9.46	11.27
1973					
Belgium	6.00	3.51	0.54	10.05	11.99
France	5.00	4.11	0.47	9.58	11.69
Germany	4.00	5.11	0.20	9.31	11.55
Ireland	6.00	3.38	0.41	9.79	11.55
Italy	4.34	2.04	0.21	6.59	7.62
Netherlands	6.00	2.49	0.39	8.88	10.27
Portugal	2.62	1.16	0.19	3.97	4.62
Spain	3.44	1.75	0.20	5.39	6.29
Sweden	6.00	2.67	0.35	9.02	10.44
UK	6.00	3.99	0.25	10.24	11.66
Japan	6.00	3.79	0.39	10.18	12.09
USA	5.95	5.02	0.80	11.77	14.58
1992					
Belgium	6.00	4.73	1.31	12.04	15.24
France	5.00	5.54	1.60	12.14	15.96
Germany	4.00	5.22	0.43	9.65	12.17
Ireland	6.00	n.a	n.a.	n.a.	n.a.
Italy	4.77	3.99	0.42	9.11	11.20
Netherlands	6.00	4.14	0.77	10.91	13.34
Portugal	3.54	3.05	0.65	7.24	9.11
Spain	3.71	4.57	0.70	8.98	11.51
Sweden	6.00	4.00	1.32	11.32	14.24
UK	6.00	4.91	0.61	11.52	14.09
Japan	6.00	5.20	0.79	11.99	14.86
USA	6.00	5.86	1.92	13.78	18.04

Source: OECD, *Educational Statistics Yearbook*, 1974, and Kotwal (1975). These figures should be regarded as crude estimates. They are based on census returns for 1950, 1960 and 1970, with extrapolation to 1992 on the basis of the average education of younger cohorts in 1970. In the last column, primary education is given a weight of 1, secondary 1.4, and higher 2.0, in line with evidence on the relative earnings potential associated with the different levels (see Maddison, 1987).

Table 2.18   Growth of education and its impact on quality of labour (annual average compound growth rates)

	Growth rate of educational stock		Average growth rate of labour quality due to education	
	1950–73	1973–92	1950–73	1973–92
Belgium	0.87	1.27	0.52	0.76
France	0.87	1.65	0.52	0.99
Germany	0.46	0.28	0.27	0.17
Ireland	0.44	n.a.	0.26	n.a.
Italy	1.44	2.05	0.86	1.23
Netherlands	1.03	1.39	0.62	0.83
Portugal	2.65	3.64	1.59	2.18
Spain	0.89	3.23	0.53	1.94
Sweden	0.41	1.65	0.25	0.99
UK	0.32	1.00	0.19	0.60
European average	0.94	1.80	0.56	1.08
Japan	1.24	1.09	0.74	0.65
USA	1.13	1.01	0.68	0.61

Source: First two columns derived from last column of Table 2.17. A 0.6 weight was applied to the first two columns, as it is generally accepted that some of the wage differential for extra education represents rewards for intelligence, family connections or the impact of credentialist rules (see Maddison, 1987, p. 661).

expenditure on all types of education in France, Japan and the UK in the 1970s and OECD *Learning Opportunities for Adults*, Vol. IV, *Participation in Adult Education*, Paris, 1977, an analysis of adult education and vocational education in the 1970s which includes surveys for Germany, Italy, The Netherlands, Sweden, the UK and the USA. A recent study of The Netherlands and UK came up with strong conclusions about the superiority of Dutch vocational training without a precise indication of its productivity impact (see Mason *et al.*, 1990).

On the cognitive quality of formal education there are many useful studies sponsored by the International Association for the Evaluation of Educational Achievement (IEA) based on carefully structured tests of thousands of students in primary and secondary education in many countries, but I have not attempted to adjust for cognitive quality here.

5   Physical capital

In the 1950s and 1960s, the literature devoted to 'explaining' economic growth relied a good deal on rates of investment to illustrate changes in

Table 2.19   Ratio of per capita human capital to per capita output level (USA = 100.0)

	1950				1989			
	Human capital per capita	GDP per capita	Human capital output ratio	Physical capital output ratio	Human capital per capita	GDP per capita	Human capital output ratio	Physical capital output ratio
Belgium	87	56	1.55	n.a.	84	75	1.12	n.a.
France	85	55	1.55	0.67	88	80	1.10	0.91
Germany	92	45	2.04	0.74	67	83	0.81	0.95
Ireland	93	37	2.51	n.a.	n.a.	47	n.a.	n.a.
Italy	49	36	1.36	n.a.	62	72	0.86	n.a.
Netherlands	72	61	1.18	0.85	74	74	1.00	0.94
Portugal	22	22	1.00	n.a.	50	48	1.04	n.a.
Spain	46	25	1.84	n.a.	64	54	1.19	n.a.
Sweden	84	70	1.20	n.a.	79	81	0.98	n.a.
UK	96	72	1.33	0.33	78	75	1.04	0.72
European average	73	48	1.56	0.65	72	71[a]	1.02	0.88
Japan	81	20	4.05	0.73	82	82	1.00	1.18

Note: [a] Average excluding Ireland.
Source: The human capital columns are derived from the last column of Table 2.17, per capita GDP from Table 2.4. The human capital–output ratio is derived from the ratio of the two preceding columns. The physical capital–output ratio is derived from Table 2.24.

the productive contribution of capital. Thus Maddison (1964) used investment–output ratios (average investment rates over a period related to output growth rates in the same period) and ECE (1964) used the same analytic tool which it called the incremental capital–output ratio (ICOR), although it was in fact an investment output ratio.

For modern growth accounts, it is necessary to have comparable capital stock estimates in order to measure joint factor productivity. In the course of the 1960s and 1970s several statistical offices began to measure capital stock using the perpetual inventory technique pioneered by Goldsmith (1951). This involves the cumulation of previous investment with allowance for depreciation (for net stock estimates) replacement (for gross stock estimates) and war damage (where appropriate). Such estimates require very long investment series because capital assets have long lives. For non-residential structures, a 40-year run of investment is required. Thus in order to calculate the stock of structures in 1950, investment estimates are needed back to 1910, and we do not have such information for all the countries under study. The position is better for equipment investment where asset lives are much shorter.

OECD (1993c) gives details of the national capital stock estimates made by 15 countries. These include Belgium, France, Germany, Italy, Sweden the UK, Japan and the USA, and the OECD has published a volume about every three years since 1983 which reproduces these estimates (which are available by sector as well as for the whole economy). The method of approach and coverage is rather similar and follows guidelines laid down in Ward (1976). The main drawback to the comparability of the estimates is that there are still significant differences in the assumptions about asset lives, and the estimates are not adjusted for differences in the purchasing power of currencies. Maddison (1995b) provides estimates for six countries which correct for these two problems. These are shown in the Appendix tables for France (1950–91), Germany (1935–91), Japan (1950–91), The Netherlands (1950–92), the UK (1940–91) and the USA (1940–92). These estimates refer to the gross non-residential fixed capital stock and are expressed in constant 1990 dollars. The conversion into dollars was made with the 1990 Geary Khamis purchasing power parity estimates for investment goods in OECD (1993a).

Table 2.20 shows the growth rates for capital which are derived from the Appendix tables. In the post-war Golden Age, there was a major investment boom in the European countries and Japan which led to very high growth of the capital stock.

In Europe the average growth rate of capital stock was 5.2% from 1950 to 1973, with the stock of machinery and equipment rising very fast (an average of 7.8% a year). In Japan the growth rates were faster, but were more marked for structures than for machinery and equipment. In the USA by contrast, the capital stock grew much more slowly in spite of the fact that the American labour supply was rising much more quickly.

The faster European and Japanese growth rates become more understandable when we look at levels of the capital stock. In 1950, the US stock of machinery and equipment per employee was more than four times that in Europe and Japan (Table 2.21). The American advantage over Europe was also very large in non-residential structures, and overwhelming compared to Japan (Table 2.23). The opportunities for catch-up with the USA were very large indeed, given the expansionary demand climate, and the liberalization of trade. The follower countries were able to mount a much larger investment effort than the USA which operated much nearer the frontier of technology and would have probably run into sharply diminishing returns if it had tried to increase capital stocks at the same rate as Europe and Japan.

Table 2.20   Rate of growth of total gross non-residential fixed capital stock (annual average compound growth rates)

	1950–73			1973–91		
	Machinery & equipment	Non-residential structures	Total	Machinery & equipment	Non-residential structures	Total
France	9.09	3.65	4.80	4.44	4.28	4.33
Germany	8.12	5.66	6.30	3.16	3.46	3.37
Netherlands	8.53	3.51	4.55	3.45[a]	2.67[a]	2.92[a]
UK	5.28	5.09	5.17	2.75	3.64	3.30
European average	7.76	4.48	5.21	3.45	3.51	3.48
USA	3.97	2.99	3.27	3.91[a]	2.76[a]	3.13[a]
Japan	8.14	9.81	9.19	7.00	6.71	6.81

Note: [a] 1973–92.
Source: Maddison (1995b).

Table 2.21   Gross stock of machinery and equipment per person employed (in 1990 Geary Khamis dollars)

	1950	1973	1991
France	2,325	15,778	32,587
Germany	3,948	18,513	30,354
Netherlands	3,878	20,394	30,044[a]
UK	4,772	13,909	21,811
European average	3,731	17,149	28,699
USA	15,091	26,093	39,646[a]
Japan	3,234	13,287	37,085

Note: [a] 1992.
Source: Maddison (1995b).

Table 2.22   Rate of growth of the stock of machinery and equipment per person employed (annual average compound growth rate)

	1950–73	1973–91
France	8.68	4.11
Germany	6.95	2.79
Netherlands	7.48	2.06[a]
UK	4.76	2.53
European average	6.86	2.90
USA	2.41	2.22[a]
Japan	6.34	5.87

Note: [a] 1992.
Source: Maddison (1995b).

Table 2.23   Stock of non-residential structures per person employed (in 1990 Geary Khamis dollars)

	1950	1973	1991
France	15,795	33,037	66,412
Germany	14,364	39,697	68,627
Netherlands	25,686	45,393	57,918[a]
UK	7,672	21,490	39,346
European average	15,879	34,904	58,076
USA	42,509	59,085	72,625[a]
Japan	4,518	26,402	70,117

Note: [a] 1992.
Source: Maddison (1995b).

Table 2.24   Ratio of total gross non-residential fixed capital stock to GDP

	1950	1973	1991
France	1.63	1.55	2.22
Germany	1.81	1.94	2.32
Netherlands	2.06	1.98	2.28[a]
UK	0.81	1.32	1.74
European average	1.58	1.70	2.14
USA	2.43	2.12	2.43[a]
Japan	1.77	1.74	2.86

Note: [a] 1992.
Source: Maddison (1995b).

Table 2.25   Average age (in years) of gross non-residential capital stock

	1950	1973	1991
France	18.12	10.54	12.60
Germany	16.46	10.53	13.87
Japan	12.05	7.72	10.61
Netherlands	17.97	11.39	14.01
UK	14.01	10.37	12.97
USA	15.92	12.21	13.91

Source: Derived from Maddison (1995b).

After the Golden Age there was a very sharp deceleration in the growth of capital stock in Europe, as the opportunities for catch-up had narrowed considerably. A deceleration was also noticeable in Japan. In the USA, by contrast, there was little change in growth rates between the two periods.

6   Growth accounts

6.1   The purpose of growth accounts

It is important to develop quantitative evidence to establish what actually happened in the past, and to assess the degree of variance in performance over time and between countries. But it is also important to deploy this evidence to establish why this happened. Causal analysis is complex because there are many interactive forces whose individual impact is difficult to quantify.

Growth accounts can do a good deal to illuminate the forces which lead to economic change. Their explanatory power is substantial compared with what was feasible forty years ago. Nevertheless they must be used with humility. They cannot provide a full causal story. They deal with 'proximate' rather than ultimate causality. They do not explain the elements of policy or circumstance, national or international which underlie them.

In combining the influence of the different measurable elements, I have used my own adaptation of Edward Denison's (1967) growth accounts which are in their turn an augmented and eclectic version of Solow's (1956) neoclassic analysis. They seem to me the most satisfactory and transparent way of merging the available evidence. Their construction forces one to merge and match data in a way that provides valuable cross-checks on the consistency and plausibility of the basic growth indicators. They are particularly useful in avoiding or identifying double counting and in tracking down complex interactions among causal components.

The transparency of the operation is a major advantage, for although there are large judgemental elements, and the quality of the evidence ranges from hard facts to hunches, the individual steps in the analysis are clearly identified and the reader has building bricks for alternative hypotheses. He or she can augment, truncate, or reweight to taste, provided that the 'explanations' of growth are logical, consistent and explicit.

The evidence assembled for growth accounts can be used quite legitimately in other ways. The econometric approach is very useful in checking the plausibility of growth accounting procedures and findings. In particular it is not constrained to the same degree by neoclassic factor weights.

The seminal articles of Romer (1986) and Lucas (1988) provoked a new wave of interest in economic growth and its causes and the 'new growth' analysts rely almost exclusively on regression analysis and econometric techniques. They have explored basic problems of the inter-relation between technical advance and formation of physical and human capital, which have proved elusive in the past. They have thrown new light on problems of convergence and divergence. They stress the possibility of technical spillovers which will produce constant or increasing returns. In my view the most illuminating articles in this new wave are those of Barro (1991) and Mankiw *et al.* (1992).

Levine and Renelt (1992) have made a critical survey with sensitivity testing of the new literature whose explanatory power they have found to be fragile. In Maddison (1995b), I give a more positive assessment. Nevertheless, the new growth literature has generally ignored the achievements of the growth accounting approach. This has sometimes led to distortions of intellectual history by suggesting that a Solow model augmented to encompass human capital and increasing returns is some-thing new. Some of the more enthusiastic disciples of the increasing returns thesis, e.g. De Long and Summers (1991), have reverted to the more or less monocausal use of evidence which Kaldor (1966) deployed to purvey simple-minded policy advice in an earlier generation. Mono-causal or over-simple explanations are much less likely and much less frequent with growth accounting than with regression analysis. A fuller review of developments in growth accounting and their relation to the new growth theory can be found in Maddison (1995a).

6.2   The growth accounts

Table 2.26 provides a summary statement of the growth accounts which can be derived from the quantitative evidence contained in the previous sections. The table covers the six countries where it is possible to provide rather complete growth accounts. For the other countries most of the components are available but the major missing item is comparable estimates for capital stock. The methodology is a simple version of that used in Maddison (1987 and 1991a), where its rationale is more fully explained.

The first entry in the accounts is the growth of GDP. This is the magnitude that the accounts are designed to explain.

6.3   Factor inputs

The next six entries describe the role of factor inputs. Rows 2–4 refer to labour inputs which are given a weight of 0.7. Rows 5–7 refer to the impact of non-residential capital which is given a weight of 0.3. The labour and capital weights correspond roughly with their factor shares.

The second entry represents the contribution of 'raw' labour input. It is derived from the changes in total working hours shown in Table 2.10, with their contribution being weighted by 0.7. The third entry shows the impact of education on labour quality and is taken from the right-hand side of Table 2.18 (weighted by 0.7).

The fourth entry represents the contribution of surplus labour which was apparently employed in 1950 and was dishoarded in 1950–73 in Japan and Germany. In normal circumstances, one would not expect labour hoarding or dishoarding to be significant in advanced capitalist economies over a period of years, because market forces cause workers to be laid off if they cease to be productive. Even in cases where labour legislation restricts freedom to hire and fire, labour turnover will permit substantial attrition over a number of years. However, there are exceptions. Japan has very high ratios of self-employed and family workers and a tradition of lifetime job security for a significant proportion of the labour force. For this reason, I assumed there was a significant degree of Japanese labour hoarding (a quarter of employment) in 1950, which was fully dishoarded by 1973. A modest 3% labour hoarding was assumed for the period of slower growth in 1973–92. The German recovery from the war was not complete in 1950 and the productive structure was in disequilibrium. There was scope for labour hoarding as 31% of the employed were self-employed or family workers.

Table 2.26 Sources of economic growth 1950–92 (annual average percentage point contribution to growth rate)

	France		Germany		Japan	
	1950–73	1973–92	1950–73	1973–92	1950–73	1973–92
GDP	5.02	2.26	5.99	2.30	9.25	3.76
Hours worked	0.01	−0.32	0.00	−0.27	1.01	0.43
Education	0.36	0.69	0.19	0.12	0.52	0.46
Labour dishoarding	0.00	0.00	0.32	0.00	0.88	−0.11
Non-res. capital	1.44	1.30	1.89	1.01	2.76	2.04
Capacity reactivation	0.00	0.00	0.19	0.00	0.38	0.00
Age effect	0.15	−0.04	0.12	−0.08	−0.08	−0.07
Foreign trade effect	0.37	0.12	0.48	0.15	0.53	0.09
Catch-up effect	0.46	0.31	0.62	0.31	0.98	0.39
Structural effect	0.36	0.15	0.36	0.17	1.22	0.20
Economies of scale	0.15	0.07	0.18	0.07	0.28	0.11
Growth explained	3.30	2.28	4.35	1.48	8.64	3.54
Growth unexplained	1.72	−0.02	1.64	0.82	0.61	0.22
Percent explained	66	101	73	64	93	94

	Netherlands		UK		USA	
GDP	4.74	2.14	2.96	1.59	3.91	2.39
Hours worked	−0.05	−0.05	−0.11	−0.40	0.81	0.86
Education	0.43	0.57	0.13	0.42	0.48	0.43
Labour dishoarding	0.00	0.00	0.00	0.00	0.00	0.00
Non-res. capital	1.37	0.88	1.55	0.99	0.98	0.94
Capacity reactivation	0.00	0.00	0.00	0.00	0.00	0.00
Age effect	0.13	−0.06	0.09	−0.06	0.07	−0.04
Foreign trade effect	1.32	0.32	0.32	0.15	0.11	0.05
Catch-up effect	0.41	0.24	0.08	0.20	0.00	0.00
Structural effect	−0.07	−0.12	0.10	−0.09	0.10	−0.17
Economies of scale	0.14	0.06	0.09	0.05	0.12	0.07
Growth explained	3.68	1.85	2.25	1.26	2.67	2.14
Growth unexplained	1.06	0.29	0.71	0.33	1.24	0.25
Percent explained	78	86	76	79	68	90

Source: See text.

I therefore assumed 10% of apparent employment represented labour hoarding in 1950, with complete dishoarding over the period 1950–73.

The fifth row shows the growth of the gross non-residential capital stock. The entries are taken from the third and sixth columns of Table 2.20 (multiplied by 0.3). In Table 2.20 the stock of machinery and equipment and of non-residential structures are shown separately, and many growth analysts might want to exploit these disaggregations to make a more complex analysis of the role of capital. It is clear that a good deal of technical progress can only be exploited by being embodied in new capital, and it seems very probable that the pace of progress is quicker for machinery and equipment than for structures. After 1973, the pace of growth of the two types of capital was less disparate than it was in many countries in the Golden Age (1950–73). There is plenty of scope for using the estimates of capital stock in Table 2.20 and the Appendix tables A.5 to A.10 in a more ambitious way than I have done here.

The sixth entry is relevant only for Japan and Germany and is analogous to the allowance for dishoarding of labour. In both these countries, I assumed that the slack in the use of physical capital paralleled that in the labour market. In the Japanese case the labour slack consisted entirely of labour hoarding. In Germany it included both labour hoarding and most of the overt unemployment. I therefore assumed slack capacity to be a quarter of the existing stock in Japan and about 15% in Germany.

The seventh entry reflects the impact of changes in the age of the capital stock. It can be seen in Table 2.25 that there was a substantial decline in the average age of capital in all six countries in the Golden Age (1950–73). After 1973, by contrast, there were significant increases in the average age. The changes in the age of the stock obviously have had some influence on economic performance. The efficiency of machinery and equipment and of structures tends to decline somewhat over time because of wear and tear, but even more significant is the impact of technical change. The older vintages of capital were installed when technological options were inferior to those available now, so the main advantage derived from rejuvenation of capital in the Golden Age was the possibility of exploiting newer vintages of technology. In estimating the age effect, I assumed a rate of embodied technical change of 1.5% per annum.

6.4   Supplementary items in the explanatory schema

Item 8 is the 'foreign trade effect'. There was a huge acceleration in the growth of foreign trade in all these countries in 1950–73. It was greatest in Germany and Japan, and most modest in the USA. After 1973 its impact was smaller and more evenly distributed between the six countries. This experience obviously played a significant role in the acceleration of growth in the golden age and the slowdown thereafter. In 1950–73, tariffs were removed on a great part of the intertrade of the European Community, and on a worldwide basis in successive GATT rounds. Quantitative restrictions on non-agricultural products were greatly reduced, and exchange controls were abolished or became marginal. By comparison, the impact of tariff reduction after 1973 was milder, and some quantitative reductions have grown. I assumed that the expansion of foreign trade produced 20% economies of scale in 1950–73 and 10% in 1973–92. The trade effect is weighted by the share of exports plus imports in GDP. This share was biggest in The Netherlands, and lowest in the USA.

The *catch-up effect* (item 9) is to some extent already explained by other items in the accounts (e.g. the acceleration of capital inputs), but it seems legitimate to assume that there is an extra efficiency bonus augmenting the yield of factor inputs and other growth components in the follower countries which is not true of the lead country. The catch-up effect was calculated by assuming a 20% bonus from the productivity convergence process (it represents 20% of the growth rates shown in Table 2.15(b)).

The tenth item in the accounts is the 'structural effect'. Economic growth has been accompanied by substantial structural changes, with a large decline in the share of agricultural employment, a big increase in the proportion of activity in services, and a rise and subsequent fall in the industrial share. Virtually all growth analysts attach importance to structural change, particularly in the form of migration from low to high productivity sectors. One must be careful not to exaggerate its autonomous role as the apparent gains are to some extent due to the increases in human and physical capital formation which are already covered elsewhere in the accounts, but I have followed the normal practice of assuming an add-on growth supplement arising from sectoral change. The structural effect is taken here to be the difference between actual output growth and the change in output which would have occurred if the structure of employment had not changed in the period under consideration, whilst assuming that productivity performance in the three major sectors (agriculture, industry and services) had remained as actually experienced.

In some cases my estimates differ from those of Bart van Ark in Chapter 3. I have not tried to reconcile the estimates in detail. However, I have mainly used employment estimates from OECD's *Labour Force*

Statistics, whilst he uses national accounts sources; my sectoral output estimates involved fewer adjustments than his; and he used a different counterfactual assumption. I used the intersectoral productivity levels in the end year of the period considered, and measured the effect of applying the initial year employment distribution to the end year productivity relatives. He has decomposed this change into two components, and only used part of what I considered to be structural influences.

The last item in the explanatory schema is 'economies of scale' at the national level which are not included in strict neoclassic growth accounts which assume constant returns, but in all Denison's studies a significant scale bonus is assumed to occur as national markets increase in size. Other analysts, e.g. Kaldor and the new growth theorists, attribute much bigger gains to scale economies. I have assumed only very modest gains, equal to 3% of GDP growth.

6.5   Degree of 'explanation' contained in the growth accounts

In earlier presentations of growth accounts for these six countries (Maddison, 1987, 1991a) I had a bigger array of explanatory elements than in Table 2.26. These included (i) a further adjustment to the 'quality' of employment by making an allowance for changes in age and sex structure, (ii) an adjustment for changes in the 'quality' of capital due to the embodiment of technical improvements in newer vintages. Here I have only taken account of such effects in relation to changes in the age structure of assets; (iii) allowance for the contribution of residential capital; (iv) adjustments for the impact of the energy price explosion of 1973–84; (v) effects of natural resource windfalls such as North Sea oil and gas for the UK, or the Groningen gas fields for The Netherlands; (vi) costs of government regulation and crime. There is therefore scope for augmenting the accounts presented in Table 2.26.

The bottom row of Table 2.26 shows the explanatory power of the influences which have been taken into account. For 1950–73, the average degree of explanation of these accounts was 76%, with a range from 66% in France to 93% for Japan. For 1973–92, the average degree of explanation was higher at 86%, with a range from 64% in Germany to 101% in France.

Appendix table A.1 GDP indices for ten countries, adjusted to eliminate impact of frontier changes (1913 = 100), 1870–1992

	Belgium	France	Germany	Ireland	Italy	Netherlands	Portugal	Spain	Sweden	UK
1870	42.5	53.1	30.4	80.9	43.8	39.2	58.1	48.8	39.8	44.6
1913	100.0	100.0	100.0	100.0	100.0	100.0	100.0	100.0	100.0	100.0
1929	125.5	134.4	121.3	100.2	131.1	177.4	127.2	149.7	135.9	111.9
1938	125.1	129.7	151.9	108.3	150.8	182.7	159.1	111.9	171.0	132.5
1947	125.4	116.5	89.5	111.1	140.8	194.8	204.8	145.2	241.4	145.6
1948	132.9	125.0	106.0	116.5	148.8	215.6	209.6	142.3	248.9	150.2
1949	138.3	142.0	123.5	122.6	159.8	234.6	213.4	142.8	258.0	155.8
1950	145.9	152.6	147.5	123.6	172.8	243.0	223.3	146.2	271.6	160.8
1951	154.2	162.0	162.0	126.7	185.7	248.1	233.3	161.7	282.4	165.6
1952	153.0	166.3	176.9	129.9	199.6	253.1	233.6	174.4	286.4	165.3
1953	157.9	171.1	192.5	133.4	214.0	275.1	249.9	176.4	294.4	171.8
1954	164.4	179.4	207.3	134.6	225.1	293.8	261.9	186.5	306.8	178.8
1955	172.2	189.7	232.2	138.1	238.2	315.6	272.7	196.2	315.7	185.3
1956	177.2	199.3	249.9	136.3	249.0	327.2	284.6	210.3	327.7	187.6
1957	180.5	211.3	264.6	136.1	263.7	336.4	297.2	219.3	342.4	190.6
1958	180.3	216.6	276.1	133.3	277.8	335.4	301.1	229.1	344.1	190.2
1959	186.0	222.8	297.6	138.7	295.1	351.8	317.4	224.8	354.6	197.9
1960	196.0	238.5	323.4	146.5	311.1	381.4	338.6	230.1	373.4	209.3
1961	205.8	251.6	338.0	153.5	337.3	382.5	357.1	257.3	394.8	216.2
1962	216.5	268.4	353.5	158.2	363.6	408.7	380.8	281.3	411.4	218.4
1963	225.9	282.8	363.3	165.3	389.5	423.5	403.4	305.9	433.3	226.8
1964	241.6	301.2	387.5	173.3	404.7	458.6	430.0	324.8	462.9	238.8
1965	250.2	315.6	408.3	176.3	413.8	482.6	462.0	356.4	480.6	245.0
1966	258.1	332.1	419.9	178.1	435.4	495.9	480.8	393.4	490.6	249.7

Appendix table A.1 *(contd)*

	Belgium	France	Germany	Ireland	Italy	Netherlands	Portugal	Spain	Sweden	UK
1967	268.1	347.6	418.6	186.9	466.4	522.0	517.1	419.1	507.2	255.3
1968	279.4	362.4	441.8	200.6	505.4	555.5	563.1	455.6	525.6	265.7
1969	298.0	387.8	474.7	211.3	534.3	591.3	575.0	506.8	551.9	271.2
1970	316.9	410.0	498.9	218.2	546.3	624.9	627.3	540.6	587.7	277.4
1971	328.5	429.5	513.9	228.1	555.1	651.3	668.9	568.7	593.2	282.9
1972	345.9	447.0	535.8	242.5	570.1	672.9	722.5	616.3	606.8	292.7
1973	366.3	471.2	561.9	255.4	610.5	704.4	803.7	665.9	630.9	314.3
1974	381.3	484.0	563.4	264.3	643.7	732.4	812.8	704.4	651.0	309.0
1975	375.6	482.4	555.5	267.6	626.7	731.7	777.4	711.4	667.7	306.7
1976	396.6	503.7	585.2	273.7	667.9	769.1	831.0	734.8	674.7	315.1
1977	398.5	521.5	601.8	272.9	690.4	787.0	877.3	758.6	664.0	322.4
1978	409.4	539.1	619.9	314.6	715.8	806.3	902.3	770.9	675.6	333.7
1979	418.1	556.2	645.3	325.3	758.7	825.4	953.1	770.7	701.5	343.1
1980	436.1	563.9	652.3	332.3	790.8	832.5	996.9	780.6	713.2	335.5
1981	431.8	570.7	652.9	341.5	795.2	826.7	1,013.2	778.7	713.1	331.2
1982	438.3	583.8	646.8	346.0	796.9	815.0	1,034.7	788.2	720.3	336.9
1983	440.3	588.4	658.2	346.7	804.6	826.5	1,033.1	802.4	732.9	349.6
1984	449.8	597.1	676.7	359.1	826.2	852.6	1,013.6	816.8	762.6	358.3
1985	453.5	608.0	690.4	368.0	847.7	875.1	1,041.9	835.7	777.3	370.8
1986	460.1	622.6	706.6	367.7	872.5	899.1	1,085.0	863.1	795.5	386.8
1987	469.5	636.1	717.1	383.8	899.8	909.7	1,142.3	909.6	820.1	405.2
1988	492.9	663.2	743.8	401.1	936.4	933.5	1,187.0	956.4	838.6	425.5
1989	511.6	688.2	770.7	427.2	963.9	977.4	1,248.1	1,000.3	858.5	434.7
1990	529.1	704.7	814.7	461.1	984.5	1,017.4	1,302.7	1,037.8	870.2	436.4
1991	539.1	709.7	851.7	469.9	996.8	1,038.8	1,330.5	1,060.1	860.5	426.5
1992	543.5	719.9	865.0	491.6	1,006.1	1,053.3	1,344.9	1,069.2	844.0	432.6

Sources for Appendix table A.1: Except as cited below, 1870–1960 from Maddison (1991a) and 1960 onwards from OECD national accounts statistics. 1960–91 from OECD, *National Accounts 1960–91*, Paris, 1993, and 1991–2 movement either from OECD, *Quarterly National Accounts*, No. 1, 1993, Paris, 1993, or from OECD, *Economic Outlook*, June, 1993.

Belgium: 1870–1950 from Maddison 1991a, 1950 onwards from OECD sources. The Belgian series before 1960 are poor and are being revised by the quantitative economic history research group in the University of Leuven.

France: 1920–38 and 1949–60 from J.-C. Toutain, *Le Produit intérieur brut de la France de 1789 à 1982*, Grenoble, 1987. Interpolation between 1938 and 1949 was based on A. Sauvy's report on national income (in 1938 francs) to the Conseil Economique, *Journal officiel*, 7 April 1954, p. 386. 1960 onwards from OECD national accounts.

Germany: 1950–87 GDP in 1985 market prices from Statistiches Bundesamt, *Volkswirtschaftliche Gesamtrechnungen, Revidierte Ergebnisse 1950 bis 1990*, Wiesbaden, updated to 1992 from *Erste Ergebnisse der Sozialproduktberechnung, 1992.*

Ireland: The estimates refer throughout to GDP in the area of the Irish Republic (i.e. Southern Ireland). The 1920 per capita level was 54% of that in the UK (excluding Southern Ireland) as estimated by C.H. Feinstein, *National Income, Expenditure and Output of the United Kingdom 1855–1965*, Cambridge University Press, 1972, Table 6. I assumed that this was valid for 1913 as well. 1926–50 from K.A. Kennedy, *Productivity and Industrial Growth: The Irish Experience*, Oxford University Press, 1971, p. 3. 1950–60 from OECD *National Accounts 1950–1968*, Paris, 1970, 1960–92 from CSO, *National Income and Expenditure 1992*, Dublin, 1993, p. ix, this publication also contains an upward revision of 3.4% in the GDP level from 1986 onwards.

Italy: 1870–1970 from Maddison (1991b). 1970–92 from OECD sources. An alternative estimate can be found in Rossi *et al.* (1992). The latter source shows slower growth for the period 1950–90 than I do. Their growth rate for 1950–90 is 4.3% a year, mine is 4.4%. They use the estimates of Golinelli and Monterastelli (1990) for 1951–90 whereas I use the latter source only for 1951–70, and OECD thereafter. Their estimate for 1890–1913 is also slower than mine, as I used five studies by Fenoaltea which they did not use.

Netherlands: 1870–99 movement supplied by J.L. van Zanden and J.P. Smits. 1900–60 from van Bochove and Huitker (1987). This official retrospective series links six separate segments: 1900-20 current price estimates of income were deflated with a fixed base cost of living index; 1921–39 is a recent official estimate by type of expenditure with annual chain weighting procedures; 1939–48 was bridged by direct comparisons of the two years with rough estimates for the intervening years of the same type as for 1900–20; 1948–68 by the commodity flow method with fixed weights; 1969 onwards is the outcome of a major revision, which raised the level of GDP by 6.2% in the link year 1969. The revised series is an annual chain index only from 1981. 1960 onwards from OECD, *National Accounts* (this incorporates the Dutch estimates and updates them).

Portugal: 1870–1913 GDP volume estimate derived from indices of agricultural and industrial output in Pedro Lains, 'How Far Can We Go? Measuring Portuguese Economic Growth (1850–1913)' and statistical annexe, paper presented to the World

Cliometric Congress, Santander, 1989; for the service sector I used population as a proxy indicator. The 1890 sector weights (agriculture 49.3, industry 24.7 and services 26.0) were taken from Lains. For 1913–53 I used an adjusted version of the GDP estimates of A.B. Nunes, E. Mata and N. Valerio, 'Portuguese Economic Growth 1833–1985', *Journal of European Economic History*, Vol. 18, 2, Fall, 1989. The Nunes, Mata, Valerio estimates have been criticized by P. Lains and J. Reis, 'Portuguese Economic Growth, 1833–1985: Some Doubts', *Journal of European Economic History*, Vol. 20, 2, Fall, 1991. The Nunes, Mata, Valerio estimates for GDP are based on three proxy indicators (exports, fiscal receipts, and government expenditures) at current prices, which they deflate by the cost of living index. These indicators are adjusted in the light of the relationship between their estimating technique and the official GDP series for 1947–85. I took their GDP estimate as representative for the material production sectors, and used population as a proxy for service sector growth. 1938–58 from *O Rendimento Nacional Português, Estudos*, No. 34, Instituto Nacional de Estatística, Lisbon, 1960; 1958–60 from R. Janes Cartado and N.E. Sequiera da Rosa, *Series Longas as Contas Nacionais Portuguesas 1958–1985*, Banco de Portugal, Lisbon, 1986. 1960 onwards from OECD, *National Accounts*, various issues. Recently (1994) the Portuguese authorities made an upward revision of 14.1545% to the 1990 GDP level, in order to incorporate the islands of the Azores and Madeira which were previously excluded, and to provide better estimates for construction and tourism; sectors which had previously been inadequately covered.

Spain: GDP by industry of origin 1870–1950 from Leandro Prados de la Escosura, 'Spain's Real Gross Domestic Product, 1850–1990: A New Series', Ministério de Economia y Hacienda, Madrid, March, 1993, Table D.1. Prados showed his results for all years at 1980 'prices', but this is simply his numeraire, as the underlying procedure was to chain successive sectors at characteristic constant prices for the relevant period. For 1950–92, Prados has since made a tapered adjustment for jumps in the GDP level between successive segments of the official national accounts. The Spanish authorities have hitherto ignored these jumps and simply linked the successive indices at the overlap year. Prados's procedure is analogous to that which I used to adjust the official Italian estimates.

Sweden: 1870–1960 GDP estimates by industry or origin supplied by Olle Krantz. His procedures are explained in O. Krantz, 'New Estimates of Swedish Historical GDP since the Beginning of the Nineteenth Century', *Review of Income and Wealth*, June, 1988. 1960 onwards from OECD, *National Accounts*.

UK: 1870–1960 from C.H. Feinstein, *National Income Expenditure and Output of the United Kingdom 1855–1965*, Cambridge, 1972, pp. T18–20. I used his 'compromise' estimates which average the results of his real expenditure, output and income estimates. 1960 onwards from OECD sources.

Appendix table A.2   Levels of GDP in ten countries in million 1990 Geary Khamis dollars, adjusted to eliminate the impact of frontier changes, 1870–1992

	Belgium	France	Germany	Ireland	Italy	Netherlands	Portugal	Spain	Sweden	UK
1870	13,456	75,999	44,101	6,836	40,900	9,545	4,722	22,295	6,927	95,651
1913	31,661	143,125	145,068	8,450	93,399	24,349	8,127	45,686	17,404	214,464
1929	39,735	192,360	175,968	8,467	122,443	43,196	10,337	68,391	23,652	239,985
1938	39,608	185,633	220,359	9,151	140,833	44,486	12,929	51,122	29,761	284,165
1947	39,703	166,740	129,836	9,388	131,506	47,432	16,643	66,335	42,014	312,260
1948	42,078	178,906	153,772	9,844	138,967	52,497	17,033	65,011	43,319	322,125
1949	43,787	203,237	179,159	10,360	149,227	57,124	17,342	65,239	44,903	334,135
1950	46,194	218,409	213,976	10,444	161,351	59,169	18,146	66,792	47,270	344,859
1951	48,821	231,862	235,011	10,706	173,476	60,411	18,959	73,874	49,149	355,153
1952	48,442	238,017	256,626	10,977	186,421	61,628	18,984	79,676	49,846	354,509
1953	49,993	244,887	279,256	11,272	199,899	66,985	20,308	80,589	51,238	368,450
1954	52,051	256,766	300,726	11,374	210,270	71,538	21,283	85,204	53,396	383,462
1955	54,520	271,508	336,848	11,669	222,475	76,846	22,161	89,635	54,945	397,402
1956	56,104	285,248	362,526	11,517	232,562	79,671	23,128	96,077	57,033	402,335
1957	57,148	302,423	383,851	11,500	246,325	81,911	24,152	100,188	59,592	408,769
1958	57,085	310,008	400,533	11,264	259,449	81,668	24,469	104,666	59,888	407,911
1959	58,890	318,882	431,723	11,720	275,630	85,661	25,794	102,701	61,715	424,425
1960	62,056	341,353	469,151	12,379	290,574	92,868	27,516	105,123	64,987	448,874
1961	65,159	360,102	490,331	12,971	315,053	93,136	29,020	117,549	68,712	463,672
1962	68,546	384,147	512,816	13,368	339,591	99,516	30,946	128,514	71,601	468,390
1963	71,522	404,757	527,033	13,968	363,813	103,119	32,782	139,752	75,412	486,405
1964	76,493	431,092	562,139	14,644	377,977	111,666	34,944	148,387	80,564	512,141
1965	79,216	451,702	592,314	14,897	386,481	117,510	37,544	162,823	83,644	525,437
1966	81,717	475,318	609,142	15,049	406,657	120,748	39,072	179,727	85,385	535,517
1967	84,883	497,502	607,256	15,793	435,584	127,103	42,022	191,468	88,274	547,527

Appendix table A.2 *(contd)*

	Belgium	France	Germany	Ireland	Italy	Netherlands	Portugal	Spain	Sweden	UK
1968	88,461	518,685	640,912	16,951	472,048	135,260	45,760	208,144	91,476	569,832
1969	94,350	555,038	688,639	17,855	498,996	143,978	46,727	231,535	96,054	581,627
1970	100,334	586,812	723,745	18,438	510,200	152,159	50,978	246,976	102,284	594,924
1971	104,007	614,721	745,506	19,274	518,457	158,587	54,358	259,814	103,241	606,719
1972	109,516	639,768	777,276	20,491	532,466	163,847	58,714	281,560	105,608	627,737
1973	115,975	674,404	815,138	21,581	570,200	171,517	65,313	304,220	109,803	674,061
1974	120,724	692,724	817,314	22,333	601,208	178,334	66,052	321,809	113,301	662,695
1975	118,919	690,434	805,854	22,612	585,330	178,164	64,175	325,007	116,208	657,762
1976	125,568	720,920	848,939	23,128	623,810	187,271	67,531	335,698	117,426	675,777
1977	126,170	746,396	873,021	23,060	644,825	191,629	71,294	346,571	115,564	691,433
1978	129,621	771,586	899,278	26,584	668,514	196,329	73,325	352,190	117,583	715,667
1979	132,375	796,061	936,125	27,488	708,617	200,979	77,454	352,099	122,090	735,827
1980	138,074	807,081	946,280	28,079	738,598	202,708	81,013	356,622	124,126	719,528
1981	136,713	816,814	947,151	28,857	742,707	201,296	82,338	355,754	124,109	710,306
1982	138,771	835,563	938,301	29,237	744,295	198,447	84,085	360,094	125,362	722,530
1983	139,404	842,147	954,839	29,296	751,487	201,247	83,955	366,581	127,555	749,767
1984	142,412	854,599	981,677	30,344	771,661	207,602	82,370	373,160	132,724	768,425
1985	143,583	870,199	1,001,551	31,096	791,741	213,081	84,670	381,794	135,283	795,233
1986	145,673	891,095	1,025,052	31,071	814,904	218,925	88,173	394,312	138,450	829,548
1987	148,649	910,417	1,040,284	32,431	840,402	221,506	92,829	415,556	142,732	869,009
1988	156,058	949,204	1,079,018	33,893	874,586	227,301	96,462	436,937	145,951	912,545
1989	161,978	984,985	1,118,041	36,098	900,271	237,942	101,427	456,993	149,415	932,276
1990	167,519	1,008,601	1,181,871	38,963	919,511	247,730	105,864	474,125	151,451	935,922
1991	170,685	1,015,757	1,235,546	39,707	930,999	252,941	108,123	484,313	149,763	914,690
1992	172,078	1,030,356	1,254,840	41,540	939,685	256,471	109,293	488,470	146,891	910,401

Source: Maddison (1995a).

Appendix table A.3 Population of ten countries adjusted to eliminate impact of frontier changes (thousands at mid-year); 1870–1992

	Belgium	France	Germany	Ireland	Italy	Netherlands	Portugal	Spain	Sweden	UK
1870	5,096	38,440	23,055	3,856	27,888	3,615	4,353	16,201	4,164	29,312
1913	7,666	41,690	38,301	3,092	37,248	6,164	6,004	20,263	5,621	42,622
1929	8,032	41,230	40,595	2,937	40,469	7,782	6,729	23,210	6,113	45,672
1938	8,374	41,960	42,990	2,937	43,419	8,685	7,575	25,279	6,298	47,484
1947	8,450	40,680	46,992	2,974	46,040	9,630	8,258	29,223	6,803	49,519
1948	8,557	41,110	48,251	2,985	46,381	9,800	8,358	27,437	6,884	50,014
1949	8,614	41,480	49,198	2,981	46,733	9,956	8,434	27,651	6,956	50,312
1950	8,640	41,836	49,983	2,969	47,105	10,114	8,512	27,868	7,015	50,363
1951	8,679	42,156	50,528	2,961	47,418	10,264	8,547	28,086	7,071	50,574
1952	8,731	42,460	50,859	2,953	47,666	10,382	8,563	28,332	7,125	50,737
1953	8,778	42,752	51,350	2,949	47,957	10,494	8,587	28,571	7,171	50,880
1954	8,820	43,057	51,880	2,941	48,299	10,616	8,607	28,812	7,213	51,066
1955	8,869	43,428	52,382	2,921	48,633	10,751	8,657	29,056	7,262	51,221
1956	8,924	43,843	53,008	2,898	48,921	10,888	8,698	29,355	7,315	51,430
1957	8,989	44,311	53,656	2,885	49,182	11,026	8,737	29,657	7,367	51,657
1958	9,053	44,789	54,292	2,853	49,476	11,187	8,789	29,962	7,415	51,870
1959	9,104	45,240	54,876	2,846	49,832	11,348	8,837	30,271	7,454	52,157
1960	9,154	45,684	55,433	2,834	50,198	11,486	8,891	30,583	7,480	52,373
1961	9,184	46,163	56,175	2,819	50,524	11,639	8,444	30,904	7,520	52,807
1962	9,218	46,998	56,837	2,830	50,844	11,806	9,002	31,158	7,562	53,292
1963	9,283	47,816	57,389	2,850	51,199	11,966	9,040	31,430	7,604	53,625
1964	9,367	48,310	57,971	2,864	51,601	12,127	9,053	31,741	7,662	53,991
1965	9,448	48,758	58,619	2,876	51,988	12,292	8,996	32,085	7,734	54,350
1966	9,508	49,164	59,148	2,884	52,332	12,455	8,871	32,453	7,807	54,643
1967	9,557	49,548	59,286	2,900	52,667	12,597	8,798	32,850	7,869	54,959

Appendix table A.3 *(contd)*

	Belgium	France	Germany	Ireland	Italy	Netherlands	Portugal	Spain	Sweden	UK
1968	9,590	49,915	59,500	2,813	52,787	12,730	8,743	33,240	7,912	55,214
1969	9,613	50,315	60,067	2,926	53,317	12,878	8,696	33,566	7,968	55,461
1970	9,638	50,772	60,651	2,950	53,661	13,039	8,663	33,876	8,043	55,632
1971	9,673	51,251	61,302	2,978	54,015	13,194	8,624	34,190	8,098	55,907
1972	9,711	51,701	61,672	3,024	54,400	13,329	8,637	34,498	8,122	56,079
1973	9,742	52,118	61,976	3,073	54,779	13,439	8,630	34,810	8,137	56,210
1974	9,772	52,460	62,054	3,124	55,130	13,545	8,879	35,147	8,160	56,224
1975	9,801	52,699	61,829	3,177	55,441	13,666	9,308	35,515	8,192	56,215
1976	9,818	52,909	61,531	3,228	55,701	13,774	9,403	35,937	8,222	56,206
1977	9,845	53,145	61,400	3,272	55,730	13,856	9,508	36,367	8,251	56,179
1978	9,872	53,376	61,327	3,314	56,127	13,942	9,609	36,778	8,275	56,167
1979	9,837	53,606	61,359	3,368	56,292	14,038	9,714	37,108	8,294	56,227
1980	9,847	53,880	61,566	3,401	56,416	14,150	9,819	37,386	8,311	56,314
1981	9,853	54,182	61,682	3,443	56,503	14,247	9,851	37,751	8,324	56,379
1982	9,856	54,480	61,638	3,480	56,639	14,313	9,877	37,961	8,327	56,335
1983	9,855	54,729	61,423	3,505	56,825	14,367	9,892	38,180	8,329	56,377
1984	9,855	54,947	61,175	3,529	56,983	14,424	9,904	38,342	8,337	56,488
1985	9,858	55,170	61,024	3,540	57,128	14,491	9,905	38,505	8,350	56,618
1986	9,862	55,394	61,066	3,541	57,221	14,572	9,903	38,668	8,370	56,763
1987	9,870	55,630	61,977	3,542	57,331	14,665	9,898	38,716	8,398	56,930
1988	9,921	55,884	61,451	3,538	57,441	14,760	9,889	38,809	8,436	57,065
1989	9,938	56,423	62,063	3,515	57,525	14,849	9,795	38,888	8,493	57,236
1990	9,967	56,735	63,254	3,503	57,647	14,951	9,908	38,959	8,559	57,411
1991	10,005	57,050	63,889	3,524	57,783	15,070	9,814	39,025	8,617	57,649
1992	10,025	57,372	64,846	3,547	57,900	15,178	9,820	39,085	8,678	57,848

Sources: Maddison (1995a). All figures are on a mid-year basis, and are adjusted to eliminate the effect of frontier changes. The figures refer throughout to population within present frontiers, except for Germany where they refer to the Federal Republic as it was before the incorporation of East Germany.

Appendix table A.4 Levels of GDP per capita in ten countries in 1990 Geary Khamis dollars, 1870–1992

	Belgium	France	Germany	Ireland	Italy	Netherlands	Portugal	Spain	Sweden	UK
1870	2,640	1,977	1,913	1,733	1,467	2,640	1,085	1,376	1,664	3,263
1913	4,130	3,433	3,788	2,733	2,507	3,950	1,354	2,255	3,096	5,032
1929	4,947	4,666	4,335	2,883	3,026	5,551	1,536	2,947	3,869	5,255
1938	4,730	4,424	5,126	3,116	3,244	5,122	1,707	2,022	4,725	5,984
1947	4,699	4,099	2,763	3,157	2,856	4,925	2,015	2,270	6,176	6,306
1948	4,917	4,352	3,187	3,298	2,996	5,357	2,038	2,369	6,293	6,441
1949	5,083	4,900	3,642	3,475	3,193	5,738	2,056	2,359	6,455	6,641
1950	5,346	5,221	4,281	3,518	3,425	5,850	2,132	2,397	6,738	6,847
1951	5,625	5,500	4,651	3,616	3,658	5,886	2,218	2,630	6,951	7,022
1952	5,548	5,606	5,046	3,717	3,911	5,936	2,217	2,812	6,996	6,987
1953	5,695	5,728	5,438	3,822	4,168	6,383	2,365	2,821	7,145	7,242
1954	5,901	5,963	5,797	3,867	4,354	6,739	2,473	2,957	7,403	7,509
1955	6,147	6,252	6,431	3,995	4,575	7,148	2,560	3,085	7,566	7,759
1956	6,287	6,506	6,839	3,974	4,754	7,317	2,659	3,273	7,797	7,823
1957	6,358	6,825	7,154	3,986	5,008	7,429	2,764	3,378	8,089	7,913
1958	6,306	6,922	7,377	3,948	5,244	7,300	2,784	3,493	8,077	7,864
1959	6,469	7,049	7,867	4,118	5,531	7,549	2,919	3,393	8,279	8,137
1960	6,779	7,472	8,463	4,368	5,789	8,085	3,095	3,437	8,688	8,571
1961	7,095	7,801	8,729	4,601	6,236	8,002	3,437	3,804	9,137	8,780
1962	7,436	8,174	9,023	4,724	6,679	8,429	3,438	4,125	9,468	8,789
1963	7,705	8,465	9,184	4,901	7,106	8,618	3,626	4,446	9,917	9,070
1964	8,166	8,923	9,697	5,113	7,325	9,208	3,860	4,675	10,515	9,486
1965	8,384	9,264	10,104	5,180	7,434	9,560	4,173	5,075	10,815	9,668
1966	8,595	9,668	10,299	5,218	7,771	9,695	4,404	5,538	10,937	9,800
1967	8,882	10,041	10,243	5,446	8,271	10,090	4,776	5,829	11,218	9,962

Appendix table A.4 (contd)

	Belgium	France	Germany	Ireland	Italy	Netherlands	Portugal	Spain	Sweden	UK
1968	9,224	10,391	10,772	6,026	8,943	10,625	5,234	6,262	11,562	10,320
1969	9,815	11,031	11,465	6,102	9,359	11,180	5,373	6,898	12,055	10,487
1970	10,410	11,558	11,933	6,250	9,508	11,670	5,885	7,291	12,717	10,694
1971	10,752	11,994	12,161	6,472	9,598	12,020	6,303	7,599	12,749	10,852
1972	11,278	12,374	12,603	6,776	9,788	12,292	6,798	8,162	13,003	11,194
1973	11,905	12,940	13,152	7,023	10,409	12,763	7,568	8,739	13,494	11,992
1974	12,354	13,205	13,171	7,149	10,905	13,166	7,439	9,156	13,885	11,787
1975	12,133	13,101	13,034	7,117	10,558	13,037	6,787	9,151	14,185	11,701
1976	12,790	13,626	13,797	7,165	11,199	13,596	7,182	9,341	14,282	12,023
1977	12,816	14,045	14,219	7,048	11,571	13,830	7,498	9,530	14,006	12,308
1978	13,130	14,456	14,664	8,022	11,911	14,082	7,631	9,576	14,209	12,742
1979	13,457	14,850	15,257	8,161	12,588	14,317	7,973	9,488	14,720	13,087
1980	14,022	14,979	15,370	8,256	13,092	14,326	8,251	9,539	14,935	12,777
1981	13,875	15,075	15,355	8,381	13,145	14,129	8,358	9,424	14,910	12,599
1982	14,080	15,337	15,223	8,401	13,141	13,865	8,513	9,486	15,055	12,826
1983	14,146	15,388	15,545	8,358	13,225	14,008	8,487	9,601	15,315	13,299
1984	14,451	15,553	16,047	8,598	13,542	14,393	8,317	9,732	15,920	13,603
1985	14,565	15,773	16,412	8,784	13,859	14,704	8,548	9,915	16,202	14,046
1986	14,771	16,086	16,786	8,775	14,241	15,024	8,904	10,197	16,541	14,614
1987	15,061	16,366	17,032	9,156	14,659	15,104	9,379	10,733	16,996	15,265
1988	15,730	16,985	17,559	9,580	15,226	15,400	9,754	11,259	17,301	15,991
1989	16,299	17,457	18,015	10,270	15,650	16,024	10,355	11,752	17,593	16,288
1990	16,807	17,777	18,685	11,123	15,951	16,569	10,685	12,170	17,695	16,302
1991	17,060	17,805	19,339	11,267	16,112	16,784	11,017	12,410	17,380	15,867
1992	17,165	17,959	19,351	11,711	16,229	16,898	11,130	12,498	16,927	15,738

Source: Maddison (1995a) which also gives updated figures.

Appendix table A.5   France: gross stock of fixed non-residential capital at 1990 prices at mid-year

Year	Gross stock of non-residential structures	Gross stock of machinery and equipment
	(million 1990 Geary Khamis $)	
1950	310,572	45,710
1951	314,613	48,289
1952	317,446	50,944
1953	319,868	53,907
1954	323,551	58,233
1955	329,306	64,597
1956	336,668	72,259
1957	346,271	81,128
1958	357,578	90,875
1959	369,453	101,437
1960	382,231	111,967
1961	396,369	122,232
1962	411,861	132,751
1963	427,462	143,780
1964	444,642	156,143
1965	463,950	169,396
1966	486,673	183,999
1967	513,414	200,322
1968	540,624	217,946
1969	568,280	238,005
1970	598,907	260,081
1971	632,618	283,658
1972	669,216	309,636
1973	708,107	338,185
1974	747,640	367,227
1975	787,484	393,250
1976	827,757	418,408
1977	868,122	444,153
1978	908,059	468,811
1979	951,144	493,772
1980	998,163	519,799
1981	1,045,833	545,101
1982	1,093,587	568,287
1983	1,140,411	587,513
1984	1,185,888	602,325
1985	1,228,951	615,997
1986	1,270,390	629,844
1987	1,311,540	643,554
1988	1,354,504	660,664
1989	1,401,342	685,327
1990	1,451,615	713,136
1991	1,505,636	738,781

Appendix table A.6   Germany: gross stock of fixed non-residential capital at 1990 prices at mid-year

Year	Gross stock of non-residential structures	Gross stock of machinery and equipment
	(million 1990 Geary Khamis $)	
1935	350,504	69,377
1936	355,085	69,605
1937	360,692	71,033
1938	367,851	74,024
1939	375,944	77,539
1940	381,942	80,903
1941	384,579	83,780
1942	383,419	86,023
1943	378,310	87,850
1944	370,593	88,676
1945	336,874	81,992
1946	304,692	75,393
1947	300,613	75,697
1948	299,989	76,762
1949	301,561	79,542
1950	303,990	83,557
1951	307,301	87,729
1952	312,544	91,745
1953	321,339	95,924
1954	333,870	101,546
1955	351,129	109,975
1956	373,324	120,663
1957	398,669	132,139
1958	425,932	145,498
1959	454,900	162,868
1960	485,639	184,221
1961	517,858	208,333
1962	552,870	233,265
1963	590,803	256,498
1964	632,491	278,996
1965	677,530	302,939
1966	722,558	326,995
1967	764,112	348,384
1968	804,004	367,821
1969	848,961	389,096
1970	902,009	414,951
1971	961,401	444,909
1972	1,021,511	475,047
1973	1,078,163	502,819
1974	1,130,917	524,908
1975	1,179,705	541,057
1976	1,225,713	556,009
1977	1,269,874	573,010

Appendix table A.6 *(contd)*

Year	Gross stock of non-residential structures	Gross stock of machinery and equipment
	(million 1990 Geary Khamis $)	
1978	1,313,644	592,477
1979	1,361,522	613,780
1980	1,413,910	637,260
1981	1,467,124	661,892
1982	1,519,800	683,494
1983	1,572,905	699,993
1984	1,626,640	711,057
1985	1,679,648	720,086
1986	1,732,950	732,412
1987	1,786,170	748,250
1988	1,837,059	770,465
1989	1,886,885	800,567
1990	1,937,481	837,445
1991	1,989,710	880,054

Appendix table A.7   Japan: gross stock of fixed non-residential capital at 1990 prices at mid-year

Year	Gross stock of non-residential structures	Gross stock of machinery and equipment
	(million 1990 Geary Khamis $)	
1950	161,223	115,409
1951	168,583	114,131
1952	177,874	112,466
1953	189,586	109,578
1954	203,314	105,315
1955	218,224	99,985
1956	235,043	95,928
1957	254,220	93,482
1958	274,949	91,559
1959	297,753	94,665
1960	325,340	106,446
1961	360,928	124,498
1962	404,161	145,999
1963	452,457	170,414
1964	505,505	198,837
1965	560,990	229,782
1966	619,398	262,217
1967	696,235	299,163
1968	785,762	345,899
1969	880,330	405,861

Appendix table A.7 *(contd)*

Year	Gross stock of non-residential structures	Gross stock of machinery and equipment
	(million 1990 Geary Khamis $)	
1970	991,034	475,090
1971	1,113,831	546,324
1972	1,245,617	618,798
1973	1,388,481	698,778
1974	1,532,674	776,379
1975	1,673,312	840,286
1976	1,814,156	898,899
1977	1,956,429	958,513
1978	2,106,106	1,021,024
1979	2,267,885	1,091,437
1980	2,439,055	1,167,072
1981	2,614,412	1,242,354
1982	2,789,110	1,312,951
1983	2,959,266	1,374,742
1984	3,128,826	1,437,830
1985	3,298,060	1,514,571
1986	3,466,384	1,601,603
1987	3,639,027	1,693,039
1988	3,821,937	1,808,504
1989	4,021,341	1,964,712
1990	4,236,974	2,153,935
1991	4,465,722	2,361,932

Appendix table A.8 Netherlands: gross stock of fixed non-residential capital at 1990 prices at mid-year

Year	Gross stock of non-residential structures	Gross stock of machinery and equipment
	(million 1990 Geary Khamis $)	
1950	105,827	15,978
1951	108,045	17,401
1952	109,954	18,362
1953	112,353	19,257
1954	115,237	21,002
1955	118,239	23,929
1956	121,668	27,809
1957	125,253	32,344
1958	128,543	36,710
1959	131,783	40,964
1960	135,580	45,491
1961	140,040	49,782

Appendix table A.8 *(contd)*

Year	Gross stock of non-residential structures	Gross stock of machinery and equipment
	(million 1990 Geary Khamis $)	
1962	145,170	53,766
1963	150,692	57,629
1964	157,328	61,472
1965	164,730	65,649
1966	172,217	70,540
1967	180,422	75,829
1968	189,472	81,246
1969	198,437	86,154
1970	207,095	90,679
1971	216,334	95,193
1972	225,449	99,737
1973	233,773	105,027
1974	241,721	110,519
1975	249,708	115,247
1976	257,814	118,886
1977	265,541	122,716
1978	272,909	127,285
1979	281,030	131,831
1980	290,300	135,688
1981	299,639	138,216
1982	308,386	139,539
1983	316,929	141,155
1984	325,709	143,463
1985	334,250	147,604
1986	341,784	154,464
1987	348,422	161,538
1988	355,095	167,646
1989	362,257	174,352
1990	369,721	182,863
1991	377,687	191,749
1992	385,443	199,945

Appendix table A.9 UK: gross stock of fixed non-residential capital at 1990 prices at mid-year

Year	Gross stock of non-residential structures	Gross stock of machinery and equipment
	(million 1990 Geary Khamis $)	
1940	175,271	92,403
1941	174,053	95,618
1942	172,123	96,778

Appendix table A.9   *(contd)*

Year	Gross stock of non-residential structures	Gross stock of machinery and equipment
	(million 1990 Geary Khamis $)	
1943	169,916	96,244
1944	167,221	94,535
1945	162,355	90,897
1946	159,755	89,203
1947	161,783	92,532
1948	164,392	97,113
1949	167,577	101,910
1950	171,863	106,884
1951	176,730	111,923
1952	181,416	116,579
1953	186,596	121,097
1954	193,307	125,923
1955	201,970	131,984
1956	212,409	139,997
1957	224,005	150,166
1958	235,992	162,601
1959	247,149	176,245
1960	259,273	189,590
1961	274,415	201,804
1962	290,843	212,699
1963	307,000	222,346
1964	324,140	232,770
1965	343,650	244,620
1966	364,303	257,942
1967	386,362	272,561
1968	410,081	287,287
1969	433,776	300,867
1970	458,425	313,894
1971	485,130	326,419
1972	512,206	337,399
1973	538,886	348,786
1974	564,291	360,936
1975	588,654	370,878
1976	612,601	380,174
1977	635,187	390,851
1978	656,359	401,728
1979	678,212	413,445
1980	701,104	424,297
1981	723,512	431,087
1982	747,269	435,013
1983	773,241	439,683
1984	800,691	446,557
1985	827,572	457,034
1986	853,483	470,458

Appendix table A.9   *(contd)*

Year	Gross stock of non-residential structures	Gross stock of machinery and equipment
	(million 1990 Geary Khamis $)	
1987	882,137	484,257
1988	914,941	500,764
1989	950,209	523,976
1990	987,330	549,102
1991	1,025,131	568,268

Appendix table A.10   USA: gross stock of fixed non-residential capital at 1990 prices at mid-year

Year	Gross stock of non-residential structures	Gross stock of machinery and equipment
	(million 1990 Geary Khamis $)	
1940	2,484,977	438,281
1941	2,508,931	448,161
1942	2,531,869	472,954
1943	2,538,743	511,343
1944	2,530,761	557,455
1945	2,522,821	610,347
1946	2,526,588	668,864
1947	2,543,146	736,514
1948	2,566,002	812,050
1949	2,591,536	875,941
1950	2,620,695	930,386
1951	2,658,250	985,605
1952	2,701,940	1,048,233
1953	2,758,111	1,117,880
1954	2,830,890	1,180,296
1955	2,910,861	1,233,434
1956	2,998,397	1,279,688
1957	3,098,349	1,309,743
1958	3,200,357	1,322,863
1959	3,293,465	1,335,407
1960	3,388,731	1,360,669
1961	3,491,483	1,382,686
1962	3,592,296	1,397,754
1963	3,694,714	1,427,915
1964	3,807,875	1,472,607
1965	3,934,062	1,529,449
1966	4,069,575	1,603,031
1967	4,208,297	1,681,563
1968	4,347,000	1,765,499

Appendix table A.10 (*contd*)

Year	Gross stock of non-residential structures	Gross stock of machinery and equipment
	(million 1990 Geary Khamis $)	
1969	4,488,452	1,859,394
1970	4,638,086	1,950,578
1971	4,802,265	2,037,060
1972	4,979,241	2,142,504
1973	5,163,463	2,280,228
1974	5,347,089	2,431,580
1975	5,508,789	2,568,874
1976	5,650,200	2,690,015
1977	5,791,755	2,822,551
1978	5,942,856	2,976,429
1979	6,114,925	3,134,464
1980	6,298,494	3,269,826
1981	6,486,419	3,387,035
1982	6,693,444	3,484,898
1983	6,904,958	3,562,727
1984	7,119,846	3,664,626
1985	7,348,410	3,804,318
1986	7,565,627	3,949,120
1987	7,762,728	4,067,936
1988	7,950,724	4,177,069
1989	8,138,481	4,321,616
1990	8,327,004	4,487,613
1991	8,500,883	4,621,782
1992	8,654,232	4,723,222

Source for Appendix tables A.5–A.10, Maddison (1995b), pp. 148–156.

NOTES

I am grateful for comments on an earlier draft from Bart van Ark, Edwin R. Dean, John Evans and David Grubb, and to Nanno Mulder for statistical help.

REFERENCES

den Bakker, G.P. (1991), 'The Choice of Index Number Formulae and Weights in the National Accounts: A Sensitivity Analysis based on Macro-economic Data for the Interwar Period', CBS Occasional Paper NA-044, The Hague.

Barro, R.J. (1991), 'Economic Growth in a Cross-Section of Countries', *Quarterly Journal of Economics*, May.

Beckerman, W. (1966), 'The Determinants of Economic Growth', in P.D. Henderson (ed.), *Economic Growth in Britain*, Weidenfeld & Nicolson, London.

Blades, D. and D. Roberts (1987), 'A Note on the New OECD Benchmark Parities for 1985', OECD *Economic Studies*, Autumn.

van Bochove, C.A. and T.A. Huitker (1987), 'Main National Accounting Series, 1900–86', CBS, Occasional Paper 17, The Hague.

CBS (1985) *Nationale rekeningen 1969–1981 met herziene reeksen voor de jaren 1969–1976*, The Hague.

CSO (1985), *United Kingdom National Accounts: Sources and Methods*, Studies in Official Statistics No. 37, London.

De Long, J.B. and L.H. Summers (1991), 'Equipment Investment and Economic Growth', *Quarterly Journal of Economics*, May.

Denison, E.F. (1967), *Why Growth Rates Differ*, Washington, DC: Brookings.

Dewhurst, J.F. and Associates (1961), *Europe's Needs and Resources*, New York: Twentieth Century Fund.

ECE (1964), *Some Factors in Economic Growth in Europe During the 1950s*, Geneva.

Elfring, T. (1988), *Service Employment in Advanced Countries: A Comparative Analysis and its Implications for Economic Growth*, Ph.D. thesis, University of Groningen.

Elsas, M.J. (1942), 'The Definition of National Income' in A.L. Bowley, *Studies in the National Income 1924–1938*, Cambridge: Cambridge University Press.

Gilbert, M. and Associates (1958), *Comparative National Products and Price Levels*, Paris: OEEC.

Gilbert, M. and I.B. Kravis (1954), *An International Comparison of National Products and the Purchasing Power of Currencies*, Paris: OEEC.

Goldsmith, R.W. (1951), 'A Perpetual Inventory of National Wealth', in M.R. Gainsburgh, *Studies in Income and Wealth*, Vol. 14, Princeton: Princeton University Press.

Golinelli, R. and M. Monterastelli (1990), 'Un metodo per la ricostruzione de serie storiche compatibili con la nuova contabilitá nazionale 1951–1989', Bologna: Prometeia.

Hill, T.P. (1971), *The Measurement of Real Product: A Theoretical and Empirical Analysis of the Growth Rates for Different Industries and Countries*, Paris: OECD.

Hofman, A. (1993), 'The Capital Stock of Spain in the 20th Century', June, ECLAC, Santiago, mimeographed.

ILO (1976), *International Recommendations on Labour Statistics*, Geneva.

ISTAT (1987), *Conti economici nazionali, anni 1980–86*, Rome.

Kaldor, N. (1966), *Causes of the Slow Rate of Growth of the United Kingdom*, Cambridge: Cambridge University Press.

Kotwal, M. (1975) 'Inequalities in the Distribution of Education between Countries, Sexes, Generations and Individuals', in *Education, Inequality and Life Chances*, Paris, OECD.

Kravis, I.B., A. Heston and R. Summers (1982), *World Product and Income*, Baltimore, MD: Johns Hopkins University Press.

Levine, R. and D. Renelt (1992), 'A Sensitivity Analysis of Cross-Country Growth Regressions', *American Economic Review*, September.

Lucas, R.E. (1988), 'On the Mechanics of Economic Development', *Journal of Monetary Economics*, **22**.

Maddison, A. (1964), *Economic Growth in the West*, London: Allen & Unwin.

Maddison, A. (1967), 'Comparative Productivity Levels in the Developed Countries', *Banca Nazionale del Lavoro Quarterly Review*, December.

Maddison, A. (1980), 'Monitoring the Labour Market: A Proposal for a Comparative Approach in Official Statistics (Illustrated by Recent Developments in France, Germany and the UK', *Review of Income and Wealth*, June.

Maddison, A. (1982), *Phases of Capitalist Development*, Oxford: Oxford University Press.

Maddison, A. (1987), 'Growth and Slowdown in Advanced Capitalist Economies: Techniques of Quantitative Assessment', *Journal of Economic Literature*, June.

Maddison, A. (1991a) *Dynamic Forces in Capitalist Development*, Oxford: Oxford University Press.

Maddison, A. (1991b) 'A Revised Estimate of Italian Economic Growth, 1861–1989', *Banca Nazionale del Lavoro Quarterly Review*, June.

Maddison, A. (1993), 'Standardised Estimates of Fixed Capital Stock: A Six Country Comparison', *Innovazione e Materie Prime*, April.

Maddison, A. (1995a), *Monitoring the World Economy 1820–1992*, Paris: OECD Development Centre.

Maddison, A. (1995b), *Explaining the Economic Performance of Nations: Essays in Time and Space*, London: Elgar.

Mankiw, N.G., D. Romer and D.N. Weill (1992), 'A Contribution to the Empirics of Economic Growth', *Quarterly Journal of Economics*, May.

Mason, G., S.J. Prais and B. van Ark (1990), 'Vocational Education and Productivity in the Netherlands and Britain', NIESR Discussion Paper 191, November.

McGibbon, J. (1964), 'The statistical comparability of rates of growth of gross national product', *Productivity Measurement Review*, OECD, Paris, February.

Mueller, B. (1965), *A Statistical Handbook for the North Atlantic Area*, New York: Twentieth Century Fund.

OEEC (1951), *National Accounts Studies: Netherlands*, Paris.

OEEC (1952a) *National Accounts Studies: France*, Paris.

OEEC (1952b) *Standardised System of National Accounts*, Paris (see also the revised 1958 version, 1968 version and forthcoming 1994 version).

OEEC (1954) *Statistics of National Product and Expenditure, 1938, 1947 to 1952*, Paris.

OECD (1961), *Manpower Statistics: 1950–60*, Paris.

OECD (1964), *Statistics of National Accounts, 1950–1961*, Paris.

OECD (1970), *National Accounts of OECD Countries, 1950–1968*, Paris.

OECD (1974), *Educational Statistics Yearbook*, Vol. 1, Paris.

OECD (1979a), *Measuring Employment and Unemployment*, Paris.

OECD (1979b), *Demographic Trends 1950–1990*, Paris.

OECD (1987), *Purchasing Power Parities and Real Expenditures: 1985*, Paris.

OECD (1991), *Flows and Stocks of Fixed Capital 1964–1989*, Paris.

OECD (1992), *Purchasing Power Parities and Real Expenditures: EKS Results 1990*, Vol. 1, Paris.

OECD (1993a), *Purchasing Power Parities and Real Expenditures: GK Results, 1990*, Paris.

OECD (1993b), *National Accounts 1960–1991*, Vol. 2, Paris.

OECD (1993c), *Methods Used by OECD Countries to Measure Stocks of Fixed Capital, National Accounts: Sources and Methods*, No. 2, Paris.

OECD (1994), *National Accounts 1960–1992*, Vol. 1., Paris.

Paige, D. and G. Bombach (1959), *A Comparison of National Output and Productivity of the United Kingdom and the United States*, Paris: OEEC.

Prados, L. (1993), Spain's Gross Domestic Product, 1850–1990: A New Series, Madrid: Ministry of Economics and Finance.

Romer, P.M. (1986) 'Increasing Returns and Long Run Growth', Journal of Political Economy, October.

Rossi, N., A. Sorgato and G. Toniolo (1992), 'Italian Historical Statistics 1890–1990', Nota di Lavoro 92–18, Dept. of Economics, Università degli Studi di Venezia, November.

Solow, R.M. (1956), 'A Contribution to the Theory of Economic Growth', Quarterly Journal of Economics, February.

Statistisches Bundesamt (1992), 'Revision der Volkswirtschaftlichen Gesamtrechnungen 1970 bis 1990', in Volkswirtschaftliche Gesamtrechnungenn 1950–1990, Fachserie 18, Reihe S.15, Wiesbaden.

Stone, R. (1956), Quantity and Price Indexes in National Accounts, Paris: OEEC.

Summers, R. and A. Heston (1991), 'The Penn World Table (Mark 5): An Expanded Set of International Comparisons, 1950–1988', Quarterly Journal of Economics, May.

Ward, M. (1976), The Measurement of Capital, Paris: OECD.

Ward, M. (1985), Purchasing Power Parities and Real Expenditures in the OECD, Paris: OECD.

Woodhall, M. (ed.)(1977), Educational Expenditure in France, Japan and the United Kingdom, Paris: OECD.

Young, A.H. (1993), 'Alternative Measures of Change in Real Output and Prices, Quarterly Estimates for 1959–92', Survey of Current Business, March.

3 Sectoral growth accounting and structural change in post-war Europe

BART VAN ARK

1 Introduction

The role of sectoral performance in economic growth has been a topic of major importance in growth studies from Adam Smith and David Ricardo onwards. Some scholars claimed that the shift of employment from low productivity to high productivity sectors was one of the main factors behind the overall rise in productivity. For example, 'structural change' was seen by Kuznets (1966) as one of the major 'stylized facts' of growth, although in his view it was more encompassing than only changes in sectoral shares of employment and output. Chenery *et al.*, (1986) defined structural transformation as 'the set of changes in the composition of demand, trade, production, and factor use that takes place as per capita income increases' (pp. 31–2).

An alleged need for structural change is also mentioned frequently as a motive behind the promotion of European economic integration. According to its supporters, liberalization of trade relations and greater mobility of factor resources between member countries of the European Union is assumed to enhance structural change, with a positive effect on the growth of GDP and productivity.

To provide empirical evidence of the effect of sectoral change on economic growth during the post-war period, this chapter analyses estimates of empirical evidence on growth and levels of output and productivity by sector of the economy. For this purpose annual sectoral accounts on real output and employment for ten sectors have been constructed which together constitute the total economy (agriculture; mining; manufacturing; public utilities; construction; trade; transport and communication; finance, insurance and real estate; community, personal and social services; and government services) for eight European countries (Denmark, France, Germany, Italy, The Netherlands, Spain, Sweden and the UK) from 1950 to 1992. For the sake of

84

comparison similar estimates are included for the USA, which go up to 1990.

The next section first discusses the concepts and sources used to obtain GDP and employment by sector. (The complete annual series for real output and employment, are shown in a statistical appendix to this chapter.) In section 3 the growth rates of labour productivity for four sub-periods (1950–60; 1960–73; 1973–79 and 1979–90) are discussed in more detail.[1] This section also presents measures of the extent to which shifts in employment between sectors accounted for the overall growth of labour productivity, as distinguished from productivity growth within the sectors.

In Section 4, the focus will be on the extent to which labour productivity for four of the countries included (France, Germany, the UK and the USA) could be accounted for by changes in capital intensity and joint factor productivity. The capital stock estimates for eight sectors which are based on the 'perpetual inventory method', i.e. the cumulation of investments with assumptions on asset lives and retirement patterns, are taken from O'Mahony's chapter in this volume (Chapter 4).

The study of structural change also greatly benefits from comparisons of *levels* of output and productivity between countries. Section 5 provides and discusses level estimates from the International Comparisons of Output and Productivity (ICOP) project for two commodity sectors (agriculture and manufacturing) and the residual part of the economy for four European countries (France, Germany, The Netherlands and the UK) in comparison to the USA.

2   Sectoral GDP and employment: concepts and sources

Despite the continuous interest in the subject, the published statistical information on sectoral output and employment for the post-war period as a whole is incomplete. Several factors affected the comparability of the existing sectoral accounts across countries.[2] Since the early 1960s OECD has presented national accounts of member countries on a more-or-less comparable basis, but so far OECD has not undertaken a backward revision of the sectoral national accounts estimates. As a result there are major breaks in the series in particular following the introduction of the 'System of National Accounts 1968'. Thanks to the work of some national statistical offices and academic scholars, there is now scope to reconstruct sectoral accounts for the post-war period on a consistent basis for quite a number of countries.[3]

In this chapter the use of the comparative framework as provided in the OECD *National Accounts*, Vol. II, is combined with the more comprehensive national statistics to construct sectoral accounts on post-war output and employment. This attempt is not the first to provide a sectoral database for European countries. For example, at OECD there are two research projects on industry statistics. The International Sectoral Database (ISDB) provides information on employment, gross domestic product, investment, capital stock, employee compensation and imports and exports for around 30 branches for 14 OECD countries (Meyer-zu-Schlochtern, 1988, 1994). ISDB is mostly based on the OECD national accounts for output and employment, but gaps are filled with information from, for example, Eurostat's national accounts (CRONOS) and the OECD labour force statistics. ISDB goes back to 1960, although even for this period the database has some gaps. Some scholars have made extensive use of ISDB for total factor productivity studies (see, for example, Dollar and Wolff (1993)).

The second OECD database is STAN, which provides similar information as ISDB but exclusively for manufacturing industries and at a more disaggregated level for 21 OECD countries from 1970 onwards (OECD, 1992, 1994). STAN, which also make use of other indicators, such as statistics on trade, research and development, etc., is much used in industry studies.

Both ISDB and STAN aim at a maximum coverage in terms of sectors, countries and indicators used. In this respect the present attempt is less ambitious because it distinguishes only ten sectors and two indicators (output and employment). On the other hand both ISDB and STAN make use only of official statistics from national and international statistical bodies. Many of the data points, in particular in STAN, are therefore estimated, as no official figures were available from the member countries. The present data set uses a wider range of data sources than ISDB and STAN, including those from academic scholars.

In all cases priority was given to keeping the sectoral accounts compatible with the macroeconomic accounts on GDP and total employment. The sectoral estimates can therefore be used in conjunction with estimates of GDP, employment and capital stock for the total economy, such as those in the chapter of Maddison in this volume (Chapter 2).

Although the sectoral accounts were constructed on a consistent basis across countries, in practice they could not always be based on exactly the same concepts, the same industry classification scheme and the same type of sources. These aspects are discussed in more detail below, but here a few general remarks will be made.

The sectoral disaggregation in this chapter is largely according to the

International Standard Industrial Classification (ISIC) which is also used by OECD:[4]

(1) agriculture, hunting, forestry and fishing
(2) mining and quarrying
(3) manufacturing
(4) electricity, gas and water
(5) construction
(6) wholesale and retail trade
(7) transport, storage and communication
(8) finance, insurance, real estate and business services
(9) community, social and personal services (CPS), including hotels and restaurants
(10) government services, including other producers

The distinction between community, social and personal services and government services was in some cases artificial, as the splitting of government and non-government services (in particular education and health) was not always unambiguous.

In cases where the national classification schemes differed very substantially from ISIC the OECD national accounts were directly used. This was for example necessary for France where mining and manufacturing could not be separated in the national statistics and where various service activities were classified on an institutional basis instead of by activity.

The general approach was to depart from the GDP level for some year in the mid-1980s (usually 1985) expressed in that year's prices. The series were subsequently linked to this benchmark figure. For the estimates of comparative levels of output and productivity between countries in Section 5, the benchmark year was 1975.

For the analysis of the data in Sections 3 and 4 the original ten sectors were collapsed into three broad sectors, i.e. agricultural (Table A.1), industry (Table A.2) and services (Table A.4), although separate tables for manufacturing (Table A.3), producer and distributive services (Table A.5) and community, social and personal services (CPS), and government services (Table A.6) are provided as well.[5]

In some cases where gaps in sectoral information could not be filled, in particular for the employment estimates of services during the early post-war periods, I used a rather straightforward estimation procedure to disaggregate the published information to the ten-sector level. This method, which assumed the productivity movement to be equal to that of a neighbouring sector or a combination of sectors, was mainly used for services. It needs to be emphasized that these estimation procedures were only used to disaggregate the information and did not affect the aggregate information on output and employment itself.

2.1   GDP estimates by sector

According to Maddison elsewhere in this volume, '(T)he international comparability of West European GDP estimates has improved markedly in the past fifty years' (Chapter 2, p. 28). Nevertheless there remain some problems which affect the comparability of the estimates. Some of the methodological differences in national accounting between countries, such as the use of different base years and the procedures to link series for sub-periods, affect the GDP estimates by sector in a similar way as the total economy estimates. However, other problems are of specific importance for the comparability of the sectoral accounts across countries.[6]

The methods of obtaining sectoral GDP estimates differ between countries. For example, output estimates for the UK and the USA are essentially derived from an overall income estimate of GDP. The GDP estimates for a benchmark year are then distributed over the different sectors on the basis of estimates from various primary sources, including production censuses, and employment surveys. In contrast, GDP by industry of origin in Germany is directly constructed from industry statistics. In France and The Netherlands output, expenditure and income estimates are first made consistent within the framework of an input–output table.

In some cases (France, Germany, The Netherlands) the full accounting procedures are repeatedly annually, but for other countries (Spain, the UK, the USA) output by industry is extrapolated from a base year by production indexes for a period of five up to ten years before a new base year is applied. In the past the latter procedure sometimes led to an underestimation of output growth, as it took insufficient account of the introduction of new products and of changes in the quality of the products.[7]

Another difference in estimation procedures which affects the sectoral accounts concerns the treatment of secondary activities. In most countries (in particular in those using input–output tables) output is distributed among industries on the basis of a clearly defined primary activity which takes place in an 'establishment', which is defined as an activity unit within an enterprise. Secondary activities of enterprises are then reallocated to other industries. However, in Germany, the output of the whole enterprise, i.e. including secondary activities, was distributed on the basis of the primary activity. This issue hardly affects the estimate of total GDP, but it can be of greater importance at sectoral level. For example, in contrast, to most other countries, repair and maintenance activities in Germany are included with manufacturing instead of with services.

Sectoral GDP in the accounts presented here is defined as the 'gross domestic product including bank service charges'. Before the introduction of the 1968 System of National Accounts bank charges were deducted for individual sectors, but since then the bank service charge has been imputed as the difference between property income received and interest paid by banks, and was not allocated to individual sectors. As a result the original estimates of GDP by sector for the earlier period are conceptually not quite the same as those for the most recent period, although for some countries (for example, for Denmark, Italy and the USA) the pre-1968 series have been adjusted. In any case, as mentioned above, all series are linked to the level estimates for a year in the mid-1980s.

Where possible, GDP measures are adjusted to a factor cost basis. The valuation at factor cost implies that indirect taxes on products (for example, value added tax, import duties and excise duties) and production (for example, levies etc.) are excluded, whereas subsidies on products and production are included in the estimates. The factor cost concept is derived from the value added at basic prices, which excludes net indirect taxes (indirect taxes minus subsidies) on products but not on production, by deducting the latter category of net indirect taxes as well. For four countries my estimates are at genuine factor cost. In one case (Sweden) the estimates are at basic prices. The OECD national accounts usually show industry GDP at producer prices, which equals value added at basic prices plus net indirect taxes on products, except VAT. In three cases (France, Germany and Spain) the estimates could not be adjusted from producer prices to a factor cost standard even though the series for Spain before 1980 were originally based on factor cost. In the case of the USA, the estimates are at market prices which means that all indirect taxes are included and subsidies excluded. These differences in valuation standards hardly affect the growth rate. In the case of the level comparisons in Section 5 all estimates for 1975 were first adjusted to a factor cost basis.

Although the sectoral accounts are conceptually consistent with the macroeconomic estimates of GDP, the sum of the sectors does not always equal aggregated GDP as directly obtained from the OECD national accounts (see Maddison, Chapter 2). One main source of difference is that adjustments for VAT and the deduction of bank service charges are made at the aggregate level and are not included in my aggregated sectoral estimates. However, in practice the difference in growth rates between the sum of the sectors and aggregated GDP is negligible, i.e. less than 0.1–0.2 percentage points of the annual compound growth rate for the period 1950 to 1990.

2.2   *Labour input by sector*

To provide standardized accounts of sectoral employment one can basically make use of two different primary sources, namely household surveys (for example, population censuses and labour force surveys) or establishment surveys (for example, production censuses or employment surveys). The former are at the basis of the OECD *Labour Force Statistics* (previously called *Manpower Statistics*), whereas the latter are mostly used as part of the national accounts including the OECD *National Accounts*, Vol. II.

Employment estimates from household surveys have limitations when used in sectoral accounts. In household surveys the respondents' statement concerning the industry where he is employed is often not in accordance with the official classification, in particular where it concerns employees in (semi-)government services, such as railways or postal services. Furthermore there are many multiple job-holders which are counted only once in the labour force survey according to their most important activity.

For sectoral accounts it is therefore preferable to estimate the number of employees per sector on the basis of returns from establishments. This means that one usually counts jobs rather than persons. During the past two decades the OECD *National Accounts* Vol. II have provided figures on employment on a fairly comprehensive scale, but, as argued by Maddison, 'these employment figures are supplied by the member countries without clearly defined OECD guidelines to standardize them' (Chapter 2, p. 47). Therefore, where possible, this chapter makes use of national sources on employment which are consistent with the national accounts. This could be done for Denmark, Germany, Italy and Sweden, and the USA. For the other countries (for example in France, Spain, and the UK for the post-1970 period) the OECD *National Accounts*, Vol. II, were used. In a few instances (for example in France and Spain for the pre-1970 period) the estimates were obtained from the OECD *Labour Force Statistics.*

For The Netherlands, which only provides figures on a man–year basis within the national accounts framework, estimates were obtained from labour force accounts and employment surveys for the period since 1973, and from the US Department of Labor (for manufacturing and the total economy) and van der Meer (1988) (for agriculture) for the period before 1973. The pre-1973 employment were divided up across the eight sectors on the basis of the distribution of the man-year estimates as reported in the Dutch national accounts.

Labour input in this chapter is defined as all persons employed, i.e. all paid employees and self-employed persons. Unfortunately, the treatment of armed forces is not fully consistent across countries, though it is mostly included. This is also the case for persons who own an enterprise but are temporarily not at work and unpaid family workers (see the Appendix for more details).

There is still much scope for improving the estimates of employment by sector in terms of international comparability. So far only a few countries have reconciled their estimates of employment from production censuses, employment censuses and household surveys. However, despite the various problems outlined above, the growth rates of total employment aggregated from the sectoral level are mostly not very different from those in the macroeconomic accounts which are almost exclusively based on OECD labour force statistics (see Maddison, Chapter 2). However, the differences in terms of numbers of persons employed are in some cases quite substantial.

Sectoral statistics on hours worked are not provided in this chapter. For growth accounting purposes one should preferably adjust measures of paid hours for time lost due to sickness, strikes, holidays, etc. (see Maddison, Chapter 2). These are only incidentally available for sectors such as agriculture and manufacturing and can seldom be obtained for all sectors of the economy. The estimation of annual hours worked is an area of great priority for future research and in particular for international standardization, as the reduction in working hours has accounted for a great deal of the changes in labour input, in particular during the 1970s and 1980s

3 Productivity growth and the effects of structural change

3.1 Agriculture

Table A.1 shows that all countries except The Netherlands and the United Kingdom experienced a relatively slow growth in agricultural output compared to the other sectors of the economy. However, the slow output growth went together with a substantial decline in agricultural employment. This resulted in labour productivity growth rates which were higher than in any other sector of the economy for all nine countries except Spain.

3.2   Industry and manufacturing

The industry sector (Table A.2), which was dominated by manufacturing (Table A.3), shows a more diverse development across the countries than agriculture. Between 1950 and 1973 real output growth was relatively fast in Germany, France, Italy, The Netherlands and Spain, but slower in Denmark, Sweden, the UK and the USA. After 1973 all countries experienced a significant decline in industrial output growth, but it was still relatively fast in Italy and Spain.

For the period as a whole employment growth in industry was moderate. However, it was clearly positive in the period up to 1973, whereas it fell in all European countries after 1973. Only in the USA was the level of employment in industry and manufacturing in 1990 similar to that in 1973.

The labour productivity growth performance in industry and manufacturing was more diverse between the countries. During the 1950–73 period it was particularly rapid in France, Germany, Italy, The Netherlands and Spain, and relatively slow in Denmark, Sweden, the UK and the USA. All countries experienced a slowdown of productivity growth in the period following 1973, but the growth rates became even more diverse than during the earlier period. The slowdown in Germany since 1973 is striking, as the country moved from a position of fastest growth in industry during the period 1950–60 to one of the slowest during the period 1973–90. The Netherlands, Sweden, the UK and the USA showed faster productivity growth during the period 1979–90 than during the period 1973–79, whereas it slowed down for the other five countries.

3.3   Services

Table A.4 shows that output growth in services for the period as a whole was not very different from that in the industrial sector in Denmark, France, Sweden and the UK. In Italy, The Netherlands and Spain services output grew slower than industrial output. Only in Germany and the USA did services output grow faster. However, in all countries the growth of employment in services has been much faster than in industry, in particular for the period since 1973.

Employment growth in community, personal and social (CPS), and government services (Table A.6) was somewhat faster than in producer and distributive services (Table A.5) in Denmark, The Netherlands, Sweden and the USA. With the exception of Spain, productivity growth was much slower in CPS and government services than in producer and distributive services

The estimation of real output in CPS and government services is clearly one of the weaker areas in national accounts. Estimation procedures of output in this area strongly differ across countries. The estimates suggest that none of the countries consistently applies a 'zero productivity growth' assumption for the sector as a whole. Some countries (for example, Germany) assume a constant productivity growth rate for some industries within this sector, whereas other countries (Italy, The Netherlands, Sweden and the USA) suggest even a decline in productivity in community and government services after 1973.

3.4 Structural changes

It is clear from these tables that the dynamics in sectoral growth rates show a great variety. One may therefore expect that the effect of structural change has played a role in explaining differences in the overall growth performance of those countries. A minimum condition for a positive effect of structural change on growth is that there has been a net shift of resources out of sectors with relatively low productivity levels to those with high productivity levels. To examine this, we therefore need to analyse two additional sets of information which can be derived from the database in this paper, i.e. the disparity in productivity levels between the sectors, and the change in employment shares from low productivity to high productivity industries.

Table A.8 shows the level of productivity for each sector compared to the productivity level of the economy as a whole. These levels are calculated by dividing the share of gross value added in current prices for each sector by the corresponding employment share. It appears that the level of productivity in agriculture is lower than the productivity in the economy as a whole, with the exception of The Netherlands (1950 to 1973) and the USA (1973 and 1979). Agricultural productivity was also relatively high in the UK, whereas it was relatively low in Germany, Italy and Spain.

During the early post-war period productivity levels in manufacturing were relatively high compared to the average for the economy as a whole, which is of course to some extent related to the lower productivity level and larger share of the agricultural sector in the economy. After 1973 the manufacturing productivity level was mostly close to that of the total economy.

With the exception of Italy (in 1950 and 1960) and Spain (1973 and 1979) the average productivity level in CPS and government services was relatively low, whereas for producer and distributive services it was significantly higher than the total economy level. In fact, productivity levels in the latter group of services were mostly well above those in manufacturing.

One can conclude from Table A.8 that any shift of resources from agriculture to manufacturing and from manufacturing to producer and distributive services would increase the contribution of structural change to growth, whereas a shift to CPS and government services would reduce this contribution.

Table A.9 shows the changes in employment shares of the individual sectors. In 1950, four of the nine countries (Denmark, France, Germany and Sweden) had an agricultural employment share of around 25%. The Netherlands (14%), the UK (6%) and the USA (11%) had clearly lower employment shares, whereas Italy and Spain still employed 45% of their labour force in agriculture. All countries experienced a strong decline in agricultural employment during the post-war period, in particular during the period 1950–73.

There has been some increase in employment shares in industry and manufacturing between 1950 and 1973, but on the whole the rise was not big except for Italy and Spain. Manufacturing employment shares were relatively high during the early post-war period in Germany and the UK, but the UK experienced a rapid decline in its manufacturing employment share during the 1980s.[8]

In 1990, the services sector accounted for about two-thirds of total employment in all eight European countries and even for three-quarters of the employment in the USA. In Denmark, Germany, France, Spain, Sweden and the USA, CPS and government services accounted for a larger share in employment than producer and distributive services, whereas the opposite was the case for the UK and The Netherlands.

The effect of shifts in sectoral shares on the productivity growth for the economy as a whole can be calculated according to a variety of different techniques. In all cases it is crucial to take account not only of the shift of employment from sectors with low productivity *growth* to sectors with high productivity *growth*, but also from sectors with low productivity *levels* to those with high productivity *levels*. The latter needs to be taken into account, because in theory it is possible that the shift of employment towards high growth sectors may be offset by a lower productivity level of the high growth sector compared to the slow growth sector.

To measure the effect of the contribution of employment shifts on the overall productivity growth, one may express the productivity for the economy as a whole as the productivity *level* by sector weighted by the sectoral employment shares:

$$P_m = \frac{Y_m}{L_m} = \sum_{k=1}^{n} \left(\frac{Y_k}{L_k}\right)\left(\frac{L_k}{L_m}\right) = \sum_{k=1}^{n} (P_k S_k) \qquad (1)$$

with Y and L representing output and employment by sector ($k = 1 \ldots n$) and the total economy (m), P representing productivity (Y/L) and S representing the sectoral employment share (L_k/L_m).

In a time perspective this expression can be rewritten as

$$\Delta P_m = \sum_{k=1}^{n}(\Delta P_k * S_k) + \sum_{k=1}^{n}(P_k * \Delta S_k) \tag{2}$$

In a discrete form the latter can be rewritten into three components as[9]

$$\frac{P_m^t - P_m^0}{P_m^0} = \frac{\sum_{k=1}^{n}(P_k^t - P_k^0)*S_k^0}{\sum_{k=1}^{n}P_k^0} + \frac{\sum_{k=1}^{n}P_k^0*(S_k^t - S_k^0)}{\sum_{k=1}^{n}P_k^0} + \frac{\sum_{k=1}^{n}(P_k^t - P_k^0)*(S_k^t - S_k^0)}{\sum_{k=1}^{n}P_k^0} \tag{3}$$

for a current year (t) and a base year (0).

The first term on the right-hand side of the latter expression represents the intrasectoral productivity growth, i.e. that part of the overall productivity change which is caused by productivity growth *within* the sectors. The second term is called the net shift effect, and measures the effect of the change in sectoral employment shares on overall growth. The third term can be derived as a residual and represents the joint effect of changes in employment shares and sectoral productivity, which is the interaction effect. The latter effect is usually small as in most cases sectors with rapid productivity growth (i.e. agriculture and industry) show an offsetting decline in employment shares.

Table 3.1 distinguishes the three components described above for the periods 1950–73 and 1973–90, which together add up to the overall growth rate. Some authors (including Maddison in Chapter 2, who uses a three-sector instead of a ten-sector disaggregation) interpret the net shift effect and the interaction effect together as representing the structural effect. However, it is useful to distinguish between these two effects, as only the former represents the pure effect of shifts from low productivity to high productivity sectors, even though the interaction effect includes a 'structural change' element as well (see below).[10]

For all countries and both sub-periods by far the largest part of the overall productivity increase is explained by the rise in intrasectoral productivity. On the whole the effect of structural change, represented by the second term of the expression, on the overall growth of labour productivity appears fairly small but it always has a positive sign. During the period 1950–73 the net shift effect was biggest in Denmark, Germany, Italy, Spain and Sweden. However, for Denmark and Sweden (and also

Table 3.1 Intrasectoral effect, net shift effect and interactive term on growth rates of labour productivity, 1950–73 and 1973–90

	Denmark	France	Germany	Italy[a]	Nether-lands	Spain	Sweden	United Kingdom	United States
1950–73									
(1)	3.45	4.35	4.84	5.31	3.83	5.37	2.99	2.08	1.91
of which:									
(2)	3.08	3.94	3.93	3.87	4.39	4.16	2.64	2.02	2.09
(3)	0.56	0.33	0.62	0.99	0.37	0.68	0.57	0.46	0.11
(4)	−0.19	0.08	0.29	0.45	−0.94	0.53	−0.22	−0.40	−0.29
1973–90									
(1)	1.72	2.31	1.98	1.97	0.97	3.64	1.27	1.34	0.48
of which:									
(2)	1.44	1.99	1.71	1.44	0.99	3.14	1.32	1.52	0.68
(3)	0.46	0.59	0.28	0.89	0.32	0.72	0.14	0.39	0.08
(4)	−0.19	−0.27	0.00	−0.36	−0.34	−0.22	−0.19	−0.57	−0.28
1973–90 minus 1950–73									
(1)	−1.73	−2.05	−2.85	−3.34	−2.85	−1.73	−1.73	−0.74	−1.42
of which									
(2)	−1.63	−1.95	−2.22	−2.43	−3.40	−1.02	−1.32	−0.50	−1.41
(3)	−0.10	0.26	−0.34	−0.10	−0.06	0.04	−0.44	−0.07	−0.03
(4)	0.01	−0.36	−0.29	−0.81	0.60	−0.75	0.03	−0.17	0.02

[a] Estimates for 1950 refer to 1951.

(1) = annual compound growth rate of labour productivity. (2) = intrasectoral effect. (3) = net-shift effect.

(4) = interaction effect.

Note: The effects were measured using productivity level estimates expressed in 1973 prices for the period 1950–73 and in 1990 prices for the period 1973–90.

The Netherlands and the UK) there were relatively large negative interaction effects which offset the net shift effect. In contrast, for Italy and Spain, and to a lesser extent for Germany, there was an additional positive interaction effect which mainly reflects the relation between the rise in sectoral productivity in industry and the increase in the industrial employment shares. The net shift effect in the USA, which had the lowest overall productivity growth, was smallest.

During the period 1973–90 productivity growth slowed down everywhere, but there has not been a substantial change in the distribution between the intrasectoral effect on the one hand and the other two effects on the other hand. Again Spain and Italy showed the biggest net shift effect, although the interaction effect was now more in line with that of the other countries. In fact the interaction effect was negative for all countries during this period. The latter indicates that employment shares declined exceptionally rapidly in sectors with relatively rapid productivity growth (i.e. agriculture and manufacturing) whereas the productivity rises were much more moderate in those sectors with rising employment shares (i.e. services).

The bottom part of Table 3.1 shows the disaggregation of the slowdown in growth between 1950–73 and 1973–90. In all cases the biggest part of the slowdown was due to the fall in intrasectoral productivity growth. Only in the case of Germany was there a significant slowdown in the net shift effect, and in Italy and Spain the interaction effect also accounted for a fair share in the productivity slowdown.

Despite the relatively small explanatory power of structural change on the basis of the conventional shift-share analysis applied here, one cannot definitively conclude that structural change has therefore played a minor role in economic growth. Firstly, it is important to look not only at differences in average productivity growth and levels by sector, but also at differences in marginal productivity performance. For example, the productivity performance of the agricultural sector might well have been much worse if the most inefficient farms had not disappeared in the process of structural change.[11]

Secondly as mentioned at the beginning of this chapter, structural transformation is about more than just the shift from low to high productivity sectors. It also includes changes in patterns of demand, trade and the use of production factors.

However, a conclusion that can safely be derived from this conventional analysis is that productivity growth within sectors has been the driving force behind growth in post-war Europe, and that the decline of growth since 1973 is mainly accounted for by the productivity slowdown within each of the sectors of the economy.

4   Capital intensity and joint factor productivity

An important element of any growth accounting study is the extent to which output per worker is accounted for by the rising intensity of factor inputs other than labour, among which is the physical capital stock. From its early times onwards the growth accounting literature has included estimates of capital stock or approximations for the stock, such as investment–output ratios.

Unfortunately, capital stock estimates could not usually be derived directly from the national accounts, but instead had to be calculated on the basis of the perpetual inventory method (PIM). The latter method is based on the accumulation of investment, mostly obtained from the national accounts, which is subsequently depreciated and scrapped on the basis of assumptions concerning the life time of assets and the pattern of depreciation and scrapping.[12]

Chapters 2 (by Maddison) and 4 (by O'Mahony) in this volume provide PIM estimates of the non-residential capital stock based on assumptions concerning asset lives and scrapping patterns which are standardized across the countries for the total economy and the sectors respectively. Here the sectoral capital stock estimates from O'Mahony were linked to the sectoral national accounts to obtain estimates of capital intensity and joint factor productivity for four countries, i.e. France, Germany, the UK and the USA.

The bottom two panels of Tables A.1 to A.7 show the index of the non-residential capital stock per person employed and joint factor productivity per sector and for the total economy. The latter was calculated on the basis of a traditional 'Solow-type' production function, in which the weights of labour and capital represent their respective factor share in the value added. They therefore add up to one suggesting constant returns to scale:

$$Y = AL^{\alpha}K^{1-\alpha} \tag{4}$$

with α as the partial elasticity of output with respect to labour and $1 - \alpha$ as the partial elasticity of output with respect to capital.

This can be reformulated by deducting the logarithmic index (which represents the growth rate) of the relative capital–labour ratio of year t and $0(K^t/L^t$ over $K^0/L^0)$ from that of the corresponding ratio of labour productivity (Y^t/L^t over Y^0/L^0):

$$\ln\frac{A^t}{A^0} = \ln\frac{Y^t/L^t}{Y^0/L^0} - (1-\alpha)\ln\frac{K^t/L^t}{K^0/L^0} \tag{5}$$

with α representing the unweighted average of the share of labour compensation in gross domestic product in year t and year 0.

To calculate the labour factor share α, the total labour compensation for employees for 1975 was obtained from the same national account sources as in the previous sections.[13] Labour compensation included the total bill of gross wages and salaries and employer contributions to social security and other insurance schemes. However, these figures do not include the compensation for self-employed persons, which is part of the operating surplus in the national accounts. For this reason, I imputed the labour compensation for self-employed persons on the assumption that the compensation per employee equalled that of a self-employed person.

Table 3.2 shows the labour factor shares for the four countries for 1975, which suggest a fairly similar picture across the countries for the total economy, but substantial differences across the sectors. Labour factor shares in agriculture were much higher in France and Germany than in the UK and the USA, representing the more capital-intensive nature of the agricultural sector in the latter two countries. On the other hand, the share of labour in value added in services (and in particular in personal and government services) appears to be of greater importance in the UK and the USA than in France and Germany. Finally, there is also a relatively larger share of manufacturing labour compensation in value added in Germany and the UK compared to France and the USA.

Table A.1 shows a faster growth of capital intensity in French and German agriculture than in the UK and the USA, though the former countries undoubtedly started from a lower level of capital intensity. Nevertheless, the joint factor productivity performance of the former two countries, and in particular that of Germany, is still better than in the UK and the USA.

The same as for agriculture can be said of the growth in capital intensity and joint factor productivity in manufacturing (Table A.3). However, the performance in UK manufacturing has improved dramatically during the 1980s, both in comparison to earlier sub-periods as well as in comparison to the other countries in the table.

The picture for the services sector is slightly different. Capital intensity clearly grew slower in the USA than in the European countries, whereas the US joint factor productivity performance in services is not better than in the other countries. As mentioned above, the USA experienced a relatively rapid growth in services employment. The rise in capital intensity in UK services was much higher than in France and Germany, whereas joint factor productivity in the UK grew more slowly than that of the two continental European countries.

Table 3.2   The share of labour compensation in total value added by sector of the economy in 1975, in percentages

	France	Germany	United Kingdom	United States
Agriculture	74	75[a]	58	34
Industry	71	85	80	82
of which:				
Manufacturing	70	86	83	76
Services	64	63	73	72
of which:				
Producer and distributive services	55	53	61	57
Community, personal, social and government services	78	75	92	90
Total economy	70	70	76	72

[a] The share for agriculture was assumed to be 75, because the imputation for self-employed led to an estimate of more than 100.
Sources: See sources of Appendix tables.

It is clear from Tables A.1 to A.7 that the rise in capital intensity was strongly related to the increase in joint factor productivity. Both factors played a crucial role in the post-war growth performance. This is one of the stylized facts which has received a great deal of attention in the growth accounting literature.[14]

Recently it has been suggested that the relationship between capital intensity and total factor productivity has not been as strong since 1973 as it was during the 1950–73 period, because the contribution of total factor productivity to the catch-up in productivity of follower countries compared to the USA has slowed down in comparison to the contribution of capital intensity.[15] Although this argument has been mainly put in terms of comparing the growth and levels of capital intensity and joint factor productivity for each country relative to the USA, it is not unlikely that this catch-up hypothesis also had its repercussions on the national growth rates as such.

It is not immediately apparent from the data presented in Tables A.1 to A.7 that the slowdown in joint factor productivity after 1973 compared to the earlier period has been significantly bigger than for capital intensity. However, to assess the issue more fully it would be desirable to test the full annual data set for both variables and to compare the relative growth rates and levels of capital intensity and joint factor productivity, which has not been done within the framework of this chapter.

5   Productivity levels and the effects of structural change

The study of structural change and economic performance can greatly benefit from international comparisons of *levels* of output and productivity by sector, in particular when such estimates take account of differences in relative price levels between countries. Unfortunately, sectoral level estimates are not available on a standardized basis in the national accounts.

International organizations such as Eurostat, OECD and the United Nations provide regular estimates of purchasing power parities from the expenditure side, which can be used to convert total GDP to a common currency. However, expenditure PPPs cannot be used for comparisons across countries of GDP by industry of origin. Expenditure PPPs include prices of imported goods, but exclude those of items which are produced and exported. Secondly, the expenditure PPPs take account of differences in trade and transport margins and indirect taxes between countries. Thirdly, there are no expenditure PPPs for many intermediate products, such as, for example, fertilizers, iron and steel, cement or paper pulp.

Exchange rates are not a good alternative to PPPs, as they do not necessarily represent the actual price relationship between two countries for each product or industry. In particular during recent decades exchange rates have been subject to substantial short-term fluctuations and capital movements.

For our purpose, one therefore needs to estimate specific purchasing power parities based on output prices by industry of origin. In the past decade a range of industry of origin studies were carried out within the framework of the International Comparisons of Output and Productivity (ICOP) project at Groningen University.[16] So far the ICOP comparisons have essentially been bilateral, with mostly the United States, which has been the world productivity leader throughout the post-war period, as the 'numeraire' country.

5.1   Methods and sources

It needs to be emphasized that the estimates in the ICOP studies are usually not directly derived from national accounts information for the various countries. Instead they are mostly based on primary sources on value added and employment, which are more detailed and disaggregated. Such primary sources also have the advantage that output and employment are derived from one and the same survey, giving a better guarantee that the same activities are covered for both variables, which is of crucial importance for level comparisons.

In the case of agriculture and mining, total output is estimated in terms of US dollars by valuing each individual item on the basis of producer prices provided by international statistics, such as those of the Food and Agriculture Organization (FAO) and the United Nations. Intermediate inputs, also valued at US prices are deducted to arrive at value added.

For manufacturing ICOP comparisons are based on production censuses or industry surveys. The latter sources contain information on output and employment for industries at a more detailed level than national accounts. Furthermore, output and employment can be derived from the same questionnaires which are returned by enterprises. Production censuses also provide figures on quantities sold and sales values for individual products to calculate the 'industry PPPs' (otherwise called 'unit value ratios').

For manufacturing, there is another important difference between the national accounts and the production censuses and surveys. The 'census concept' of value added is defined as gross value of output minus cost of raw materials, packaging, energy inputs and contract work. This concept of value added is not exclusive of the value of purchased industrial and non-industrial services, such as repair and maintenance, advertising, accountancy, etc., and is therefore somewhat broader than is common practice in the national accounts. In ICOP comparisons with the USA as the numeraire country it appeared not possible to obtain the 'national accounts concept' of value added directly from the *US Census of Manufacturers* (see van Ark, 1993).

A recent ICOP study by Maddison and van Ark (1994) has therefore adjusted the ICOP estimates to a 'national accounts basis' for four commodity sectors (i.e. agriculture, forestry and fishing, mining and manufacturing). These adjustments implied that:

(1) the estimates of purchasing power parities, value added in national currencies and employment were rebased to a single benchmark year, i.e. 1975.
(2) value added was adjusted to the so-called 'present national accounts concept', i.e. gross value added at factor cost including bank service charges.
(3) value added and employment were increased to achieve full coverage, i.e. to include smaller establishments with less than ten or less than twenty employees.

The estimates from the Maddison–van Ark paper were taken as the starting point here, but in addition the PPPs were adjusted from a

Paasche basis to a Fisher basis. The latter PPP is the geometric average of the Laspeyres and the Paasche PPPs, and is not biased towards either the denominator country or the numerator country.

Table 3.3 shows the Fisher PPPs for two commodity sectors (i.e. agriculture, including forestry and fishing, and manufacturing) in terms of national currencies to the US dollar for France, Germany, The Netherlands and the UK for 1975.[17] Column (4) shows the expenditure Fisher PPP which was obtained from Kravis et al. (1982). These PPPs were used to calculate the value added in US dollars for agriculture, manufacturing and the economy as a whole, which is shown in Table 3.4. The value added in US dollars for the rest of the economy is then derived as a residual by subtracting the value added in agriculture and manufacturing from the PPP-converted GDP for the economy as a whole. By comparing the value added for the residual part of the economy expressed in US dollars to that expressed in the currencies of the countries themselves, the PPPs for the residual sector of the economy are implicitly obtained (see column (5) of Table 3.3).

Table 3.3 shows that the PPPs are quite different across the industries in 1975. The PPPs for manufacturing are relatively close to the official exchange rate, which might have been expected because of the largely tradeable nature of most manufacturing products. The PPPs for agriculture were clearly higher than the manufacturing PPPs, which indicates the relatively high price levels of agricultural products in European countries compared to the USA. The average of the PPPs for the two commodity sectors are somewhat below the GDP PPPs for France and The Netherlands, 16% below the GDP PPP for Germany, but 22% above the GDP PPP in the case of the UK. As a result, price levels in services relative to the commodity sectors were low in the UK and high in Germany in 1975.

Table 3.4 shows the value added for each of the countries converted to US dollars as well as the corresponding employment and labour productivity in 1975.[18] In Table 3.5 the 1975 benchmark estimates of labour productivity are extrapolated backwards to 1950 and forwards to 1990. In agriculture, The Netherlands emerged as the best performer after the USA during the post-war period. By 1990 it had a productivity level which was 1.3 to 1.4 times that in France and the UK and 2.4 times that in Germany.

In manufacturing, Germany reached the highest productivity level of the four countries in 1960, and was less than 10% behind the US productivity level in 1979. After 1979 the German productivity advantage eroded rapidly. The Netherlands reached the highest productivity levels among the four European countries by 1990. During the 1980s only the

Table 3.3 Purchasing power parities by industry of origin, ICP expenditure PPPs and the exchange rate in 1975 (national currencies to the US dollar), Fisher type

	Agri-culture (1)	Manu-facturing (2)	Two com-modity sectors (3)	ICP Fisher PPP for GDP (4)	Rest of the economy (residual) (5)	Exchange rate (6)
France	6.03	4.39	4.57	4.73	4.81	4.29
Germany	3.20	2.39	2.43	2.88	3.25	2.46
Netherlands	3.97	2.64	2.80	1.99	3.06	2.53
UK	0.581	0.466	0.474	0.388	0.359	0.45
USA	1.00	1.00	1.00	1.00	1.00	1.00

Sources: Agriculture and Manufacturing from Maddison and Van Ark (1994), adjusted from Paasche to Fisher PPPs. ICP Paasche PPP from Kravis et al. (1982), pp. 255–82.

Table 3.4 Gross value added at factor cost in US dollars, converted at industry of origin PPPs, employment and labour productivity in 1975

	France	Germany	Nether-lands	United Kingdom	United States
Gross value added (min. US$)					
Agriculture[a]	12,800	6,391	2,456	4,756	51,386
Manufacturing	70,859	131,760	16,994	67,468	336,063
Total economy	296,110	341,866	71,636	256,792	1,499,684
Other sectors (residual)	212,451	203,715	52,186	184,567	1,112,235
Employment					
Agriculture[a]	2,156	1,801	263	687	3,507
Manufacturing	5,085	8,460	1,142	7,467	18,302
Total economy	21,452	26,110	4,743	25,055	88,026
Other sectors (residual)	14,211	15,849	3,338	16,901	66,217
Labour productivity (gross value added per person)					
Agriculture[a]	5,937	3,549	9,340	6,924	14,652
Manufacturing	13,935	15,574	14,887	9,035	18,362
Total economy	13,803	13,093	15,104	10,249	17,037
Other sectors (residual)	14,950	12,854	15,632	10,921	16,797

[a] Including forestry and fisheries.
Sources: Agriculture, Manufacturing and Total economy from Maddison and Van Ark (1994), adjusted from Paasche to Fisher PPPs.

Table 3.5   Relative levels of gross value added per person employed
(USA = 100)

	France	Germany	Netherlands	UK
Agriculture (including forestry and fisheries)				
1950	26.0	10.8	33.2	31.9
1960	26.3	13.9	40.0	31.6
1973	41.5	22.7	65.3	48.9
1979	50.2	29.1	74.1	52.1
1990	60.0	34.1	80.4	55.7
Manufacturing				
1950	36.9	39.8	37.9	46.0
1960	50.3	66.3	56.0	48.2
1973	71.1	79.4	81.7	49.4
1979	84.6	91.8	86.8	48.5
1990	80.9	75.9	83.8	53.1
Total economy				
1950	44.2	38.0	55.0	58.3
1960	54.1	54.2	60.7	55.0
1973	76.3	73.0	84.6	60.7
1979	90.0	86.3	92.3	65.1
1990	103.7	94.0	91.9	70.1
Other sectors of the economy (residual)				
1950	56.0	49.1	63.9	64.4
1960	67.1	59.1	66.2	60.3
1973	84.4	73.8	87.9	65.8
1979	96.5	84.5	94.9	72.4
1990	112.1	96.9	93.1	75.8

Source: see Table 3.4 and time series from the appendix.

UK managed to keep its comparative productivity level in manufacturing
up relative to the USA, but it was still way behind the continental
European countries in 1990.[19]

In the residual sector of the economy, which represented all sectors
other than agriculture and manufacturing, the continental European
countries had reached productivity levels close to those of the USA by
1979. In 1990, France even showed a productivity advantage of 12%
over the USA on the basis of these measures. The UK stayed behind in
productivity performance, although its relative performance was better
than in agriculture and manufacturing.[20]

To measure the degree to which the productivity gaps between each
country and the productivity leader can be accounted for by differences

Table 3.6   Effect of differences in sectoral distribution of employment on comparative productivity levels

	France	Germany	Netherlands	UK
Value added per person (USA = 100) on basis of intrasectoral productivity gaps				
1950	50.3	45.4	57.3	58.3
1960	61.9	58.4	62.9	56.5
1973	80.0	72.8	85.0	61.5
1979	92.5	84.0	92.6	66.2
1990	103.7	90.8	90.3	69.7
Effect of employment structure on productivity gap (USA = 100) in percentage points				
1950	−6.8	−8.1	−1.9	0.9
1960	−5.4	−4.9	−1.9	−1.2
1973	−0.6	1.1	0.2	1.2
1979	0.4	2.6	0.1	1.8
1990	4.0	8.8	2.5	2.6
Interaction effect on productivity gap (USA = 100) in percentage points				
1950	0.8	0.7	−0.4	−0.9
1960	−2.4	0.6	−0.3	−0.3
1973	−3.0	−0.9	−0.6	−2.1
1979	−2.9	−0.2	−0.5	−2.9
1990	−4.0	−5.6	−0.9	−2.2
Value added per person (USA = 100) using own country employment weights				
1950	44.2	38.0	55.0	58.3
1960	54.1	54.0	60.7	55.0
1973	76.3	73.0	84.6	60.7
1979	90.0	86.3	92.3	65.1
1990	103.7	94.0	91.9	70.1

Source: see Table 3.5 Employment weights calculated from Table 3.3 and time series on employment from the appendix.

in the structure of sectoral employment, a measure analogous to that for the shift effect in Section 3 can be calculated by substituting country variables by time variables from equation (3):

$$\frac{P_m^x - P_m^u}{P_m^u} = \frac{\sum_{k=1}^{n}(P_k^x - P_k^u) * S_k^u}{\sum_{k=1}^{n} P_k^u} + \frac{\sum_{k=1}^{n} P_k^u * (S_k^x - S_k^u)}{\sum_{k=1}^{n} P_k^u} + \frac{\sum_{k=1}^{n}(P_k^x - P_k^u) * (S_k^x - S_k^u)}{\sum_{k=1}^{n} P_k^u} \quad (6)$$

for a country X and a country U (in this case the USA).

The results are shown in Table 3.6. It appears that structural effects hardly played a role in accounting for the productivity gaps between The Netherlands and the UK on the one hand and the USA on the other. They were somewhat more important for France and Germany in 1950 and 1960, but the effect became negligible in later years. In Germany, the sectoral employment distribution even turned in favour of that country, which can be explained by the relatively high employment share in manufacturing. On the other hand, in particular for 1990, there were fairly strong offsetting effects from the interaction effect.

There is much scope for improvement of comparative estimates of output and productivity, for example by expanding these comparisons to services sectors so that in the future the structural effects of differences in employment distribution between producer and distributive services on the one hand and community, personal, social and government services on the other can be calculated as well. Furthermore it is important to adjust the labour productivity measures for differences in working hours, which up to present has only been feasible for manufacturing and the whole economy on a cross-country basis.

6   Conclusions and the future research agenda on sectoral growth accounting

In this chapter I introduced a set of sectoral accounts which were presented for eight European countries and the USA for the post-war period. The accounts can be used complementarily to the macroeconomic accounts, such as those presented by Maddison in this volume. Use has also been made of O'Mahony's estimates of capital stock by sector (Chapter 4) to obtain joint factor productivity estimates. In Section 5 of the paper the sectoral accounts were linked to the comparative estimates of output and productivity levels from the ICOP project.

The data from the sectoral accounts were analysed for the extent to which structural change, in terms of its narrow definition (i.e. shifts in employment from low productivity to high productivity sectors), has contributed to each country's productivity performance. On the whole the net shift effect was found to have a relatively small but positive impact on the overall productivity growth between 1950 and 1973 and between 1973 and 1990. Furthermore, the decline in growth after 1973 could hardly be explained by a slowdown in the net shift effect although fairly strong negative interaction effects set in during the latter period. Similar results were found for the comparisons of the productivity levels.

On the basis of these estimates one may conclude that intrasectoral change in productivity has been the major explanation for productivity growth at the aggregate level in post-war Europe. However, another question is what the intrasectoral productivity growth would have been in case there had been no significant shifts in employment shares. This counterfactual question needs to be addressed in more detail, because differences in marginal productivity between the sectors may have been bigger than the differences in average productivity. Furthermore, as mentioned in the introduction, structural change in terms of its broader definition, including changes in trade and demand patterns and in the use of factor resources, may be more strongly associated with growth and differences in economic performance between countries.

As far as the use of factor resources are concerned, this paper also looked into the contribution of physical capital intensity and joint factor productivity to the change in labour productivity. It was concluded that there was a fairly diverse performance of these two factors across the countries at sectoral level. However, on the whole the rise in physical capital intensity and joint factor productivity developed in parallel during most of the period. The sectoral accounts developed in this chapter, in combination with O'Mahony's capital stock estimates, provide a good starting point to test recent suggestions about the greater slowdown in joint factor productivity compared to capital intensity since 1973.

Table A.1   Agricultural gross domestic product, employment and labour productivity, capital intensity and joint factor productivity, 1950–90 (1950 = 100)

	Denmark	France	Germany	Italy[a]	Nether-lands	Spain	Sweden	United Kingdom	United States
Agricultural GDP in constant prices									
1950	100	100	100	100	100	100	100	100	100
1960	122	130	141	125	142	133	101	126	106
1973	130	166	182	167	208	179	111	179	109
1979	156	177	181	178	257	196	100	184	117
1990	232	216	231	191	442	228	129	258	173
Employment									
1950	100	100	100	100	100	100	100	100	100
1960	82	86	73	76	79	91	71	86	71
1973	44	48	40	38	49	62	35	54	50
1979	39	40	29	34	50	46	31	49	51
1990	27	26	20	25	51	28	22	42	49
Agricultural GDP per person employed									
1950	100	100	100	100	100	100	100	100	100
1960	149	151	192	165	179	145	142	147	149
1973	297	346	456	439	426	287	313	331	217
1979	403	447	626	526	518	425	326	378	232
1990	855	822	1,130	769	864	806	594	621	356
Non-residential capital stock per person employed									
1950		100	100					100	100
1960		189	211					165	181
1973		600	658					393	359
1979		864	965					496	464
1990		1,400	1,359					561	416
Agricultural GDP per joint unit of labour capital									
1950		100	100					100	100
1960		128	160					119	101
1973		218	285					185	94
1979		257	355					191	85
1990		393	545					290	128

[a] Estimates for 1950 refer to 1951.
Source: For GDP see Appendix tables 1.1 to 1.9. For employment see Appendix tables 2.1 to 2.9. For capital stock, see O'Mahony (Chapter 4).

Table A.2   Industrial gross domestic product, employment and labour productivity, capital intensity and joint factor productivity, 1950–90 (1950 = 100)

	Denmark	France	Germany	Italy[a]	Netherlands	Spain	Sweden	United Kingdom	United States
Industrial GDP in constant prices									
1950	100	100	100	100	100	100	100	100	100
1960	146	165	255	210	176	190	141	132	141
1973	286	370	449	444	417	750	280	185	226
1979	292	423	488	538	425	1,028	292	195	240
1990	364	479	540	683	463	1,424	363	220	290
Employment									
1950	100	100	100	100	100	100	100	100	100
1960	116	103	140	129	118	137	116	109	107
1973	125	120	143	145	119	204	115	101	130
1979	111	111	130	147	110	195	108	94	142
1990	109	94	127	132	100	176	105	75	137
Industrial GDP per person employed									
1950	100	100	100	100	100	100	100	100	100
1960	126	161	182	163	149	138	122	121	132
1973	228	309	313	307	350	367	243	183	173
1979	262	380	376	365	386	527	270	207	170
1990	332	512	426	519	461	807	347	292	212
Non-residential capital stock per person employed									
1950		100	100					100	100
1960		108	173					142	143
1973		167	398					279	191
1979		220	514					346	218
1990		325	622					448	269
Industrial GDP per joint unit of labour capital									
1950		100	100					100	100
1960		157	167					113	119
1973		266	253					149	144
1979		302	292					162	136
1990		359	316					218	158

[a] Estimates for 1950 refer to 1951.
Source: See Table A.1.

Table A.3   Manufacturing gross domestic product, employment and labour productivity, capital intensity and joint factor productivity, 1950–90 (1950 = 100)

	Denmark	France	Germany	Italy[a]	Nether-lands	Spain	Sweden	United Kingdom	United States
Manufacturing GDP in constant prices									
1950	100	100	100	100	100	100	100	100	100
1960	141	168	289	186	209	192	146	139	131
1973	271	423	549	490	467	829	301	205	241
1979	298	496	607	701	468	1,180	311	196	268
1990	345	544	687	960	597	1,567	379	220	339
Employment									
1950	100	100	100	100	100	100	100	100	100
1960	117	103	144	119	117	134	114	111	109
1973	120	119	149	140	117	199	112	103	130
1979	106	111	135	150	105	194	108	96	138
1990	109	92	134	130	100	168	102	71	126
Manufacturing GDP per person employed									
1950	100	100	100	100	100	100	100	100	100
1960	121	164	200	156	178	143	128	126	120
1973	226	356	368	350	398	416	270	198	185
1979	282	447	449	467	446	609	289	205	195
1990	315	590	512	738	595	935	370	310	269
Non-residential capital stock per person employed									
1950		100	100					100	100
1960		152	159					130	131
1973		363	373					244	179
1979		497	477					299	216
1990		745	558					403	285
Manufacturing GDP per joint unit of labour capital									
1950		100	100					100	100
1960		145	188					121	113
1973		242	308					170	161
1979		277	363					171	162
1990		320	395					245	208

[a] Estimates for 1950 refer to 1951.
Source: See Table A.1.

Table A.4 Services gross domestic product, employment and labour productivity, capital intensity and joint factor productivity, 1950–90 (1950 = 100)

	Denmark	France	Germany	Italy[a]	Nether-lands	Spain	Sweden	United Kingdom	United States
Services GDP in constant prices									
1950	100	100	100	100	100	100	100	100	100
1960	143	146	203	151	143	170	141	119	144
1973	273	271	359	293	252	387	231	169	244
1979	324	332	443	369	320	480	272	188	296
1990	404	458	624	495	409	676	354	256	406
Employment									
1950	100	100	100	100	100	100	100	100	100
1960	116	105	146	129	117	112	130	108	126
1973	164	135	180	164	153	168	173	124	178
1979	185	150	199	192	179	177	202	134	213
1990	207	179	237	250	224	223	240	170	280
Services GDP per person employed									
1950	100	100	100	100	100	100	100	100	100
1960	123	140	139	117	122	152	109	110	114
1973	166	200	199	179	165	231	133	137	137
1979	175	222	223	192	179	272	134	140	139
1990	195	256	263	198	183	303	148	151	145
Non-residential capital stock per person employed									
1950		100	100					100	100
1960		119	102					130	103
1973		185	194					258	121
1979		236	234					311	125
1990		310	293					419	135
Services GDP per joint unit of labour capital									
1950		100	100					100	100
1960		134	138					103	113
1973		163	158					107	127
1979		166	166					105	129
1990		172	177					109	131

[a] Estimates for 1950 refer to 1951.
Source: See Table A.1.

Table A.5 Gross domestic product in producer and distributive services, employment and labour productivity, capital intensity and joint factor productivity, 1950–90 (1950 = 100)

	Denmark	France	Germany	Italy[a]	Nether-lands	Spain	Sweden	United Kingdom	United States
GDP in producer and distributive services at constant prices									
1950	100	100	100	100	100	100	100	100	100
1960	152	157	225	171	163	167	148	127	145
1973	315	346	422	383	290	407	253	189	259
1979	360	425	524	485	392	498	290	207	323
1990	465	604	720	655	546	666	407	308	447
Employment									
1950	100	100	100	100	100	100	100	100	100
1960	111	106	157	139	124	130	137	113	116
1973	135	141	172	170	150	240	161	127	156
1979	136	155	175	197	171	246	171	134	188
1990	147	181	189	241	215	273	203	168	237
GDP in producer and distributive services per person employed									
1950	100	100	100	100	100	100	100	100	100
1960	137	149	143	123	131	128	108	113	125
1973	234	245	245	225	194	170	150	149	166
1979	265	275	300	246	230	202	170	155	172
1990	315	334	380	272	254	244	200	184	189
Non-residential capital stock per person employed									
1950		100	100					100	100
1960		111	101					136	106
1973		146	194					260	131
1979		189	238					327	138
1990		239	302					452	174
GDP in producer and distributive services per joint unit of labour capital									
1950		100	100					100	100
1960		142	143					100	122
1973		207	179					102	148
1979		206	199					98	150
1990		226	219					104	150

[a] Estimates for 1950 refer to 1951.
Source: See Table A.1.

Table A.6   Gross domestic product in community, personal and social (CPS), and government services, employment and labour productivity, capital intensity and joint factor productivity, 1950–90 (1950 = 100)

	Denmark	France	Germany	Italy[a]	Nether-lands	Spain	Sweden	United Kingdom	United States
GDP in CPS and government services at constant prices									
1950	100	100	100	100	100	100	100	100	100
1960	133	136	187	133	122	175	134	109	142
1973	228	204	312	210	212	356	209	144	226
1979	285	250	384	262	244	453	254	163	265
1990	338	328	553	347	265	690	302	185	359
Employment									
1950	100	100	100	100	100	100	100	100	100
1960	122	104	137	119	108	100	122	103	137
1973	207	130	188	157	157	125	186	121	200
1979	256	145	222	187	188	135	234	134	237
1990	293	178	281	259	234	193	277	172	324
GDP in CPS and government services per person employed									
1950	100	100	100	100	100	100	100	100	100
1960	109	131	137	111	113	174	110	105	104
1973	110	156	166	134	135	285	112	119	113
1979	112	172	173	140	130	336	109	121	112
1990	115	184	197	134	113	358	109	108	111
Non-residential capital stock per person employed									
1950		100	100					100	100
1960		115	103					121	97
1973		206	180					227	106
1979		259	210					251	102
1990		346	254					267	92
GDP in CPS and government services per joint unit of labour capital									
1950		100	100					100	100
1960		127	136					104	106
1973		133	143					111	109
1979		139	144					112	110
1990		138	152					102	117

[a] Estimates for 1950 refer to 1951.

Source: See Table A.1.

Table A.7   Gross domestic product of the total economy, employment and labour productivity, capital intensity and joint factor productivity, 1950–90 (1950 = 100)

	Denmark	France	Germany	Italy[a]	Nether-lands	Spain	Sweden	United Kingdom	United States
Total economy GDP at constant prices									
1950	100	100	100	100	100	100	100	100	100
1960	142	150	222	163	152	167	138	125	141
1973	262	291	389	318	298	420	235	176	229
1979	298	345	451	391	348	535	262	191	265
1990	375	442	572	509	426	740	337	241	348
Employment									
1950	100	100	100	100	100	100	100	100	100
1960	107	100	126	105	112	108	110	107	114
1973	120	109	131	102	126	126	119	110	149
1979	123	110	129	109	134	119	127	111	172
1990	129	113	138	117	152	121	138	120	208
Total economy GDP per person employed									
1950	100	100	100	100	100	100	100	100	100
1960	133	151	176	156	136	155	125	116	123
1973	218	267	296	312	237	333	197	161	154
1979	242	314	350	359	259	448	207	172	154
1990	291	393	414	435	280	611	244	201	168
Non-residential capital stock per person employed									
1950		100	100					100	100
1960		119	137					137	118
1973		207	300					262	147
1979		271	381					315	154
1990		374	480					384	167
Total economy GDP per joint unit of labour capital									
1950		100	100					100	100
1960		143	160					108	118
1973		214	213					127	138
1979		253	256					130	137
1990		284	276					148	145

[a] Estimates for 1950 refer to 1951.
Source: See Table A.1.

Table A.8   Relative level of gross value added per person employed for each industry compared to the total economy

	Denmark	France	Germany	Italy[a]	Nether-lands	Spain	Sweden	United Kingdom	United States
Agriculture									
1950	73	61	45	44	105	66	49	96	63
1960	64	46	43	39	111	53	51	84	62
1973	72	67	42	48	104	47	59	99	112
1979	65	58	44	47	75	44	63	80	105
1990	78	64	45	38	92	44	76	85	79
Industry									
1950	107	136	115	141	102	121	130	102	112
1960	103	134	111	118	104	134	121	104	122
1973	94	106	103	103	102	113	110	101	116
1979	95	104	103	106	106	115	112	108	123
1990	98	104	101	106	116	110	113	118	127
Manufacturing									
1950	106	155	119	135	107	132	148	103	110
1960	96	147	109	107	108	141	140	103	117
1973	85	112	103	95	97	114	104	96	110
1979	93	108	103	102	90	133	101	96	114
1990	91	109	101	103	105	109	102	112	122
Services									
1950	111	92	120	152	97	137	102	99	100
1960	114	97	107	141	95	130	98	97	93
1973	108	103	106	116	98	119	98	99	92
1979	107	104	103	111	99	110	97	96	91
1990	103	101	103	107	95	105	96	93	93
Producer and distributive services									
1950	132	104	160	180	104	229		105	124
1960	136	111	126	165	95	193		100	132
1973	138	132	123	138	105	121	118	118	127
1979	144	131	123	137	106	105	116	116	124
1990	143	134	125	130	116	137	125	119	124
Community, personal, social and government services									
1950	81	82	83	123	88	82		92	78
1960	85	86	86	112	94	80		94	61
1973	81	75	92	93	90	115	82	76	66
1979	79	79	88	82	90	116	83	72	65
1990	74	72	89	85	71	78	75	63	71

[a] 1950 refers to 1951.
Source: See Table A.1.

Table A.9   Share of employment by sector, 1950–1990 (as a percentage of total employment)

	Denmark	France	Germany	Italy[a]	Netherlands	Spain	Sweden	United Kingdom	United States
Agriculture									
1950	26	24	24	45	13	47	23	6	11
1960	20	21	14	33	9	40	15	5	7
1973	10	11	7	17	5	23	7	3	4
1979	8	9	5	14	5	18	6	3	3
1990	6	6	3	10	5	11	4	2	3
Industry									
1950	32	35	43	26	38	22	38	45	33
1960	35	36	48	32	41	28	39	46	31
1973	34	38	47	38	37	36	36	42	29
1979	29	35	44	36	32	36	32	38	27
1990	27	29	40	30	26	32	29	28	22
Manufacturing									
1950	24	25	32	18	28	16	28	34	25
1960	26	25	37	20	29	20	29	35	24
1973	24	27	37	24	26	25	26	32	22
1979	20	25	34	24	22	25	24	29	20
1990	20	20	31	20	18	22	21	20	15
Services									
1950	42	41	33	28	48	31	39	49	56
1960	45	43	38	35	50	32	46	49	62
1973	57	51	45	46	58	41	57	55	67
1979	63	56	51	50	63	46	62	59	70
1990	67	65	57	61	70	57	68	69	76
Producer and distributive services									
1950	24	19	16	14	26	12	20	26	28
1960	26	20	20	19	29	14	24	28	28
1973	27	25	21	24	31	22	26	30	29
1979	27	27	22	26	33	24	26	32	31
1990	28	31	22	30	37	26	29	37	32
Community, personal, social and government services									
1950	17	22	17	14	21	19	19	23	28
1960	20	23	19	16	21	18	21	22	34
1973	30	26	25	22	27	19	30	25	38
1979	36	29	30	24	30	22	36	27	39
1990	39	35	35	31	33	31	39	33	44

[a] 1950 refers to 1951.

Source: See Table A.1.

Appendix

1   Gross value added in constant prices

(Figures printed in shadow are estimated as described in the notes.)

Denmark

Notes:

The estimates are all at factor cost.

Original GDP estimates for 1947–66 were expressed in '1955 prices', for 1966–71 in '1970 prices' and for 1972–92 in '1980 prices', although the base years in the original accounts have changed more frequently.

Sources:

GDP 1947–66 from Danmarks Statistik, 'Reviderede tideserier for produktionsvaerdi og bruttofaktorindkomst for perioden 1947–65', Kopenhagen, mimeographed. GDP 1966–90 from Danmarks Statistik, *Nationalregnskabsstatistik 1982, 1987* and *1993*, Copenhagen.

France

Notes:

Before 1962 original series are at market prices, linked to series at producer prices after 1962. The classification of activities in the French national accounts (INSEE, *Les Comptes de la Nation*, various issues) differed in some respects from the International Standard Industrial Classification. Most important are the inclusion of mining activities in manufacturing, and the distinction between 'market' and 'non-market' services instead of between 'government' and 'non-government'. OECD adjusted the estimates to their common classification scheme, which I could not do directly on the basis of the French national accounts. I therefore relied on the OECD National Accounts for the whole period.

Sources:

1950–58 (in 1954 prices) from OECD, *Statistics of National Accounts 1950–1961*; 1958–62 (in 1958 prices) from OECD, *National Accounts 1955–1964*; 1962–71 (in 1970 prices) from OECD, *National Accounts of OECD Countries 1950–78*, Vol. I; 1971–77 (in 1970 prices) from OECD, *National Accounts, Detailed Tables*, Vol. II, 1977–90 (in 1980 prices) from OECD, *National Accounts, Detailed Tables*, Vol. II, 1980–92.

Germany

Notes:

Figures for the whole period are at producer prices.

Original GDP estimates in Germany for 1960–90 were expressed in '1985 prices' and for 1950–60 in '1976 prices', although the base years in the original accounts were changed more frequently.

Original series for 1950–59 exclude Saarland and Berlin.

The figures for repair and maintenance are included with manufacturing

Sources:

1950–59 from Statistisches Bundesamt, *Volkswirtschaftlich Gesamtrechnungen, Lange Reihen, 1950–84*, pp. 72–73; 1960–87 from *Volkswirtschaftliche Gesamtrechungen, Revidierte Ergebnisse 1950–1990*, Fachserie 18, Reihe S. 15, pp. 117–120. GDP 1987–92 from *Volkswirtschaftliche Gesamtrechnungen, Hauptbericht 1993 and 1994*, Fachserie 18.

Italy

Notes:

The estimates for the whole period are at factor cost.

Sources:
Updated series belonging to R. Golinelli and M. Monterastelli, *Un metodo per la ricostruzione de serie storiche compatibili con la nuova contabilità nazionale (1959–1989)*, Nota di lavoro no. 9001, Promoteia, November 1990. The updated series which go up to 1992 and are rebased from 1980 to 1985 prices, were kindly provided by Roberto Golinelli (October 1993). These series are entirely compatible with the Italian national accounts from ISTAT, *Contabilità nazionale 1970–1992*.

The Netherlands

Notes:
Government excludes government organisations outside the 'government sector', which are included in the industry estimates.
The estimates for the whole period are at factor cost. The 1985 estimate is also at factor cost but unadjusted for the difference in value tax received and value added tax paid.
1950–63: mining, public utilities and construction were obtained on the basis of the assumption that their productivity movement equalled that of the three sectors taken together. Wholesale and retail trade and finance, insurance and real estate were obtained on the basis of the assumption that their productivity movement equalled that of the transport and communication sector. 1950–66: community, personal and social services and government services were obtained on the basis of the assumption that their productivity movement equalled that of the two sectors taken together. 1963–84: finance, insurance and real estate was obtained on the basis of the assumption that its productivity movement equalled that of the wholesale and retail trade sector and the transport and communication sector taken together. Community, personal and social services was obtained on the basis of the assumption that its productivity movement equalled that of government services.
Sources:
1985–92 from CBS, *Nationale Rekeningen 1993*, with services weighted at 1990 factor values. 1984–85 from CBS, *Nationale Rekeningen 1990*; 1977–84 from CBS (1987), *Nationale Rekeningen, Tijdreeksen 1969–84*. 1969–77 from CBS (1985), *Nationale Rekeningen, Herziene Reeksen 1969–76*, except manufacturing which was calculated by the author separately by deflating value added in current prices by a producer price index. 1963–69 from CBS, *Nationale Rekeningen 1972*, except for manufacturing (as above) and mining which was derived as a residual from the industry index. 1960–63 from CBS, *Nationale Rekeningen 1966*, except for manufacturing (as above) and mining, utilities and construction which was derived as a residual from the industry index. Wholesale and retail trade, finance and insurance, community and social services and government services were obtained by using 1963 value added weights. 1955–60 from CBS, *Nationale Rekeningen 1963*, otherwise procedure as for 1960 using value added weights for 1958. 1949–55 from CBS, *Nationale Rekeningen 1960*, otherwise procedure as for 1960 using value added weights for 1953.

Spain

Notes:
The series before 1980 refer to GDP at factor cost linked to series after 1980 at producer prices.
Sources:
1950–64 (in 1958 prices) from Leandro Prados de la Escosura, *Spain's Gross Domestic Product, 1850–1990: A New Series*, Documentos de Trabajo D-93002, Ministeria de Economia y Hacienda, March 1993. 1964–71 (in 1970 prices) except industry from OECD, *National Accounts of OECD Countries 1950–78*, Vol. I; 1971–80 (in 1970 prices) except industry from OECD, *National Accounts, Detailed Tables*, Vol. II, 1971–83; 1964–81 industry from R. Gandoy Juste (1988), *Evolucion de la productividad global en la industria Española. Un analisis desagregado para el periodo 1964–1981*, Editorial de la Universidad Complutense de Madrid. 1980–87 (in 1980 prices) from OECD, *National Accounts, Detailed*

Tables, Vol. II, 1975–87; 1986–90 (in 1986 prices) from OECD, *National Accounts, Detailed Tables*, Vol. II, 1979–91. 1990–92 from updated provided by OECD.

Sweden

Notes:
The series for the whole period refer to basic values, i.e. net indirect taxes on production are included, but those on commodities are excluded.

Source:
Figures for 1950–70 from SCB (1972), *Nationalraekenskaper 1950–1971*, apart from 'hotels and restaurants' which were shifted to 'community, social and personal services' on the basis of shares (in 1968 prices) from OECD, *National Accounts of OECD Countries 1950–78*, Vol. I; figures for 1970–90 from SCB (1991), *Nationalraekenskaper 1950–1990*. 1990–92 updated provided by OECD.

United Kingdom

Notes:
The series for the whole period are at factor cost.

Sources:
1947–65 index series from C. H. Feinstein, *Statistical Tables of National Income, Expenditure and Output of the United Kingdom 1855–1965*. The series are weighted at the 1958 distribution of GDP from OECD, *National Accounts Statistics 1955–1964*. 1965–73, 1973–78, 1978–83, 1983–86 and 1986–93 on the basis of index series from CSO, *National Income and Expenditure* and (subsequently) *United Kingdom National Accounts*, making use of 1970, 1975, 1980, 1985 and 1990 current price weights respectively from OECD national accounts.

United States

Notes:
The series for the whole period are at market prices. The series up to 1987 are at 1982 prices, and from 1987 onwards at 1987 prices.

Sources:
1947–77 from BEA, *National Income and Product Accounts of the United States, 1929–1982*, Washington, DC, 1986 (printout), linked in 1977 to new series; 1977–87 from BEA, *Survey of Current Business*, January and April 1991; 1987–90 from BEA, *Survey of Current Business*, November 1993.

Appendix table 1.1   Gross value added at factor cost. Denmark, 1947–92, millions of kroner (1980 prices)

Year	Agriculture	Mining	Manufacturing	Public utilities	Construction	Wholesale and retail trade	Transport and communication	Finance, insurance and real estate	Community, social and personal services	Government services	GDP at factor cost
1947	8,637	616	16,209	240	6,700	10,760	11,433	9,436	13,043	18,027	95,101
1948	8,901	539	16,971	276	7,466	10,869	10,684	9,751	12,989	19,074	97,521
1949	9,661	284	18,754	322	8,709	11,763	11,140	10,053	12,859	19,238	102,785
1950	10,990	204	20,632	401	9,762	12,901	11,320	10,343	13,089	19,033	108,676
1951	10,863	344	20,396	434	9,706	12,552	12,502	10,485	12,844	20,121	110,247
1952	11,685	310	19,762	442	10,287	12,625	12,300	10,831	12,897	20,891	112,030
1953	12,698	190	20,577	525	11,453	13,490	12,345	11,417	13,312	22,533	118,539
1954	11,462	188	21,705	585	11,571	14,282	12,626	11,917	13,619	23,211	121,166
1955	11,733	216	21,509	719	10,990	14,322	13,707	12,071	13,734	24,073	123,074
1956	12,127	262	21,551	761	11,196	14,359	15,171	12,343	13,596	24,597	125,961
1957	13,767	301	23,250	719	11,622	15,620	15,210	12,867	13,887	25,521	132,764
1958	13,224	272	24,169	693	11,931	16,994	15,103	13,417	14,301	25,326	135,429
1959	12,405	284	27,049	897	13,837	18,768	16,139	14,460	14,808	26,640	145,286
1960	13,370	284	29,075	938	15,050	20,488	16,854	15,336	15,306	27,379	154,080
1961	14,209	296	31,034	955	17,310	21,840	17,422	15,947	15,736	28,046	162,796
1962	14,437	286	33,416	1,113	18,518	23,229	17,056	16,570	15,897	31,506	172,029
1963	13,517	272	33,537	1,302	18,847	23,567	18,115	17,434	16,488	32,656	175,733
1964	14,721	281	36,631	1,416	22,171	26,075	18,751	19,119	16,879	34,031	190,077
1965	15,025	272	38,480	1,514	23,702	27,696	19,696	20,792	16,971	35,468	199,617
1966	14,592	262	39,299	1,727	25,084	28,649	20,479	23,137	17,079	37,984	208,291
1967	14,940	224	40,913	1,791	27,064	30,029	20,152	25,358	16,918	40,909	218,297
1968	15,253	205	43,550	2,065	25,124	31,446	22,333	29,169	17,082	42,737	228,965
1969	15,269	195	46,501	2,576	27,881	33,237	23,127	33,094	17,708	45,137	244,726
1970	13,621	177	48,049	2,758	28,957	33,565	23,839	35,012	17,430	48,192	251,601

Appendix table 1.1 (*contd*)

Year	Agriculture	Mining	Manufacturing	Public utilities	Construction	Wholesale and retail trade	Transport and communication	Finance, insurance and real estate	Community, social and personal services	Government services	GDP at factor cost
1971	14,964	166	48,853	2,798	29,913	33,650	23,608	38,059	17,727	49,648	259,386
1972	15,417	344	53,042	2,706	32,171	34,188	24,109	41,214	17,846	52,301	273,338
1973	14,285	344	55,978	3,076	29,328	38,345	25,261	45,341	18,095	55,113	285,166
1974	17,388	240	56,846	3,097	27,365	37,592	23,411	46,027	18,673	57,066	287,705
1975	16,259	264	55,471	3,407	24,442	37,309	22,223	46,214	18,549	58,402	282,540
1976	14,631	287	58,130	3,557	25,694	41,540	24,005	48,671	19,508	61,123	297,146
1977	16,633	784	58,387	3,953	25,091	41,498	24,717	48,878	20,072	64,008	304,021
1978	17,025	761	58,223	4,496	25,094	41,307	24,132	51,853	20,048	67,390	310,329
1979	17,107	857	61,530	4,936	23,286	42,714	26,966	54,660	20,404	71,187	323,647
1980	17,818	373	64,311	4,520	24,383	41,228	25,899	52,303	20,259	74,725	325,819
1981	19,294	948	62,267	4,183	20,169	40,004	26,215	51,790	20,355	78,208	323,433
1982	21,228	2,271	63,257	4,970	19,073	42,464	25,842	51,697	20,469	81,669	332,940
1983	19,404	2,508	67,510	5,153	18,499	44,893	25,532	53,771	20,382	82,180	339,832
1984	23,289	3,125	70,673	5,244	20,124	45,575	26,726	58,369	20,610	82,092	355,827
1985	23,191	4,991	72,920	6,064	21,431	49,131	26,477	60,030	21,080	83,924	369,239
1986	22,368	7,841	72,920	6,528	25,486	52,270	26,816	64,293	21,970	85,351	385,843
1987	21,311	10,074	69,933	6,356	26,573	53,018	30,349	65,132	21,336	85,801	389,883
1988	23,447	10,242	71,036	6,544	24,749	52,991	32,489	65,967	21,817	87,198	396,480
1989	25,274	12,402	71,869	6,397	23,045	51,055	34,130	68,775	21,430	87,140	401,517
1990	25,486	12,671	71,130	6,903	22,054	53,343	37,578	69,702	21,174	87,333	407,374
1991	25,175	15,163	70,301	6,249	18,923	55,488	38,114	67,377	22,077	87,311	406,178
1992	25,503	16,232	70,750	7,346	17,879	56,951	41,033	66,284	22,396	87,992	412,366

Appendix table 1.2   Gross value added at producer prices. France, 1950–92, million francs (1980 prices)

Year	Agricul- ture	Mining	Manufac- turing	Public utilities	Construc- tion	Wholesale and retail trade	Transport and communi- cation	Finance, insurance and real estate	Community, social and personal services	Govern- ment services	GDP at producer prices
1947											
1948											
1949											
1950	68,414	17,380	137,838	5,230	62,478	87,214	34,867	98,262	50,333	196,518	758,532
1951	66,499	18,704	150,883	6,044	64,912	91,935	37,898	98,932	54,268	205,854	795,928
1952	67,966	19,797	153,458	6,451	63,623	95,191	38,808	100,049	56,649	217,449	819,442
1953	73,100	19,164	157,769	6,607	64,482	99,913	37,898	106,525	57,840	218,052	841,350
1954	77,704	19,912	164,963	7,265	70,852	105,449	39,977	110,321	60,254	220,310	877,008
1955	77,623	21,408	174,733	7,923	78,152	114,458	42,923	115,458	64,123	225,280	922,079
1956	70,289	21,523	191,221	8,706	81,014	122,598	45,998	116,574	67,529	234,165	959,617
1957	75,993	22,732	202,026	9,363	85,165	130,251	50,026	125,061	72,192	237,176	1,009,985
1958	76,238	23,940	209,024	10,271	89,459	130,251	51,888	138,013	73,945	238,381	1,041,411
1959	80,629	24,986	213,626	10,797	95,403	131,848	53,359	140,889	75,605	248,231	1,075,370
1960	89,057	26,458	231,670	12,373	97,519	143,070	56,468	147,245	80,813	255,977	1,140,649
1961	84,312	26,506	243,616	13,161	106,031	154,081	59,661	154,660	85,563	263,171	1,190,762
1962	93,831	27,503	259,461	14,474	113,990	170,473	63,358	156,324	89,941	270,586	1,259,943
1963	91,812	26,907	278,795	16,695	118,234	181,264	68,567	170,222	92,921	274,006	1,319,424
1964	94,234	28,235	307,582	16,733	132,419	191,300	74,610	182,193	96,935	282,288	1,406,528
1965	97,804	27,913	324,366	17,962	141,827	195,954	78,187	195,698	100,530	288,739	1,468,979
1966	97,320	27,320	354,451	19,050	148,787	208,379	83,322	199,650	106,781	293,133	1,538,192
1967	103,514	26,772	372,709	19,972	157,756	220,826	85,692	213,773	108,268	303,088	1,612,369
1968	106,057	26,084	394,499	21,441	158,913	231,619	86,577	231,193	106,758	319,009	1,682,149
1969	101,370	26,358	441,671	23,445	166,029	247,878	93,217	255,699	111,643	328,046	1,795,356
1970	105,525	26,446	481,283	25,772	175,169	249,227	98,566	278,358	116,522	337,773	1,894,641

Appendix table 1.2 *(contd)*

Year	Agriculture	Mining	Manufacturing	Public utilities	Construction	Wholesale and retail trade	Transport and communication	Finance, insurance and real estate	Community, social and personal services	Government services	GDP at producer prices
1971	107,354	24,581	512,181	27,422	179,997	269,687	103,116	294,882	121,822	350,095	1,991,136
1972	107,878	24,072	544,431	30,032	189,519	284,714	112,160	314,395	129,276	360,963	2,097,441
1973	113,885	23,857	582,366	33,486	185,506	298,741	119,436	343,654	135,514	367,477	2,203,922
1974	113,620	23,420	601,105	35,767	192,478	307,900	122,328	370,214	143,006	371,712	2,281,550
1975	105,383	22,033	588,750	37,349	196,082	303,872	122,043	373,312	150,588	379,463	2,278,875
1976	101,174	22,319	630,296	39,570	190,354	323,449	131,034	390,952	159,128	401,743	2,390,018
1977	101,437	22,140	653,759	42,993	188,137	326,671	137,533	413,632	166,061	409,375	2,461,738
1978	112,086	24,114	667,908	45,611	187,507	334,447	146,936	420,411	172,661	425,787	2,537,438
1979	121,389	24,407	684,036	47,432	187,414	341,015	156,115	438,882	176,155	439,845	2,616,690
1980	119,024	23,821	679,520	50,308	193,609	337,760	164,194	472,578	178,547	448,211	2,667,572
1981	118,226	22,801	674,873	56,782	192,832	345,165	168,903	484,236	182,169	457,139	2,703,126
1982	138,019	19,313	680,762	57,846	192,720	351,810	174,577	493,065	191,857	472,369	2,772,338
1983	131,217	21,209	683,532	63,797	187,519	355,744	179,319	490,559	200,653	481,600	2,795,149
1984	137,323	20,407	671,038	70,040	183,153	361,274	184,483	507,082	210,245	489,752	2,834,797
1985	138,441	21,700	668,425	74,085	180,406	366,488	191,249	528,799	217,022	498,414	2,885,029
1986	139,457	20,745	667,256	77,261	185,861	377,092	198,339	566,336	226,552	505,807	2,964,706
1987	141,354	21,054	661,095	81,682	187,684	383,296	209,271	601,553	230,655	512,351	3,029,995
1988	140,801	20,275	700,521	83,221	202,688	391,035	228,695	623,157	240,118	526,532	3,157,043
1989	145,962	19,729	736,640	82,712	212,123	406,652	246,655	649,334	254,810	531,650	3,286,287
1990	147,909	19,869	750,295	85,126	213,303	421,007	258,759	650,613	268,873	540,572	3,356,326
1991	143,938	21,227	738,670	89,068	214,092	419,392	266,592	657,575	277,757	552,102	3,380,413
1992	153,784	20,962	740,283	90,117	214,990	421,570	276,523	656,925	285,641	563,156	3,423,951

Appendix table 1.3   Gross value added at producer prices. Germany, 1950–92, millions of deutschmark (1985 prices)

Year	Agricul- ture	Mining	Manufac- turing	Public utilities	Construc- tion	Wholesale and retail trade	Transport and communi- cation	Finance, insurance and real estate	Community, social and personal services	Govern- ment services	GDP at producer prices
1947											
1948											
1949											
1950	15,842	23,101	94,288	5,316	29,680	33,246	21,234	29,510	45,598	67,685	365,000
1951	18,295	25,796	108,505	6,263	33,092	35,463	23,464	32,390	48,795	70,133	402,196
1952	18,481	26,781	123,118	6,856	36,934	38,096	24,641	36,388	54,400	75,103	440,797
1953	18,625	26,256	137,643	7,181	44,650	41,464	25,682	40,131	60,268	78,768	480,667
1954	19,107	26,624	154,118	8,099	47,570	44,651	27,361	43,938	64,661	82,447	518,576
1955	18,912	29,119	180,749	9,121	55,286	49,876	31,453	48,688	71,250	87,476	581,929
1956	18,811	31,117	195,347	10,113	58,837	55,170	34,296	53,007	77,019	91,830	625,546
1957	19,394	31,179	208,671	10,794	57,822	59,632	35,803	57,054	83,247	99,218	662,814
1958	20,663	29,896	219,825	10,972	59,805	61,641	35,435	61,564	86,247	105,903	691,951
1959	21,390	30,432	240,623	11,831	66,691	67,268	37,923	67,354	91,934	110,081	745,527
1960	22,380	32,930	272,780	13,030	69,780	74,280	40,790	74,120	97,540	114,230	811,860
1961	20,490	32,380	289,120	13,240	72,970	78,130	42,610	78,090	102,120	119,620	848,770
1962	21,980	32,980	302,790	13,890	76,010	82,620	44,170	82,570	105,040	124,470	886,520
1963	22,700	33,020	308,770	14,790	77,750	84,730	45,700	86,410	108,450	129,690	912,010
1964	22,260	31,310	336,160	16,950	87,710	90,930	47,840	92,010	113,750	133,120	972,040
1965	21,180	29,950	361,750	17,400	91,130	96,900	49,780	96,420	121,000	138,420	1,023,930
1966	22,280	29,660	368,000	18,770	94,520	99,280	50,780	102,150	124,740	144,560	1,054,740
1967	24,160	25,990	359,770	19,420	90,560	99,090	50,510	108,750	127,730	148,830	1,054,810
1968	25,660	25,830	397,070	21,090	89,990	103,720	54,800	115,860	130,420	153,010	1,117,450
1969	24,980	25,610	443,490	24,280	91,920	113,710	59,890	121,450	138,310	157,270	1,200,910
1970	25,770	28,610	466,000	26,290	95,790	118,470	64,160	126,660	142,100	165,630	1,259,480

125

Appendix table 1.3 (*contd*)

Year	Agriculture	Mining	Manufacturing	Public utilities	Construction	Wholesale and retail trade	Transport and communication	Finance, insurance and real estate	Community, social and personal services	Government services	GDP at producer prices
1971	27,030	25,660	470,920	28,090	101,770	123,300	64,480	132,300	148,890	172,770	1,295,210
1972	26,200	23,120	486,250	30,970	108,460	128,180	66,230	143,780	157,210	181,990	1,352,390
1973	28,860	23,640	517,310	34,370	109,250	133,070	70,280	151,070	163,110	190,870	1,421,830
1974	30,250	23,910	512,250	36,530	100,640	131,980	72,280	150,190	168,090	198,770	1,424,890
1975	28,730	19,920	488,080	36,130	94,600	130,500	70,250	162,850	171,800	204,800	1,407,660
1976	27,600	20,150	525,440	40,430	98,760	138,190	75,460	169,660	180,010	208,370	1,484,070
1977	29,180	18,420	535,130	42,540	100,900	144,580	79,440	177,980	189,410	211,910	1,529,490
1978	30,040	17,240	545,330	45,060	102,440	149,860	83,180	186,700	199,170	218,890	1,577,910
1979	28,670	18,800	572,390	47,310	105,260	154,170	89,970	195,700	208,660	226,120	1,647,050
1980	29,310	18,310	561,430	48,570	106,720	153,080	93,970	202,690	217,240	232,180	1,663,500
1981	29,440	17,730	555,850	47,760	102,150	151,090	95,640	208,650	224,580	237,830	1,670,720
1982	34,810	17,580	536,360	46,440	98,270	146,060	96,750	215,840	227,340	240,210	1,659,660
1983	32,100	16,630	543,600	47,400	100,020	148,990	97,780	220,390	236,240	242,150	1,685,300
1984	34,110	16,130	559,520	49,060	100,390	155,750	101,220	224,420	248,110	245,510	1,734,220
1985	31,920	16,050	578,850	50,480	94,810	156,410	105,050	231,870	258,960	249,940	1,774,340
1986	35,250	13,870	587,020	51,960	96,220	159,750	105,090	242,800	271,530	254,580	1,818,070
1987	32,120	13,950	575,590	54,860	94,540	162,230	109,500	251,830	286,780	258,640	1,840,140
1988	34,480	12,900	593,760	55,450	96,430	168,100	117,220	262,350	307,600	262,460	1,910,750
1989	34,970	13,897	614,123	57,389	100,489	175,117	123,073	271,455	325,584	264,573	1,980,670
1990	36,540	12,275	647,787	58,742	103,774	188,917	132,487	282,913	356,015	270,116	2,089,566
1991	34,080	13,645	671,966	62,236	104,123	210,322	138,436	290,120	388,295	276,127	2,189,350
1992	41,390	13,042	653,490	61,984	106,641	210,729	145,040	296,461	414,842	283,281	2,226,900

Appendix table 1.4 Gross value added at factor cost. Italy, 1951–92, billions of lira (1985 prices)

Year	Agriculture	Mining	Manufacturing	Public utilities	Construction	Wholesale and retail trade[a]	Transport and communication	Finance, insurance and real estate	Community, social and personal services[a]	Government services	GDP at factor cost
1947											
1948											
1949											
1950											
1951	20,540	3,383	21,989	4,750	16,859	24,059	9,064	21,714	22,011	37,580	181,948
1952	20,204	3,804	22,559	5,034	19,729	26,090	9,546	22,497	22,624	38,678	190,764
1953	22,479	4,250	24,265	5,207	22,663	27,606	10,437	23,287	23,333	39,737	203,264
1954	21,239	4,898	26,421	5,426	25,086	29,136	10,751	24,100	23,557	42,414	213,028
1955	22,443	5,705	28,163	5,782	28,086	30,978	12,058	25,300	24,254	43,777	226,546
1956	22,591	6,275	30,309	6,437	29,001	32,853	13,128	26,783	24,592	44,779	236,748
1957	22,996	6,887	32,211	6,888	31,557	35,199	13,852	28,202	25,364	46,465	249,621
1958	25,674	7,196	32,868	7,690	33,922	36,921	14,129	29,482	25,912	48,199	261,992
1959	26,707	7,969	36,473	8,386	36,429	39,549	15,133	31,235	26,708	50,121	278,710
1960	25,723	9,018	40,852	10,047	38,518	43,387	16,837	33,543	27,684	51,581	297,188
1961	28,132	9,954	45,320	11,016	41,645	48,221	18,636	35,811	28,836	53,390	320,980
1962	28,028	11,072	49,794	11,453	45,253	52,071	20,744	38,126	29,397	54,421	340,358
1963	28,789	11,397	53,930	12,160	48,126	57,181	21,129	40,386	30,376	55,624	359,098
1964	30,073	11,398	54,017	13,562	48,362	59,693	21,443	42,475	31,138	57,298	369,458
1965	31,047	12,499	56,360	14,811	45,500	61,385	22,006	44,852	31,813	59,405	379,679
1966	31,860	13,257	61,915	15,850	46,984	65,810	23,231	46,689	34,446	62,188	402,229
1967	33,376	14,936	67,832	17,392	49,458	72,068	24,046	48,499	36,185	63,542	427,334
1968	33,499	16,352	74,053	18,833	54,210	79,547	26,826	50,477	39,681	65,285	458,742
1969	34,694	17,196	79,019	20,425	57,529	87,339	30,021	51,870	41,848	66,440	486,382
1970	35,199	17,934	87,322	21,984	56,378	94,668	31,715	53,542	44,992	67,480	511,214

Appendix table 1.4 *(contd)*

Year	Agriculture	Mining	Manufacturing	Public utilities	Construction	Wholesale and retail trade[a]	Transport and communication	Finance, insurance and real estate	Community, social and personal services[a]	Government services	GDP at factor cost
1971	35,219	18,453	88,683	22,741	54,209	96,815	32,606	57,168	46,587	69,940	522,421
1972	31,983	19,356	93,485	24,001	53,856	99,450	33,065	61,382	48,935	73,063	538,578
1973	34,214	18,525	107,755	26,333	55,807	107,495	35,333	67,233	49,847	75,517	578,059
1974	34,640	17,541	116,848	28,008	57,107	114,034	40,116	68,494	50,121	77,853	604,762
1975	36,018	15,740	111,104	21,800	54,713	113,289	36,477	68,742	50,266	80,092	588,241
1976	34,473	18,720	127,100	22,309	52,662	121,052	38,341	72,506	56,140	82,507	625,810
1977	34,368	19,546	131,674	23,491	52,104	125,746	39,205	74,999	58,455	84,821	644,409
1978	34,891	19,566	138,819	23,654	52,546	130,971	42,105	77,376	63,156	86,891	669,975
1979	36,616	21,117	154,188	23,684	53,634	138,723	48,245	78,964	67,771	88,386	711,328
1980	38,403	22,125	162,570	24,103	55,110	143,627	51,670	79,882	70,635	89,882	738,007
1981	38,178	21,242	159,854	23,668	54,735	144,897	52,995	82,418	72,691	91,065	741,743
1982	37,228	19,875	159,190	23,379	52,922	146,517	54,427	82,291	75,769	92,344	743,942
1983	40,865	19,898	160,548	22,593	53,273	147,674	54,269	83,295	77,888	93,495	753,798
1984	38,759	21,138	167,611	22,758	51,500	152,546	56,360	84,224	84,174	94,736	773,806
1985	39,237	21,602	173,371	22,793	51,527	154,700	59,077	87,764	89,064	96,007	795,142
1986	39,734	21,390	178,253	23,938	51,854	157,806	62,022	92,333	92,494	97,426	817,250
1987	41,466	22,619	185,613	24,594	52,589	164,080	64,291	93,847	95,754	98,845	843,698
1988	40,128	24,624	199,178	24,966	53,952	171,120	69,197	97,546	98,019	100,160	878,890
1989	40,653	25,488	206,795	25,681	55,850	174,736	73,121	101,831	101,495	101,031	906,681
1990	39,328	25,757	211,134	26,611	57,267	178,197	75,750	105,202	105,151	101,821	926,218
1991	42,646	24,500	210,975	26,937	57,992	180,545	77,944	106,638	107,499	102,517	938,193
1992	42,841	25,158	209,170	27,213	57,480	181,283	80,397	113,490	109,775	103,077	949,884

[a] Hotels and restaurants are included with wholesale and retail trade.

Appendix table 1.5   Gross value added at factor cost. The Netherlands, 1950–92, million DFL (1985 prices)

Year	Agriculture	Mining	Manufacturing	Public utilities	Construction	Wholesale and retail trade	Transport and communication	Finance, insurance and real estate	Community, social and personal services	Government services	GDP at factor cost
1947											
1948											
1949	4,630		14,116				5,066				103,300
1950	4,731	9,062	14,170	921	7,731	18,987	5,637	12,323	14,984	20,356	108,901
1951	4,983		12,767				6,137				110,432
1952	5,184		13,636				6,565				111,765
1953	5,033		15,781				7,136				119,635
1954	5,234		18,507				7,778				127,927
1955	5,486		19,793				8,420				137,938
1956	5,082		21,428				8,988				143,412
1957	5,428		22,943				9,556				147,049
1958	5,775		22,836				9,461				147,758
1959	5,197		25,306				9,934				155,158
1960	6,699	13,040	29,567	1,292	12,193	24,813	10,975	24,340	15,238	27,915	166,072
1961	6,229	13,178	30,750	1,377	13,337	25,785	11,097	26,062	15,495	28,585	171,895
1962	6,287	13,478	31,815	1,435	14,465	26,886	11,584	27,643	16,044	29,316	178,954
1963	5,876	13,515	33,175	1,545	15,508	28,398	12,194	29,003	16,878	30,201	186,296
1964	6,898	13,045	37,601	1,748	18,462	31,279	13,091	32,053	17,315	30,945	202,437
1965	6,898	12,434	41,378	1,952	19,200	33,337	17,395	37,386	16,200	28,840	215,019
1966	6,728	15,736	42,032	2,195	20,431	33,337	14,167	36,119	19,070	31,465	221,279
1967	7,494	14,500	44,851	2,602	22,400	34,983	14,525	39,285	19,722	31,874	232,236
1968	7,835	16,761	48,129	3,090	24,616	36,218	15,960	41,048	19,903	33,100	246,659
1969	8,090	20,017	52,787	3,537	23,877	38,276	17,036	48,788	16,869	34,734	264,011
1970	8,464	22,712	54,943	3,953	24,770	40,495	18,517	50,976	17,430	36,691	278,950

Appendix table 1.5 *(contd)*

Year	Agriculture	Mining	Manufacturing	Public utilities	Construction	Wholesale and retail trade[a]	Transport and communication	Finance, insurance and real estate	Community, social and personal services[a]	Government services	GDP at factor cost
1971	8,713	26,176	57,668	4,369	25,885	41,049	19,258	52,865	18,779	38,159	292,921
1972	8,961	31,566	59,866	4,994	25,885	41,604	19,505	53,648	19,665	39,626	305,320
1973	9,833	35,415	66,170	5,479	25,885	44,378	19,999	42,668	33,395	41,583	324,805
1974	10,455	38,495	68,642	5,826	24,323	46,597	20,986	47,632	33,238	43,051	339,243
1975	10,331	39,649	61,537	6,034	23,877	47,151	20,739	50,771	34,804	43,051	337,945
1976	10,455	41,959	65,410	6,520	23,431	49,370	21,727	53,642	36,251	45,008	353,772
1977	10,828	41,189	62,404	6,520	23,654	51,589	22,468	57,746	36,953	46,475	359,827
1978	11,589	37,936	64,277	6,891	23,475	53,182	22,966	61,343	38,033	47,558	367,250
1979	12,174	40,130	66,333	6,849	22,129	55,490	24,163	65,257	37,902	48,445	378,873
1980	12,461	37,823	66,665	7,010	22,421	54,940	24,936	67,799	38,619	49,232	381,907
1981	14,205	34,381	66,665	6,989	20,627	52,578	25,984	68,456	39,984	50,168	380,037
1982	15,377	29,388	65,798	7,207	19,573	52,083	25,660	69,186	40,352	50,315	374,939
1983	15,863	31,733	66,917	7,263	18,968	51,919	26,059	71,017	39,962	50,118	379,819
1984	16,834	32,490	70,798	7,347	19,528	54,226	27,804	76,137	37,750	50,168	393,083
1985	16,199	35,251	72,639	7,543	19,663	56,204	28,627	80,640	36,491	50,660	403,917
1986	17,662	32,726	74,415	7,873	20,247	59,183	29,356	84,079	36,638	51,797	413,975
1987	16,889	33,911	75,430	7,983	20,691	59,454	29,980	86,342	37,790	52,554	421,023
1988	17,767	29,859	78,305	8,203	22,722	61,283	30,952	88,989	38,072	53,041	429,192
1989	19,000	30,856	81,856	8,203	23,072	64,465	32,687	94,928	38,450	53,529	447,046
1990	20,902	31,168	84,562	8,456	23,353	67,716	34,699	99,425	39,417	54,124	463,822
1991	21,550	33,880	84,901	8,744	23,119	70,763	37,163	101,700	40,275	54,449	476,542
1992	21,780	34,160	84,309	8,803	22,699	71,169	39,141	102,454	39,970	54,828	479,312

Appendix table 1.6 Gross value added at producer prices. Spain, 1947–92, billion pesetas (1986 prices)

Year	Agriculture	Mining	Manufacturing	Public utilities	Construction	Wholesale and retail trade	Transport and communication	Finance, insurance and real estate	Community, social and personal services	Government services	GDP at producer pices
1947	921	86	596	28	222	980	153	919	749	613	5,266
1948	871	91	581	29	224	980	161	902	753	577	5,169
1949	874	94	561	27	227	976	165	896	765	588	5,171
1950	883	98	615	33	238	1,007	176	921	761	573	5,304
1951	1,093	105	654	39	238	1,075	174	934	796	651	5,760
1952	1,082	114	771	44	244	1,142	198	1,038	824	691	6,148
1953	1,034	116	788	47	265	1,203	221	1,033	839	721	6,269
1954	1,092	118	842	49	318	1,244	220	1,107	887	825	6,702
1955	1,060	122	930	56	357	1,343	229	1,181	905	810	6,993
1956	1,040	129	1,002	64	370	1,360	265	1,271	951	1,035	7,486
1957	1,126	139	1,063	68	386	1,424	289	1,362	993	1,073	7,923
1958	1,105	144	1,135	76	440	1,494	301	1,426	1,038	1,090	8,250
1959	1,165	135	1,146	80	427	1,571	303	1,458	1,058	1,047	8,392
1960	1,172	138	1,180	86	463	1,694	306	1,504	1,132	1,196	8,871
1961	1,242	142	1,392	96	456	1,824	345	1,655	1,175	1,285	9,613
1962	1,222	136	1,566	105	504	1,981	371	1,860	1,206	1,555	10,506
1963	1,438	136	1,655	119	584	2,098	414	2,143	1,323	1,702	11,611
1964	1,312	134	1,831	135	667	2,171	463	2,412	1,369	1,709	12,202
1965	1,240	154	2,111	147	785	2,259	508	2,558	1,455	1,751	12,969
1966	1,310	149	2,395	157	908	2,447	551	2,654	1,548	1,780	13,898
1967	1,362	142	2,640	165	1,062	2,572	622	2,791	1,618	1,803	14,777
1968	1,364	143	2,836	184	1,143	2,697	655	2,951	1,768	1,845	15,586
1969	1,387	179	3,279	215	1,222	2,966	717	3,093	1,964	1,935	16,957
1970	1,375	179	3,607	231	1,297	3,084	793	3,230	2,085	1,985	17,867

Appendix table 1.6 (*contd*)

Year	Agriculture	Mining	Manufacturing	Public utilities	Construction	Wholesale and retail trade[a]	Transport and communication	Finance, insurance and real estate	Community, social and personal services[a]	Government services	GDP at producer prices
1971	1,520	196	3,904	242	1,338	3,189	865	3,395	2,209	2,052	18,912
1972	1,523	205	4,527	272	1,477	3,419	964	3,606	2,334	2,130	20,456
1973	1,580	199	5,095	343	1,740	3,658	1,065	3,849	2,490	2,251	22,270
1974	1,694	219	5,689	388	1,935	3,823	1,163	4,042	2,595	2,419	23,966
1975	1,691	222	5,939	416	1,976	3,868	1,212	4,257	2,725	2,529	24,836
1976	1,765	217	6,384	434	1,986	3,973	1,291	4,437	2,796	2,678	25,960
1977	1,690	229	6,774	467	2,021	4,072	1,384	4,626	2,914	2,802	26,979
1978	1,802	222	7,071	542	2,013	4,186	1,450	4,645	2,993	2,934	27,859
1979	1,729	228	7,250	623	2,017	4,186	1,495	4,792	2,980	3,060	28,360
1980	1,883	251	7,608	596	2,035	4,211	1,525	4,924	2,936	3,163	29,132
1981	1,704	247	7,421	658	2,013	4,127	1,566	4,983	3,011	3,264	28,996
1982	1,678	229	7,552	677	2,067	4,152	1,577	5,059	3,156	3,401	29,548
1983	1,783	219	7,730	678	2,069	4,235	1,618	5,088	3,191	3,525	30,134
1984	1,936	215	7,774	750	1,941	4,324	1,663	5,247	3,265	3,634	30,749
1985	1,997	209	7,918	787	1,985	4,406	1,725	5,355	3,290	3,786	31,458
1986	1,815	246	8,322	859	2,103	4,560	1,755	5,423	3,474	3,941	32,499
1987	2,025	224	8,751	899	2,278	4,756	1,829	5,697	3,685	4,165	34,311
1988	2,092	226	9,128	969	2,509	4,968	1,904	6,017	3,832	4,419	36,063
1989	1,953	251	9,491	956	2,848	5,190	2,016	6,327	4,067	4,725	37,824
1990	2,017	255	9,628	987	3,137	5,319	2,113	6,591	4,153	5,045	39,246
1991	1,979	(a)	10,898	(a)	3,251	(b)	(b)	(b)	15,998	5,290	37,416
1992	1,936	(a)	10,781	(a)	3,109	(b)	(b)	(b)	16,432	5,458	37,716

[a] Included with manufacturing. [b] Included with community, social and personal services.

132

Appendix table 1.7 Gross value added at basic prices. Sweden, 1950–92, million kronor (1985 prices)

Year	Agriculture	Mining	Manufacturing	Public utilities	Construction	Wholesale and retail trade	Transport and communication	Finance, insurance and real estate	Community, social and personal services	Government services	GDP at basic prices
1947											
1948											
1949											
1950	23,984	1,815	52,971	2,308	22,291	25,983	12,608	42,585	27,119	54,457	266,120
1951	24,570	2,066	56,010	2,544	20,678	25,906	13,458	45,436	28,448	56,861	275,977
1952	25,135	2,326	54,684	2,695	20,722	26,293	13,370	47,473	28,613	59,396	280,708
1953	23,646	2,287	55,750	2,873	23,838	26,968	13,112	49,002	29,210	61,669	288,354
1954	23,999	2,078	58,309	3,265	25,879	29,198	14,010	51,132	30,614	63,527	302,011
1955	22,320	2,397	60,990	3,265	25,330	30,309	14,890	52,814	30,942	64,942	308,193
1956	22,954	2,598	63,760	3,484	25,435	31,914	14,894	54,911	31,495	67,899	319,342
1957	23,973	2,637	67,052	3,659	25,868	32,703	15,368	56,867	31,779	69,527	329,433
1958	23,809	2,535	68,138	3,847	27,482	33,943	15,880	59,171	31,554	72,718	339,077
1959	22,954	2,530	71,222	3,988	28,197	35,908	16,572	61,788	31,659	75,723	350,541
1960	24,137	2,931	77,288	4,349	27,620	36,604	18,508	65,354	32,331	76,936	366,058
1961	24,385	3,217	82,772	4,842	29,295	38,857	18,902	68,091	33,406	79,854	383,621
1962	24,549	3,135	89,216	5,465	32,406	40,261	19,697	70,555	33,765	83,253	402,301
1963	22,764	3,276	93,736	5,688	34,646	42,731	20,375	72,658	35,139	89,515	420,527
1964	24,727	3,737	105,140	6,174	36,644	45,435	21,695	76,188	35,599	92,152	447,488
1965	24,175	4,146	113,143	6,643	39,183	47,464	23,073	79,120	35,943	95,896	468,785
1966	23,145	3,996	118,866	6,708	41,500	48,585	24,314	82,681	36,022	99,465	485,281
1967	25,569	4,264	121,371	7,061	42,416	49,509	24,675	85,634	35,786	105,001	501,285
1968	26,244	4,976	128,940	7,673	41,823	57,772	26,208	87,986	31,664	112,117	525,403
1969	23,840	5,177	137,470	7,965	44,348	60,439	27,021	90,534	32,103	118,106	547,002
1970	25,673	5,365	146,672	8,258	44,486	61,866	28,320	93,064	32,739	126,655	573,096

133

Appendix table 1.7 (*contd*)

Year	Agriculture	Mining	Manufacturing	Public utilities	Construction	Wholesale and retail trade[a]	Transport and communication	Finance, insurance and real estate	Community, social and personal services[a]	Government services	GDP at basic prices
1971	27,295	5,061	147,916	9,525	44,689	61,342	30,133	97,923	30,717	129,176	583,776
1972	26,268	4,957	148,809	10,795	46,150	64,069	30,757	101,755	31,425	134,167	599,151
1973	26,624	5,567	159,340	11,595	45,869	67,805	33,198	104,634	32,447	138,010	625,089
1974	27,832	5,574	167,952	10,873	42,591	71,616	38,803	106,756	32,207	143,455	649,659
1975	25,279	4,552	168,511	12,058	45,682	71,947	37,216	109,794	36,190	149,232	660,462
1976	25,291	4,424	168,552	12,147	47,674	74,981	38,190	111,908	36,581	153,978	673,724
1977	23,610	3,775	158,891	12,866	47,593	73,158	38,996	114,277	36,554	157,953	667,673
1978	24,022	3,124	154,595	14,225	47,340	72,034	39,806	115,680	35,995	164,306	671,128
1979	23,919	4,063	164,543	14,718	48,273	75,847	41,888	117,364	36,417	170,957	697,989
1980	24,761	4,118	165,183	14,905	48,628	76,345	44,816	120,216	36,535	175,123	710,630
1981	24772	3,542	160,847	15,935	46,932	74,808	46,250	124,635	37,445	179,358	714,524
1982	26,131	2,915	161,382	15,175	48,800	75,123	47,248	130,385	37,775	182,020	726,954
1983	28,331	2,808	170,760	17,033	47,590	76,763	45,306	134,012	37,954	185,571	746,128
1984	28,939	3,445	183,266	20,613	49,977	79,709	45,887	135,591	38,468	188,849	774,744
1985	28,350	3,688	186,750	22,629	51,136	82,271	47,025	138,745	38,135	190,524	789,253
1986	28,138	3,780	189,001	23,817	52,015	87,112	49,866	142,628	38,742	192,846	807,945
1987	26,638	3,776	193,642	25,164	54,189	92,718	54,224	147,818	40,756	195,102	834,027
1988	26,215	3,619	199,566	25,195	55,049	96,688	58,743	153,223	41,359	196,807	856,464
1989	29,417	3,283	201,892	24,200	59,286	100,335	59,986	158,869	42,178	201,037	878,483
1990	30,874	3,404	200,579	24,705	59,486	101,254	68,785	160,167	41,291	205,283	895,828
1991	28,080	3,259	189,405	24,929	59,359	100,558	67,754	163,838	40,913	206,280	884,375
1992	28,015	3,337	187,948	24,511	58,964	98,334	67,604	163,068	40,475	201,590	873,846

Appendix table 1.8 Gross value added at factor cost. United Kingdom, 1947–92, million pounds (1985 prices)

Year	Agricul-ture	Mining	Manufac-turing	Public utilities	Construc-tion	Wholesale and retail trade	Transport and communi-cation	Finance, insurance and real estate	Community, social and personal services	Govern-ment services	GDP at factor cost
1947	2,068	8,396	33,888	1,814	10,522	19,234	8,884	17,630	7,060	34,272	143,788
1948	2,224	8,901	36,962	1,928	11,468	19,981	9,556	17,765	7,171	31,517	147,473
1949	2,390	9,196	39,316	2,062	11,993	21,289	9,784	18,035	6,840	31,268	152,172
1950	2,447	9,295	42,020	2,248	12,008	22,222	10,006	18,370	6,729	31,152	156,498
1951	2,502	9,603	43,810	2,389	11,553	21,849	10,455	18,426	6,729	32,487	159,802
1952	2,558	9,738	42,234	2,462	11,898	21,289	10,569	18,426	6,619	33,286	159,079
1953	2,613	9,689	44,841	2,585	12,729	22,596	10,791	18,863	6,729	33,764	165,200
1954	2,668	9,812	47,856	2,796	13,230	23,903	10,905	19,491	6,840	33,837	171,337
1955	2,640	9,701	50,910	2,946	13,260	24,837	11,132	20,008	6,950	33,457	175,841
1956	2,781	9,726	50,657	3,083	13,995	25,210	11,355	20,324	6,950	33,769	177,850
1957	2,836	9,664	51,786	3,192	13,950	25,770	11,355	20,896	7,060	33,735	180,245
1958	2,781	9,246	51,124	3,336	13,885	26,144	11,241	21,468	7,171	33,380	179,775
1959	2,890	8,999	54,198	3,423	14,661	27,824	11,690	22,543	7,502	33,346	187,077
1960	3,086	8,679	58,594	3,686	15,482	28,758	12,368	23,362	7,832	33,395	195,243
1961	3,086	8,556	58,692	3,856	16,588	29,692	12,590	23,934	8,053	34,053	199,100
1962	3,197	8,790	58,945	4,163	16,759	29,692	12,703	24,339	8,274	34,579	201,441
1963	3,306	8,778	61,357	4,437	16,799	30,626	13,153	25,158	8,494	35,271	207,378
1964	3,501	8,802	66,201	4,584	18,786	31,746	13,939	26,121	9,046	35,881	218,606
1965	3,588	8,482	68,399	4,847	19,171	32,493	14,502	26,795	9,156	36,753	224,187
1966	3,588	7,997	69,648	5,035	19,494	32,842	15,014	27,575	9,469	37,480	228,142
1967	3,706	7,941	70,117	5,217	20,240	33,192	15,184	29,557	9,569	38,876	233,599
1968	3,706	7,726	74,724	5,557	20,844	34,240	15,696	29,954	9,672	39,282	241,402
1969	3,746	7,276	77,613	5,836	20,562	34,240	16,379	31,115	9,748	38,962	245,475
1970	3,943	6,936	78,081	6,067	20,159	34,939	17,061	32,334	10,933	46,518	258,970

Appendix table 1.8 (*contd*)

Year	Agriculture	Mining	Manufacturing	Public utilities	Construction	Wholesale and retail trade[a]	Transport and communication	Finance, insurance and real estate	Community, social and personal services[a]	Government services	GDP at factor cost
1971	4,179	6,915	77,769	6,303	20,744	35,288	17,232	33,934	9,948	40,967	253,279
1972	4,258	5,826	79,643	6,746	21,207	37,035	18,085	34,344	10,111	42,566	280,821
1973	4,376	6,492	86,124	7,146	21,671	39,481	18,767	37,268	10,511	43,903	275,739
1974	4,429	5,294	85,095	7,139	19,427	38,187	18,805	38,220	10,602	44,812	272,010
1975	4,086	5,902	79,158	7,248	18,396	36,967	18,674	38,784	10,933	46,667	266,815
1976	3,759	7,442	80,741	7,415	18,139	37,263	18,506	39,948	11,690	48,534	273,435
1977	4,233	11,119	82,245	7,712	18,065	36,782	19,029	40,724	11,802	48,522	280,232
1978	4,577	13,757	82,641	7,951	19,298	38,667	19,533	42,133	12,121	48,737	289,414
1979	4,507	17,389	82,490	8,300	19,426	39,811	20,483	44,564	12,382	49,293	298,645
1980	5,002	17,456	75,333	8,122	18,361	36,896	20,220	46,232	13,033	49,790	290,447
1981	5,122	18,488	70,813	8,081	16,507	36,158	20,018	47,899	12,772	50,068	285,927
1982	5,552	20,151	70,964	8,000	16,819	36,860	19,897	50,632	12,642	49,905	291,421
1983	5,322	21,474	72,998	8,178	17,498	38,040	20,605	53,042	13,033	50,183	300,373
1984	6,431	20,251	75,800	6,933	18,326	39,911	21,617	56,191	13,912	50,183	309,555
1985	6,096	22,222	77,823	8,414	18,400	41,574	22,494	58,914	14,644	50,458	321,039
1986	6,102	22,930	78,835	9,247	19,154	43,861	23,461	63,608	15,376	50,733	333,307
1987	5,913	22,368	82,959	9,499	20,774	46,771	25,306	68,302	16,548	51,558	349,997
1988	5,822	20,922	88,796	9,575	23,110	49,930	26,858	72,731	17,280	52,153	367,178
1989	6,112	17,684	92,778	9,536	24,437	51,922	28,232	74,111	17,211	52,462	374,585
1990	6,321	16,955	92,592	9,801	25,038	51,546	28,505	75,977	17,297	52,781	376,813
1991	6,435	17,311	87,592	10,349	23,010	49,592	27,968	75,482	17,436	53,111	368,286
1992	6,751	18,057	87,037	10,349	22,084	49,496	28,474	73,897	17,782	53,279	367,205

Year	Agriculture	Mining	Manufacturing	Public utilities	Construction	Wholesale and retail trade	Transport and communication	Finance, insurance and real estate	Community, social and personal services	Government services	GDP at market prices
1947	56,907	77,942	233,010	14,376	73,020	142,782	73,010	103,054	128,271	156,230	1,058,602
1948	62,712	83,457	245,823	16,347	85,610	146,544	72,093	107,767	132,662	155,564	1,108,579
1949	62,442	75,783	233,237	18,118	85,050	150,317	66,260	112,299	132,693	164,020	1,100,219
1950	65,815	83,924	265,611	19,702	95,200	164,765	69,631	119,762	137,645	169,254	1,191,309
1951	64,035	93,173	297,234	22,819	105,557	166,282	76,613	126,476	140,850	214,091	1,307,131
1952	65,728	93,911	307,358	24,509	110,325	171,493	76,306	134,761	143,373	231,994	1,359,759
1953	67,846	97,244	329,720	26,426	114,112	177,044	77,905	142,293	146,836	230,996	1,410,422
1954	69,753	96,065	305,643	29,068	118,740	178,393	73,633	149,601	150,083	225,470	1,396,449
1955	70,690	106,031	337,718	30,440	126,814	194,585	80,101	160,233	157,454	223,482	1,487,547
1956	69,396	111,219	340,753	32,828	135,803	200,433	83,291	168,879	165,768	225,649	1,534,021
1957	67,454	110,931	342,660	35,031	135,529	203,723	83,687	178,389	173,464	229,244	1,580,113
1958	69,879	102,879	312,763	36,534	140,380	203,612	79,048	184,549	179,290	230,164	1,538,999
1959	67,311	108,441	348,347	40,029	152,654	217,859	83,246	196,034	188,815	232,815	1,635,551
1960	69,841	108,606	349,040	42,969	155,244	222,061	85,036	206,584	195,635	240,386	1,675,403
1961	69,088	110,220	349,808	45,179	157,076	224,236	85,383	215,109	203,392	249,287	1,708,777
1962	68,673	113,139	379,543	47,490	164,185	238,852	89,414	226,581	213,650	258,476	1,800,003
1963	68,802	117,879	409,600	49,953	168,896	247,879	94,496	235,976	223,714	264,615	1,881,808
1964	66,717	121,824	438,488	53,387	176,926	263,053	97,964	245,920	237,373	274,095	1,975,747
1965	68,203	126,088	476,680	55,831	184,336	280,412	106,279	259,894	247,335	284,333	2,089,391
1966	63,893	132,589	513,182	59,296	185,032	295,526	115,339	271,263	261,201	305,571	2,202,893
1967	66,972	138,589	511,791	62,197	181,447	303,511	116,738	282,515	272,843	322,359	2,258,963
1968	65,030	143,728	538,032	68,162	180,969	321,084	122,717	296,181	282,578	332,685	2,351,166
1969	66,785	148,663	553,109	72,537	174,710	327,388	129,347	314,189	296,048	340,302	2,423,078
1970	70,449	155,125	522,302	74,437	159,841	332,696	131,270	320,854	304,227	339,694	2,410,894

137

Appendix table 1.9 *(contd)*

Year	Agriculture	Mining	Manufacturing	Public utilities	Construction	Wholesale and retail trade[a]	Transport and communication	Finance, insurance and real estate	Community, social and personal services[a]	Government services	GDP at market prices
1971	72,261	152,628	531,262	79,678	154,873	349,078	132,780	336,061	311,120	340,094	2,459,834
1972	72,502	154,967	578,427	82,108	158,599	375,415	143,776	351,068	329,228	340,594	2,586,684
1973	71,934	153,756	640,296	92,619	162,124	395,507	153,544	367,876	350,010	343,495	2,731,161
1974	71,371	150,221	609,719	95,165	154,441	385,732	156,946	381,783	357,521	350,697	2,713,596
1975	74,809	144,790	564,273	99,712	142,209	391,977	151,395	387,786	362,562	355,098	2,674,610
1976	73,163	143,375	618,995	98,710	150,449	411,255	161,972	403,293	378,303	357,799	2,797,313
1977	73,300	145,500	664,800	99,400	157,100	433,700	171,800	417,900	399,600	363,000	2,926,100
1978	73,000	148,300	694,700	97,800	166,900	466,600	186,200	442,800	421,500	371,600	3,069,400
1979	77,000	142,200	712,200	95,000	167,400	488,000	196,400	461,100	436,900	376,500	3,152,700
1980	76,400	143,500	673,900	97,300	153,300	481,800	196,600	468,900	450,900	382,800	3,125,400
1981	87,400	145,700	678,600	99,300	150,300	499,100	194,600	476,100	463,000	385,400	3,179,500
1982	89,596	132,122	634,648	92,049	140,908	506,484	196,392	475,139	463,633	383,922	3,114,893
1983	76,700	129,900	674,200	92,100	146,100	530,000	215,700	492,900	480,400	387,300	3,225,300
1984	84,200	137,900	752,400	104,300	159,400	588,900	221,800	509,800	509,700	391,900	3,460,300
1985	95,800	139,000	779,200	109,200	166,300	621,500	222,200	528,300	538,600	400,500	3,600,600
1986	103,600	128,200	803,400	111,900	174,600	662,200	230,500	535,600	565,800	407,900	3,723,700
1987	105,100	127,500	852,200	119,400	177,500	655,900	251,900	560,600	592,600	415,600	3,858,300
1988	101,062	144,705	896,567	125,135	176,417	687,687	261,426	586,079	615,547	423,679	4,018,303
1989	104,506	127,961	905,013	130,612	177,583	711,813	266,818	599,233	640,462	432,139	4,096,142
1990	113,769	141,018	901,421	130,869	175,167	702,303	278,321	601,172	658,411	443,190	4,145,642

2   Number of persons employed by industry
(Figures printed in shadow are estimated as described in the notes.)

Denmark
Notes:
Before 1975 data on armed forces are not available. 1948–75: finance, insurance and real estate was obtained on the basis of the assumption that its productivity movement equalled that of transport and communication and wholesale and retail trade; community, personal and social services was obtained on the basis of the assumption that its productivity movement equalled that of government services. The combined employment of finance, insurance and real estate and community, personal and social services was obtained as a residual from total employment minus the employment of the other sectors.
Sources:
1948–75 from the database of the ADAM Macroeconomic Model, which was kindly provided by Danmarks Statistik. The self-employed in non-agriculture were distributed over the industries on the basis of the ratio of self-employed to employees in 1975 from Danmarks Statistik, *Nationalregnskabsstatistik 1982*. 1975–90 from Danmarks Statistik, *Nationalregnskabsstatistik 1982, 1987* and *1993*, Copenhagen.

France
Notes:
1950–64: finance, insurance and real estate was obtained on the basis of the assumption that its productivity movement equalled that of transport and communication and wholesale and retail trade. 1950–70: community, personal and social services and government services were obtained on the basis of the assumption that their productivity movement equalled that of the two sectors taken together. The combined employment of finance, insurance and real estate, community, personal and social services and government services was obtained as a residual from total employment minus the employment of the other sectors.
Sources:
1950 from Maddison (Chapter 2) distributed over the industries on the basis of 1954 shares from OECD, *Manpower Statistics 1950–1962*, and linked to the 1954. 1954–56 from OECD, *Manpower Statistics 1950–1962*. 1956–65 from OECD *Labour Force Statistics 1956–1966*. 1965–69 from OECD, *Labour Force Statistics 1965–1985* and 1970–71 from OECD *Labour Force Statistics 1970–1990*. 1971–79 from OECD *National Accounts, Detailed Tables*, Vol. II, 1971–83; 1979–90 from OECD, *National Accounts, Detailed Tables*, Vol. II, 1980–92.

Germany
Notes:
1950–59: wholesale and retail trade and finance, insurance and real estate were obtained on the basis of the assumption that their productivity movement equalled that of the two sectors taken together. The combined employment of the two sectors was obtained as a residual from total employment minus the employment of the other sectors.
Sources:
1950–87 'Erwerbstätige' from *Volkswirtschaftliche Gesamtrechnungen, Revidierte Ergebnisse 1950–1990*, Fachserie 18, Reihe S. 15, p. 88 and pp. 117–20. 1987–92 from *Volkswirtschaftliche Gesamtrechnungen, Hauptbericht 1993*, Fachserie 18. From 1950–59 disaggregated to industries on the basis of W. G. Hoffman, *Das Wachstum der Deutschen Wirtschaft seit der Mitte des 19. jahrhunderts*, Springer Verlag, 1965. 1960–69 disaggregated to industries on the basis of Institut für Arbeitsmarkt und Berufsforschung, *Arbeitszeit und Arbeitsvolumen in der Bundesrepublik Deutschland 1960–1986*, Nuremberg.

Italy

Source:
See notes on gross value added in constant prices.

The Netherlands

Notes:
The figures on employment published in the Dutch national accounts are for 'man-years'. It appeared not possible to rework these estimates to the number of persons. However, the man-year estimates were used to divide the estimates of persons employed up into sectors where independent estimates were not available, which was for the government sector for the whole period, and for all sectors except agriculture and manufacturing before 1973.
Sources:
1987–92 from CBS, *Arbeidsrekeningen 1989–1992.* 1977–87: adjusted series (provided by CBS) for employees based on the *Statistiek Werkzame Personen.* Includes adjustments for changes in definitions and for persons working less than 15 hours per week. Armed forces from OECD, *Labour Force Statistics,* various issues. 1973–77 from *Statistiek Werkzame Personen,* but adjusted for persons working less than 15 hours per week derived from the *Arbeidskrachtentelling 1973, 1975* and *1977* and with intermediate years interpolated. 1973–87: self-employed from CBS, *Volkstelling 1971* and *Arbeidskrachtentelling,* various issues, and with intermediate years interpolated. 1950–73: total economy supplied by US Department of Labor. Manufacturing from US Department of Labor, 'International Comparisons of Manufacturing Productivity and Unit Labor Cost Trends, 1991', USDL: 92–752, Washington, DC. Agriculture from C. L. J. van der Meer, 'Employment and Labour Input in Dutch Agriculture 1849–1986', Research Memorandum no. 259, University of Groningen.

Spain

Notes:
1950–69: finance, insurance and real estate was obtained on the basis of the assumption that its productivity movement equalled that of transport and communication and wholesale and retail trade. 1950–79: community, personal and social services and government services were obtained on the basis of the assumption that their productivity movement equalled that of the two sectors taken together. The combined employment of finance, insurance and real estate, community, personal and social services and government services was obtained as a residual from total employment minus the employment of the other sectors.
Sources:
1950 from OECD, *Manpower Statistics 1950–1962.* 1956–63 from OECD, *Labour Force Statistics 1956–1966.* 1963–70 except industry from OECD, *Labour Force Statistics 1959–1970* and 1970–71 except industry from OECD, *Labour Force Statistics 1970–1990.* 1971–80 except industry from OECD, *National Accounts, Detailed Tables,* Vol. II. 1971–83 with services split off on the basis of shares from OECD, *Labour Force Statistics 1965–1985.* 1964–81 industry from R. Gandoy Juste (1988), *Evolucion de la productividad global en la industria Española. Un analisis desagregado para el periodo 1964–1981,* Editorial de la Universidad Complutense de Madrid. 1980–85 from OECD, *National Accounts, Detailed Tables,* Vol. II. 1975–87 and 1985–89 from OECD, *National Accounts, Detailed Tables,* Vol. II, 1978–90. 1990–92 from updated data provided by OECD.

Sweden

Notes:
1950–60: wholesale and retail trade and finance, insurance and real estate were obtained on the basis of the assumption that their productivity movement equalled that of the two sectors taken together. 1950–60: community, personal and social services and government services were obtained on the basis of the assumption that their productivity movement

equalled that of the two sectors taken together. The combined employment of wholesale and retail trade and finance, insurance and real estate, community, personal and social services and government services was obtained as a residual from total employment minus the employment of the other sectors.

Source:
1950 from B. R. Mitchell, *International Historical Statistics Europe, 1750–1988*, 1992. 1960–69 obtained as index series from SCB (1972), *Sysselsättnung 1960–1971* (Employment), Supplement II SM N 1972:93 National Accounts, including correction for break in series in 1968. 1970–85 from SCB (1986), *Nationalraekenskaper 1970–1985*, Appendix 5. 1985–90 from SCB (1991), *Nationalraekenskaper 1970–1990*, Appendix 5. 1990–92 provided by OECD.

United Kingdom

Sources:
1947–65 index series from C. H. Feinstein, *Statistical Tables of National Income, Expenditure and Output of the United Kingdom 1855–1965*. 1965–74 from OECD, *National Accounts of OECD Countries 1950–78*, Vol. I. For 1965–74 employment shares for services sectors were obtained from OECD *Labour Force Statistics 1965–85*. 1975–91 from OECD, *National Accounts, Detailed Tables*, Vol. II, 1971–83 and OECD, *National Accounts, Detailed Tables*, Vol. II, 1980–92.

United States

Notes:
Number of persons employed is calculated as full-time and part-time employees plus self-employed.
Sources:
1982–90 from BEA, *Survey of Current Business*, various issues, 1947–82 from BEA, *National Income and Product Accounts of the United States, 1929–1982*, Washington, DC, 1986.

Appendix table 2.1 Number of persons employed. Denmark 1948–92 (thousands)

Year	Agriculture	Mining	Manufacturing	Public utilities	Construction	Wholesale and retail trade	Transport and communication	Finance, insurance and real estate	Community, social and personal services	Government services	Total employment
1947											
1948	534.4	21.0	437.3	10.7	130.5	257.3	131.9	85.6	143.4	192.1	1,944.1
1949	527.1	20.0	447.4	10.7	135.6	257.4	134.0	84.9	144.8	194.2	1,956.1
1950	519.9	19.1	472.2	11.0	141.0	269.6	135.3	83.2	146.1	195.8	1,993.1
1951	512.8	18.1	479.3	11.1	137.8	273.7	136.4	81.2	148.2	217.6	2,016.3
1952	501.9	17.1	461.8	11.2	142.7	279.0	130.2	83.0	145.9	224.5	1,997.3
1953	497.1	16.2	468.5	11.1	156.3	275.2	138.5	81.4	147.9	249.2	2,041.6
1954	488.5	15.2	485.0	11.3	161.4	289.5	140.0	85.5	142.9	240.1	2,059.4
1955	480.1	14.3	478.8	11.2	152.5	294.6	142.6	85.6	145.3	248.5	2,053.3
1956	468.7	13.2	475.2	11.1	154.9	284.0	152.9	86.4	146.8	248.8	2,042.1
1957	457.1	12.2	491.1	11.2	153.4	284.2	151.5	87.7	148.0	250.0	2,046.3
1958	448.0	11.3	487.6	11.2	153.7	289.4	151.2	84.3	154.1	264.3	2,053.1
1959	436.8	10.3	522.2	11.2	168.4	294.0	152.5	87.8	152.9	257.0	2,093.1
1960	424.4	9.4	550.5	11.2	174.6	301.3	155.3	87.5	154.9	263.3	2,132.3
1961	412.5	8.6	562.6	11.4	181.3	307.1	155.8	83.9	161.8	286.7	2,171.7
1962	399.2	7.8	575.4	11.6	185.9	308.5	158.9	91.5	154.0	302.8	2,205.5
1963	384.0	7.0	572.8	11.7	186.3	316.7	161.0	94.9	166.3	307.5	2,208.1
1964	371.7	6.3	579.8	11.9	205.4	320.1	161.3	98.6	172.9	321.7	2,249.6
1965	357.2	5.4	586.7	12.1	210.0	341.3	159.3	101.7	169.8	339.8	2,283.3
1966	337.7	5.6	581.4	12.7	204.6	322.6	149.0	102.9	175.0	372.7	2,264.1
1967	317.4	4.8	554.3	12.8	221.9	300.3	145.5	105.6	177.1	405.2	2,244.8
1968	297.9	4.0	557.7	12.9	218.3	295.7	150.8	115.7	178.1	413.6	2,244.7
1969	277.5	3.3	569.2	13.0	227.9	330.6	156.6	119.7	165.0	445.6	2,308.3
1970	258.2	2.5	569.4	13.1	233.1	344.7	159.3	127.7	158.1	466.8	2,332.6

Appendix table 2.1 *(contd)*

Year	Agriculture	Mining	Manufacturing	Public utilities	Construction	Wholesale and retail trade	Transport and communication	Finance, insurance and real estate	Community, social and personal services	Government services	Total employment
1971	246.4	2.4	547.2	13.3	231.0	340.1	157.2	*132.7*	*168.3*	520.6	2,357.0
1972	230.0	2.4	559.1	13.6	222.1	329.0	157.2	*145.9*	*173.6*	531.5	2,364.3
1973	227.8	2.1	566.9	13.7	223.2	338.3	166.8	*151.4*	*168.2*	540.1	2,398.7
1974	223.7	2.1	546.7	13.9	205.7	325.4	170.5	*151.5*	*175.4*	587.0	2,401.9
1975	224.0	2.0	504.0	14.0	191.0	321.0	159.0	158.0	178.0	586.0	2,337.0
1976	218.0	2.0	505.5	15.0	203.0	327.0	164.0	160.0	183.0	603.0	2,380.0
1977	214.0	2.0	503.0	15.0	199.0	325.0	166.0	165.0	182.0	628.0	2,399.0
1978	206.0	2.0	500.0	15.0	203.0	312.0	165.0	175.0	190.0	655.0	2,423.0
1979	201.0	2.0	499.0	15.0	201.0	308.0	168.0	186.0	184.0	690.0	2,454.0
1980	192.0	2.0	490.0	15.0	189.0	294.0	169.0	193.0	178.0	720.0	2,442.0
1981	186.0	2.0	472.0	15.0	165.0	281.0	170.0	196.0	176.0	747.0	2,410.0
1982	185.0	2.0	470.0	15.0	154.0	278.0	171.0	197.0	176.0	773.0	2,421.0
1983	183.0	2.0	471.0	16.0	152.0	276.0	172.0	200.0	177.0	779.0	2,428.0
1984	179.0	2.0	495.0	16.0	163.0	278.0	173.0	210.0	181.0	773.0	2,470.0
1985	175.0	2.0	523.0	16.0	169.0	284.0	176.0	223.0	185.0	778.0	2,531.0
1986	169.0	3.0	542.0	16.0	186.0	290.0	179.0	237.0	190.0	785.0	2,597.0
1987	163.0	3.0	535.0	17.0	191.0	287.0	184.0	253.0	198.0	791.0	2,622.0
1988	155.0	2.0	523.0	16.0	186.0	287.0	188.0	260.0	194.0	793.0	2,604.0
1989	148.0	2.0	517.0	17.0	175.0	284.0	184.0	262.0	194.0	807.0	2,590.0
1990	141.0	2.0	517.0	17.0	168.0	279.0	182.0	258.0	193.0	808.0	2,565.0
1991	134.0	2.0	509.0	17.0	159.0	273.0	178.0	255.0	190.0	804.0	2,521.0
1992	130.0	2.0	503.0	17.0	159.0	273.0	176.0	253.0	192.0	811.0	2,516.0

Appendix table 2.2   Number of persons employed. France 1950–92 (thousands)

Year	Agriculture	Mining	Manufacturing	Public utilities	Construction	Wholesale and retail trade	Transport and communication	Finance, insurance and real estate	Community, social and personal services	Government services	Total employment
1947											
1948											
1949											
1950	4,800.2	414.1	4,937.2	99.5	1,482.6	2,088.6	872.0	858.1.2	798.4	3,603.6	19,954.4
1951											
1952											
1953											
1954	4,808.9	414.8	4,946.1	99.7	1,485.3	2,092.4	873.6	811.2	853.0	3,605.4	19,990.4
1955	4,599.0	402.1	4,986.7	103.6	1,556.8	2,132.5	874.5	795.9	900.4	3,656.7	20,008.3
1956	4,808.9	414.8	4,946.1	99.7	1,485.3	2,092.4	873.6	740.1	904.4	3,625.1	19,990.4
1957	4,588.9	418.2	5,075.1	102.2	1,540.7	2,151.1	887.7	761.6	960.2	3,646.5	20,132.3
1958	4,413.4	414.8	5,119.7	106.1	1,532.7	2,202.6	899.2	849.6	954.7	3,558.0	20,050.7
1959	4,295.5	408.0	5,045.0	109.2	1,538.7	2,225.2	905.3	860.5	939.0	3,564.0	19,890.5
1960	4,147.8	391.0	5,063.4	112.4	1,557.9	2,268.6	915.9	849.7	983.7	3,602.0	19,892.4
1961	4,000.1	369.5	5,109.0	114.3	1,591.1	2,311.0	929.1	848.3	1,012.5	3,600.1	19,885.2
1962	3,854.4	359.3	5,174.9	117.5	1,639.5	2,359.8	945.0	799.8	1,040.4	3,618.2	19,909.0
1963	3,713.3	351.3	5,294.9	119.9	1,734.8	2,416.6	974.4	836.8	1,056.7	3,602.2	20,101.1
1964	3,576.5	339.8	5,401.0	121.5	1,846.9	2,464.7	1,000.4	860.1	1,079.2	3,633.0	20,323.1
1965	3,442.5	329.5	5,358.3	123.9	1,933.9	2,509.3	1,016.8	910.4	1,107.7	3,677.3	20,409.5
1966	3,314.6	321.1	5,386.3	125.5	1,978.1	2,553.3	1,024.8	959.8	1,177.5	3,736.7	20,577.7
1967	3,191.7	308.0	5,355.3	127.9	2,000.2	2,603.4	1,035.4	1,017.2	1,183.7	3,830.4	20,653.2
1968	3,044.0	291.3	5,279.6	129.6	2,023.3	2,632.4	1,038.9	1,074.6	1,148.1	3,965.8	20,627.6
1969	2,876.5	275.7	5,429.1	131.2	2,078.1	2,694.8	1,054.8	1,155.0	1,194.6	4,057.7	20,947.6
1970	2,726.8	260.2	5,577.7	131.2	2,106.5	2,744.9	1,065.4	1,228.5	1,244.2	4,169.3	21,254.7

Appendix table 2.2 *(contd)*

Year	Agriculture	Mining	Manufacturing	Public utilities	Construction	Wholesale and retail trade	Transport and communication	Finance, insurance and real estate	Community, social and personal services	Government services	Total employment
1971	2,589.1	249.5	5,660.5	130.4	2,088.6	2,770.4	1,068.9	1,283.6	1,279.8	4,251.7	21,372.4
1972	2,440.9	236.5	5,730.4	130.4	2,082.3	2,785.1	1,079.0	1,330.5	1,326.6	4,321.1	21,462.6
1973	2,311.6	222.3	5,855.7	131.9	2,103.4	2,950.6	1,096.1	1,341.3	1,337.4	4,402.8	21,753.1
1974	2,204.1	212.8	5,918.3	135.0	2,092.9	2995.7	1,125.2	1,382.7	1,378.7	4,451.6	21,897.0
1975	2,115.6	205.7	5,756.0	136.6	2,001.8	2,968.6	1,126.2	1,412.3	1,408.2	4,524.7	21,655.9
1976	2,050.0	195.1	5,698.5	137.4	1,985.9	3,023.7	1,132.5	1,457.1	1,492.1	4,601.5	21,773.7
1977	1,989.3	184.4	5,673.9	138.9	1,979.5	3,056.8	1,156.5	1,513.0	1,562.2	4,658.8	21,913.3
1978	1,942.5	176.2	5,583.5	143.6	1,938.2	3,081.0	1,178.8	1,580.1	1,617.1	4,738.0	21,979.1
1979	1,904.7	169.1	5,485.9	144.4	1,919.2	3,088.8	1,185.0	1,633.8	1,655.8	4,746.6	21,933.1
1980	1,849.7	164.7	5,405.7	147.0	1,913.1	3,102.8	1,188.0	1,700.8	1,669.1	4,801.0	21,941.9
1981	1,781.4	161.0	5,232.2	150.2	1,878.3	3,108.6	1,197.1	1,739.6	1,707.3	4,880.5	21,836.2
1982	1,717.3	160.8	5,150.0	156.5	1,831.6	3,128.3	1,221.5	1,765.1	1,769.7	4,995.1	21,895.9
1983	1,659.9	157.7	5,048.6	164.0	1,752.6	3,143.5	1,240.0	1,779.4	1,807.0	5,112.5	21,865.2
1984	1,604.2	152.3	4,904.3	165.7	1,639.8	3,100.5	1,248.0	1,819.8	1,844.0	5,194.3	21,672.9
1985	1,547.1	143.6	4,773.5	164.9	1,579.4	3,043.9	1,247.2	1,877.0	1,867.7	5,363.8	21,608.1
1986	1,496.0	137.2	4,687.1	165.1	1,577.2	3,042.9	1,251.1	1,934.0	1,925.8	5,477.1	21,693.5
1987	1,438.5	130.8	4,569.9	164.7	1,588.4	3,089.9	1,256.1	2,015.8	1,991.1	5,518.1	21,763.3
1988	1,382.1	123.7	4,504.0	164.6	1,612.3	3,133.3	1,268.0	2,141.7	2,061.5	5,565.9	21,957.1
1989	1,322.7	118.9	4,528.1	163.4	1,649.5	3,168.1	1,274.9	2,294.2	2,134.6	5,591.9	22,246.3
1990	1,262.0	113.3	4,557.2	161.9	1,662.2	3,198.7	1,292.0	2,405.1	2,203.8	5,620.7	22,476.9
1991	1,206.0	108.3	4,482.8	160.9	1,651.3	3,177.8	1,304.0	2,439.7	2,234.2	5,718.5	22,483.5
1992	1,151.9	104.7	4,366.8	160.0	1,606.9	3,148.9	1,314.6	2,415.5	2,286.5	5,820.4	22,376.2

Appendix table 2.3 Number of persons employed. Germany 1950–92 (thousands)

Year	Agricul- ture	Mining	Manufac- turing	Public utilities	Construc- tion	Wholesale and retail trade	Transport and communi- cation	Finance, insurance and real estate	Community, social and personal services	Govern- ment services	Total employ- ment
1947											
1948											
1949											
1950	4,873.4	599.2	6,661.9	151.4	1,516.7	2,089.8	969.4	215.8	1,398.3	2,147.8	20,623.7
1951	4,693.4	618.5	7,061.9	155.4	1618.1	2,240.1	991.9	238.0	1,397.1	2,173.7	21,188.2
1952	4,553.9	651.8	7,224.5	164.0	1,704.2	2,374.9	1,023.8	263.9	1,439.4	2,255.7	21,656.1
1953	4,427.5	667.5	7,485.1	166.6	1,822.3	2,535.5	1,047.4	285.5	1,489.9	2,324.8	22,252.1
1954	4,307.1	661.1	7,794.5	170.5	1,958.2	2,072.3	1,079.7	306.0	1,545.0	2,401.4	22,895.8
1955	4,205.0	659.4	8,358.2	171.8	2,096.3	2,851.6	1,114.1	323.9	1,580.2	2,424.0	23,784.5
1956	4,096.8	672.0	8,711.2	178.4	2,186.1	3,021.4	1,159.1	337.8	1,629.2	2,496.3	24,488.0
1957	4,037.1	683.9	8,974.5	181.6	2,144.0	3,210.2	1,160.2	357.3	1,646.8	2,607.4	25,003.0
1958	3,919.8	666.5	8,988.4	182.5	2,190.2	3,332.0	1,209.0	387.2	1,725.4	2,689.4	25,290.3
1959	3,766.1	610.5	9,049.2	184.2	2,299.7	3,433.7	1,229.7	400.0	1,821.4	2,800.5	25,595.0
1960	3,581.0	616.0	9,624.0	131.0	2,126.0	3,299.0	1,460.0	383.0	1,981.0	2862.0	26,063.0
1961	3,449.0	586.0	9,905.0	136.0	2,178.0	3,344.0	1,464.0	411.0	1,995.0	2,958.0	26,426.0
1962	3,307.0	550.0	9,948.0	148.0	2,272.0	3,348.0	1,464.0	432.0	2,027.0	3,022.0	26,518.0
1963	3,144.0	517.0	9,883.0	148.0	2,379.0	3,376.0	1,469.0	452.0	2,089.0	3,124.0	26,581.0
1964	3,002.0	497.0	9,885.0	157.0	2,447.0	3,344.0	1,473.0	466.0	2,124.0	3,209.0	26,604.0
1965	2,876.0	474.0	10,059.0	171.0	2,454.0	3,327.0	1,464.0	485.0	2,167.0	3,278.0	26,755.0
1966	2,790.0	435.0	9,953.0	193.0	2,436.0	3,359.0	1,441.0	513.0	2,206.0	3,347.0	26,673.0
1967	2,638.0	378.0	9,418.0	204.0	2,249.0	3,292.0	1,417.0	536.0	2,238.0	3,434.0	2,5804.0
1968	2,523.0	337.0	9,488.0	210.0	2,285.0	3,300.0	1,392.0	554.0	2,283.0	3,454.0	25,826.0
1969	2,395.0	318.0	9,883.0	221.0	2,305.0	3,330.0	1,384.0	573.0	2,310.0	3,509.0	26,228.0
1970	2,262.0	310.0	10,117.0	241.0	2,319.0	3,348.0	1,407.0	597.0	2,336.0	3,623.0	26,560.0

Appendix table 2.3 *(contd)*

Year	Agriculture	Mining	Manufacturing	Public utilities	Construction	Wholesale and retail trade	Transport and communication	Finance, insurance and real estate	Community, social and personal services	Government services	Total employment
1971	2,128.0	305.0	10,051.0	245.0	2,350.0	3,332.0	1,437.0	633.0	2,406.0	3,781.0	26,668.0
1972	2,034.0	282.0	9,862.0	249.0	2,360.0	3,399.0	1,473.0	663.0	2,469.0	3,983.0	26,774.0
1973	1,946.0	260.0	9,926.0	254.0	2,368.0	3,455.0	1,495.0	687.0	2,546.0	4,129.0	27,066.0
1974	1,845.0	251.0	9,690.0	257.0	2,201.0	3,418.0	1,500.0	704.0	2,637.0	4,235.0	26,738.0
1975	1,749.0	251.0	9,097.0	252.0	2,024.0	3,369.0	1,503.0	703.0	2,721.0	4,351.0	26,020.0
1976	1,617.0	244.0	8,892.0	253.0	2,016.0	3,387.0	1,500.0	711.0	2,817.0	4,445.0	25,882.0
1977	1,534.0	242.0	8,927.0	255.0	1,997.0	3,379.0	1,499.0	712.0	2,867.0	4,507.0	25,919.0
1978	1,493.0	235.0	8,906.0	255.0	2,013.0	3,412.0	1,500.0	722.0	2,970.0	4,624.0	26,130.0
1979	1,410.0	227.0	9,011.0	259.0	2,083.0	3,470.0	1,511.0	739.0	3,101.0	4,757.0	26,568.0
1980	1,403.0	230.0	9,094.0	263.0	2,134.0	3,512.0	1,520.0	755.0	3,215.0	4,854.0	2,6980.0
1981	1,368.0	234.0	8,930.0	266.0	2,098.0	3,508.0	1,525.0	767.0	3,313.0	4,942.0	26,951.0
1982	1,322.0	235.0	8,669.0	267.0	2,006.0	3,465.0	1,513.0	774.0	3,377.0	5,002.0	26,630.0
1983	1,280.0	232.0	8,379.0	270.0	1,961.0	3,409.0	1,490.0	780.0	3,400.0	5,050.0	26,251.0
1984	1,239.0	223.0	8,341.0	273.0	1,954.0	3,426.0	1,481.0	786.0	3,478.0	5,092.0	26,293.0
1985	1,196.0	219.0	8,445.0	273.0	1,863.0	3,430.0	1,489.0	793.0	3,598.0	5,183.0	26,489.0
1986	1,117.0	216.0	8,580.0	276.0	1,840.0	3,449.0	1,507.0	808.0	3,710.0	5,293.0	25,856.0
1987	1,125.0	210.0	8,585.0	280.0	1,814.0	3,484.0	1,528.0	828.0	3,826.0	5,370.0	27,050.0
1988	1,078.0	200.0	8,569.0	283.0	1,810.0	3,540.0	1,539.0	839.0	3,979.0	5,424.0	27,261.0
1989	1,028.0	190.0	8,692.0	282.0	1,833.0	3,601.0	1,557.0	850.0	4,142.0	5,483.0	27,658.0
1990	995.0	181.0	8,932.0	285.0	1,911.0	3,727.0	1,587.0	892.0	4,402.0	5,567.0	28,479.0
1991	970.0	173.0	9,060.0	287.0	1,930.0	3,901.0	1,646.0	919.0	4,673.0	5,630.0	29,189.0
1992	930.0	163.0	8,902.0	288.0	1,953.0	3,992.0	1,663.0	941.0	4,900.0	5,723.0	29,455.0

Appendix table 2.4 Number of persons employed. Italy 1951–92 (thousands)

Year	Agriculture	Mining	Manufacturing	Public utilities	Construction	Wholesale and retail trade[a]	Transport and communication	Finance, insurance and real estate	Community, social and personal services[a]	Government services	Total employment
1947											
1948											
1949											
1950											
1951	8,978.3	490.2	3,505.2	118.4	1,137.8	2,082.7	658.7	111.6	969.1	1,828.2	19,880.1
1952	8,757.8	514.5	3,513.8	122.0	1,298.0	2,191.4	671.8	112.9	987.0	1,876.4	20,045.7
1953	8,539.3	519.8	3,590.9	125.1	1,471.2	2,287.5	684.1	118.8	1,004.2	1,918.1	20,259.0
1954	8,387.2	541.4	3,704.8	130.5	1,575.2	2,403.3	697.4	123.4	1,021.4	1,950.3	20,534.9
1955	8,059.3	565.9	3,716.2	134.1	1,653.1	2,513.1	726.6	128.0	1,041.8	1,988.3	20,526.5
1956	7,756.5	578.7	3,860.1	135.5	1,630.8	2,660.9	738.3	134.7	1,080.3	2,020.2	20,596.0
1957	7,396.5	585.4	4,017.0	138.4	1,664.6	2,794.5	761.2	140.9	1,120.8	2,067.2	20,686.5
1958	7,248.6	581.7	4,036.8	138.6	1,689.8	2,888.8	769.6	148.1	1,167.8	2,088.9	20,758.7
1959	7,123.7	586.1	4,094.8	140.6	1,714.7	2,912.8	781.1	151.3	1,154.7	2,128.5	20,788.4
1960	6,814.4	614.3	4,176.2	146.1	1,824.6	2,963.1	831.2	161.6	1,138.5	2,202.4	20,872.3
1961	6,427.0	622.0	4,296.7	148.9	1,947.7	3,035.6	888.8	165.3	1,119.3	2,255.1	20,906.3
1962	6,004.2	624.5	4,360.9	151.1	2,042.8	3,050.5	918.5	171.3	1,024.9	2,327.6	20,676.2
1963	5,454.8	636.8	4,443.9	153.1	2,117.3	3,073.8	949.5	179.7	946.0	2,385.7	20,340.8
1964	5,128.2	624.8	4,435.8	155.8	2,145.5	3,141.4	961.9	184.1	1,036.8	2,436.9	20,251.1
1965	5,111.9	605.2	4,354.1	159.2	1,996.6	3,110.8	980.2	185.6	938.2	2,479.8	19,921.6
1966	4,803.1	581.2	4,354.4	163.4	1,926.4	3,106.3	990.1	188.9	962.5	2,531.2	19,607.6
1967	4,693.1	590.5	4,471.6	169.0	1,955.7	3,185.1	997.5	190.3	1,005.8	2,587.4	19,845.9
1968	4,371.1	602.5	4,544.8	173.9	1,969.5	3,232.2	998.6	196.3	1,069.9	2,645.9	19,804.8
1969	4,131.7	603.0	4,644.1	177.3	2,024.7	3,332.9	1,012.0	199.8	1,079.9	2,703.7	19,909.1
1970	3,781.2	622.8	4,783.2	179.4	2,024.1	3,415.6	1,031.7	202.0	1,134.8	2,774.8	19,949.4

Appendix table 2.4 *(contd)*

Year	Agriculture	Mining	Manufacturing	Public utilities	Construction	Wholesale and retail trade[a]	Transport and communication	Finance, insurance and real estate	Community, social and personal services[a]	Government services	Total employment
1971	3,763.5	625.6	4,865.5	183.2	1,911.6	3,296.7	1,038.8	206.8	1,133.6	2,902.4	19,927.7
1972	3,465.8	611.6	4,762.4	177.5	1,907.5	3,432.1	1,059.2	213.2	1,171.3	3,015.8	19,816.4
1973	3,407.5	610.6	4,902.4	179.3	1,905.0	3,524.6	1,103.6	224.7	1,251.3	3,134.0	20,243.0
1974	3,336.7	622.1	5,065.1	182.8	1,867.6	3,666.3	1,136.8	239.9	1,318.5	3,210.2	20,646.0
1975	3,209.1	617.5	5,034.6	183.3	1,803.0	3,766.8	1,158.3	255.4	1,356.7	3,284.2	20,668.9
1976	3,207.5	617.4	5,089.5	183.5	1,722.3	3,884.9	1,195.9	277.3	1,415.0	3,395.4	20,988.7
1977	3,094.4	623.2	5,207.5	185.2	1,716.9	3,910.0	1,205.4	292.7	1,454.1	3,511.0	21,200.9
1978	3,094.5	615.0	5,178.0	187.1	1,682.0	3,933.5	1,222.8	315.1	1,547.8	3,539.7	21,315.3
1979	3,044.4	620.5	5,266.4	187.1	1,688.8	4,046.2	1,243.5	335.6	1,633.7	3,594.6	21,640.8
1980	2,993.8	607.2	5,359.0	189.6	1,762.3	4,161.0	1,257.3	349.8	1,736.3	3,646.3	22,062.6
1981	2,845.2	597.2	5,152.8	192.0	1,791.8	4,272.6	1,293.0	359.5	1,822.7	3,733.5	22,060.3
1982	2,683.3	589.0	5,013.2	189.9	1,790.6	4,425.6	1,317.6	367.3	1,994.2	3,811.1	22,181.8
1983	2,745.3	562.7	4,819.3	187.4	1,778.5	4,540.7	1,353.0	373.9	2,081.8	3,881.9	22,324.5
1984	2,686.5	534.9	4,604.6	190.2	1,675.0	4,719.2	1,354.6	383.4	2,304.7	3,959.8	22,412.9
1985	2,580.7	502.3	4,567.3	192.9	1,651.5	4,789.2	1,364.8	388.7	2,537.1	4,038.2	22,612.7
1986	2,562.1	509.9	4,532.6	195.9	1,633.2	4,841.5	1,411.2	393.0	2,635.8	4,071.1	22,786.3
1987	2,507.8	510.0	4,483.4	199.6	1,615.0	4,924.7	1,439.3	398.1	2,670.2	4,129.4	22,877.5
1988	2,396.1	517.1	4,543.6	199.2	1,610.0	4,946.5	1,465.5	404.6	2,793.0	4,197.4	23,073.0
1989	2,276.6	531.8	4,553.3	196.2	1,598.3	4,919.0	1,492.4	414.1	2,884.0	4,221.5	23,087.2
1990	2,234.9	524.7	4,560.0	197.0	1,633.5	4,968.0	1,485.7	422.8	2,993.0	4,251.6	23,271.2
1991	2,236.3	497.8	4,466.6	195.1	1,673.8	5,048.8	1,492.1	433.8	3,104.4	4,301.1	23,449.8
1992	2,141.4	494.8	4,297.7	189.5	1,688.4	5,021.7	1,490.0	441.8	3,127.3	4,351.8	23,244.2

[a] Hotels and restaurants are included with wholesale and retail trade.

Appendix table 2.5 Number of persons employed. Netherlands 1950–92 (thousands)

Year	Agricul-ture	Mining	Manufac-turing	Public utilities	Construc-tion	Wholesale and retail trade^a	Transport and communi-cation	Finance, insurance and real estate	Community, social and personal services^a	Govern-ment services	Total employ-ment
1947											
1948											
1949											
1950	559.2	60.4	1,156.1	39.5	360.3	632.3	306.9	144.0	432.5	455.7	4,147.1
1951	551.7										
1952	543.2										
1953	535.6										
1954	526.2										
1955	514.9		1,261.4								
1956	501.7										4,535.6
1957	486.6										4,560.8
1958	468.7										4,518.5
1959	450.8										4,564.8
1960	441.3	66.8	1,358.1	42.6	436.5	746.4	340.9	257.0	397.3	564.4	4,651.4
1961	420.6	63.3	1,390.8	42.6	447.9	768.0	342.0	272.4	400.0	572.2	4,719.8
1962	417.8	61.8	1,427.0	42.3	463.2	788.1	346.6	284.4	407.6	577.6	4,816.4
1963	398.0	60.5	1,441.6	44.5	485.2	812.8	347.1	291.4	418.7	581.1	4,880.8
1964	385.7	57.9	1,464.5	45.4	512.8	831.6	346.0	299.1	429.3	580.9	4,953.3
1965	370.6	56.9	1,476.6	47.8	527.6	848.3	345.7	309.3	442.3	586.7	5,011.7
1966	348.9	50.0	1,473.0	48.9	533.3	866.5	348.0	324.7	453.2	600.4	5,046.9
1967	339.5	40.9	1,435.5	48.9	519.7	885.9	345.7	339.3	464.7	610.7	5,030.8
1968	315.0	33.2	1,431.9	49.2	542.2	915.0	334.3	358.2	479.1	622.2	5,090.2
1969	293.3	25.5	1,454.9	46.5	538.6	1,025.1	333.6	437.7	393.4	626.1	5,174.8
1970	281.0	21.2	1,454.9	46.6	552.6	1,027.5	337.3	459.4	416.1	634.7	5,231.1

Appendix table 2.5 (*contd*)

Year	Agriculture	Mining	Manufacturing	Public utilities	Construction	Wholesale and retail trade[a]	Transport and communication	Finance, insurance and real estate	Community, social and personal services[a]	Government services	Total employment
1971	275.4	18.9	1,428.3	46.6	541.8	1,029.1	341.9	472.9	448.5	653.9	5,257.3
1972	273.5	15.6	1,378.7	47.8	517.8	1,018.8	335.5	476.6	474.4	673.3	5,212.0
1973	272.5	13.7	1,355.7	50.1	506.4	960.6	314.8	344.6	749.5	646.3	5,214.0
1974	282.1	10.3	1,347.3	46.5	508.8	971.4	319.8	379.1	760.5	667.6	5,293.4
1975	283.2	7.9	1,317.8	47.4	479.6	978.0	330.5	384.5	772.3	686.4	5,287.5
1976	285.6	7.6	1,262.2	47.2	479.2	976.9	321.6	391.9	821.5	719.8	5,313.5
1977	287.0	7.0	1,241.1	46.9	486.9	986.6	320.7	418.3	854.1	739.1	5,387.7
1978	283.3	7.2	1,222.6	47.3	498.5	1,009.0	324.1	439.8	868.4	748.6	5,448.6
1979	278.0	7.1	1,213.1	47.8	511.8	1,037.4	340.8	470.8	895.5	775.0	5,577.3
1980	276.2	7.3	1,201.1	48.3	518.2	1,055.4	348.0	494.0	932.0	808.9	5,689.5
1981	272.8	8.0	1,182.0	48.7	456.0	1,044.3	345.3	498.1	969.6	834.9	5,659.8
1982	277.1	8.4	1,139.1	48.9	403.0	1,017.9	340.7	494.3	990.6	853.0	5,572.9
1983	281.0	8.5	1,090.7	43.2	358.7	1,003.2	335.3	503.5	991.1	849.6	5,464.8
1984	282.9	8.6	1,051.6	48.0	354.7	995.4	334.0	534.8	988.1	855.5	5,453.5
1985	280.9	9.0	1,056.8	48.4	356.9	998.3	338.9	572.7	997.6	867.8	5,527.3
1986	284.2	9.6	1,081.6	47.8	370.1	1,024.1	348.4	617.6	1,050.9	895.4	5,729.6
1987	286.0	10.0	1,093.0	48.0	376.0	1,065.0	353.0	643.0	1,103.3	894.7	5,872.0
1988	288.0	10.0	1,107.0	47.0	386.0	1,096.0	355.0	684.0	1,112.3	914.7	6,000.0
1989	289.0	10.0	1,137.0	48.0	399.0	1,140.0	370.0	719.0	1,102.1	924.9	6,139.0
1990	286.0	10.0	1,160.0	46.0	406.0	1,195.0	377.0	759.0	1,128.8	947.2	6,315.0
1991	285.0	11.0	1,164.0	45.0	408.0	1,241.0	388.0	785.0	1,206.0	1,012.0	6,545.0
1992	288.0	11.0	1,155.0	45.0	402.0	1,275.0	398.0	803.0	1,168.4	980.6	6,526.0

Appendix table 2.6   Number of persons employed. Spain 1950–92 (thousands)

Year	Agriculture	Mining	Manufacturing	Public utilities	Construction	Wholesale and retail trade[a]	Transport and communication	Finance, insurance and real estate	Community, social and personal services[a]	Government services	Total employment
1947											
1948											
1949											
1950	5,074.1	152.3	1,685.8	47.6	485.2	695.9	430.5	130.1	1,075.0	1,012.7	10,789.1
1951											
1952											
1953											
1954											
1955											
1956	4,849.4	183.1	2,092.2	60.4	719.3	837.5	522.5	157.9	903.6	1,229.9	11,555.7
1957	4,818.3	186.6	2,191.1	62.9	733.4	868.9	536.0	165.8	925.6	1,252.0	11,740.5
1958	4,762.8	189.2	2,291.8	65.5	774.9	902.3	566.0	172.9	961.7	1,263.6	11,950.7
1959	4,709.3	184.8	2,256.7	67.2	811.8	910.4	558.8	169.6	948.8	1,174.5	11,791.7
1960	4,626.7	176.0	2,263.9	68.9	745.7	920.5	552.6	164.2	901.5	1,192.5	11,612.4
1961	4,545.0	172.5	2,348.4	69.7	782.5	962.0	586.7	175.3	911.5	1,247.9	11,801.4
1962	4,473.0	169.0	2,460.8	70.6	853.3	999.4	606.4	188.4	840.6	1,356.2	12,017.5
1963	4,377.7	161.9	2,548.9	71.4	888.2	1,043.9	639.5	212.9	850.8	1,370.5	12,165.8
1964	4,174.8	154.0	2,637.7	74.9	909.3	1,181.1	651.8	248.9	849.6	1,327.9	12,210.1
1965	3,673.1	148.8	2,736.6	77.9	999.4	1,336.3	660.8	273.8	844.8	1,272.7	12,024.3
1966	3,947.7	140.2	2,813.8	76.6	1,025.7	1,390.0	674.3	271.0	877.3	1,262.5	12,478.9
1967	3,904.3	131.8	2,840.1	77.0	1,062.7	1,323.6	686.6	260.5	982.4	1,370.2	12,639.2
1968	3,886.1	126.0	2,898.2	78.0	1,090.1	1,260.5	700.1	256.0	1,107.7	1,446.8	11,868.4
1969	3,789.2	117.7	2,973.4	78.9	1,129.2	1,200.3	711.3	238.1	1,240.9	1,530.3	13,009.3
1970	3,696.3	114.2	3,044.5	78.8	1,150.9	1,143.0	720.3	230.2	1,395.6	1,662.4	13,236.3

Appendix table 2.6 *(contd)*

Year	Agriculture	Mining	Manufacturing	Public utilities	Construction	Wholesale and retail trade[a]	Transport and communication	Finance, insurance and real estate	Community, social and personal services[a]	Government services	Total employment
1971	3,586.3	110.2	3,102.4	79.3	1,163.3	1,107.6	689.1	230.9	*1,350.9*	*1,570.8*	12,990.9
1972	3,246.2	104.2	3,197.6	80.4	1,282.0	1,768.0	723.8	392.9	*1,157.9*	*1,322.3*	13,275.4
1973	3,157.3	99.4	3,358.9	80.5	1,300.9	1,887.7	710.3	418.3	*1,220.3*	*1,380.6*	13,614.1
1974	3,022.1	97.5	3,454.0	80.7	1,337.6	1,947.5	725.1	465.9	*1,204.6*	*1,405.2*	13,740.1
1975	2,825.2	100.6	3,475.4	75.2	1,292.6	1,890.4	702.4	493.2	*1,187.3*	*1,379.1*	13,426.1
1976	2,735.4	100.0	3,440.5	76.9	1,292.6	1,869.9	726.6	498.4	*1,243.3*	*1,490.2*	13,473.7
1977	2,592.1	99.4	3,402.0	79.0	1,305.4	1,876.9	698.7	516.5	*1,258.0*	*1,513.6*	13,341.5
1978	2,461.9	97.4	3,343.1	79.2	1,259.6	1,851.3	679.2	493.9	*1,257.9*	*1,543.3*	13,066.7
1979	2,335.7	95.6	3,264.7	77.5	1,188.4	1,858.7	724.0	507.7	*1,231.5*	*1,582.5*	12,866.3
1980	2,141.9	93.8	3,220.9	78.8	1,099.6	1,778.1	701.5	487.9	1,183.8	1,595.7	12,382.1
1981	2,016.7	92.8	3,012.4	80.9	978.8	1,753.6	705.3	491.1	1,205.9	1,665.2	12,002.7
1982	1,969.6	91.3	2,808.6	87.1	964.3	1,727.0	712.9	489.5	1,256.7	1,698.7	11,805.6
1983	1,960.3	90.3	2,732.9	85.0	936.4	1,700.4	719.6	492.7	1,267.0	1,747.6	11,732.2
1984	1,889.5	88.0	2,602.3	83.0	814.3	1,633.9	696.7	486.2	1,288.4	1,802.9	11,385.2
1985	1,828.0	57.0	2,475.0	84.0	776.0	1,640.0	690.0	483.0	1,267.0	1,875.0	11,175.0
1986	1,646.6	55.6	2,513.5	82.7	831.3	1,743.1	686.2	508.4	1,292.0	1,939.0	11,298.4
1987	1,608.8	54.3	2,600.7	82.2	930.2	1,875.4	685.2	546.0	1,367.8	2,057.3	11,807.9
1988	1,591.1	52.6	2,651.7	82.2	1,025.4	1,940.3	689.2	575.5	1,447.2	2,151.7	12,206.9
1989	1,488.2	50.4	2,735.7	81.8	1,139.4	1,997.9	698.9	601.9	1,536.9	2,293.9	12,625.0
1990	1,437.9	48.1	2,825.8	80.0	1,230.4	2,078.3	713.0	635.7	1,598.5	2,423.9	13,071.6
1991	1,302.3	(a)	2,870.2	(a)	1,284.0	(b)	(b)	(b)	5,167.1	2,510.3	13,133.9
1992	1,211.5	(a)	2,796.4	(a)	1,206.3	(b)	(b)	(b)	5,212.7	2,554.4	12,981.3

[a] Included with manufacturing.
[b] Included with community, social and personal services.

153

Appendix table 2.7 Number of persons employed. Sweden 1950–92 (thousands)

Year	Agriculture	Mining	Manufacturing	Public utilities	Construction	Wholesale and retail trade[a]	Transport and communication	Finance, insurance and real estate	Community, social and personal services[a]	Government services	Total employment
1947											
1948											
1949											
1950	774.4	15.4	931.8	23.8	267.4	335.7	246.9	65.1	246.8	392.7	3,300.0
1951											
1952											
1953											
1954											
1955											
1956											
1957											
1958											
1959											
1960	547.7	23.6	1,058.5	27.1	322.0	538.1	238.1	113.6	269.3	507.9	3,645.9
1961	521.2	24.0	1,084.3	27.1	323.3	547.7	238.6	119.6	272.8	515.8	3,674.5
1962	507.6	22.8	1,090.8	27.1	333.6	547.5	239.2	126.4	278.8	519.4	3,693.2
1963	463.9	21.2	1,090.6	27.2	344.1	551.2	239.8	137.9	285.5	550.1	3,711.4
1964	443.8	20.9	1,104.2	27.2	357.2	558.4	240.5	153.4	276.5	573.6	3,755.7
1965	419.3	20.9	1,109.5	27.2	377.1	562.0	241.2	161.8	271.8	588.8	3,779.6
1966	394.5	20.3	1,094.8	27.4	384.9	559.7	243.7	172.9	269.0	613.4	3,780.6
1967	374.7	19.2	1,058.8	27.1	399.3	549.0	244.6	179.2	253.2	645.2	3,750.1
1968	348.8	18.2	1,041.2	27.1	403.6	572.2	247.4	182.6	254.2	689.2	3,784.5
1969	331.6	17.6	1,059.6	27.4	398.7	580.1	248.0	187.8	255.9	740.1	3,846.8
1970	326.1	17.9	1,075.8	27.9	369.6	578.2	246.2	197.0	260.9	812.8	3,912.4

Appendix table 2.7 (*contd*)

Year	Agriculture	Mining	Manufacturing	Public utilities	Construction	Wholesale and retail trade[a]	Transport and communication	Finance, insurance and real estate	Community, social and personal services[a]	Government services	Total employment
1971	310.1	17.2	1,040.0	28.6	344.9	582.6	251.5	208.6	255.4	865.9	3,904.8
1972	290.8	16.9	1,023.7	28.6	347.5	575.1	255.5	214.1	255.5	910.3	3,917.6
1973	274.4	17.0	1,039.1	29.0	340.8	569.8	256.7	214.4	249.9	941.1	3,932.3
1974	270.8	17.0	1,061.4	29.5	331.6	580.3	261.9	217.5	244.2	996.1	4,010.3
1975	261.7	17.8	1,070.0	29.8	325.3	597.4	267.0	226.5	247.5	1,046.3	4,089.4
1976	250.7	17.7	1,066.4	30.0	314.9	598.6	268.2	225.2	243.8	1,095.7	4,111.1
1977	242.6	16.9	1,029.3	30.6	298.3	597.5	270.2	229.2	246.4	1,142.5	4,103.5
1978	242.6	15.6	1,000.1	30.6	297.2	587.6	270.4	233.0	248.5	1,201.6	4,127.3
1979	237.0	16.2	1,002.4	31.9	290.1	593.6	273.2	239.2	243.6	1,253.6	4,180.8
1980	231.3	15.7	1,001.6	32.5	301.7	588.8	280.4	240.0	242.2	1,299.6	4,233.8
1981	222.8	15.2	972.2	32.9	299.1	586.2	281.7	240.4	244.9	1,345.2	4,240.6
1982	218.7	14.3	933.8	33.8	293.0	578.3	288.1	247.2	248.7	1,376.7	4,232.6
1983	214.0	13.6	915.9	34.2	279.9	581.4	283.5	258.5	248.8	1,412.5	4,242.3
1984	211.6	13.1	924.0	33.7	272.2	582.7	282.4	271.9	244.7	1,441.3	4,277.6
1985	206.9	13.0	944.1	34.1	272.0	592.5	288.9	276.4	248.6	1,445.2	4,321.7
1986	201.4	12.2	948.0	34.1	273.1	593.1	288.3	310.5	248.8	1438.9	4,348.4
1987	181.0	11.1	968.3	34.0	279.9	603.3	289.1	326.2	255.3	1,434.9	4,383.1
1988	178.4	10.8	986.7	33.3	280.9	620.1	289.1	339.7	255.2	1,449.0	4,443.2
1989	169.8	12.1	979.8	33.5	291.1	642.5	293.1	358.3	257.6	1,470.3	4,508.1
1990	167.8	12.1	953.0	33.0	299.2	638.0	297.9	378.8	264.2	1,505.7	4,549.7
1991	160.0	10.0	872.0	32.0	297.0	621.0	300.0	385.0	267.0	1,538.0	4,482.0
1992	155.0	10.0	796.0	32.0	268.0	595.0	288.8	377.0	268.0	1,493.0	4,282.0

155

Appendix table 2.8 Number of persons employed. United Kingdom, 1948–92 (thousands)

Year	Agriculture	Mining	Manufacturing	Public utilities	Construction	Wholesale and retail trade^a	Transport and communication	Finance, insurance and real estate	Community, social and personal services^a	Government services	Total employment
1947											
1948	1,385.2	887.8	7,412.3	310.3	1,387.3	3,418.6	1,727.2	726.3	1,892.7	3,459.9	22,607.6
1949	1,381.7	885.8	7,548.3	323.6	1,376.1	3,518.7	1,725.3	744.3	1,830.6	3,351.3	22,685.7
1950	1,365.8	863.7	7,737.6	341.6	1,375.2	3,553.7	1,730.0	736.1	1,815.4	3,372.8	22,891.9
1951	1,329.9	865.7	7,914.6	350.2	1,388.2	3,610.0	1,693.3	744.3	1,784.3	3,493.1	23,173.7
1952	1,301.1	885.8	7,797.6	359.6	1,380.8	3,632.5	1,699.9	754.1	1,817.7	3,564.0	23,193.1
1953	1,276.9	890.8	7,917.4	359.6	1,386.4	3,702.6	1,676.4	763.9	1,772.2	3,564.9	23,311.2
1954	1,264.3	879.8	8,133.4	360.6	1,407.8	3,803.9	1,657.6	786.7	1,777.5	3,600.7	23,672.4
1955	1,258.5	873.8	8,318.0	364.4	1,440.4	3,899.0	1,653.8	806.3	1,777.5	3,583.7	23,975.4
1956	1,222.8	868.8	8,328.4	363.4	1,493.5	3,997.8	1,665.1	812.8	1,771.5	3,625.0	24,149.2
1957	1,215.9	876.8	8,333.2	365.3	1,473.9	4,059.1	1,652.0	843.9	1,740.4	3,585.5	24,146.0
1958	1,198.6	862.7	8,194.3	361.5	1,451.6	4,054.1	1,636.9	853.7	1,737.4	3,563.1	23,913.9
1959	1,189.4	843.7	8,227.6	363.4	1,482.3	4,135.4	1,624.7	901.0	1,758.6	3,584.6	24,110.7
1960	1,168.7	776.5	8,566.3	360.6	1,524.2	4,239.2	1,618.1	923.8	1,762.4	3,599.9	24,539.7
1961	1,131.9	744.4	8,673.8	369.1	1,582.0	4,271.7	1,641.6	953.2	1,773.0	3,644.7	24,785.4
1962	1,092.7	719.3	8,567.2	374.8	1,618.3	4,328.0	1,646.3	981.0	1,825.3	3,722.8	24,875.8
1963	1,083.5	691.2	8,443.6	384.3	1,655.6	4,358.1	1,624.7	1,026.7	1,837.4	3,820.6	24,925.6
1964	1,040.9	665.1	8,586.3	390.0	1,736.7	4,376.8	1,612.5	1,062.6	1,911.6	3,843.9	25,226.4
1965	982.2	632.0	8,696.6	397.6	1,778.6	4,388.1	1,600.3	1,085.4	1,927.5	3,941.7	25,430.0
1966	944.4	583.9	8,726.0	410.8	1,815.8	4,372.2	1,574.9	1,100.5	1,985.5	4,072.5	25,586.5
1967	909.7	558.4	8,461.6	407.7	1,752.0	4,225.7	1,571.9	1,114.7	1,986.1	4,230.3	25,218.0
1968	880.3	492.9	8,393.7	397.6	1,739.3	4,169.1	1,554.6	1,154.1	1,956.1	4,323.2	25,060.9
1969	843.5	447.9	8,501.1	382.4	1,699.9	4,162.8	1,529.3	1,188.3	1,951.0	4,363.1	25,069.3
1970	808.9	420.3	8,484.9	368.2	1,591.5	4,120.2	1,567.8	1,255.6	1,876.6	4,458.0	24,951.9

Appendix table 2.8 *(contd)*

Year	Agriculture	Mining	Manufacturing	Public utilities	Construction	Wholesale and retail trade^a	Transport and communication	Finance, insurance and real estate	Community, social and personal services^a	Government services	Total employment
1971	758.4	406.0	8,212.3	347.9	1,536.2	4,029.7	1,569.8	1,283.8	1,861.5	4,584.8	24,590.5
1972	733.2	388.6	7,942.8	326.6	1,620.2	4,377.8	1,555.6	1,499.8	1,336.7	4,743.6	24,525.0
1973	737.4	372.2	7,993.4	314.4	1,779.7	4,523.0	1,545.5	1,574.8	1,388.9	4,881.5	25,110.9
1974	704.9	357.9	8,043.1	349.9	1,718.0	4,481.0	1,577.9	1,620.5	1,420.5	4,923.4	25,197.2
1975	687.0	361.0	7,654.0	355.0	1,617.0	4,516.0	1,582.0	1,622.0	1,441.0	5,218.0	25,053.0
1976	685.0	357.0	7,411.0	354.0	1,577.0	4,504.0	1,539.0	1,622.0	1,466.0	5,320.0	24,835.0
1977	684.0	359.0	7,461.0	349.0	1,504.0	4,555.0	1,533.0	1,642.0	1,499.0	5,279.0	24,885.0
1978	680.0	361.0	7,427.0	341.0	1,524.0	4,591.0	1,551.0	1,692.0	1,552.0	5,296.0	25,015.0
1979	666.0	359.0	7,395.0	349.0	1,590.0	4,729.0	1,567.0	1,767.0	1,586.0	5,384.0	25,392.0
1980	654.0	361.0	7,081.0	353.0	1,617.0	4,818.0	1,580.0	1,837.0	1,677.0	5,349.0	25,327.0
1981	639.0	351.0	6,365.0	350.0	1,526.0	4,705.0	1,526.0	1,901.0	1,663.0	5,318.0	2,4344.0
1982	632.0	338.0	6,005.0	336.0	1,474.0	4,671.0	1,477.0	1,976.0	1,734.0	5,265.0	23,908.0
1983	622.0	323.0-	5,664.0	322.0	1,461.0	4,639.0	1,439.0	2,067.0	1,784.0	5,306.0	23,627.0
1984	615.0	301.0	5,579.0	313.0	1,509.0	4,851.0	1,460.0	2,174.0	1,957.0	5,476.0	24,235.0
1985	616.0	284.0	5,561.0	303.0	1,500.0	4,885.0	1,432.0	2,330.0	2,131.0	5,494.0	24,536.0
1986	603.0	244.0	5,430.0	295.0	1,484.0	4,880.0	1,411.0	2,444.0	2,198.0	5,573.0	24,562.0
1987	591.0	210.0	5,395.0	289.0	1,559.0	4,920.0	1,442.0	2,585.0	2,399.0	5,685.0	25,075.0
1988	580.0	188.0	5,476.0	288.0	1,645.0	5,070.0	1,464.0	2,792.0	2,668.0	5,746.0	25,917.0
1989	566.0	178.0	5,512.0	283.0	1,793.0	5,231.0	1,521.0	3,050.0	2,927.0	5,717.0	26,778.0
1990	568.0	189.0	5,494.0	278.0	1,829.0	5,331.0	1,520.0	3,245.0	3,218.0	5,697.0	27,369.0
1991	560.0	173.0	5,118.2	276.0	1,664.7	5,200.7	1,477.2	3,176.0	3,366.5	5,482.0	26,494.3
1992	540.8	150.9	4,908.1	258.8	1,524.0	5,119.8	1,447.4	3,133.6	3,545.2	5,249.0	25,877.4

Appendix table 2.9 Number of persons employed. United States 1950–92 (thousands)

Year	Agriculture	Mining	Manufacturing	Public utilities	Construction	Wholesale and retail trade[a]	Transport and communication	Finance, insurance and real estate	Community, social and personal services[a]	Government services	Total employment
1947											
1948											
1949											
1950	6,834	959	15,639	556	3,452	11,685	3,708	2,082	8,707	8,884	62,508
1951	6,441	974	16,866	568	3,687	12,232	3,906	2,189	8,948	10,442	66,253
1952	6,284	951	17,174	574	3,681	12,437	3,913	2,283	9,008	11,190	67,495
1953	6,091	912	17,998	587	3,628	12,578	3,949	2,386	9,219	11,216	68,564
1954	6,112	837	16,774	592	3,512	12,456	3,729	2,488	9,229	11,211	66,940
1955	5,911	841	17,327	597	3,608	12,773	3,781	2,572	9,775	11,286	68,471
1956	5,623	879	17,674	605	3,752	13,181	3,879	2,663	10,298	11,524	70,078
1957	5,377	876	17,577	609	3,669	13,292	3,862	2,714	10,577	11,825	70,378
1958	5,221	782	16,234	624	3,557	13,206	3,578	2,764	10,856	11,878	68,700
1959	5,066	749	16,967	619	3,696	13,468	3,582	2,820	11,242	12,068	70,277
1960	4,873	728	17,088	623	3,655	13,774	3,587	2,903	11,622	12,412	71,265
1961	4,800	694	16,636	624	3,630	13,677	3,481	2,962	12,047	12,775	71,326
1962	4,662	675	17,199	620	3,710	13,850	3,482	3,025	12,458	13,143	72,824
1963	4,445	656	17,320	622	3,792	13,993	3,478	3,100	12,760	13,408	73,574
1964	4,189	651	17,614	626	3,913	14,400	3,527	3,179	13,208	13,855	75,162
1965	4,012	654	18,398	635	4,064	14,884	3,597	3,285	13,595	14,300	77,424
1966	3,712	650	19,579	642	4,143	15,417	3,727	3,378	14,232	15,524	81,004
1967	3,592	634	19,811	656	4,105	15,689	3,818	3,503	14,668	16,385	82,861
1968	3,550	629	20,154	667	4,236	16,133	3,870	3,672	15,152	16,899	84,962
1969	3,449	639	20,574	684	4,432	16,771	3,973	3,830	15,724	17,236	87,312
1970	3,383	642	19,713	701	4,374	17,119	4,013	3,954	15,900	17,321	87,120

Appendix table 2.9 *(contd)*

Year	Agriculture	Mining	Manufacturing	Public utilities	Construction	Wholesale and retail trade^a	Transport and communication	Finance, insurance and real estate	Community, social and personal services^a	Government services	Total employment
1971	3,324	630	18,860	712	4,458	17,445	3,978	4,049	16,215	17,309	86,980
1972	3,374	638	19,328	726	4,687	17,907	4,019	4,184	16,939	17,309	89,111
1973	3,450	654	20,405	742	5,041	18,709	4,142	4,444	17,668	17,569	92,824
1974	3,535	715	20,387	752	5,039	19,145	4,214	4,584	18,103	17,940	94,414
1975	3,462	769	18,658	741	4,529	19,181	4,067	4,660	18,508	18,303	92,878
1976	3,493	806	19,375	741	4,618	19,893	4,080	4,772	19,147	18,303	95,228
1977	3,375	847	20,113	754	4,969	20,761	4,202	4,988	20,024	18,482	98,515
1978	3,425	903	21,000	784	5,550	21,880	4,419	5,359	21,122	18,891	103,333
1979	3,453	976	21,530	819	5,877	22,633	4,626	5,652	21,998	19,683	107,247
1980	3,547	1,068	20,800	834	5,679	22,755	4,626	5,828	22,656	20,122	107,915
1981	3,522	1,186	20,699	866	5,504	23,034	4,651	5,946	23,500	20,064	108,972
1982	3,475	1,167	19,308	881	5,173	22,953	4,561	6,065	24,143	20,059	107,785
1983	3,520	987	18,934	885	5,273	23,466	4,486	6,252	25,057	20,197	109,057
1984	3,436	998	19,888	900	5,828	24,795	4,639	6,499	26,481	20,500	113,964
1985	3,242	947	19,700	914	6,186	25,577	4,703	6,753	27,595	20,915	116,532
1986	3,224	800	19,465	920	6,400	26,180	4,712	7,065	28,553	21,235	118,554
1987	3,290	744	19,511	926	6,532	26,980	4,852	7,374	30,020	21,650	121,879
1988	3,301	746	19,940	936	6,741	27,715	4,998	7,519	31,523	21,861	125,279
1989	3,320	714	19,990	943	6,790	28,519	5,086	7,558	33,009	22,228	128,157
1990	3,316	737	19,734	956	6,785	28,521	5,221	7,609	34,297	22,679	129,856

NOTES

To construct the database for this chapter I received a great deal of statistical assistance from Gjalt de Jong and Erik Monnikhof, for which I am very grateful. I am also indebted to Mary O'Mahony for letting me use her capital stock estimates presented elsewhere in this volume. I received useful suggestions for improvement from participants in the N.W. Posthumus seminar on 'Comparative Historical National Accounts' which was held in June 1994 in Groningen, and in particular from Erik Buyst, Steve Broadberry, Nick Crafts and Angus Maddison. Furthermore I am grateful to Frits Bos and Simon Kuipers for further comments. I would like to acknowledge the Centre for Economic Policy Research (London) for the financial support for constructing the database.

1 Although the series in the appendix go up to 1992, the analysis of the results in this paper concerns only the period 1950–1990. The year 1992 was a depression year in many countries, which would affect comparisons between beginning and end point estimates for the period as a whole and the most recent sub-period. My beginning and end point estimates are for relatively 'normal' years in the business cycle.

2 The term 'sectoral national accounts' should not be confused with 'sector accounts' as sometimes used in another context. The latter shows separately the various kinds of transactions by institutional sectors and which are primarily distinguished to highlight differences in their financial role, behaviour and experience in the economy (United Nations, 1968).

3 See, for example, Danmarks Statistik (1992) for Denmark; Statistisches Bundesamt (1991) for Germany; Golinelli and Monterastelli (1990) for Italy; Prados (1993) for Spain; Feinstein (1972) for the UK; US Department of Commerce (1986, 1992) for the USA.

4 The major exception compared to the OECD classification is that, where possible, I transferred 'hotels and restaurants' from 'wholesale and retail trade' to 'community, social and personal services', as I regard the productivity performance of hotels and restaurants rather different from that of the trade sector. See also note 5.

5 Here I follow the distinction made by Elfring (1988). Producer services include business and professional services, finance and insurance and real estate. Distribution services include retail and wholesale trade, transport and communication; personal services include hotels and restaurants, domestic services and repair; social services include government services, health and education.

6 For the discussion of differences in weighting procedures and adjustment for inadequate coverage, see Maddison, Chapter 2 in this volume.

7 See van Ark (1993) for a sensitivity test of the series of UK manufacturing value added from 1950 to 1989 by comparing the official national accounts series with a series from the UK Census of Production deflated by a producer price index. It appears that the underestimation of output growth in the UK national accounts was particularly important for the period 1948–73.

8 It should be emphasized that the German estimate for manufacturing may be somewhat overstated because repair and maintenance is included with manufacturing. On the other hand, the publishing sector in Germany is included with services.

9 See also, for example, Fabricant (1942), Maddison (1952) and Badulescu (1993).

10 The three effects were measured at two levels of disaggregation. Firstly I used the ten-sector breakdown which is also represented in Table 3.1. In addition I calculated the effect for a more aggregated breakdown of the three broad sectors, i.e. agriculture, industry and services. On the whole the differences between the different aggregation levels were fairly small for the period 1950–73, which suggests that the shift among the three broad sectors dominated any other shifts at more disaggregated levels. For the period 1973–90 the three-sector disaggregation systematically tended to give a somewhat bigger weight to the intrasectoral effect, whereas the ten-sector disaggregation leaves more of the explanation to structural change.

11 See Denison (1967) for a discussion of the effect on growth of the reduction of excessive allocation of labour to the agricultural sector during the 1950s. Denison estimated the effect of shift of labour out of agriculture on the productivity performance of agriculture itself, and concluded it accounted for 12% of the growth of national income per person employed in Northwest Europe from 1950 to 1962.

12 See Chapter 4 by O'Mahony which provides details on the perpetual inventory method.

13 It might have been better to use annual changing weights instead of one constant weight for the whole period, which would have made equation (5) a genuine translog index. However, there was insufficient information for many of the sectors to calculate annual weights. The year 1975 was chosen as a year close to the middle of the period under consideration, and it provides a link with the comparative level estimates in Section 5 which are also benchmarked on 1975.

14 For a specific account of the relation between capital intensity and total factor productivity growth; see Wolff (1991).

15 See, for example, Dollar and Wolff (1993) and Englander and Gurney (1994).

16 There are some important pioneering studies of this type for earlier years, in particular between the UK and the USA (Rostas, 1948; Paige and Bombach, 1959; Smith *et al.*, 1982). For an historical overview of industry of origin studies, see van Ark (1993), table 2.2. See also Broadberry (1993). For a general overview of the ICOP project, see Maddison and van Ark (1994). Most ICOP studies are available for the manufacturing sector covering approximately twenty countries, including six of the countries covered in this paper, i.e. France, Germany, The Netherlands, Spain, the UK and the USA. For a specific account of ICOP studies on manufacturing, see van Ark (1993). There are also studies for agriculture (Maddison and van Ooststroom, 1993) and mining (Wieringa and Maddison, 1985) covering thirteen countries. So far the comparisons for other sectors of the economy cover a more limited number of countries. For example, there is a study of output and productivity in France and the USA for transport and communication and for wholesale and retail distribution (Mulder, 1994).

17 Mining is excluded because there were no Fisher PPPs available for that sector. Spain is excluded from the comparison, because the binary comparison is only with the United Kingdom as the benchmark country (see van Ark, 1994).

18 The value added and employment estimates from Maddison and van Ark

(1994) for the commodity sectors for 1975 were mostly fairly similar to the national accounts estimates. The most important differences are for agriculture in Germany, for which ICOP value added was 33% below national accounts value added and ICOP employment was 10% below national accounts employment; for manufacturing in France, for which ICOP value added was 22% below national accounts value added and ICOP employment 10% below national accounts employment, and for manufacturing in the UK, for which ICOP value added was 13% above national accounts value added and ICOP employment 3% below national accounts employment. Some of these differences may be due to differences in valuation systems as the German and French national accounts are at producer prices rather than at factor cost (see Section 2). See also van Ark (1993) for a more detailed discussion.

19 The estimates of relative productivity levels in manufacturing presented here are very similar to those based on census value added from van Ark (1993).

20 Here I show no estimates of comparative levels of joint factor productivity, which in principle can be done using the same method as for the growth estimates in Section 4. See Chapter 4 in this volume by O'Mahony for estimates of that kind for the total economy and for manufacturing.

REFERENCES

Ark, B. van (1993), *International Comparisons of Output and Productivity*, Monograph Series No. 1, Groningen Growth and Development Centre.

Ark, B. van (1994), 'Comparative Output and Productivity in Spanish Manufacturing, 1950–1989', University of Groningen, mimeographed.

Badulescu, P. (1993), 'Measuring Technical and Structural Changes', Working Paper Series, Dept. of Economics, Uppsala University.

Broadberry, S.N. (1993), 'Manufacturing and the Convergence Hypothesis: What the Long Run Data Show', *Journal of Economic History*, **53**, 772–95.

Chenery, H., S. Robinson and M. Syrquin (1986), *Industrialization and Growth. A Comparative Study*, World Bank, Oxford: Oxford University Press.

Danmarks Statistik (1992), 'Reviderede tideserier for produktionsvaerdi og bruttofaktorindkomst for perioden 1947–1965', Copenhagen, mimeographed.

Denison, E.F. (1967), *Why Growth Rates Differ*, Washington, DC: The Brookings Institution.

Dollar, D. and E.N. Wolff (1993), *Competitiveness, Convergence and International Specialization*, Cambridge, MA: MIT Press.

Elfring, T. (1988), *Service Sector Employment in Advanced Countries*, Aldershot: Avebury.

Englander, A.S. and A. Gurney (1994), 'Medium Determinants of OECD Productivity', OECD Economic Studies, No. 22, Spring, 49–109.

Fabricant, S. (1942), *Employment in Manufacturing, 1899–1939, An Analysis of its Relation to the Volume of Production*, New York: National Bureau of Economic Research.

Feinstein, C.H. (1972), *National Income, Expenditure and Output of the United Kingdom 1855–1965*, Cambridge: Cambridge University Press.

Golinelli, R. and M. Monterastelli (1990), 'Un metodo per la ricostruzione de serie storiche compatibili con la nuova contabilità nazionale (1959–1989)', Nota di lavoro no. 9001, Promoteia, November.

Kravis, I.B., A. Heston and R. Summers (1982), *World Product and Income: International Comparisons of Real Gross Product*, Baltimore: Johns Hopkins University Press.

Kuznets, S. (1966), *Modern Economic Growth*, Oxford: Oxford University Press.

Maddison, A. (1952), 'Productivity in an Expanding Economy', *The Economic Journal*, LXII (247), 585–98.

Maddison, A. (1991), *Dynamic Forces in Capitalist Development*, Oxford: Oxford University Press.

Maddison, A. (1995), *Monitoring the World Economy 1820–1992*, Paris: OECD Development Centre.

Maddison, A. and H. van Ooststroom (1993), 'The International Comparison of Value Added, Productivity and Purchasing Power Parities in Agriculture', Research Memorandum GD-1, Groningen Growth and Development Centre.

Maddison, A. and B. van Ark (1994), 'The International Comparison of Real Product and Productivity', Research Memorandum GD-6, Groningen Growth and Development Centre.

Meer, C.L.J. van der (1988), 'Employment and Labour Input in Dutch Agriculture 1849–1986', Research Memorandum no. 259, Institute of Economic Research, University of Groningen.

Meyer-zu-Schlochtern, F.J.M. (1988), 'An International Sectoral Data Base for Thirteen OECD Countries', OECD Working Papers No. 57, Paris.

Meyer-zu-Schlochtern, F.J.M. (1994), 'An International Sectoral Data Base for Fourteen OECD Countries', OECD Working Papers No. 145, Paris.

Mulder, N. (1994), 'New Perspectives on Services Output and Productivity: a Comparison of French and US Productivity in Transport, Communication, Wholesale and Retail Trade', Research Memorandum GD-14, Groningen Growth and Development Centre.

OECD (1992, 1994), *The OECD STAN Database for Industrial Analysis*, Paris: OECD.

Paige, D. and G. Bombach (1959), *A Comparison of National Output and Productivity of the United Kingdom and the United States*, Paris: OEEC.

Prados de la Escosura, L. (1993), 'Spain's Gross Domestic Product, 1850–1990: A New Series', Documentos de Trabajo D-93002, Ministeria de Economia y Hacienda, March.

Rostas, L. (1948), *Comparative Productivity in British and American Industry*, Cambridge: NIESR.

SCB (1972), *Nationalraekenskaper 1950–1971*, Stockholm: SCB.

Smith, A.D., D.M.W.N. Hitchens and S. W. Davies (1982), *International Industrial Productivity: A Comparison of Britain, America and Germany*, NIESR, Cambridge: Cambridge University Press.

Statistisches Bundesamt (1991), *Volkswirtschaftliche Gesamtrechnungen, Revidierte Ergebnisse 1950–1990*, Fachserie 18, Reihe S. 15, Wiesbaden.

United Nations (1968), 'A System of National Accounts', Studies in Methods, Series F, No. 2, Rev. 3, New York: Statistical Office of the United Nations.

US Department of Commerce (1986), *The National Income and Product Accounts of the United States, 1929–1982*, Washington DC: Bureau of Economic Analysis.

US Department of Commerce (1992), *The National Income and Product Accounts of the United States, 1959–1988*, Vol. 2, Washington DC: Bureau of Economic Analysis.

Wieringa, P. and A. Maddison (1985), 'An International Comparison of Levels of Real Output in Mining and Quarrying in 1975', University of Groningen, mimeographed.

Wolff, E.N. (1991), 'Capital Formation and Productivity Convergence over the Long Term', *American Economic Review*, June, pp. 565–579.

4 Measures of fixed capital stocks in the post-war period: a five-country study

MARY O'MAHONY

1 Introduction

Comparing the levels and growth rates of fixed capital stocks is an important input into explaining differences in labour productivity and ultimately in standards of living across countries. To do so requires estimates of fixed capital which are measured in a consistent way across countries. Statistical offices in most countries do use the same measurement technique, the perpetual inventory method (PIM), which estimates current capital stocks as the sum of past real investments in fixed capital which have survived up to the current period. However each country differs in the assumptions they employ to implement the PIM, in particular, those on the service lives of assets.

This chapter attempts to shed more light on the issues involved in comparing fixed capital stocks across countries focusing on the impact of differences in mean service lives and the form retirement distributions are assumed to take around the average service life. It also considers in some detail problems which arise from differences in methods used to calculate investment deflators. The paper then presents capital stock measures for three European countries, the UK, Germany, and France. It is helpful to contrast the capital experience of the European countries with that in the USA, the world productivity leader, and with Japan which has experienced a marked improvement in relative productivity in the post-war period. The chapter therefore also presents capital stock estimates for these two countries.

The chapter begins with a description of the PIM. It examines the basis for international differences in service lives and attempts to gauge their plausibility in the light of information, both direct and indirect, on service lives. Section 3 describes the construction of the data series and Section 4 presents the estimates of fixed capital stocks for the five nations using various assumptions on asset lives and mortality distributions and shows how sensitive the estimates are to methodological differences. Finally Section 5 estimates the contribution of fixed capital to explaining differences in both the levels and growth rates of labour productivity across countries and shows how sensitive the conclusions are to different measures of capital stocks.

2   The perpetual inventory method

Gross capital stocks, at constant replacement cost, measure the value of investment in fixed assets which are currently available for productive use. Each year's assets are revalued to a constant base year's prices so that the capital stocks do not depend on inflation in producer goods prices. In the gross capital stock calculation, assets are assumed to be equally productive until they become obsolete, at which time they are assumed to be discarded from the stock. Net capital stocks allow additionally for depreciation.

The issue of whether gross or net stocks should be used to explain international differences in productivity has been the subject of much debate. For example, Kendrick (1976, 1993) is in favour of using gross capital stocks in the analysis of production and growth since capital assets are likely to retain their output-producing capacity throughout their working lives. Net capital stocks with geometric depreciation is favoured by Jorgenson *et al.* (1987) since only in this case is the measure of capital stocks consistent with the rental price of assets which are used to weight capital's contribution to productivity. Denison (1967, 1974) uses an average of gross and net stocks.

Jorgenson *et al.* criticize both the Kendrick and Denison measures by showing that neither imply a consistent pattern of relative efficiency in both their capital stock measures and their estimates of the rental prices of capital services. On the other hand, the use of net capital stocks as a measure of the productive capacity of an economy or sector is correct only if depreciation measures the rate of wear and tear or obsolescence of the asset. But, as argued by Kendrick (1993), depreciation measures the decline in net income-producing capacity of assets as they age, and this is likely to be much larger than any out-producing capacity decline. In this section we discuss the sensitivity of both gross and net stocks to variations in service lives but the empirical analysis below is largely confined to measures of gross capital stock.

The perpetual inventory method calculates gross capital stock at time t as:

$$K_t^G = K_{t-1}^G + I_t - R_t \tag{1}$$

where K^G = gross capital stock, I = real gross investment, and R = real retirements.

Suppose initially that investment consists of a single asset with average service life denoted by v and that retirements occur exactly v years after the asset is purchased. With this 'sudden death' assumption retirements are given by $R_t = I_{t-v}$ so that (1) can be rewritten as:

$$K_t = K_{t-1} + I_t - \sum_{i=0}^{v} I_{t-i}$$ (2)

In general, investment consists of a number of different asset types so that retirements will occur during a range of years around the average service life. Then retirements at time t can be written as:

$$R_t = \sum_{i=-s}^{s} \lambda_i \, I_{t-v+i}$$ (3)

with $\lambda_i > 0$, and $\sum_i \lambda_i = 1$

Thus retirements at time t are a weighted average of the investment which occurred in the years from $t-v-s$ to $t-v+s$. Countries differ in their assumptions regarding the weights λ_i. For example the UK assumes equal weights for years 20% above and below the average service life whereas both the USA and Germany assume a bell-shaped distribution around v. In Japan, the sudden death assumption is employed.

Net capital stocks allow additionally for depreciation. In general, the net capital stock at time t can be written as:

$$K_t^N = I_t + \sum_{i=1}^{T} p_i I_{t-i}$$ (4)

where p_i is the undepreciated proportion of period $t-i$ investment. Two approaches to modeling depreciation are exponential decay and straight line depreciation. In the former, if δ is the depreciation rate, it is easy to show that:

$$K_t^{Ne} = (1 - \delta) K_{t-1}^{Ne} + I_t$$ (5)

With straight line depreciation, $p_i = i/v$ so that the net capital stock is given by:

$$K_t^{Ns} = K_{t-1}^{Ns} + I_t - (1/v) \sum_{i=1}^{v} I_{t-1}$$ (6)

Since gross investment is always non-negative, it is clear from (2) and

(3) that an increase in the service life never lowers the gross capital stock. In equation (3) an increase in the average service life from v to $v + 1$ years, increases period t gross capital stock by:

$$\sum_{i=-v+s}^{-v-s} \lambda_{-v-i} I_{t-i}$$

To see the impact of increases in service lives on net capital stocks in equation (5) we need to relate the depreciation rate, δ, to the average service life, v. A frequently used assumption is 'double declining balance' which sets $\delta = 2/v$. The greater is v the lower is $1 - \delta$ so that net capital stock levels, with exponential depreciation, also increase with v. Depreciation in (6) is of the same form as retirements in (3) with fixed weights. Therefore increases in v also raise net capital stocks.

The sensitivity of the measures above to variations in service lives will depend on the rate of investment. O'Mahony (1993) presents the results of simulations showing the impact of changing service lives when investment is assumed to grow at a constant rate per annum. The simulations suggest that a one year difference in service lives can have a very large impact on capital stock levels, either net or gross, when both the service life and the annual rate of investment are relatively small. The simulations also show that the proportionate impact of a one-year increase in service lives is not always greater for gross than for net capital stocks. In the gross capital stock calculation a one-year increase in the service life adds the total investment for one more year whereas the net stock calculation adds only the undepreciated proportion of that year's investment. But since the depreciation rate generally depends on the service life, a greater proportion of all periods' investment remains in the net capital stocks when the service life is increased. This latter effect will be greater, the higher is the growth rate of investment. In most of the simulations, the proportionate impact of an increase in the service life is in fact larger using net capital stocks with straight line depreciation than gross stocks with 'sudden death' retirements.

Table 4.1 shows the actual service life assumptions, by sector, currently in use in the five countries. In general, the assumed service lives for equipment are very similar in the USA, Germany and France but, with the exception of agriculture and transport, service lives tend to be much longer in the UK. The latter seem implausible, in particular, in distribution, finance and services since equipment in these sectors is largely composed of furniture and fixtures, vehicles and office machinery, all of which are relatively short-lived. The service lives for Japanese equipment in Table 4.1 are considerably shorter than in all other countries.

Table 4.1   Official service lives (years)

	USA	UK	Germany	France	Japan
A. Equipment					
Agriculture, forestry & fishing	12	13	15	11	6
Mining & utilities	18	25	16	16	14
Manufacturing	17	24	15	17	10
Construction	10	20	10	12	5
Transport & communication	18	18	14	16	8
Distribution & repairing	11	22	11	16	10
Finance, insurance & real estate	15	24	13	16	10
Services & government	15	20	14	16	10
Total	15	23	14	15	10
B. Structures					
Agriculture, forestry & fishing	38	31	69	40	43
Mining & utilities	26	49	44	37	35
Manufacturing	31	60	41	37	43
Construction	35	80	47	30	43
Transport & communication	42	67	41	40	37
Distribution & repairing	35	80	65	30	43
Finance, insurance & real estate	41	80	77	30	43
Services & government	49	75	74	30	43
Total	40	66	57	34	42

Notes: Estimates are based on weighted averages, both across asset types and sub-sectors, of service lives for the period 1948–89 with weights equal to investment shares.
Sources: USA: Table B, p. xxii, *Fixed Reproducible Tangible Wealth in the United States, 1925–85*, US Dept. of Commerce, Bureau of Economic Analysis, 1987. UK: unpublished data from the Central Statistical Office, London. Germany: Tabelle 1, p. 503, 'Reproduzierbares Anlagevermögen in erweiterter Bereichsgliederung', *Wirtschaft und Statistik*, 7/1986, Statistisches Bundesamt. France: Blades (1983), Tables 2–4, p. 12–14. Japan: equipment, Blades (1983), Tables 2–4, pp. 12–14 and structures, estimate from Uno (1987, p. 103).

In the case of structures, the US, French and Japanese lives are similar but the average life for aggregate economy investment in structures is much longer in the UK and Germany. The latter, however, hides large discrepancies at the sectoral level. The big differences between Germany, on the one hand, and France and the USA on the other, occurs in agriculture and the three service sectors. In the UK, the service lives of structures in most sectors are considerably longer than those used in the other four countries.

The data in Table 4.1 are the service lives in use in the 1980s but not all the statistical offices assume these service lives have been fixed over time.

The German statistical office assumes declining service lives in all sectors whereas the UK CSO assumes declining lives in some sectors, mainly in manufacturing. The issue of fixed versus declining lives is considered further below.

Blades (1991) describes the data sources used by statisticians to gather information on the service lives of assets in the major industrialized nations. The primary sources are service lives for tax purposes, information from company accounts, surveys of firms and expert advice. The first of these formed the basis of the service lives for both the UK and the USA in the inter-war period but in more recent times, the fact that most countries allow some accelerated depreciation of assets renders the tax lives unreliable as a measure of the physical durability of assets. In practice most countries' current estimates of service lives tend to be based on a combination of small-scale surveys and expert advice.

Evidence on the implausibility of the longer than average lives for equipment in the UK can be found in Smith (1987). This study presented alternative capital stock estimates for a sample of firms who used current cost accounting methods in the early 1980s. The implicit service lives for equipment derived by Smith from his capital stock estimates were considerably below the lives employed by the CSO and were in fact close to those used in other European countries and the USA.

Some direct evidence on the average age of machinery is available from the periodic international censuses of machine tools. Using the results of the UK and US censuses, Bacon and Eltis (1974) calculate that the average age of machine tools were 12 and 12.75 years, respectively. Prais (1986) gives the distribution of machine tools by age for the five countries considered in this chapter for a number of years and shows a similar distribution in the UK, the USA, France and Germany, with Britain having the lowest percentage of long-lived machinery (over twenty years). In Japan the proportion in the longest age class was very small. Thus the machine tool data are not consistent with the assumption of longer UK service lives but do lend some support to shorter lives in Japan.

Evidence on differences in the age of machinery in use across countries is presented in a series of matched plant visits between the UK, Germany, France and The Netherlands carried out at NIESR (e.g. Daly et al. (1985), Steedman and Wagner (1987, 1989), Prais and Wagner (1988), Jarvis and Prais (1989) and Mason et al. (1993)). These visits covered such diverse areas in manufacturing as engineering, furniture, women's clothing and biscuits, and hotels in non-manufacturing. Most of the studies concluded that the age of the machinery stock was similar in the UK, Germany and France. The exception was women's clothing where UK machinery was found to be slightly older but even in this case the difference between the UK and Germany was not as large as the assumptions underlying the official service lives. The small amount of direct evidence therefore does not support the large differences in official lives. In the PIM calculation countries estimate capital stocks at different levels of disaggregation, both by asset type and sector. Maddison (1991, and Chapter 2, this volume) estimates standardized capital stocks using a single service life for equipment and one service life for structures for the whole economy. Our estimates for the total economy below are derived by standardizing asset lives in eight broad sectors and then aggregating so that we allow to some extent for compositional differences. Comparing these estimates with one derived using a single service life shows only small compositional effects.

It has been argued that the relatively higher labour costs in the USA to those in European countries implies relatively higher maintenance costs and hence provides an incentive for firms to replace assets earlier in the USA. It is clear that higher relative labour costs in the USA should lead to greater capital intensity in that country than in say the UK. But if the official service lives are employed for manufacturing, then capital per worker turns out to be higher in the UK. This suggests that relative input prices on their own are not sufficient to justify the magnitude of the official service life differences in those two countries. Also, in comparison with Germany, France and Japan the US assumptions on equipment are generally longer despite the likelihood of higher American maintenance costs.

When comparing Britain with the continental countries, it is obvious from the matched plant comparisons, cited above, that British workers in general possess fewer skills than their continental European counterparts and that this deficiency implies lower levels of machinery maintenance, in particular preventive maintenance, in Britain. The lack of the required skilled maintenance workers in Britain should, other things equal, lead to a faster rate of physical obsolescence in Britain than in France and Germany but the official service lives imply the opposite.

A recent report on the tax treatment of manufacturing assets in OECD countries, OECD (1991), shows that the tax system is not, in general, neutral and that there is considerable variation across countries. Using data on tax rates (both corporate and personal) and investment tax allowances for 1991, the report shows that the tax system in the USA puts a higher tax burden on marginal investment, for both equipment and structures, than in the UK, France and Germany. The tax burden in Japan is similar to that in the USA whereas there is very little difference between the European countries in the tax rates on equipment. The effective tax rates on structures in France were slightly higher than in the UK or Germany. The calculation of the effective tax rates were carried out only for manufacturing and the tax rates and allowances were for a very recent year, 1991. Nevertheless, the information on tax rates does tend to question the validity of the service lives in Table 4.1.

In summary, the evidence on international differences in service lives, both direct and indirect, is not generally supportive of the lives shown in Table 4.1. In international comparisons an alternative is to assume service lives are equal across countries. The case for standardizing service lives is not based on the assumption that service lives are identical across countries but rather is based on the belief that the actual differences are largely unknown and are unlikely to be as large as the differences in official estimates. With standard asset lives the relative magnitudes of capital stocks across countries depend on differences in investment, which are known with a considerable degree of accuracy, rather than being overly dependent on unreliable service life assumptions.

Finally in this section we look at the issue of whether asset lives show a tendency to decline over time. In the USA capital stock calculations the service life is assumed to be unchanged in the post-war period. Service lives are assumed to have declined in Germany in all sectors and in the UK in some sectors, mainly manufacturing. There are a number of reasons why the service life of an asset may decline over time. The economic or physical lives of a particular type of asset, say metal-working machinery, may decline due to higher costs of keeping old assets in operation or to a faster pace of technical progress.

Blades (1991) casts doubt on the notion that, in the absence of more rapid technical change, the economic life of assets has declined in the post-war period. Economic lives are likely to be cyclically sensitive with firms keeping machinery in operation for longer periods in booms when they face capacity constraints and engaging in more rapid scrapping in recessions. But in the long run these cyclical effects may cancel each other so that the evidence for a long-run decline in service lives is not strong. Also Abramovitz (1991) suggests that the pace of technological change may have, in fact, slowed since the 1960s.

If countries merely report an average life for all types of equipment used in each sector, as is the case for the UK, then compositional change can lead to changes in these aggregate lives over time. O'Mahony (1993) examines the composition of assets with different assumed physical durations in the USA where sufficiently detailed data exists. The Bureau of Economic Analysis (US Department of Commerce) gathers data on investment for fifty different asset types and sixty-one sectors. The average life of each asset was multiplied by its share in investment for each year from 1948 to 1990 for each separate industry and then aggregated to broad sectors to yield an average expected service life of assets invested in each year.

The results showed that the average life of both equipment, excluding office machinery, and structures have fallen by approximately one year in the 1970s and 1980s relative to the 1950s and 1960s. When computers are included there is a more pronounced fall in the expected life of equipment. This is partially caused by the hedonic price deflator for computers used in the USA (which is discussed further below) but even if computers are deflated by a general machinery price deflator the reduction in the expected equipment life remains. Office machinery is assumed to live for an average of eight years which is considerably shorter than other types of equipment. Therefore, the US data does lend some support to the idea that asset lives have been declining over time due to the increased share of short-lived assets. Evidence on the increased share of office machinery in total investment is also available for Germany (see OECD (1993)).

The assumption of declining asset lives in Germany and the UK and the implicit decline in the USA introduces a further source of non-comparability into the official capital stock series. It is likely for example that all countries experienced some decline due to the greater share of investment in office machinery in recent years but only the USA and possibly the German official estimates take account of this. In the UK the CSO assumes declining lives in manufacturing but not in services where the trend towards increased shares of short-lived office machinery is probably greatest. International evidence on the extent of decreases in the average service lives of assets is not available. The estimates of capital stocks below therefore assume fixed lives in all sectors for both equipment and structures.[1]

3   Data

The capital stock estimates, presented in the next section, are built up from real investment series which distinguish two asset types, equipment and structures. Equipment includes all types of machinery, furniture and fixtures and vehicles. 'Structures' includes all types of buildings, mine shafts, railway tracks and infrastructure such as roads, dams and harbours. Most countries follow the United Nations System of National Accounts (SNA) in deciding which assets to include in investment. There are some deviations from the SNA but these are deemed to be minor (OECD (1993)).

Data series were obtained directly for the USA, from the Bureau of

Economic Analysis, US Department of Commerce, and for the UK, from the Central Statistical Office. The official German series were available from 1960 and before then we use estimates from Kirner (1968) which is the source used by the Statistisches Bundesamt in their capital stock calculations. Official series for France from 1970 were obtained from INSEE and these were combined with series from the OECD national accounts and from Carré et al. (1976). Japanese data from the Economic Planning Agency were used together with data from the OECD national accounts and from Ohkawa and Shinohara (1979) and Ohkawa and Rosovsky (1973). Adjustments were made to take account of war damage using estimates presented in Maddison (1991). Details of the data series for all five countries are given in the data appendix.

One source of non-comparability in the investment data may be differences in the methods used to construct investment deflators. O'Mahony (1993) looks at the correspondence between the international relative prices of investment goods as implied by each country's investment deflators and those implied by the relative 'purchasing power parities' (PPPs) of producer durables and non-residential structures estimated periodically since the 1950s. The results show that for the three European countries the investment deflators imply a greater rise in producer durables prices in each country relative to prices in the USA than do the purchasing power parities. The investment deflators were not available for Japan. In general one would not expect the PPPs and investment deflators to give identical answers since they are based on different bundles of commodities. However, it would be worrying if there was some systematic error in either series. The use of hedonic price indexes to deflate the prices of office machinery in the USA could introduce such a bias in the investment deflators.

Baily and Gordon (1991) discuss the impact of different methods of deflating investment in the statistical offices in the USA, Germany, France and the UK. In particular they focus on the use of hedonic price indexes to deflate investment in office machinery in the USA. There are significant cross-country differences in the treatment of computer deflators in the five countries. Figure 4.1 shows the price indexes for office machinery relative to the producer price indexes for all manufactured products in three countries, the USA, Germany and the UK. The adjustment for quality change in the UK is minimal whereas the German statistical office estimates that the price of office machinery has more than halved in the past two decades. But differences between Germany and the UK are small relative to differences between these two countries and the USA. Baily and Gordon (1991) show that the reduction in the relative price of computers in France is similar to that in the UK. In

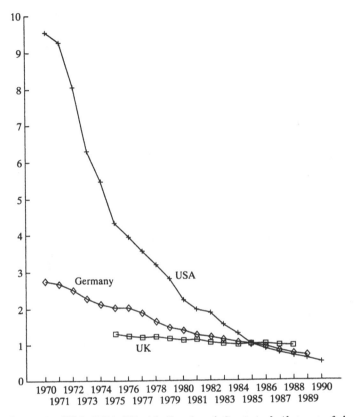

Sources: USA: BEA 'Wealth Tape' and *Statistical Abstract of the USA*. UK: *Annual Abstract of Statistics*, CSO. Germany: *Statistisches Jahrbuch*, Statistisches Bundesamt.

Figure 4.1 Price of office machinery relative to producer prices for manufactured goods, 1985 = 100

Japan, a single deflator is used for all assets so it is not clear if any adjustment is made for falling relative prices of office machinery.

Since computer technology is internationally transferable it seems unlikely that the differences in Figure 4.1 reflect the true relative price of office machinery to investors in each country. This is confirmed by an examination of purchasing power parities for closely matched types of office equipment which show only small differences in relative prices across countries; see O'Mahony (1993) for details. That paper also shows that the PPPs and investment deflators are closer together when office machinery in the USA is deflated by a general equipment price index. Therefore the use of the hedonic price deflator in the USA is introducing some non-comparability into the estimates. In the empirical section below we consider again the quantitative impact of different methods of deflating office machinery in the USA.

Finally, on the issue of deflators, the capital stock estimates need to be converted to a common currency in order to measure the contribution of capital to comparative productivity levels. Therefore we need to use some years' purchasing power parities to undertake the conversion. The inconsistency between investment deflators and PPPs suggest that the results will be sensitive to which years' PPPs are used. Below we also show the impact of using various PPPs for the 1970s and 1980s.

The estimates presented below do not make allowance for any premature scrapping of capital which may have occurred in the 1970s and 1980s. Baily (1981) suggested that the energy price rises after 1973 may have led to early obsolescence of energy-intensive equipment. Mendis and Muellbauer (1984) suggest that the collapse of British manufacturing industry in 1980–81 may also have led to wholesale scrapping in that sector. It is difficult to derive reliable estimates of the extent of premature scrapping and the many attempts to do so, generally for British manufacturing, have yielded a large range of values. Since the energy price rise was worldwide this source of premature scrapping may not have a significant impact on international comparisons of capital stocks. The collapse of British manufacturing in the early 1980s, however, may imply that the British estimates below are overstated since then.

4   The measurement of capital stocks in five nations

The focus in this section is on the impact of different measurement assumptions on the relative size and growth rates of capital stocks in the five countries. The analysis is confined largely to gross capital stocks but we briefly consider the impact of service lives on net stocks. Gross capital stocks were estimated for each of the five countries using two alternative service life assumptions, those in use in the USA and the official lives given in Table 4.1 above, assuming uniform retirements in the range of 20% around the average service lives. Capital stocks were estimated for eight sectors[2] and then aggregated to yield measures for the whole economy. Purchasing power parities for the year 1985 for producer durables and non-residential structures, published in OECD (1985), were used to convert each country's gross capital stocks to constant 1985 prices. Table 4.2 summarizes the results for 1989 and Appendix table B

Table 4.2   Gross tangible physical capital stocks, 1989 (1985 $)

	Total economy			Manufacturing		
	Value (billion $)	per Worker-hour ($)	(UK = 100)	Value (billion $)	per Worker-hour ($)	(UK = 100)
USA	10,762	51.8	173	1,572	42.0	137
UK	1,338	30.0	100	267	30.7	100
Germany	2,589	58.3	194	578	41.1	134
France	1,741	44.4	148	296	41.5	135
Japan	5,035	39.1	131	1,132	34.6	113

Sources: Investment series: see data appendix. Labour input: (a) Total economy: Employment from OECD *National Accounts*, Annual average hours worked per year: USA from OECD *National Accounts* (total man-hours divided by total employment); UK, own calculations using hours per week from *The New Earnings Survey, 1989*, Department of Employment, and weeks per year using data on holidays and time lost due to strikes from *The Department of Employment Gazette*, Department of Employment, various issues, and data on time lost due to illness and maternity leave from *Social Security Statistics*, Department of Health and Social Security, various issues; Germany, France and Japan from Maddison (1991). (b) Manufacturing: employment and hours worked – USA from van Ark (1992); UK from census of production and hours as for total economy; Germany from O'Mahony (1992a); France from van Ark (1990) and Japan from Pilat and van Ark (1992).

shows the sectoral capital stock estimates, using standard US service lives, annually from 1948 to 1989.

Table 4.2 shows that in 1989 real capital stock levels were highest in the USA and lowest in the UK for both the total economy and manufacturing. This reflects to some extent the relative size of the economies. Table 4.2 also shows capital per unit of labour input (annual average hours worked) for the five countries. In 1989, in the aggregate economy, each unit of German labour had more capital at its disposal than had US labour but capital intensity in the USA was marginally higher than Germany in manufacturing. Capital intensity was lowest in the UK for both the aggregate economy and manufacturing.

How sensitive are these results to changes in service lives? Table 4.3 shows the percentage by which gross capital stocks in 1989 using official lives were above or below those using US lives. For both the aggregate economy and manufacturing the use of official service lives results in considerably higher total capital stocks for the UK; this is true for both equipment and structures. In Germany and France the use of official

Table 4.3   The sensitivity of capital stocks to asset lives (percentage, 1989)

| | Total economy | | | Manufacturing | | |
	T	E	S	T	E	S
UK	25.9	31.4	20.5	44.9	39.4	61.2
Germany	4.9	−7.7	12.4	0.8	−10.9	23.4
France	−0.4	1.6	−1.7	1.6	0.0	5.4
Japan	−10.4	−26.9	−0.2	−19.5	−29.8	4.1

Notes: T = total assets, E = equipment, S = structures. The figures shown are estimates using official lives minus estimates using US lives, as a percentage of the latter. As in Table 4.2 the estimates for the total economy are aggregates of capital stocks for eight sectors.

lives makes little difference to the size of the total capital stock although for Germany this results from non-negligible offsetting differences in equipment and structures. For Japan official lives yield considerably lower equipment and hence total capital stocks. From Tables 4.2 and 4.3 we see that capital per worker-hour in UK manufacturing is about two-thirds the American level using standardized lives, whereas capital per worker is about the same in the two countries if official lives are used. The latter is not consistent with what we would expect given the relatively higher cost of labour to capital in the USA.

It is useful to compare gross capital stocks using constant US service lives with official estimates produced by the statistical offices in each country. This was possible only for the USA, the UK and Germany. In the USA and Germany the official capital stocks for the total economy were close to the standardized estimates given in this chapter but the official German capital stocks in manufacturing were some 10% below the standardized estimates. The largest differences were for the UK where the official capital stocks were about 30% and 60% higher than the standardized estimates for the total economy and manufacturing, respectively. The latter are somewhat greater than the estimates above but this reflects also differences in the form of the mortality distributions and the level of aggregation at which the calculations are carried out. The lives of some assets are also assumed to decline in the official estimates in the UK and Germany whereas the Americans assume constant lives throughout. This comparison does suggest, however, that differences in service lives are likely to be the most important component of non-comparability in international capital stock measurement.

Are relative capital stock levels sensitive to which service life is used as

Table 4.4   The ratio of capital stocks using own country lives to those using US lives. Total economy, gross and net capital stocks

	Equipment		Structures	
	net	gross	net	gross
UK	38.8	39.6	45.5	15.5
Germany	−5.4	−5.4	22.5	8.9
France	0.0	0.0	−9.0	−5.3
Japan	−22.5	−22.2	−1.2	0.6

Note: The gross capital stocks employed in this table were derived using aggregate economy investment and so will differ from the estimates in Table 4.3 which were built up from sector investment series.

the standard? We estimated gross capital stocks using service lives which were the average of those employed in the UK and the USA.[3] We then compared relative (to US) capital stocks using this assumption to those where the standard was US service lives and found little difference in the two estimates. Therefore relative capital stocks do not appear to be very sensitive to which service life is used as the standard.

We now consider the sensitivity of net capital stocks to changes in service lives. This is carried out using only straight line depreciation – estimation of capital stocks assuming exponential depreciation requires either more historical data than was possible to obtain for the five countries or benchmark estimates of capital stocks which are dependent on differences in service lives some time in the past. Table 4.4 shows the impact of changing service lives on net capital stocks with straight-line depreciation.

In 1989 both net and gross stocks of equipment were about equally sensitive to changes in service lives. However, there were large differences in the sensitivity of net and gross stocks of structures to variations in service lives, in particular in the UK and Germany. The stock of equipment is derived from investment flows in the 1970s and 1980s when investment grew very slowly in all countries whereas the stock of structures is comprised of investment flows from the 1950s to the current period when the average annual rate of growth of investment was higher. The simulations in O'Mahony (1993) suggest a greater sensitivity of net capital stocks to changes in service lives when investment is growing rapidly.

The service life is generally considered to be an average over many types of assets, so that retirements will occur in a range of years around this life. Blades (1991) suggests that, for the distributions used in most industrialized countries, which are generally some approximation to a bell-shaped distribution, the form of the retirement distribution would have a negligible impact on capital stock levels. O'Mahony (1993) examines three retirement distributions, the US Winfrey S-3 curve, where retirements occur between 45% and 155% of the mean life and the distribution of retirements between these two points is bell-shaped, the uniform distribution with retirements occurring 20% above and below the mean life, as used in the UK, and the 'sudden death' assumption, as used in Japan. The results showed that the impact of different retirement distributions on relative capital stock levels was indeed very small with differences in the retirement distribution accounting for less than 2% of gross capital stocks. We can conclude, therefore, that differences in the assumed forms of mortality distributions have only a minor impact on cross-country comparisons of capital stocks.

It was suggested above that the use of a hedonic price index for office machinery in the US may introduce some bias into international measures of capital stocks. O'Mahony (1993) recalculated US capital stocks using a general equipment deflator rather than the hedonic index for office machinery. In general, gross stocks of equipment in the USA were found to be about 10% lower when the hedonic price index is used rather than a general equipment deflator and total gross capital stocks were about 4% lower.

In the aggregate productivity calculations shown below, the use of the hedonic index for office machinery in capital input is almost exactly counterbalanced by its use in deriving real output series in the USA. But in more open economies the two effects would not necessarily cancel each other and so would be distortionary. Also in the manufacturing sector, which produces the office machinery, output will be more affected than capital. (See Denison (1989) for a discussion of the distortions introduced into productivity calculations by the use of the hedonic index.) Since the remaining four countries do not produce separate investment series for office machinery it is not possible to take account of this source of non-comparability in the capital stock estimate. Hence, it should be borne in mind that the capital stock levels for the USA are likely to be slightly overestimated.

Next we examine the impact of the use of alternative base years to compare capital stock levels across countries. Table 4.5 shows the ratio of capital stocks in the three European countries to US capital stocks using 1980 or 1975 purchasing power parities relative to that ratio using 1985 PPPs. The 1980 PPP for producer durables implies about a 10% smaller ratio of UK to US gross capital stock than using either the 1985 or 1975 PPP. For other countries the main impact of using different years'

Table 4.5   Ratio of relative capital stocks using 1980 and 1975 PPPs

	Gross capital stocks		
	UK/USA	Germany/USA	France/USA
1980 relative to 1985 base			
Equipment	0.84	0.95	0.92
Structures	0.89	0.95	1.08
Total capital	0.87	0.95	1.03
1975 relative to 1985 base			
Equipment	0.75	0.77	0.94
Structures	1.09	1.01	0.99
Total capital	0.98	0.93	0.97

Table 4.6   Relative gross capital stocks, 1989. Comparison with Maddison (Chapter 2, this volume) (USA = 100)

	This chapter	Maddison
UK	12.4	11.8
Germany	24.1	21.6
France	16.2	16.7
Japan	46.8	48.0

PPPs is to alter the relative shares of equipment and structures in total investment relative to those in the USA.

It is interesting to compare the estimates in this chapter for the aggregate economy with those produced by Maddison (Chapter 2, this volume) who also standardizes the service lives of assets. Table 4.6 shows that the two estimates of the 1989 capital stocks for the four countries relative to those in the USA[4] are reasonably close. The small differences can be explained by slight variations in the investment series used in the two papers and in the methodology employed. For example Maddison uses the sudden death retirement assumption and his estimates are derived from investment series for the total economy whereas the estimates in this paper are built up from sectoral investment series.

Finally in this section we consider the impact of differences in service lives on growth rates of capital stocks. Table 4.7 shows the growth rates of gross capital stocks over selected time periods using both official and

Table 4.7   The impact of service lives on growth rates of capital

	UK	Germany	USA	France	Japan
Equipment, US lives					
1948–89	3.93	6.34	4.08	4.57	5.94
1948–73	4.82	8.38	4.12	5.41	6.02
1973–89	2.53	3.16	4.02	3.27	5.82
1948–65	5.03	9.30	3.73	4.93	2.93
1965–73	4.38	6.43	4.94	6.42	12.57
1973–79	2.98	3.67	5.00	4.33	6.01
1979–89	2.26	2.85	3.44	2.63	5.70
Equipment, own country lives					
1948–89	3.98	6.27	4.08	4.71	6.11
1948–73	4.55	8.39	4.12	5.56	6.53
1973–89	3.08	2.96	4.02	3.39	5.45
1948–65	4.39	9.43	3.73	5.13	3.86
1965–73	4.89	6.18	4.94	6.50	12.20
1973–79	3.54	3.46	5.00	4.50	4.13
1979–89	2.81	2.67	3.44	2.72	6.25
Structures, US lives					
1948–89	3.56	4.02	2.67	2.78	NA
1948–73	3.90	4.63	3.00	1.91	NA
1973–89	3.03	3.08	2.16	4.16	5.99
1948–65	3.24	4.37	2.74	0.52	NA
1965–73	5.31	5.19	3.53	4.84	8.98
1973–79	3.51	3.74	2.38	4.73	7.25
1979–89	2.75	2.68	2.03	3.82	5.23
Structures, own country lives					
1948–89	3.02	3.61	2.67	2.80	NA
1948–73	3.18	4.00	3.00	1.89	NA
1973–89	2.78	2.99	2.16	4.22	5.90
1948–65	2.67	3.78	2.74	0.63	NA
1965–73	4.26	4.48	3.53	4.58	8.73
1973–79	3.07	3.46	2.38	4.93	7.09
1979–89	2.61	2.71	2.03	3.80	5.05

US service lives. It is obvious from Table 4.7 that growth rates of capital stocks are generally insensitive to the service life assumed. Generally the differences in growth rates are less than half a percentage point. The one exception is the growth rate of the Japanese stock of equipment in the post-1973 period. In this case use of Japanese service lives implies about two percentage points lower growth in capital than using US service lives in the period 1973–79. In general, however, we can conclude that differences in service lives impact mainly on international comparisons of capital stock levels but have little effect on growth rates.

5 Capital's contribution to relative productivity levels

Growth accounting is the most commonly used method to measure the contribution of inputs to relative output. Suppose the production function is Cobb–Douglas with constant returns to scale and assume its parameters are the same across countries. Let Y denote real output, let L denote labour input (annual hours worked) and, as before, let K denote real tangible physical capital stocks, then joint factor productivity in country j relative to that in the UK (u) is given by:

$$\ln RJFP = \ln(Y_j/Y_u) - \alpha \ln(L_j/L_u) - (1 - \alpha) \ln(K_j/K_u) \qquad (7)$$

where α is labour's share in value added. With constant returns to scale (7) can be rewritten as:

$$\ln(Y_j/Y_u) - \ln(L_j/L_u) = (1-\alpha) \ln(K_j/L_j)/(K_u/L_u) + \ln RJFP \quad (8)$$

The first term on the right-hand side of equation (8) measures the contribution of physical capital to explaining relative labour productivity and RJFP measures the residual relative labour productivity when account is taken of differences in capital intensity in the two countries.

Estimates of relative joint factor productivity from (8) are subject to the usual limitations of growth accounting, in particular its dependence on the assumptions of price taking behaviour and constant returns to scale. Recent contributions to growth theory (e.g. Romer (1990a)) have questioned the validity of the growth accounting coefficients and suggest that they may understate the importance of capital in explaining relative levels or growth of productivity. In these models some of the benefits to capital accumulation are assumed to be external to the firms or agents undertaking the investments and hence raise the social value of capital accumulation above that implied by traditional growth accounting. The external benefits are generally based on some idea of learning effects from capital accumulation. In this case joint factor productivity is given by:

$$\ln RJFP = \ln(Y_j/Y_u) - \alpha_1 \ln(L_j/L_u) - \alpha_2 \ln(K_j/K_u) \qquad (9)$$

where $\alpha_1 + \alpha_2 > 1$, and relative output per unit of labour input is given by:

$$\ln(Y_j/Y_u) - \ln(L_j/L_u) = (1 - \alpha_1) \ln(K_j/L_j)/(K_u/L_u) +$$
$$(\alpha_1 + \alpha_2 - 1) \ln(K_j/K_u) + \ln RJFP \qquad (10)$$

so that the absolute values of capital stocks, and not just capital intensity, affect relative productivity.

Empirical evidence from a wide range of sources, however, suggests that external effects from physical capital are unimportant, i.e. $(\alpha_1 + \alpha_2)$ is close to one. For example, econometric evidence in Barro and Sala-i-Martin (1991) for states of the USA, Mankiw et al. (1992) for a cross-section of nations, Oulton (1992) for UK manufacturing growth and O'Mahony (1992b) for UK and German manufacturing all yield coefficients on physical capital close to its share of value added, the growth accounting weight. In what follows we therefore employ these growth accounting weights.

Table 4.8 shows the percentage of relative labour productivity explained by differences in physical capital and relative joint factor productivity for 1989. For the aggregate economy about half the UK productivity gap with the USA and almost all the gap with France can be explained by differences in capital intensity whereas the UK productivity gap with Germany is more than explained by differences in capital intensity. Therefore in comparison with these three countries the UK's lower stocks of capital per worker-hour is an important determinant of her lower output per man-hour. With Japan the opposite conclusion emerges, i.e. Japan's relatively low labour productivity compared to the UK cannot be explained by differences in capital intensity. When account is taken of differences in capital at the aggregate economy level Japan's joint factor productivity is reduced to about 30% below that in the UK in 1989.

Table 4.8 shows that, in manufacturing, differences in physical capital explain considerably less of the UK's lower labour productivity with the USA, Germany and France than was the case for the aggregate economy but some of the gap with Japan can now be explained by differences in capital intensity. This partly reflects the fact that capital's share of value added at about 0.33 for the aggregate economy is greater than capital's share of manufacturing value added (about 0.25). In manufacturing the UK's productivity disadvantage remains substantial against the USA when allowance is made for differences in capital intensity. The

Table 4.8 The contribution of physical tangible capital to explaining relative productivity with the UK, 1989 (UK = 100)

	Total economy			Manufacturing		
	RLP	RJFP	Contribution of capital[a]	RLP	RJFP	Contribution of capital[a]
USA	134.1	111.7	58.7	158.1	146.1	14.0
Germany	113.1	90.6	190.1	116.3	108.1	46.4
France	115.2	101.0	92.4	124.2	115.3	32.4
Japan	82.0	75.0	− 51.5	124.3	120.7	12.5

Notes: RLP is relative labour productivity (output per hour worked).
[a] This is calculated as $\exp(\beta \ln(RKL)) - 1$ divided by the productivity gaps from Table 4.1 where RKL is relative capital intensity and β is one minus labour's share of value added. We use values of β equal to 0.33 and 0.25, respectively, for the aggregate economy and for manufacturing. These coefficients are averages over a number of countries from OECD data. Ideally we should include each countries actual shares of labour but this would involve difficult comparisons of relative labour costs which is beyond the scope of this chapter.
Sources: Total economy: GDP in 1985 prices and employment primarily from OECD *National Accounts*, converted to US$ using 1985 GDP purchasing power parities from OECD (1985), and from Summers and Heston (1991). Annual average hours worked per year for the USA from OECD *National Accounts* (total man-hours divided by total employment); UK, own calculations using hours per week from *The New Earnings Survey, 1989*, Department of Employment, and weeks per year using data on holidays and time lost due to strikes from *The Department of Employment Gazette*, Department of Employment, various issues, and data on time lost due to illness and maternity leave from *Social Security Statistics*, Department of Health and Social Security, various issues; Germany, France and Japan from Maddison (1991). Manufacturing: USA/UK from van Ark (1992), Germany/UK from O'Mahony (1992a), France/UK from van Ark (1990) and Japan/USA from Pilat and van Ark (1992), updated to 1989 using national accounts estimates for real output and employment in manufacturing for each country.

manufacturing joint factor productivity gap also remains large against France and Japan but is close to being eliminated against Germany.

We now consider the time pattern of relative productivity from 1950 to 1989. We first consider the aggregate economy and then look at trends in manufacturing productivity. There is ample evidence of a narrowing of GDP labour productivity gaps in industrialized nations over time (see Baumol (1986)). We will be interested to see this is also true for joint factor productivity at the aggregate level and for both labour and joint factor productivity in manufacturing.

Table 4.9 shows relative labour productivity, capital intensity and joint

Table 4.9 Relative productivity and capital intensity, 1950. Total economy (UK = 100)

	Output per worker-hour	Capital per worker-hour	Joint factor productivity
USA	170.0	367.2	110.7
Germany	54.9	122.0	51.2
France	73.1	169.2	65.5
Japan[a]	31.3	67.5	34.5

[a]   1953.
Sources: as in Table 4.8.

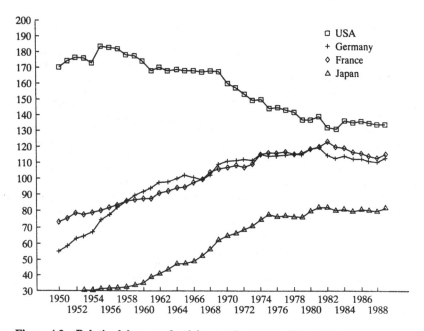

Figure 4.2   Relative labour productivity: total economy (UK = 100)

factor productivity for the aggregate economy in 1950. Figures 4.2 to 4.4 show the time series for the three decades from 1950 to 1989. For the aggregate economy the dispersion of labour productivity levels across the five countries was greater in 1950 than in 1989 and, to a lesser extent, this is also true of joint factor productivity. But examination of the figures shows that any trend towards convergence in the latter occurred primarily in the 1950s and 1960s.

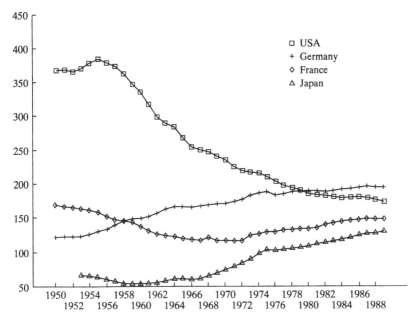

Figure 4.3   Relative capital–labour ratios: total economy (UK = 100)

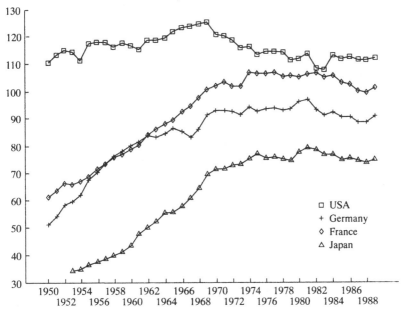

Figure 4.4   Relative joint factor productivity: total economy (UK = 100)

Table 4.10   Relative productivity and capital intensity, 1950. Manufacturing (UK = 100)

	Output per worker-hour	Capital per worker-hour	Joint factor productivity
USA	281.3	207.2	254.5
Germany	86.8	80.1	91.8
France	81.8	72.6	88.7
Japan	32.5	47.1	45.8

Sources: As in Table 4.8.

In 1950 both labour productivity and capital intensity were considerably higher in the USA relative to the UK than in 1989, but relative US to UK joint factor productivity was similar in the two years. Therefore the UK's relatively greater investment in physical capital in the past four decades can explain much of the narrowing of her labour productivity gap with the USA. The UK's position relative to the other three countries is, however, very different. Table 4.9 shows a deterioration in the UK's relative performance, both for labour and joint factor productivity, relative to all three countries, but the graphs show that much of those occurred in the first two decades. Britain's lower investment in physical capital can partly explain her deterioration against Germany and Japan. In comparison with France, Britain invested more per unit of labour up to the early 1970s but invested less thereafter.

Turning now to manufacturing, Table 4.10, which shows the position in 1950, implies considerable narrowing of both the labour and joint factor productivity gaps. Figures 4.5 to 4.7 show that the trend in US/UK labour productivity can be partly explained by the decline in capital intensity in the USA relative to the UK but its explanatory power is much less than for the aggregate economy since there was also a considerable narrowing of the joint factor productivity gap between these two countries. In manufacturing the deterioration in Britain's productivity relative to Germany, France and Japan continued well into the 1970s. The manufacturing sectors in all three countries invested more in physical capital than did British manufacturing but only relative to Japan does this explain a significant amount of Britain's relative decline.

6   Conclusion

There are a number of differences in methodology used by statistical offices in constructing gross capital stocks. This chapter has shown that

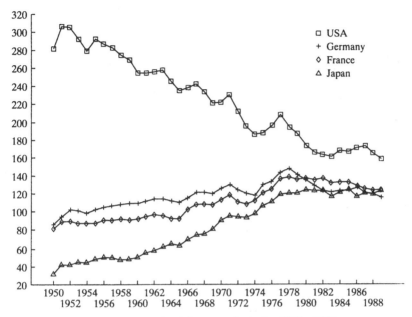

Figure 4.5   Relative labour productivity: manufacturing (UK = 100)

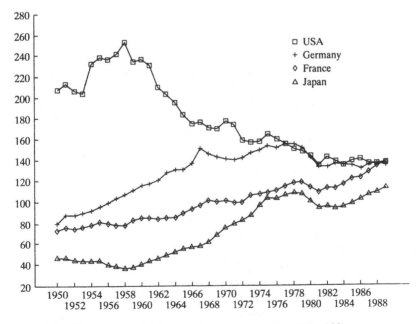

Figure 4.6   Relative capital–labour ratios: manufacturing (UK = 100)

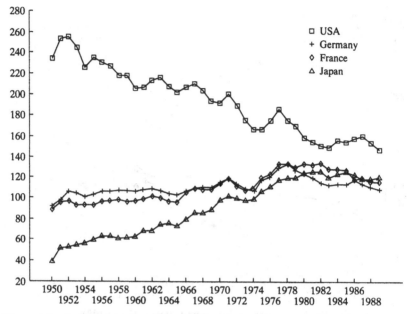

Figure 4.7   Relative joint factor productivity: manufacturing (UK = 100)

differences in assumptions on the service lives of assets have the greatest impact. In evaluating the relative productivity performance of the five countries and its relation to fixed capital this chapter uses a standardized methodology which, as far as possible, takes account of these differences. We believe that this approach gives a more accurate picture than merely taking published official data without regard to differences in method.

The chapter shows that, in explaining relative productivity growth rates and levels, capital has an important role. Thus differences in capital intensity explain much of the variation in labour productivity between the European countries, but this is more important for the aggregate economy than for manufacturing. Also higher rates of investment in physical capital help explain the convergence of European productivity levels to those in the USA in the post-war period but this is most pronounced in the 1950s and 1960s.

There is a general impression in the economics literature that differences in fixed capital across countries does not matter. This partly stems from the conclusion of the neoclassical growth model that capital has no impact on steady-state growth. But at any one time the economy may be very far from steady-state growth. Also the weight given to fixed capital in traditional growth accounting is small. This has been attacked by the new growth theorists but the empirical evidence does not support a higher weight. However, even a small weight can have a significant impact if differences in capital across countries are large. This chapter shows that the impression that fixed capital is unimportant is misleading, i.e. differences in physical capital remain important in understanding differences in labour productivity levels and growth rates across industrialized nations.

The conclusions of this chapter are, however, dependent on the assumptions used to measure relative capital stocks. We acknowledge that much work needs to be done to have confidence in cross-country differences in capital stocks. This would involve comprehensive surveys of the lives of assets and would probably require more international cooperation by statistical offices than is at present the case.

Appendix A: Data and sources

A.   United Kingdom

The primary source for investment in both current and constant prices is an unpublished series from the CSO which is used in their construction of post-war stocks. The CSO series distinguish ten sectors and three asset types. The ten sectors are (1) agriculture, forestry and fishing, (2) extraction of mineral oil and natural gas, (3) other energy (including gas, electricity and water, mineral oil refining and mining & quarrying), (4) manufacturing, (5) construction, (6) transport, (7) communication, (8) distribution, hotels and catering, (9) finance, insurance and business services and (10) public, social and other services.

The three asset types are buildings (other than dwellings), plant & machinery and vehicles. Buildings includes most civil engineering and construction work and railway track and gas and water mains. Agricultural tractors, cranes etc. are classified to plant & equipment as are road making vehicles but machinery and equipment which form an integral part of buildings such as lifts are classified to buildings. Vehicles includes railway rolling stock, ships and aircraft.

The CSO post-war investment series come from data on capital expenditure in the censuses of production and company accounts (see CSO 1985). The inter-war data, in general are based on Feinstein's estimates in Feinstein (1965). The CSO use Dean's backward projections of Feinstein's inter-war series for the years before 1920. We have continued to use the CSO series from 1920 but have altered the pre-1920 data to take account of new estimates of investment available in Feinstein and Pollard (1988). These new data were spliced onto the CSO series in 1920. War damage was assumed to equal 3% of the capital stock between 1939 and 1945. This estimate was taken from Maddison (1991). The use of Feinstein's revised pre-1920 and his inter-war investment data in calculating standardized capital stocks may lead to inconsistencies since his capital formation series are frequently based not on measures of annual capital expenditure but rather on direct estimates of the gross stock and assumed service lives. Feinstein frequently estimates gross capital formation as the difference between two years' capital stocks plus scrapping, the latter being investment from some previous period depending on the service life assumed. Therefore, reducing the UK service lives to those in the USA *within* the period covered by Feinstein would lead to results inconsistent with his estimated stocks. Post-war capital formation data are, however, based on flows of capital expenditures so that reducing the asset life does not lead to an inconsistency but does involve the implicit assumption that the service life has declined in the post-war period.

B.   United States

The US investment data come directly from the BEA, US Department of Commerce. Detailed data are available for 61 sectors (21 in manufacturing) and 50 asset types both at current and constant prices. The BEA data source contains series from 1921 for most types of equipment (including vehicles). Some equipment series, notably office machinery and trucks, were only available from 1933 but in most industries investment in these assets was very small relative to the total in 1933. The growth rates of equipment investment for which information from 1921 to 1933 was available were applied to the series with missing values to yield consistent equipment data from 1921. Information on investment was available from 1900 for most types of structures but missing values were extrapolated backwards using a similar technique to that employed for equipment.

C.   Germany

Investment data for West Germany come from two sources. Data for the period 1850–1960 are available in Kirner (1968). These distinguish equipment and structures for 20 sectors and adjust for changes in the geographic boundaries in Germany over this period. The data are presented in constant prices but Kirner also presents the price deflators used. Kirner adjusted his investment data for war damage. Data for the period 1960–88 are contained in Statistisches Bundesamt (1991). These data distinguish structures and equipment and are available for over 50 sectors at 1985 prices. Separate data on investment in vehicles are not recorded. The German statistical office does not follow accounting conventions in that both the values of breeding livestock and the value of social infrastructure capital such as roads and bridges are not included (see Lützel (1977)). For both reasons the value of German aggregate capital will be underestimated.

D.   France

In many respects the French data is the least complete, the historical data is about equivalent in coverage to that of Japan but the recent detailed data are available only from 1970. Against this, these current data are more detailed, in terms of their disaggregation into asset types, than those for the other European countries. Unpublished data on investment by industry and asset type, at both current and constant prices, were obtained from INSEE. These cover 36 sectors of which 19 are in manufacturing and distinguish 10 asset types, i.e. agricultural products (livestock), building and other materials, metal products, mechanical products, electrical & electronic products, household durable goods, cars & other transport equipment, ships & aircraft, furniture & fixtures, and buildings & civil engineering; the data include a separate estimate for transfer costs.

From 1959 to 1970 real investment by broad sector were available from the OECD national accounts, and Carré et al. (1976) present real investment data by broad sector. Neither source gives a breakdown by asset type but a division into buildings and equipment, for selected years from 1949 to 1966, is given in Carré et al. This series, completed by linear interpolation, was used to derive the proportions of structures and equipment by applying the aggregate proportions to all sectors.

The pre-1949 data is very sparse. Carré et al. give a single figure for investment from 1946 to 1949 and indexes of aggregate investment both for structures and equipment from 1896 to 1913 and 1922 to 1938. No data appear to be available for the years covering the two world wars. We completed these series by assuming that investment during the wars were half their pre-war values during the wars and equalled their immediate pre-war estimate in the year after the end of hostilities. These indexes were spliced onto the post-war series in 1949 for each sector so that movements in investment in structures and equipment were assumed to be the same across all sectors. War damage was assumed to be 8% of the pre-1919 capital stock and a further 8% of the pre-1945 capital stock – these estimates come from Maddison (1991).

E. Japan

In terms of coverage, the Japanese data is by far the poorest of the five countries considered here. From 1965 to 1988 data are available for private enterprises from the Economic Planning Agency (EPA) at constant 1985 prices for ten broad industrial sectors and, in addition, for fifteen sub-sectors in manufacturing. The industrial sectors were agriculture, mining, manufacturing, construction, retail, transport & communication, utilities, finance & insurance, real estate and other services. These data are limited in that they do not distinguish investment by asset type or include estimates for the public sector. Also a single deflator (not published) is used for all forms of investment. Despite these shortcomings the EPA data were the most readily available by sector and so are used in this study (but see Dean *et al.* (1990) for a discussion of various sources of manufacturing capital input).

Data on private enterprise investment are available, at current prices, from the OECD national accounts for the years 1952 to 1970, for six industrial sectors. These were deflated by the investment deflator for those years given in Ohkawa and Shinohara (1979). The average proportions for the first five years of the 1970s were used to break down these six sectors into the ten available in the EPA data. From 1905 to 1940 Ohkawa and Rosovsky (1973) give investment at constant prices for five sectors, agriculture, mining & manufacturing, facilitating industries (transport and communication and public utilities), construction and services. There are no data by industry from 1941 to 1951 but Ohkawa and Rosovsky present estimates of non-residential investment, in constant prices, in the private sector. The average proportions for the early 1950s were used to breakdown investment data into sectors pre-1952.

For the public sector, investment data were taken from the OECD national accounts, for the years 1970 to 1989, excluding investment in residential buildings by public enterprises. From 1940 to 1970 data were taken from Ohkawa and Rosovsky (1973) and for the pre-1940 period from Ohkawa and Shinohara (1979). All series were available at constant prices. Following Maddison (1991) war damage was assumed to equal 27.5% of the 1939–45 capital stock.

The Economic Planning Agency has not published investment data by asset type since World War II. Nevertheless, the OECD national accounts do include such a breakdown, for aggregate investment, from

1970. Ohkawa and Shinohara (1979) include a breakdown into structures and plant & machinery for aggregate investment for the period before 1940. The proportions for the aggregate economy in the intervening years were estimated by simple linear interpolation from 1946 to 1970 where the proportions in 1946 were set equal to their 1935 values. The share of structures declined dramatically after 1935 with the pre-war build-up. This emphasis on plant & machinery probably continued throughout the war so the 1940 structures share was used for the years 1941–45.

Examination of the data by sector for other countries showed that the importance of structures in total investment varied considerably across sectors so that use of the single aggregate proportions for all sectors would not be appropriate. For the immediate post-war years the proportions of structures in each sector's total investment were assumed to be as follows: agriculture, 30%; energy, 50%; manufacturing, 25%; construction, 15%; transport & communications, 40%; retailing, 40%; finance & insurance, 65%; and other services & government, 80%. These proportions were based approximately on averages over the other four countries. For remaining years the proportions of structures in each sector was assumed to follow the trends for the aggregate economy.

Appendix table B.   Gross capital stocks by sector, billions 1985 $.
I. United States, equipment

	AF	MU	MF	CR	TC	RR	FI	SE	TOT
1948	73.6	63.2	225.0	31.3	118.6	47.7	19.5	212.5	791.4
1949	83.2	68.4	237.3	33.5	126.5	50.1	22.0	216.0	837.0
1950	92.6	74.8	250.6	37.0	134.0	54.0	26.1	220.7	890.0
1951	100.5	80.9	267.9	41.0	143.3	58.4	30.2	226.9	949.0
1952	107.4	89.2	285.2	44.8	153.1	62.5	33.5	236.7	1,012.4
1953	114.1	98.2	301.9	47.8	163.5	68.1	38.6	245.4	1,077.5
1954	119.2	106.7	317.3	50.2	170.5	74.1	43.5	248.1	1,129.6
1955	124.7	114.3	331.6	53.0	178.3	82.0	50.3	243.9	1,178.1
1956	128.4	122.5	350.2	53.9	188.8	87.1	57.2	233.2	1,221.3
1957	130.9	131.1	368.5	54.4	200.4	90.6	62.6	218.9	1,257.3
1958	132.7	138.6	379.1	54.4	206.0	92.1	66.1	202.6	1,271.6
1959	133.2	146.6	387.9	54.7	214.6	94.6	71.8	187.3	1,290.7
1960	130.9	153.1	397.6	54.9	224.3	98.0	75.7	174.4	1,308.8
1961	127.6	158.8	403.7	54.5	233.0	101.0	78.9	165.3	1,322.8
1962	124.8	164.4	410.9	54.5	243.0	105.5	81.6	162.3	1,347.1
1963	123.6	170.2	419.0	55.3	252.2	110.6	84.6	165.3	1,380.8
1964	124.0	176.0	431.1	57.5	262.6	116.3	88.8	172.3	1,428.5
1965	126.5	182.8	449.2	60.1	275.8	124.1	94.2	179.9	1,492.6
1966	130.8	191.6	472.7	62.7	289.7	133.7	101.7	187.7	1,570.5
1967	135.8	199.4	493.9	63.9	303.1	141.6	110.7	195.3	1,643.7
1968	140.2	208.1	515.2	65.8	318.9	152.7	122.2	202.1	1,725.3
1969	144.7	217.3	539.0	68.6	337.6	165.8	134.8	209.3	1,817.2
1970	151.5	228.1	559.8	71.3	353.4	176.5	146.7	216.4	1,903.6
1971	158.4	239.0	575.7	73.5	367.8	186.9	159.2	224.9	1,985.4
1972	165.5	251.9	596.7	75.7	383.6	201.0	175.3	235.7	2,085.4
1973	176.7	267.3	622.4	80.6	408.5	220.5	194.6	244.8	2,215.4
1974	186.8	286.1	657.6	84.7	431.5	234.5	211.4	254.5	2,347.1
1975	194.0	301.1	686.5	85.3	448.7	242.4	225.1	262.9	2,445.9
1976	202.1	313.9	715.5	85.1	466.5	254.1	239.3	271.1	2,547.6
1977	211.1	332.3	750.6	86.2	490.6	267.6	258.1	280.6	2,677.0
1978	218.5	349.1	792.3	90.5	524.8	283.4	280.0	290.7	2,829.3
1979	227.8	367.4	832.9	94.2	564.1	299.4	305.0	299.0	2,990.0
1980	231.9	385.0	872.2	95.5	598.3	308.8	325.3	306.9	3,124.0
1981	233.2	401.4	907.0	96.7	628.1	320.1	344.8	314.4	3,245.8
1982	229.9	415.1	931.2	90.7	649.7	330.1	362.6	321.7	3,331.0
1983	224.4	423.0	942.2	84.8	671.4	350.5	386.2	331.7	3,414.2
1984	217.4	430.5	960.0	80.0	690.5	382.4	419.9	343.4	3,524.1
1985	208.2	445.5	982.5	76.3	707.9	411.0	459.7	359.7	3,650.8
1986	197.0	454.8	997.1	73.1	727.2	455.6	503.6	375.6	3,774.0
1987	185.7	462.8	1,011.2	69.4	744.7	482.7	552.3	394.8	3,903.5
1988	175.0	468.1	1,029.3	65.6	761.9	526.2	613.8	417.7	4,057.7
1989	164.5	463.9	1,054.5	61.5	778.3	570.4	681.7	443.4	4,218.2

Notes: AF = agriculture, forestry & fishing; MU = mining & utilities; MF = manufacturing; CR = construction; TC = transport & communication; RR = retailing & repairing; FI = finance, insurance, business services & real estate; SE = other services and public administration.

Appendix table B. Gross capital stocks by sector, billions 1985 $. II. United States, structures

	AF	MU	MF	CR	TC	RR	FI	SE	TOT
1948	73.9	260.5	183.0	2.2	426.7	114.4	218.5	910.3	2,189.4
1949	75.1	269.7	182.0	2.2	418.8	114.8	220.4	935.7	2,218.6
1950	76.3	279.7	181.4	2.3	410.0	115.7	224.7	965.0	2,255.0
1951	77.3	290.0	185.0	2.4	402.2	115.0	228.9	996.2	2,297.0
1952	78.7	301.9	188.9	2.5	394.9	113.3	232.3	1,030.2	2,342.6
1953	79.6	316.7	191.6	2.5	388.5	113.6	236.9	1,067.1	2,396.6
1954	80.4	331.9	193.4	2.6	381.8	114.7	244.3	1,109.8	2,458.9
1955	81.2	348.3	195.4	2.7	375.6	116.3	253.3	1,151.8	2,524.6
1956	82.1	367.0	202.6	2.8	371.5	117.8	261.9	1,194.0	2,599.7
1957	82.8	385.9	209.4	2.9	367.4	120.0	270.7	1,238.8	2,677.9
1958	83.6	403.6	212.6	3.0	360.3	123.2	280.4	1,288.7	2,755.3
1959	85.3	420.5	214.9	3.1	355.3	127.5	291.6	1,340.4	2,838.7
1960	86.7	437.5	221.4	3.2	351.2	132.0	303.2	1,293.7	2,928.8
1961	88.4	454.5	228.1	3.6	346.4	137.4	316.3	1,451.0	3,025.8
1962	90.5	471.8	234.6	4.0	341.8	142.7	331.9	1,509.6	3,126.8
1963	92.7	487.6	242.0	4.7	339.0	149.2	345.4	1,574.2	3,234.9
1964	95.1	505.8	250.9	5.1	336.5	157.3	360.1	1,642.4	3,353.3
1965	97.8	525.8	266.3	5.6	334.7	166.8	379.1	1,714.3	3,490.5
1966	100.8	545.7	286.8	6.3	334.0	176.1	397.3	1,789.9	3,636.8
1967	104.6	566.0	306.3	7.3	333.3	185.4	413.6	1,867.2	3,783.7
1968	108.1	588.3	323.1	8.2	334.0	195.0	431.4	1,947.2	3,935.3
1969	111.7	610.6	340.7	9.4	335.9	205.3	451.7	2,019.8	4,085.1
1970	116.1	630.6	355.8	10.8	338.9	217.2	470.6	2,085.9	4,225.9
1971	120.4	647.8	367.0	12.1	341.8	229.9	491.5	2,149.0	4,359.5
1972	124.0	666.2	376.5	13.5	344.7	243.7	513.5	2,209.0	4,491.0
1973	129.0	684.6	386.3	15.3	349.2	260.1	535.9	2,269.9	4,630.3
1974	135.0	702.0	399.3	17.6	354.3	276.3	551.1	2,331.0	4,766.5
1975	141.4	717.4	409.0	19.7	359.0	289.3	561.3	2,386.8	4,883.8
1976	148.0	730.1	418.4	21.9	365.5	299.8	571.1	2,437.8	4,992.6
1977	154.5	744.9	426.7	23.7	370.7	309.0	585.1	2,483.1	5,097.6
1978	161.4	760.7	436.9	25.4	376.6	323.2	600.0	2,531.2	5,215.4
1979	167.7	776.8	450.4	27.0	383.6	339.9	619.5	2,575.0	5,339.9
1980	172.7	798.9	462.0	28.3	390.3	356.7	642.7	2,617.7	5,469.2
1981	176.1	829.4	472.9	29.4	397.0	374.9	668.0	2,653.4	5,601.0
1982	178.0	855.7	482.2	30.4	402.6	392.0	695.9	2,684.5	5,721.2
1983	179.2	873.0	486.4	31.2	407.0	409.2	722.5	2,715.1	5,823.5
1984	180.1	895.7	492.4	32.1	412.2	430.0	754.7	2,748.5	5,945.6
1985	180.0	916.7	499.5	32.9	418.0	457.3	792.6	2,787.9	6,084.7
1986	179.5	928.8	503.9	33.6	422.5	480.0	828.9	2,830.5	6,207.7
1987	178.8	931.5	507.3	34.4	426.7	500.9	865.1	2,877.5	6,322.1
1988	178.0	936.6	510.9	35.1	431.2	521.4	901.1	2,920.6	6,434.9
1989	176.8	935.0	517.0	35.8	434.6	541.5	935.9	2,967.3	6,543.9

Notes: AF = agriculture, forestry & fishing; MU = mining & utilities; MF = manufacturing; CR = construction; TC = transport & communication; RR = retailing & repairing; FI = finance, insurance, business services & real estate; SE = other services and public administration.

Appendix table B.   Gross capital stocks by sector, billions 1985 $.
III. United States, total assets

	AF	MU	MF	CR	TC	RR	FI	SE	TOT
1948	147.5	323.7	408.0	33.5	545.3	162.1	238.0	1,122.8	2,980.8
1949	158.3	338.1	419.3	35.8	545.3	164.9	242.4	1,151.7	3,055.6
1950	168.9	354.5	432.0	39.3	544.0	169.7	250.8	1,185.7	3,145.0
1951	177.8	370.9	452.9	43.4	545.4	173.4	259.1	1,223.1	3,246.0
1952	186.1	391.0	474.1	47.3	548.0	175.8	265.8	1,266.9	3,355.0
1953	193.7	414.9	493.5	50.3	552.0	181.8	275.5	1,312.5	3,474.1
1954	199.6	438.6	510.7	52.8	552.3	188.7	287.7	1,357.9	3,588.5
1955	206.0	462.6	527.0	55.7	553.9	198.3	303.6	1,395.7	3,702.7
1956	210.5	489.5	552.8	56.7	560.3	204.9	319.1	1,427.2	3,821.0
1957	213.7	517.0	577.9	57.3	567.8	210.6	333.3	1,457.7	3,935.2
1958	216.3	542.2	591.7	57.4	566.3	215.3	346.5	1,491.3	4,027.0
1959	218.5	567.1	602.8	57.8	569.9	222.1	363.4	1,527.7	4,129.4
1960	217.6	590.5	618.9	58.1	575.5	230.0	378.9	1,568.1	4,237.6
1961	215.9	613.3	631.8	58.1	579.6	238.3	395.2	1,616.4	4,348.6
1962	215.3	636.2	645.5	58.5	584.8	248.2	413.5	1,671.9	4,473.9
1963	216.3	657.8	661.0	60.0	591.2	259.8	430.0	1,739.5	4,615.7
1964	219.0	681.8	682.0	62.6	599.1	273.6	449.0	1,814.7	4,781.8
1965	224.2	708.7	715.4	65.7	610.5	290.9	473.4	1,894.2	4,983.1
1966	231.5	737.3	759.5	69.0	623.6	309.8	499.1	1,977.6	5,207.3
1967	240.4	765.4	800.3	71.2	636.4	326.9	524.3	2,062.5	5,427.4
1968	248.3	796.4	838.4	74.1	652.9	347.7	553.6	2,149.3	5,660.6
1969	256.4	827.9	879.7	78.0	673.6	371.1	586.5	2,229.1	5,902.3
1970	267.6	858.7	915.7	82.1	692.3	393.6	617.3	2,302.3	6,129.5
1971	278.8	886.8	942.7	85.6	709.6	416.9	650.6	2,373.9	6,344.9
1972	289.5	918.1	973.2	89.2	728.2	444.7	688.8	2,444.7	6,576.4
1973	305.7	951.9	1,008.7	95.9	757.7	480.6	730.5	2,514.6	6,845.7
1974	321.8	988.2	1,056.8	102.3	785.8	510.8	762.5	2,585.5	7,113.6
1975	335.4	1,018.5	1,095.4	105.0	807.6	531.7	786.3	2,649.7	7,329.8
1976	350.1	1,044.0	1,133.9	107.0	832.0	553.8	810.3	2,709.0	7,540.1
1977	365.6	1,077.1	1,177.3	109.9	861.3	576.6	843.1	2,763.7	7.774.6
1978	379.9	1,109.8	1,229.1	115.9	901.5	606.6	880.0	2,822.0	8,044.7
1979	395.6	1,144.3	1,283.3	121.2	947.7	639.2	924.5	2,874.0	8,329.8
1980	404.6	1,183.9	1,334.1	123.8	988.7	665.5	968.0	2,924.6	8,593.1
1981	409.3	1,230.8	1,379.9	126.1	1,025.1	695.0	1,012.8	2,967.8	8846.8
1982	407.9	1,270.8	1,413.4	121.0	1,052.3	722.0	1,058.5	3,006.2	9,052.2
1983	403.6	1,296.0	1,428.6	116.1	1,078.2	759.7	1,108.7	3,046.8	9,237.8
1984	397.6	1,326.2	1,452.4	112.1	1,102.7	812.4	1,174.6	3,091.9	9,469.8
1985	388.2	1,362.2	1,482.0	109.2	1,125.8	868.3	1,252.2	3,147.5	9,735.5
1986	376.5	1,383.6	1,501.0	106.7	1,149.8	925.6	1,332.4	3,206.1	9,981.7
1987	364.5	1,394.4	1,518.5	103.7	1,171.4	983.6	1,417.3	3,272.2	10,225.6
1988	353.0	1,404.8	1,540.3	100.7	1,193.1	1,047.6	1,515.0	3,338.2	10,492.6
1989	341.4	1,398.9	1,571.5	97.3	1,212.9	1,111.8	1,617.7	3,410.7	10,762.1

Notes: AF = agriculture, forestry & fishing; MU = mining & utilities; MF = manufacturing; CR = construction; TC = transport & communication; RR = retailing & repairing; FI = finance, insurance, business services & real estate; SE = other services and public administration.

Appendix table B.   Gross capital stocks by sector, billions 1985 $.
IV. United Kingdom, equipment

	AF	MU	MF	CR	TC	RR	FI	SE	TOT
1948	8.4	28.9	53.5	1.0	29.6	3.6	0.9	2.6	128.5
1949	9.3	29.8	55.9	1.3	30.6	3.8	0.9	2.8	134.3
1950	10.1	30.8	58.9	1.5	31.2	4.2	0.9	3.2	140.7
1951	10.8	32.0	62.0	1.9	31.6	4.6	1.0	3.5	147.5
1952	11.4	33.3	64.6	2.2	31.6	5.2	1.1	3.8	153.3
1953	11.9	34.8	66.9	2.6	31.9	6.0	1.2	4.2	159.3
1954	12.4	36.7	68.7	3.0	32.6	6.8	1.4	4.6	166.1
1955	13.0	39.1	70.6	3.3	33.6	7.8	1.6	5.1	174.1
1956	13.3	41.4	73.0	3.6	35.0	8.6	1.8	5.7	182.5
1957	13.6	43.9	76.1	3.9	37.1	9.3	2.0	6.4	192.4
1958	14.0	46.9	79.3	4.2	39.1	10.1	2.2	7.1	202.9
1959	14.4	50.5	82.7	4.4	41.2	11.1	2.4	8.0	214.7
1960	14.5	53.9	87.5	4.7	43.9	12.1	2.7	8.8	228.1
1961	14.6	57.4	94.2	5.1	46.7	13.3	2.9	9.7	243.9
1962	14.5	61.3	100.4	5.4	48.8	14.4	3.2	10.6	258.7
1963	14.6	66.2	105.6	5.8	51.0	15.7	3.6	11.5	274.1
1964	14.8	71.5	111.5	6.5	53.3	17.2	4.0	12.5	291.4
1965	14.9	76.6	118.3	7.2	55.8	18.6	4.3	13.3	309.2
1966	15.1	82.5	124.9	7.8	58.2	19.8	4.7	14.3	327.2
1967	15.3	88.6	130.7	8.4	60.9	20.9	5.0	15.3	345.1
1968	15.6	92.8	137.1	9.1	64.2	22.2	5.7	16.4	363.0
1969	15.6	95.4	143.9	9.7	67.0	23.5	6.5	17.6	379.2
1970	15.7	96.9	151.2	10.2	70.5	24.6	7.8	18.9	395.8
1971	15.7	98.2	157.1	10.4	73.7	25.9	9.3	20.4	410.7
1972	15.9	98.9	161.6	10.7	76.4	27.7	10.7	21.8	423.7
1973	16.3	99.0	166.8	11.1	79.8	29.7	12.8	23.4	439.1
1974	16.5	99.3	173.0	11.6	82.6	31.6	14.9	24.9	454.4
1975	16.5	100.2	177.4	11.7	84.2	32.7	17.0	26.3	466.0
1976	16.7	102.1	181.2	11.7	86.1	33.7	19.6	27.6	478.7
1977	16.9	103.1	185.3	11.6	87.8	35.4	22.9	28.9	492.0
1978	17.1	104.2	189.8	11.6	89.9	37.4	27.6	29.9	507.5
1979	17.0	105.2	194.4	11.7	92.4	39.8	33.5	31.2	525.1
1980	16.5	105.9	196.8	11.5	94.8	41.4	39.7	32.5	539.0
1981	15.9	106.3	195.9	11.1	95.4	42.5	46.1	33.5	546.8
1982	15.4	106.2	194.7	10.8	95.2	43.6	52.7	34.7	553.3
1983	14.8	106.0	193.4	10.5	95.8	44.5	58.9	36.1	560.1
1984	14.1	104.9	193.1	10.1	96.5	46.1	66.9	37.6	569.1
1985	13.1	103.8	193.5	9.6	97.6	47.8	77.4	39.2	582.0
1986	12.2	102.9	193.8	9.1	98.6	49.5	87.0	40.9	593.9
1987	11.1	101.5	194.7	8.8	99.7	51.5	99.0	42.4	608.8
1988	10.2	100.5	196.6	8.9	102.7	54.4	114.3	44.5	632.0
1989	9.6	98.5	199.3	9.3	105.6	58.0	130.6	47.1	658.0

Notes: AF = agriculture, forestry & fishing; MU = mining & utilities; MF = manufacturing; CR = construction; TC = transport & communication; RR = retailing & repairing; FI = finance, insurance, business services & real estate; SE = other services and public administration.

Appendix table B.   Gross capital stocks by sector, billions 1985 $.
V. United Kingdom, structures

	AF	MU	MF	CR	TC	RR	FI	SE	TOT
1948	5.3	14.5	33.3	0.9	13.0	7.6	11.3	67.5	153.4
1949	5.5	15.0	33.6	0.9	13.1	7.6	11.4	67.5	154.6
1950	5.7	15.8	34.1	1.0	13.2	7.8	11.6	67.7	156.8
1951	5.8	16.3	34.4	1.0	13.3	7.9	11.8	68.0	158.6
1952	5.9	17.0	34.9	1.0	13.5	8.1	12.1	68.4	160.8
1953	6.1	17.9	35.4	1.1	13.7	8.2	12.4	68.9	163.7
1954	6.2	18.9	36.1	1.2	13.9	8.5	12.8	69.6	167.2
1955	6.4	20.0	37.2	1.2	14.1	8.9	13.3	70.6	171.9
1956	6.6	21.1	39.0	1.4	14.4	9.3	14.0	71.8	177.7
1957	6.8	22.5	40.8	1.4	14.9	9.8	14.7	73.4	184.4
1958	7.0	23.8	42.4	1.5	15.7	10.3	15.5	75.5	191.7
1959	7.4	25.2	44.0	1.6	16.6	10.9	16.4	76.7	198.6
1960	7.8	26.4	45.9	1.6	17.6	11.7	17.6	79.4	208.0
1961	8.3	27.6	48.4	1.7	18.7	12.6	18.9	83.0	219.2
1962	8.8	29.0	50.6	1.8	19.5	13.5	20.4	87.5	231.1
1963	9.4	30.4	52.2	1.8	20.1	14.4	21.9	92.1	242.4
1964	10.0	32.3	54.0	2.0	21.0	15.5	23.6	97.9	256.2
1965	10.6	34.5	56.1	2.1	21.9	17.1	25.3	103.8	271.4
1966	11.1	37.0	57.9	2.3	23.1	18.6	26.9	109.8	286.7
1967	11.8	40.0	59.2	2.4	24.2	20.1	28.9	117.3	303.9
1968	12.5	42.8	60.6	2.6	25.4	21.7	30.9	125.6	322.2
1969	13.3	45.2	62.5	2.8	26.6	23.5	33.0	133.9	340.8
1970	14.2	47.5	64.4	2.9	27.7	25.3	35.2	143.0	360.3
1971	15.2	49.7	65.9	2.9	28.9	27.4	37.8	152.1	379.9
1972	16.2	51.5	66.9	3.0	30.0	29.4	40.1	161.3	398.3
1973	17.1	53.1	67.7	3.1	31.0	31.2	42.9	171.1	417.2
1974	18.0	55.7	68.4	3.2	32.0	32.8	45.9	178.9	434.9
1975	18.7	60.2	69.0	3.4	33.0	34.1	48.3	186.0	452.7
1976	19.3	65.0	69.2	3.5	34.1	35.3	51.0	193.0	470.3
1977	19.8	69.2	69.6	3.6	35.3	36.7	53.5	198.6	486.2
1978	20.5	72.9	70.3	3.7	36.5	38.2	55.5	203.5	501.2
1979	21.2	75.8	71.1	3.7	37.7	40.1	57.9	208.1	515.8
1980	21.9	78.6	71.5	3.8	38.6	41.9	60.4	212.4	529.1
1981	22.5	81.7	71.4	3.8	39.3	43.4	63.2	216.4	541.5
1982	23.2	84.9	70.9	3.8	39.9	45.0	66.4	221.5	555.6
1983	24.0	87.9	70.2	3.9	40.8	46.6	69.7	226.6	569.6
1984	24.8	91.0	69.7	3.9	41.8	48.6	73.0	232.6	585.3
1985	25.4	93.6	69.4	3.9	42.8	50.8	76.2	238.8	600.9
1986	25.8	95.9	68.8	3.9	43.8	53.5	80.0	245.5	617.0
1987	26.3	97.8	68.2	3.9	44.8	56.9	85.5	252.5	636.1
1988	26.7	99.5	67.9	4.0	46.2	60.8	92.6	259.6	657.4
1989	27.0	100.7	67.3	4.0	47.6	65.1	100.3	268.0	680.0

Notes: AF = agriculture, forestry & fishing; MU = mining & utilities; MF = manufacturing; CR = construction; TC = transport & communication; RR = retailing &
repairing; FI = finance, insurance, business services & real estate; SE = other
services and public administration.

Appendix table B. Gross capital stocks by sector, billions 1985 $.
VI. United Kingdom, total assets

	AF	MU	MF	CR	TC	RR	FI	SE	TOT
1948	13.6	43.5	86.8	1.9	42.6	11.2	12.2	70.1	281.8
1949	14.8	44.8	89.6	2.2	43.6	11.4	12.2	70.3	288.9
1950	15.8	46.6	92.9	2.5	44.4	11.9	12.5	70.9	297.5
1951	16.6	48.4	96.5	2.9	44.9	12.5	12.8	71.5	306.1
1952	17.3	50.3	99.5	3.3	45.1	13.3	13.1	72.2	314.1
1953	17.9	52.6	102.2	3.7	45.7	14.2	13.6	73.1	323.0
1954	18.6	55.6	104.7	4.1	46.5	15.3	14.2	74.2	333.3
1955	19.4	59.1	107.8	4.6	47.7	16.7	15.0	75.7	346.0
1956	19.9	62.5	112.0	5.0	49.5	17.9	15.8	77.6	360.2
1957	20.5	66.4	116.9	5.3	52.0	19.1	16.7	79.8	376.7
1958	21.1	70.7	121.7	5.6	54.7	20.4	17.7	82.6	394.6
1959	21.8	75.7	126.7	5.9	57.8	22.0	18.8	84.6	413.3
1960	22.3	80.2	133.4	6.3	61.6	23.8	20.2	88.3	436.2
1961	22.9	85.0	142.6	6.8	65.3	25.9	21.8	92.8	463.1
1962	23.4	90.3	151.0	7.1	68.3	27.9	23.7	98.1	489.9
1963	24.0	96.6	157.8	7.7	71.1	30.1	25.5	103.6	516.5
1964	24.8	103.8	165.6	8.5	74.3	32.7	27.7	110.3	547.6
1965	25.5	111.1	174.4	9.4	77.7	35.7	29.6	117.1	580.6
1966	26.2	119.5	182.8	10.0	81.3	38.3	31.6	124.1	613.9
1967	27.1	128.6	189.9	10.9	85.1	40.9	33.9	132.6	649.0
1968	28.1	135.5	197.7	11.7	89.6	43.9	36.6	142.0	685.2
1969	29.0	140.6	206.4	12.4	93.6	46.9	39.5	151.6	720.0
1970	29.9	144.5	215.6	13.0	98.2	49.9	43.1	161.9	756.1
1971	30.9	148.0	223.1	13.4	102.5	53.3	47.1	172.5	790.7
1972	32.1	150.4	228.4	13.6	106.5	57.0	50.8	183.1	822.0
1973	33.5	152.1	234.5	14.2	110.9	60.8	55.7	194.4	856.2
1974	34.5	154.9	241.4	14.8	114.6	64.4	60.8	203.8	889.2
1975	35.2	160.3	246.4	15.1	117.3	66.8	65.3	212.3	918.7
1976	36.0	167.0	250.4	15.2	120.2	69.0	70.6	220.7	949.1
1977	36.8	172.3	254.9	15.2	123.1	72.1	76.2	227.5	978.2
1978	37.6	177.2	260.2	15.3	126.4	75.6	83.1	233.4	1,008.7
1979	38.2	181.0	265.5	15.4	130.2	79.9	91.4	239.3	1,040.9
1980	38.4	184.5	268.3	15.3	133.4	83.3	100.1	244.9	1,068.2
1981	38.4	188.0	267.3	14.9	134.7	85.9	109.2	249.9	1,088.3
1982	38.6	191.1	265.6	14.6	135.1	88.6	119.2	256.1	1,108.9
1983	38.8	193.9	263.6	14.4	136.6	91.2	128.5	262.7	1,129.7
1984	38.9	195.9	262.8	14.0	138.3	94.7	139.8	270.2	1,154.4
1985	38.5	197.4	262.9	13.5	140.4	98.6	153.6	278.0	1,182.9
1986	38.0	198.8	262.6	13.1	142.4	102.8	167.0	286.3	1,210.9
1987	37.4	199.3	263.0	12.7	144.6	108.4	184.5	294.9	1,244.9
1988	36.9	200.0	264.5	13.0	148.8	115.2	206.9	304.1	1,289.3
1989	36.7	199.3	266.7	13.3	153.2	123.1	230.8	315.0	1,338.0

Notes: AF = agriculture, forestry & fishing; MU = mining & utilities; MF = manufacturing; CR = construction; TC = transport & communication; RR = retailing & repairing; FI = finance, insurance, business services & real estate; SE = other services and public administration.

Appendix table B. Gross capital stocks by sector, billions 1985 $.
VII. Germany, equipment

	AF	MU	MF	CR	TC	RR	FI	SE	TOT
1948	7.0	9.7	32.1	1.3	14.1	2.5	0.2	4.9	71.8
1949	6.9	10.4	34.2	1.3	15.0	3.0	0.3	4.8	75.9
1950	7.3	11.4	37.1	1.5	15.9	3.6	0.3	4.8	81.9
1951	6.9	12.7	40.5	1.6	16.8	4.2	0.4	4.8	88.1
1952	7.6	14.1	43.9	1.8	17.8	4.9	0.5	4.8	95.7
1953	8.0	16.0	47.5	2.2	19.4	5.6	0.7	4.9	104.2
1954	9.0	18.1	51.8	2.7	21.0	6.4	0.8	5.0	114.8
1955	10.6	20.2	57.5	3.5	23.0	7.6	0.9	5.4	128.7
1956	12.3	21.8	63.3	4.5	25.0	9.2	1.1	6.0	143.1
1957	14.0	23.5	69.0	5.4	26.8	10.8	1.2	6.7	157.3
1958	16.0	25.4	74.9	6.2	28.7	12.3	1.4	7.5	172.4
1959	18.3	27.3	81.7	7.5	30.9	13.8	1.5	8.9	189.9
1960	20.8	29.2	91.2	9.0	33.2	15.7	1.6	10.6	211.4
1961	23.7	31.3	102.4	10.9	36.0	17.6	1.8	12.6	236.2
1962	26.3	33.8	114.5	12.8	39.1	19.9	1.9	14.7	262.9
1963	28.5	36.2	126.3	14.5	42.7	22.2	2.1	17.0	289.4
1964	31.1	38.8	139.5	16.2	46.0	24.4	2.2	19.5	317.8
1965	34.1	41.2	154.1	17.7	49.3	26.6	2.4	22.5	347.9
1966	36.3	43.1	168.3	18.5	52.3	28.8	2.5	25.8	375.7
1967	37.5	45.0	179.8	19.3	55.6	30.1	2.7	29.2	399.1
1968	38.3	46.3	192.0	20.1	59.0	31.6	2.8	32.7	422.7
1969	39.7	47.2	207.6	21.3	62.7	33.0	3.2	37.1	451.8
1970	40.9	48.6	225.9	22.6	67.2	34.6	3.6	42.4	485.7
1971	41.3	50.8	243.5	23.9	72.5	36.1	4.0	47.9	519.9
1972	41.6	53.4	258.3	24.9	77.6	37.4	4.4	53.5	551.2
1973	42.3	55.9	270.8	25.3	82.2	38.8	4.9	60.2	580.3
1974	42.1	58.7	280.6	24.7	86.3	38.9	5.4	65.8	602.4
1975	41.7	61.5	288.6	24.3	89.3	38.9	5.9	72.3	622.6
1976	41.6	63.6	297.1	24.1	92.2	39.4	6.5	79.7	644.1
1977	42.0	64.9	305.5	24.0	95.3	40.4	7.1	89.1	668.3
1978	42.7	66.2	313.3	24.1	98.7	41.5	7.8	100.5	694.7
1979	43.3	67.2	322.0	24.4	101.8	42.5	8.4	114.2	723.8
1980	43.6	68.4	331.2	24.2	105.0	43.2	9.1	128.0	752.8
1981	43.6	70.0	338.7	23.2	108.6	43.3	9.7	141.1	778.3
1982	43.5	72.9	343.7	22.0	111.4	42.9	10.4	151.2	798.0
1983	43.6	75.6	348.4	21.2	114.7	42.8	11.4	161.5	819.3
1984	43.4	78.5	350.8	20.6	117.5	42.6	12.2	172.7	838.3
1985	43.3	81.1	355.2	20.2	121.1	42.7	13.1	184.1	860.7
1986	43.1	83.5	360.5	19.9	124.0	43.2	14.1	195.9	884.3
1987	42.6	85.8	366.7	19.5	126.2	44.4	14.9	209.2	909.4
1988	42.4	87.5	373.3	18.9	128.3	46.2	15.9	224.8	937.3
1989	41.9	89.0	380.1	18.2	130.4	48.0	16.9	240.5	965.1

Notes: AF = agriculture, forestry & fishing; MU = mining & utilities; MF = manufacturing; CR = construction; TC = transport & communication; RR = retailing & repairing; FI = finance, insurance, business services & real estate; SE = other services and public administration.

Appendix table B.   Gross capital stocks by sector, billions 1985 $.
VIII. Germany, structures

	AF	MU	MF	CR	TC	RR	FI	SE	TOT
1948	24.7	11.5	36.6	0.7	69.3	7.7	3.3	155.2	309.0
1949	24.2	12.0	39.0	0.8	69.7	7.9	3.8	155.7	313.1
1950	24.1	12.9	42.3	0.8	69.2	8.4	4.5	157.8	320.1
1951	23.9	14.0	45.7	0.9	68.4	8.8	5.1	159.3	326.1
1952	23.6	15.2	48.8	0.9	67.7	9.1	5.8	160.6	331.7
1953	23.6	17.0	51.8	1.0	67.5	9.8	6.7	164.2	341.6
1954	23.6	19.2	55.4	1.1	67.6	10.5	7.6	168.3	353.2
1955	23.8	21.6	60.8	1.3	67.9	11.8	8.6	173.7	369.4
1956	24.2	24.0	66.7	1.5	68.5	13.6	9.9	180.1	388.6
1957	24.7	26.4	72.0	1.8	69.6	16.0	10.9	187.5	409.1
1958	25.5	29.0	77.3	2.1	70.8	18.4	11.9	197.3	432.4
1959	26.7	31.4	83.5	2.5	72.3	20.9	12.9	208.0	458.2
1960	27.9	33.6	91.3	2.9	73.6	23.9	13.9	218.2	485.4
1961	29.1	36.0	99.5	3.4	75.2	26.7	15.0	229.9	514.9
1962	30.3	38.6	106.3	4.0	77.0	29.5	16.2	243.6	545.6
1963	31.4	41.2	112.5	4.6	78.8	32.2	17.3	259.9	578.0
1964	32.6	44.0	118.6	5.3	80.5	35.1	18.6	281.2	615.8
1965	33.8	47.0	124.9	5.9	82.2	38.2	20.2	303.0	655.1
1966	35.0	49.8	131.1	6.5	84.1	41.3	21.9	325.6	695.2
1967	36.1	53.0	135.4	7.1	86.2	44.3	23.5	343.5	729.2
1968	37.3	55.8	138.9	7.5	89.1	47.4	25.2	364.0	765.2
1969	38.3	58.5	144.4	8.0	92.8	51.0	27.1	386.1	806.2
1970	39.0	61.3	15.20	8.5	97.3	54.4	29.0	411.7	853.2
1971	39.5	64.8	159.6	9.1	102.6	58.0	30.9	437.9	902.5
1972	39.9	68.4	165.6	9.9	108.2	62.0	33.1	465.1	952.1
1973	40.3	71.7	170.9	10.7	113.6	65.8	35.3	491.7	999.9
1974	40.8	74.8	175.0	11.1	118.4	68.5	37.7	519.1	1,045.4
1975	41.4	78.5	177.9	11.5	122.7	70.9	39.9	544.6	1,087.4
1976	42.1	82.0	180.5	11.8	126.8	74.3	42.3	568.1	1,128.1
1977	42.9	85.1	183.8	12.3	131.0	77.7	44.3	591.4	1,168.5
1978	43.8	87.9	186.6	12.7	135.3	80.6	45.9	616.0	1,208.9
1979	44.5	90.7	189.9	13.1	139.9	83.8	47.3	642.4	1,251.5
1980	45.1	93.8	193.3	13.6	144.5	86.8	49.1	668.6	1,294.8
1981	45.6	96.4	195.7	14.0	148.8	89.3	51.2	693.6	1,334.6
1982	46.1	98.8	197.1	14.3	153.1	91.6	53.3	718.0	1,372.2
1983	46.7	100.9	197.5	14.7	157.6	94.0	55.6	741.0	1,408.0
1984	47.2	103.0	197.7	15.0	162.6	96.4	58.1	763.3	1,443.2
1985	47.6	104.8	197.4	15.2	168.0	98.5	59.9	785.4	1,476.8
1986	47.9	106.8	197.7	15.4	174.0	100.7	61.9	808.6	1,513.0
1987	48.1	108.2	198.2	15.5	180.3	103.0	63.4	832.4	1,549.1
1988	48.2	109.8	198.2	15.7	186.1	106.1	65.3	856.4	1,585.9
1989	48.2	111.5	198.1	15.7	192.1	109.2	67.2	881.6	1,623.7

Notes: AF = agriculture, forestry & fishing; MU = mining & utilities; MF = manufacturing; CR = construction; TC = transport & communication; RR = retailing & repairing; FI = finance, insurance, business services & real estate; SE = other services and public administration.

Appendix table B.   Gross capital stocks by sector, billions 1985 $.
IX. Germany, total assets

	AF	MU	MF	CR	TC	RR	FI	SE	TOT
1948	31.7	21.2	68.7	2.1	83.4	10.2	3.5	160.1	380.8
1949	31.1	22.4	73.2	2.1	84.7	10.9	4.0	160.6	389.0
1950	31.4	24.4	79.4	2.3	85.1	12.0	4.8	162.6	402.0
1951	30.8	26.6	86.3	2.5	85.2	13.0	5.6	164.1	414.2
1952	31.3	29.3	92.7	2.8	85.5	14.1	6.3	165.4	427.4
1953	31.5	33.0	99.3	3.2	86.9	15.4	7.3	169.1	445.8
1954	32.6	37.2	107.2	3.8	88.6	16.9	8.4	173.3	468.0
1955	34.4	41.7	118.2	4.8	90.9	19.4	9.6	179.1	498.1
1956	36.5	45.8	130.0	6.0	93.6	22.8	11.0	186.1	531.7
1957	38.8	49.9	141.0	7.1	96.4	26.8	12.2	194.2	566.3
1958	41.6	54.4	152.2	8.3	99.5	30.6	13.3	204.8	604.8
1959	45.0	58.6	165.2	9.9	103.3	34.8	14.4	216.9	648.1
1960	48.7	62.9	182.5	12.0	106.8	39.7	15.5	228.9	696.9
1961	52.8	67.3	201.9	14.4	111.2	44.3	16.8	242.5	751.2
1962	56.5	72.5	220.8	16.7	116.1	49.4	18.1	258.3	808.6
1963	59.8	77.4	238.8	19.1	121.5	54.4	19.4	276.9	867.3
1964	63.6	82.8	258.1	21.5	126.5	59.5	20.8	300.7	933.6
1965	67.8	88.2	279.1	23.6	131.5	64.8	22.5	325.5	1,003.0
1966	71.3	92.9	299.4	25.0	136.4	70.1	24.4	351.4	1,070.9
1967	73.6	98.0	315.3	26.3	141.8	74.4	26.2	372.7	1,128.2
1968	75.5	102.0	330.9	27.6	148.1	78.9	28.0	396.7	1,187.8
1969	78.0	105.7	352.0	29.3	155.5	84.0	30.3	423.2	1,258.0
1970	79.9	109.9	377.9	31.1	164.6	89.0	32.6	454.0	1,338.9
1971	80.9	115.6	403.1	33.0	175.2	94.0	34.9	485.9	1,422.4
1972	81.5	121.8	424.0	34.8	185.8	99.4	37.5	518.6	1,503.3
1973	82.5	127.6	441.6	36.0	195.8	104.5	40.3	551.9	1,580.3
1974	82.9	133.5	455.6	35.8	204.8	107.4	43.0	584.8	1,647.8
1975	83.2	140.0	466.5	35.8	212.0	109.8	45.8	616.9	1,710.0
1976	83.8	145.6	477.6	35.9	219.0	113.7	48.8	647.8	1,772.3
1977	85.0	150.0	489.3	36.2	226.2	118.1	51.4	680.5	1,836.7
1978	86.5	154.1	499.9	36.7	234.0	122.2	53.7	716.5	1,903.6
1979	87.8	157.8	511.9	37.5	241.7	126.3	55.7	756.7	1,975.3
1980	88.7	162.1	524.6	37.8	249.5	130.0	58.3	796.6	2,047.5
1981	89.2	166.4	534.4	37.2	257.4	132.6	60.9	834.7	2,112.8
1982	89.6	171.6	540.8	36.3	264.5	134.5	63.7	869.2	2,170.2
1983	90.3	176.5	545.9	35.9	272.3	136.8	67.0	902.5	2,227.3
1984	90.6	181.4	548.5	35.6	280.1	139.0	70.2	936.0	2,281.5
1985	90.9	185.9	552.6	35.4	289.0	141.2	73.1	969.5	2,337.5
1986	90.9	190.3	558.2	35.3	298.0	143.9	76.0	1,004.6	2,397.3
1987	90.7	194.1	564.9	35.0	306.4	147.5	78.3	1,041.6	2,458.6
1988	90.6	197.3	571.5	34.5	314.4	152.3	81.2	1,081.2	2,523.2
1989	90.1	200.6	578.2	34.0	322.6	157.2	84.1	1,122.1	2,588.8

Notes: AF = agriculture, forestry & fishing; MU = mining & utilities; MF = manufacturing; CR = construction; TC = transport & communication; RR = retailing & repairing; FI = finance, insurance, business services & real estate; SE = other services and public administration.

Appendix table B. Gross capital stocks by sector, billions 1985 $.
X. France, equipment

	AF	MU	MF	CR	TC	RR	FI	SE	TOT
1948	13.1	23.6	25.9	3.2	19.9	3.2	0.2	8.3	97.5
1949	13.5	23.8	26.2	3.4	20.1	3.3	0.2	8.5	99.0
1950	14.1	24.0	26.9	3.7	20.3	3.6	0.2	8.7	101.3
1951	15.1	24.0	27.7	4.1	20.2	4.2	0.3	8.9	104.5
1952	16.2	24.1	28.5	4.5	20.3	4.6	0.3	9.3	107.6
1953	17.4	24.2	29.4	4.9	20.5	5.1	0.3	9.6	111.4
1954	19.0	24.3	30.5	5.3	20.9	5.7	0.3	10.2	116.2
1955	21.1	24.5	32.3	5.8	21.5	6.6	0.4	10.9	123.0
1956	23.2	25.0	34.7	6.3	22.1	7.0	0.4	11.9	130.7
1957	25.6	25.8	38.0	7.0	23.0	7.4	0.5	13.0	140.2
1958	27.6	27.0	41.4	7.6	24.0	7.7	0.5	14.1	149.9
1959	29.3	28.3	45.0	8.0	25.2	8.0	0.6	15.1	159.4
1960	30.7	29.4	49.2	8.5	26.6	8.3	0.6	16.4	169.7
1961	32.6	30.4	54.3	9.3	28.1	8.7	0.7	17.9	182.0
1962	34.4	31.2	60.1	10.2	29.8	9.3	0.8	19.7	195.3
1963	36.5	31.8	66.2	11.1	31.4	10.0	0.9	21.7	209.6
1964	38.8	32.3	72.7	12.2	33.0	10.7	1.0	24.0	224.7
1965	41.0	32.8	79.0	13.1	34.7	11.6	1.1	26.6	240.0
1966	43.6	33.2	85.9	14.1	36.6	12.8	1.2	29.5	256.9
1967	45.9	33.6	92.6	15.1	38.5	14.2	1.4	32.7	274.0
1968	48.3	34.0	99.3	16.0	40.4	15.8	1.5	36.2	291.6
1969	50.6	34.1	107.1	17.1	42.4	17.7	1.7	39.7	310.6
1970	52.3	34.3	115.8	18.4	44.1	19.5	1.9	43.3	329.4
1971	54.4	34.2	124.8	19.6	46.9	21.5	2.1	47.8	351.4
1972	56.8	34.3	133.5	20.5	50.7	23.6	2.3	52.9	374.5
1973	59.6	34.5	143.3	21.3	55.3	25.8	2.7	58.6	401.0
1974	62.2	34.7	151.2	21.9	60.1	27.8	3.1	63.8	424.8
1975	63.9	35.0	156.1	22.6	64.9	29.3	3.5	68.2	443.5
1976	65.2	35.4	161.8	23.7	70.6	31.0	3.8	72.9	464.4
1977	65.8	36.3	167.0	24.6	76.3	32.2	4.1	77.1	483.4
1978	66.6	37.3	171.7	25.3	81.4	33.2	4.6	81.6	501.7
1979	67.5	39.0	175.8	26.2	86.1	34.2	5.0	86.1	519.9
1980	68.2	41.3	180.2	27.0	90.9	35.1	5.5	91.1	539.3
1981	68.8	43.5	183.2	27.5	95.0	36.1	5.9	96.0	556.1
1982	69.4	46.0	185.4	28.0	99.2	36.9	6.3	101.2	572.3
1983	69.6	48.1	186.8	28.1	102.5	37.3	6.7	106.4	585.6
1984	69.4	49.7	188.0	27.9	105.7	37.5	7.1	111.1	596.5
1985	69.0	51.4	190.3	27.7	109.2	38.0	7.5	116.8	610.0
1986	68.0	52.3	193.4	27.3	112.0	38.3	8.0	124.6	623.7
1987	66.7	53.4	196.8	26.8	114.2	38.9	8.6	133.0	638.4
1988	66.0	54.0	201.5	26.4	117.4	39.4	9.3	142.3	656.4
1989	66.1	54.3	207.2	26.2	121.3	39.4	10.0	151.7	676.2

Notes: AF = agriculture, forestry & fishing; MU = mining & utilities; MF = manufacturing; CR = construction; TC = transport & communication; RR = retailing & repairing; FI = finance, insurance, business services & real estate; SE = other services and public administration.

Appendix table B. Gross capital stocks by sector, billions 1985 $.
XI. France, structures

	AF	MU	MF	CR	TC	RR	FI	SE	TOT
1948	15.9	98.1	16.0	7.8	58.6	12.0	3.9	98.4	310.8
1949	16.1	99.0	16.2	7.9	59.0	12.2	3.9	99.7	314.0
1950	16.3	99.0	16.5	8.1	59.3	12.3	4.0	100.6	316.2
1951	16.5	98.3	16.8	8.2	59.4	12.7	4.0	101.4	317.2
1952	16.7	96.8	17.0	8.3	59.4	12.9	4.1	102.3	317.5
1953	16.9	94.9	17.1	8.4	59.7	13.2	4.1	103.2	317.5
1954	17.1	92.6	17.2	8.5	59.9	13.5	4.2	104.3	317.2
1955	17.3	90.1	17.3	8.6	60.1	13.9	4.3	105.5	317.2
1956	17.6	88.0	17.4	8.7	60.3	14.1	4.3	107.0	317.5
1957	17.9	86.1	17.6	8.9	60.6	14.2	4.4	108.5	318.1
1958	18.2	84.8	17.9	9.0	60.9	14.3	4.5	110.2	319.7
1959	18.5	83.9	18.1	9.2	61.3	14.3	4.6	112.3	322.2
1960	18.8	82.8	18.4	9.3	61.8	14.5	4.8	114.9	325.2
1961	19.1	81.7	18.9	9.5	62.3	14.7	4.9	118.2	329.3
1962	19.4	80.9	19.6	9.7	63.0	15.0	5.1	122.2	334.8
1963	19.7	80.4	20.3	10.0	63.5	15.3	5.4	126.8	341.3
1964	20.1	80.5	21.2	10.3	64.2	15.8	5.7	132.3	350.0
1965	20.5	81.1	22.1	10.6	64.9	16.4	6.0	138.7	360.3
1966	21.0	82.2	23.3	11.0	65.9	17.1	6.4	145.8	372.6
1967	21.6	83.8	24.7	11.5	67.0	18.1	6.9	154.7	388.1
1968	22.4	85.8	26.4	12.1	68.5	19.5	7.5	164.8	407.0
1969	23.4	87.9	28.6	12.9	70.3	21.3	8.3	176.6	429.3
1970	24.4	90.2	31.7	14.0	72.4	23.4	9.2	190.6	455.7
1971	25.4	92.3	35.3	15.2	74.2	25.6	10.0	204.8	482.9
1972	26.6	94.3	39.5	16.6	76.0	28.1	11.1	219.5	511.7
1973	28.1	95.8	43.7	18.1	78.4	30.7	12.3	234.6	541.7
1974	29.6	97.7	47.4	19.7	81.6	33.2	13.8	249.8	572.8
1975	30.9	99.4	50.6	20.9	84.7	35.7	15.1	265.9	603.2
1976	32.2	101.0	53.8	22.0	87.9	38.2	16.2	282.7	634.0
1977	33.6	102.1	57.2	23.0	91.9	40.7	17.6	297.5	663.7
1978	35.0	103.8	60.5	24.0	96.0	43.2	18.9	311.4	692.7
1979	36.5	106.1	64.0	25.0	99.9	45.8	20.4	326.4	724.2
1980	37.9	109.1	67.5	25.9	103.8	48.4	21.7	342.0	756.3
1981	39.3	112.1	70.2	26.7	107.6	51.0	23.1	358.7	788.7
1982	40.7	115.0	72.5	27.4	110.9	53.6	24.5	376.2	820.9
1983	42.1	117.7	74.7	28.1	114.0	55.9	26.0	392.9	851.3
1984	43.3	120.2	76.6	28.8	116.6	58.4	27.8	409.6	881.3
1985	44.6	122.6	78.5	29.3	119.5	60.8	29.8	427.0	912.0
1986	46.0	125.0	80.5	29.8	122.3	64.0	32.0	445.8	945.4
1987	47.4	126.6	82.7	30.3	126.1	67.4	34.5	465.9	980.8
1988	49.1	128.5	85.6	31.0	129.4	71.7	37.3	488.3	1,020.8
1989	50.9	130.3	89.2	31.7	133.0	76.7	40.4	513.0	1,065.3

Notes: AF = agriculture, forestry & fishing; MU = mining & utilities; MF = manufacturing; CR = construction; TC = transport & communication; RR = retailing & repairing; FI = finance, insurance, business services & real estate; SE = other services and public administration.

Appendix table B.   Gross capital stocks by sector, billions 1985 $.
XII. France, total assets

	AF	MU	MF	CR	TC	RR	FI	SE	TOT
1948	29.0	121.7	41.9	11.1	78.5	15.2	4.1	106.8	408.3
1949	29.5	122.8	42.4	11.3	79.1	15.5	4.2	108.1	413.1
1950	30.3	123.0	43.4	11.7	79.6	15.9	4.2	109.3	417.5
1951	31.6	122.3	44.5	12.3	79.6	16.9	4.3	110.4	421.8
1952	32.9	121.0	45.5	12.7	79.7	17.5	4.3	111.5	425.1
1953	34.3	119.1	46.5	13.2	80.1	18.3	4.4	112.8	428.9
1954	36.1	116.8	47.7	13.8	80.8	19.2	4.5	114.5	433.4
1955	38.4	114.6	49.6	14.4	81.6	20.5	4.6	116.5	440.2
1956	40.8	113.0	52.2	15.1	82.5	21.1	4.8	118.9	448.2
1957	43.5	111.9	55.6	15.9	83.6	21.5	4.9	121.4	458.3
1958	45.8	111.8	59.3	16.6	84.9	22.0	5.0	124.2	469.7
1959	47.8	112.2	63.1	17.1	86.5	22.3	5.2	127.4	481.6
1960	49.4	112.2	67.6	17.8	88.5	22.7	5.4	131.2	494.9
1961	51.7	112.0	73.3	18.8	90.5	23.4	5.6	136.0	511.3
1962	53.7	112.1	79.6	19.9	92.7	24.3	5.9	141.9	530.2
1963	56.2	112.2	86.5	21.1	94.8	25.3	6.2	148.5	550.9
1964	58.8	112.9	93.8	22.5	97.2	26.5	6.6	156.3	574.7
1965	61.5	113.9	101.2	23.8	99.6	28.0	7.1	165.3	600.3
1966	64.6	115.4	109.2	25.2	102.5	29.9	7.6	175.3	629.5
1967	67.5	117.4	117.3	26.6	105.4	32.3	8.2	187.4	662.2
1968	70.7	119.8	125.7	28.1	108.9	35.3	9.1	201.0	698.6
1969	74.0	122.1	135.8	30.0	112.7	39.0	10.0	216.3	739.8
1970	76.7	124.4	147.4	32.4	116.5	42.8	11.1	233.8	785.1
1971	79.8	126.5	160.1	34.8	121.2	47.1	12.1	252.6	834.2
1972	83.4	128.6	173.0	37.1	126.7	51.6	13.4	272.3	886.2
1973	87.6	130.4	186.9	39.5	133.7	56.5	15.0	293.1	942.7
1974	91.9	132.4	198.6	41.7	141.7	61.1	16.9	313.6	997.7
1975	94.8	134.4	206.7	43.5	149.6	65.0	18.5	334.1	1,046.7
1976	97.4	136.4	215.5	45.7	158.6	69.1	20.0	355.6	1,098.4
1977	99.4	138.4	224.2	47.6	168.3	72.9	21.7	374.6	1,147.1
1978	101.6	141.1	232.3	49.3	177.4	76.4	23.4	393.0	1,194.5
1979	104.0	145.1	239.8	51.2	186.0	80.1	25.4	412.5	1,244.0
1980	106.1	150.4	247.7	53.0	194.7	83.5	27.1	433.1	1,295.6
1981	108.1	155.7	253.5	54.2	202.6	87.1	29.0	454.7	1,344.8
1982	110.1	161.0	257.8	55.4	210.1	90.4	30.8	477.5	1,393.2
1983	111.6	165.8	261.5	56.2	216.4	93.2	32.7	499.3	1,436.8
1984	112.8	169.9	264.6	56.7	222.4	96.0	34.9	520.7	1,477.8
1985	113.6	173.9	268.8	57.0	228.8	98.7	37.3	543.8	1,522.0
1986	113.9	177.3	273.8	57.1	234.3	102.2	40.0	570.4	1,569.1
1987	114.1	180.0	279.5	57.1	240.3	106.3	43.1	598.8	1,619.2
1988	115.1	182.5	287.1	57.4	246.9	111.0	46.5	630.6	1,677.2
1989	117.0	184.6	296.4	57.9	254.3	116.1	50.5	664.7	1,741.4

Notes: AF = agriculture, forestry & fishing; MU = mining & utilities; MF = manufacturing; CR = construction; TC = transport & communication; RR = retailing & repairing; FI = finance, insurance, business services & real estate; SE = other services and public administration.

Appendix table B. Gross capital stocks by sector, billions 1985 $. XIII. Japan, equipment

	AF	MU	MF	CR	TC	RR	FI	SE	TOT
1948	16.5	14.6	31.9	1.9	11.8	1.3	1.2	48.2	127.3
1949	15.8	14.5	32.8	1.8	11.7	1.3	1.1	49.3	128.4
1950	15.2	14.4	33.8	1.7	11.6	1.2	1.1	49.6	128.7
1951	14.6	14.4	34.9	1.7	11.5	1.2	1.0	49.8	128.9
1952	14.1	14.4	36.0	1.6	11.4	1.1	0.9	48.3	127.7
1953	13.7	14.5	37.2	1.6	11.5	1.2	0.9	46.8	127.3
1954	13.5	14.4	37.7	1.6	11.3	1.3	0.9	45.3	126.1
1955	13.7	14.4	38.1	1.7	11.1	1.6	1.1	43.7	125.4
1956	14.1	14.3	40.2	1.9	11.2	2.0	1.2	41.8	126.7
1957	14.7	14.4	42.7	2.3	11.2	2.3	1.4	40.4	129.5
1958	15.4	14.6	44.4	2.6	11.2	2.7	1.6	39.6	132.0
1959	16.9	14.9	48.9	3.1	11.3	3.2	1.8	39.3	139.5
1960	18.3	15.5	58.0	3.9	11.7	3.9	2.2	39.8	153.4
1961	20.2	16.5	70.6	5.1	12.6	4.9	2.8	41.1	173.7
1962	21.9	17.6	81.7	6.0	13.7	6.4	3.7	44.0	195.0
1963	23.9	18.9	94.3	7.1	15.1	8.2	4.7	48.2	220.4
1964	25.9	20.2	108.4	8.2	16.8	10.6	6.1	52.9	249.2
1965	28.2	22.1	120.8	9.1	18.9	12.5	7.1	58.3	277.0
1966	31.2	24.4	133.9	10.3	21.5	14.8	8.1	65.3	309.5
1967	35.4	26.7	154.1	11.9	24.4	17.4	9.1	73.0	352.1
1968	40.8	29.3	180.9	13.7	27.9	20.8	10.3	82.0	405.8
1969	47.0	32.5	213.4	16.2	32.8	25.7	12.0	92.4	472.1
1970	54.6	36.1	252.3	19.1	38.0	31.1	13.8	100.8	545.9
1971	62.0	39.9	286.4	22.4	43.4	35.9	15.5	108.4	613.8
1972	69.6	43.8	316.8	26.3	49.0	41.6	17.1	115.8	680.0
1973	78.3	48.4	352.0	31.1	54.1	49.5	18.9	124.9	757.3
1974	86.7	52.0	385.6	34.7	58.7	56.2	20.3	130.5	824.7
1975	95.8	55.6	409.3	38.2	63.3	62.3	21.3	133.7	879.4
1976	106.0	59.6	431.0	41.9	67.1	67.9	21.7	137.9	932.7
1977	114.5	64.1	450.3	45.1	70.6	72.7	22.1	142.3	981.6
1978	124.1	69.8	466.0	48.1	74.4	77.4	22.2	147.6	1,029.6
1979	132.3	75.6	486.6	51.5	78.9	83.2	22.8	155.3	1,086.2
1980	140.3	81.3	512.1	55.1	83.3	88.8	23.2	162.6	1,146.6
1981	146.0	88.0	538.8	57.9	87.7	93.3	23.6	172.0	1,207.3
1982	150.8	94.3	564.6	60.4	92.2	96.5	24.1	183.4	1,266.2
1983	154.9	100.8	587.4	62.6	95.8	99.1	24.5	197.7	1,322.8
1984	159.0	107.3	615.4	65.0	99.5	102.1	25.7	218.5	1,392.6
1985	163.2	114.3	649.4	66.0	106.8	105.1	27.9	243.8	1,476.5
1986	166.5	121.4	678.7	67.9	116.3	109.9	30.8	272.4	1,563.9
1987	169.5	129.7	704.0	70.6	127.6	117.3	35.2	304.2	1,658.2
1988	173.1	137.0	738.7	74.6	140.1	127.0	41.5	345.3	1,777.3
1989	175.9	144.6	788.9	79.9	153.4	138.9	49.0	389.8	1,920.3

Notes: AF = agriculture, forestry & fishing; MU = mining & utilities; MF = manufacturing; CR = construction; TC = transport & communication; RR = retailing & repairing; FI = finance, insurance, business services & real estate; SE = other services and public administration.

Appendix table B. Gross capital stocks by sector, billions 1985 $. XIV. Japan, structures

	AF	MU	MF	CR	TC	RR	FI	SE	TOT
1948	NA	11.3	7.2	0.3	NA	1.0	NA	NA	NA
1949	NA	11.4	7.7	0.3	NA	1.0	NA	NA	NA
1950	NA	11.4	8.1	0.3	NA	1.0	NA	NA	NA
1951	NA	11.6	8.7	0.4	NA	1.1	NA	NA	NA
1952	15.9	11.7	9.3	0.4	NA	1.1	NA	NA	NA
1953	16.2	12.1	10.1	0.4	NA	1.3	NA	NA	271.3
1954	16.6	12.4	10.8	0.5	NA	1.5	2.8	NA	279.8
1955	16.9	12.7	11.5	0.5	10.7	1.7	3.2	NA	289.0
1956	17.2	13.1	12.9	0.6	11.1	2.0	3.6	NA	298.9
1957	17.5	13.8	14.5	0.7	11.6	2.3	4.0	NA	310.3
1958	17.8	14.6	15.9	0.7	12.0	2.5	4.4	NA	323.0
1959	18.2	15.4	18.1	0.8	12.5	2.9	5.0 ˎ	NA	338.7
1960	18.7	16.5	21.8	1.0	13.1	3.3	5.7	NA	358.8
1961	19.4	17.9	26.5	1.2	13.9	4.0	6.8	NA	384.5
1962	20.1	19.3	30.6	1.4	14.9	5.1	8.4	NA	415.8
1963	20.9	20.9	35.1	1.6	16.0	6.3	10.3	NA	452.1
1964	21.7	22.4	40.1	1.8	17.2	8.0	13.0	NA	492.1
1965	22.8	24.3	44.3	2.0	18.6	9.4	15.1	397.1	533.6
1966	24.1	26.6	48.8	2.3	20.4	11.1	17.1	431.2	581.6
1967	26.0	29.1	55.7	2.7	22.2	13.0	19.3	467.0	635.0
1968	28.4	31.7	64.8	3.0	24.6	15.5	21.8	507.4	697.3
1969	31.2	35.2	75.7	3.6	27.8	19.0	25.2	552.8	770.6
1970	35.0	39.5	90.0	4.3	31.6	23.3	29.6	606.3	859.7
1971	38.9	44.3	103.0	5.1	35.7	27.5	34.3	663.0	951.9
1972	43.1	49.5	115.1	6.1	40.1	32.7	39.4	725.9	1,052.0
1973	47.9	55.3	128.9	7.2	44.1	39.7	45.0	793.9	1,161.9
1974	52.8	60.5	142.9	8.1	47.8	46.1	50.4	852.9	1,261.7
1975	58.5	66.0	154.5	9.1	51.9	52.8	55.8	916.0	1,364.5
1976	64.7	72.0	165.5	10.1	55.4	58.8	59.6	980.6	1,466.6
1977	70.4	78.6	176.0	11.2	58.7	65.0	63.6	1,052.8	1,576.3
1978	77.1	86.8	185.7	12.2	62.4	71.3	67.2	1,136.2	1,698.8
1979	83.3	94.6	197.2	13.4	66.6	78.6	71.4	1,221.7	1,826.8
1980	89.8	102.2	210.6	14.8	70.8	86.1	75.7	1,304.5	1,954.4
1981	95.5	110.6	224.5	16.1	75.0	93.0	80.0	1,390.1	2,084.8
1982	101.0	118.1	238.3	17.3	79.3	99.6	84.4	1,473.9	2,211.9
1983	106.2	125.4	251.3	18.5	831	105.7	88.8	1,555.6	2,334.7
1984	111.2	131.6	265.6	19.7	86.8	111.7	93.7	1,634.4	2,454.7
1985	115.9	137.3	280.9	20.6	92.3	117.3	99.1	1,709.0	2,572.8
1986	120.6	143.7	294.9	21.6	99.0	123.9	105.0	1,786.1	2,694.8
1987	125.2	150.6	308.4	22.7	106.8	131.5	112.6	1,866.5	2,824.3
1988	129.9	156.2	323.8	24.0	114.8	139.9	121.3	1,953.1	2,963.1
1989	134.5	162.1	342.8	25.5	123.3	149.5	131.2	2,045.4	3,114.3

Notes: AF = agriculture, forestry & fishing; MU = mining & utilities; MF = manufacturing; CR = construction; TC = transport & communication; RR = retailing &

repairing; FI = finance, insurance, business services & real estate; SE = other services and public administration.

It was not possible to calculate stocks of structures for some sectors for the earliest years due to the lack of historical investment series. The figure for the total economy from 1953 to 1964 is derived from an estimate using a single service life for aggregate economy investment. This was spliced onto the later series in 1965.

Appendix table B.   Gross capital stocks by sector, billions 1985 $.
XV. Japan, total assets

	AF	MU	MF	CR	TC	RR	FI	SE	TOT
1948	NA	25.8	39.1	2.2	NA	2.3	NA	NA	0
1949	NA	25.9	40.4	2.1	NA	2.3	NA	NA	0
1950	NA	25.9	41.9	2.1	NA	2.3	NA	NA	0
1951	NA	25.9	43.5	2.0	NA	2.3	NA	NA	0
1952	30.0	26.1	45.3	2.0	NA	2.2	NA	NA	0
1953	29.9	26.5	47.3	2.0	NA	2.5	NA	NA	398.6
1954	30.1	26.8	48.5	2.1	NA	2.8	3.7	NA	405.9
1955	30.6	27.1	49.6	2.2	21.8	3.4	4.2	NA	414.4
1956	31.3	27.3	53.1	2.5	22.3	3.9	4.8	NA	425.6
1957	32.2	28.2	57.2	2.9	22.8	4.6	5.4	NA	439.8
1958	33.2	29.2	60.3	3.3	23.2	5.2	6.0	NA	455.0
1959	35.1	30.4	67.0	3.9	23.8	6.1	6.8	NA	478.2
1960	37.0	32.0	79.8	4.9	24.8	7.2	7.9	NA	512.2
1961	39.6	34.4	97.2	6.3	26.5	9.0	9.6	NA	558.3
1962	42.0	36.9	112.3	7.4	28.5	11.5	12.1	NA	610.8
1963	44.8	39.7	129.4	8.7	31.1	14.5	15.0	NA	672.4
1964	47.6	42.7	148.5	10.0	34.0	18.7	19.1	NA	741.3
1965	51.0	46.4	165.1	11.1	37.5	21.8	22.2	455.5	810.5
1966	55.2	51.0	182.8	12.6	41.9	25.8	25.3	496.6	891.1
1967	61.3	55.8	209.9	14.6	46.7	30.4	28.4	540.0	987.0
1968	69.3	61.0	245.6	16.7	52.5	36.4	32.1	589.4	1,103.1
1969	78.2	67.7	289.2	19.8	60.6	44.8	37.2	645.2	1,242.7
1970	89.6	75.6	342.4	23.4	69.6	54.4	43.4	707.1	1,405.6
1971	100.9	84.2	389.4	27.5	79.1	63.4	49.8	771.4	1,565.7
1972	112.8	93.3	431.9	32.3	89.2	74.4	56.6	841.7	1,732.0
1973	126.2	103.7	480.9	38.3	98.2	89.2	63.9	918.8	1,919.2
1974	139.5	112.5	528.5	42.9	106.6	102.3	70.8	983.4	2,086.3
1975	154.3	121.6	563.7	47.3	115.2	115.2	77.1	1,049.6	2,243.9
1976	170.7	131.5	596.5	52.0	122.5	126.3	81.3	1,118.5	2,399.3
1977	184.9	142.7	626.3	56.3	129.3	137.6	85.7	1,195.0	2,557.9
1978	201.3	156.6	651.7	60.3	136.8	148.7	89.4	1,283.7	2,728.4
1979	215.7	170.3	683.7	65.0	145.4	161.8	94.2	1,377.1	2,913.1
1980	230.1	183.4	722.7	69.8	154.1	174.9	98.9	1,467.0	3,101.0
1981	241.5	198.6	763.3	74.0	162.7	186.3	103.6	1,562.1	3,292.0
1982	251.8	212.4	802.4	77.7	171.5	196.1	108.51	1,657.3	3,478.2

Appendix table B. XV *(contd)*

	AF	MU	MF	CR	TC	RR	FI	SE	TOT
1983	261.1	226.2	838.7	81.2	179.0	204.8	113.3	1,753.3	3,657.5
1984	270.2	238.9	881.0	84.7	186.4	213.8	119.4	1,852.9	3,847.3
1985	279.1	251.9	930.2	86.7	199.2	222.4	127.0	1,952.8	4,049.2
1986	287.1	265.2	973.6	89.4	215.3	233.8	135.7	2,058.4	4,258.6
1987	294.7	280.3	1,012.4	93.3	234.4	248.9	147.8	2,170.7	4,482.5
1988	303.1	293.2	1,062.5	98.6	254.8	266.9	162.7	2,298.5	4,740.4
1989	310.4	306.6	1,131.7	105.5	276.7	288.4	180.2	2,435.2	5,034.6

Notes: AF = agriculture, forestry & fishing; MU = mining & utilities; MF = manufacturing; CR = construction; TC = transport & communication; RR = retailing & repairing; FI = finance, insurance, business services & real estate; SE = other services and public administration.

NOTES

This research was funded by a grant from the Leverhulme Trust to which I owe thanks. I am particularly grateful to Angus Maddison who initially encouraged me to work on the issue of international measures of physical capital stocks and for comments received. Helpful comments were also received from Bart van Ark, Andrew Britton, Steve Broadberry, David Mayes, Nick Oulton, Sig Prais and Dirk Pilat.

1   We do not make use of the detailed investment data by asset type for the USA but rather assume one service life for equipment in each sector.
2   The eight sectors were: agriculture, forestry and fishing; mining and utilities (gas, electricity and water); manufacturing; construction; transport and communication; retailing and repairing; finance, insurance, business services and real estate; and other services including public administration.
3   The average service life over all five countries was very similar to the US lives and so was not an interesting alternative.
4   The absolute levels of gross capital stocks differ in both chapters since we use slightly different standard lives – Maddison assumes 39 and 14 years, respectively, for structures and equipment whereas our estimates are close to 40 and 15 years. This, however, has no effect on relative (to US) capital stocks.

REFERENCES

Abramovitz, M. (1991), 'The Postwar Productivity Spurt and Slowdown. Factors of Potential and Realisation', in *Technology and Productivity: The Challenge for Economic Policy*, Paris: OECD.

van Ark, B. (1990), 'Manufacturing Productivity Levels in France and the United Kingdom', *National Institute Economic Review*, No. 133, August, 62–77.

van Ark, B. (1992), 'Comparative Productivity in British and American manufacturing', *National Institute Economic Review*, No. 142, November, 63–74.

Bacon, R.W. and W.A. Eltis (1974), *The Age of US and UK Machinery*, London: NEDO.

Baily, M.N. (1981), 'Productivity and the Services of Capital and Labour', *Brookings Papers on Economic Activity*, No. 1, 1–50.

Baily, M.N. and R.J. Gordon (1991), 'Measurement Issues and the Productivity Slowdown in Five Major Industrial Countries', in *Technology and Productivity: the Challenge for Economic Policy*, Paris: OECD.

Barro, R. and X. Sala-i-Martin (1991), 'Convergence across Regions and States', *Brookings Papers on Economic Activity*, No. 1.

Baumol, W.J. (1986), 'Productivity Growth Convergence and Welfare: What the Long Run Data Show', *American Economic Review*, 76,(5), 1072–85.

Blades, D.W. (1983), 'Service Lives of Fixed Assets', OECD working paper No. 4, March.

Blades, D.W. (1991), 'Capital Measurement in the OECD Countries: An Overview', in *Technology and Productivity: the Challenge for Economic Policy*, Paris: OECD.

Carré, J.J., P. Dubois and E. Malinvaud (1976), *French Economic Growth*, Stanford, CA: Stanford University Press.

CSO (Central Statistical Office) (1985), *United Kingdom National Accounts: Sources and Methods*, London: HMSO.

Daly, A., D.M.W.N. Hitchens and K. Wagner (1985), 'Productivity, machinery and skills in a sample of British and German manufacturing plants', *National Institute Economic Review*, No. 111, February, 48–61.

Dean, E., M. Darrough and A. Neef (1990), 'Alternative Measures of Capital Inputs in Japanese Manufacturing', in C. Hulten (ed.), *Productivity Growth in Japan and the United States*, Chicago: University of Chicago Press.

Dean, G.A. (1964), 'The Stock of Fixed Capital in the United Kingdom in 1961', *Journal of the Royal Statistical Society*, Series A, 127, 327–58.

Denison, E. (1967), *Why Growth Rates Differ*, Washington, DC: The Brookings Institution.

Denison, E. (1974), *Accounting for United States Economic Growth, 1929–1969*, Washington, DC: The Brookings Institution.

Denison, E. (1989), *Estimates of Productivity Change by Industry*, Washington, DC: The Brookings Institution.

Economic Planning Agency (1991), 'Gross Capital Stock of Private Enterprises', Department of National Accounts, Economic Research Institute, Tokyo.

Feinstein, C. (1965), *Domestic Capital Formation in the United Kingdom*, Cambridge: Cambridge University Press.

Feinstein, C. (1972), *National Income, Expenditure and Output of the United Kingdom*, Cambridge: Cambridge University Press.

Feinstein, C. and S. Pollard (eds.) (1988), *Studies in Capital Formation in the United Kingdom, 1750–1920*, Oxford: Clarendon Press.

Gilbert, M. and I.B. Kravis (1954), *An International Comparison of National Products and the Purchasing Power of Currencies*, Paris: OEEC.

Helliwell, J. and A. Chung (1992), 'Convergence and Growth Linkages between North and South', NBER Working Paper No. 3948, January.

Jarvis, V. and S.J. Prais (1989), 'Two nations of shopkeepers: training for retailing in France and Britain', *National Institute Economic Review*, May

Jorgenson, D., F. Gollop and B. Fraumeni (1987), *Productivity and U.S. Economic Growth*, Cambridge, MA: Harvard University Press.

Kendrick, J. (1976), *The Formation and Stocks of Total Capital*, New York: National Bureau of Economic Research.

Kendrick, J. (1993), 'How Much Does Capital Explain', in A. Szirmai, B. van Ark and D. Pilat (eds.), *Explaining Economic Growth: Essays in Honour of Angus Maddison*, Amsterdam: North Holland.

Kirner, W. (1968), *Zeitreihen für das Anlagevermögen der Wirtschaftsbereiche in der Bundesrupublik Deutschland*, Deutsches Institut für Wirtschaftsforschung Beiträge zur Strukturforschung, Heft 5, Berlin: Duncker & Humblot.

Kravis, I.B., Z. Kenessey, A. Heston and R. Summers (1975), *A System of International Comparisons of Gross Product and Purchasing Power*, Baltimore, MD: The Johns Hopkins University Press.

Kravis, I.B., A. Heston and R. Summers (1982), *World Product and Income: International Comparisons of Real Gross Product*, Baltimore, MD: The Johns Hopkins University Press.

Lützel, H. (1977), 'Estimates of Capital Stocks by Industries in the Federal Republic of Germany', *Review of Income and Wealth*, series 23, number 1, pp. 63–78.

Maddison, A. (1991), *Dynamic Forces in Capitalist Development*, Oxford: Oxford University Press.

Mankiw, N.G., P. Romer and D. Weil (1992), 'A Contribution to the Empirics of Economic Growth', *Quarterly Journal of Economics*, May, 407–438.

Mason, G., B. van Ark and K. Wagner (1993), 'Productivity, Product Quality and Workforce Skills: Food Processing in Four European Countries', National Institute of Economic and Social Research Discussion Paper No. 34, March.

Mendis, L. and J. Muellbauer (1984), 'British Manufacturing Productivity 1955–83: Measurement Problems, Oil Shocks and Thatcher Effects', CEPR Discussion Paper No. 32, London.

OECD (1985), *Purchasing Power Parities and Real Expenditures, 1985*, Department of Economics and Statistics, OECD, Paris.

OECD (1991), *Taxing Profits in a Global Economy: Domestic and International Issues*, Paris: OECD.

OECD (1993), *Methods Used by OECD Countries to Measure Stocks of Fixed Capital*, National Accounts: Sources and Methods No. 2, OECD, Paris.

Ohkawa, K. and H. Rosovsky (1973), *Japanese Economic Growth*, Oxford: Oxford University Press.

Ohkawa, K. and M. Shinohara (1979), *Patterns of Japanese Economic Development—A Quantitative Appraisal*, New Haven, CT: Yale University Press.

O'Mahony, M. (1992a), 'Productivity Levels in British and German Manufacturing', *National Institute Economic Review*, No. 139, February, 46–63.

O'Mahony, M. (1992b), 'Productivity and Human Capital Formation in UK and German Manufacturing', National Institute of Economic and Social Research, Discussion Paper No. 28, October.

O'Mahony, M. (1993), 'International Measures of Fixed Capital Stocks: a Five-Country Study', National Institute of Economic and Social Research, Discussion Paper No. 51, September.

Oulton, N. (1992), 'Investment, Increasing Returns and the Pattern of Productivity Growth in UK Manufacturing, 1954–86', NIESR Discussion Paper, No. 5, February.

Oulton, N. and M. O'Mahony (1994), *Productivity and Growth: A Disaggregated Study of British Industry, 1954–1986*, Cambridge: Cambridge University Press.

Pilat, D. (1992), 'Productivity Growth and Levels by Sector, Japan and the United States, 1885–1990', University of Groningen, mimeo.

Pilat, D. and B. van Ark, (1992), 'Productivity Leadership in Manufacturing, Germany, Japan and the United States, 1973–1989', Research Memorandum No. 456, University of Groningen, March.

Prais, S.J. (1986), 'Some International Comparisons of the Age of the Machine Stock, *The Journal of Industrial Economics*, March, 261–277.

Prais, S.J. and K. Wagner (1988), 'Productivity and Management: The Training of Foremen in Britain and Germany', *National Institute Economic Review*, No. 123, February, 34–47.

Prais, S.J., V. Jarvis and K. Wagner (1989), 'Productivity and Vocational Skills in Services in Britain and Germany: Hotels', *National Institute Economic Review*, November, pp. 52–74.

Romer, P. (1986), 'Increasing Returns and Long Run Growth', *Journal of Political Economy*, **94**, 1002–37.

Romer, P. (1990a), 'Endogenous Technological Change', *Journal of Political Economy*, October, S71–S102.

Romer, P. (1990b), 'Capital, Labour and Productivity', *Brookings Papers, Microeconomics*.

Smith, A.D. (1987), 'A Current Cost Accounting Measure of Britain's Stock of Equipment', *National Institute Economic Review*, May, 42–57.

Statistisches Bundesamt (1991), *Volkswirtschaftliche Gesamtrechnungen, Revidierte Ergebnisse, 1950 bis 1990*, Fachserie 18, Reihe S. 15, Wiesbaden.

Steedman, H. and K. Wagner (1987), 'A Second Look at Productivity, Machinery and Skills in Britain and Germany', *National Institute Economic Review*, No. 122, November, 84–96.

Steedman, H. and K. Wagner (1989), 'Productivity, Machinery and Skills: Clothing Manufacture in Britain and Germany', *National Institute Economic Review*, No. 128 May, 40–57.

Summers, R. and A. Heston (1991), 'The Penn world table (mark 5): an expanded set of international comparisons, 1950–1988', *The Quarterly Journal of Economics*, May, 327–368.

Uno, K. (1987), *Japanese Industrial Performance*, Amsterdam: North Holland.

Ward, M. (1985), *Purchasing Power Parities and Real Expenditures in the OECD*, Paris: OECD.

5 Technology indicators and economic growth in the European area: some empirical evidence

BART VERSPAGEN

1 Introduction

Technological change is obviously a main factor behind growth in modern capitalist economies. As such, it is subject to much debate, both in the academic and the policy context. In the academic environment, the event of new growth theory (for example, Romer (1986) and Grossman and Helpman (1991); for an overview see Verspagen (1991b)) has put the issue of endogenous technological change back into the centre of attention. Policy debates around technological and economic competitiveness in the European Community are now more relevant than ever, with 'traditional' forms of integration (like the ERM) finding less and less support.

The impact of technological progress on economic activity is manifold. New technologies create and destroy jobs, have an impact on the quality of work, cause structural change, have an influence on specialization and trade-patterns, provide 'windows' of opportunity for backward nations, or, on the other hand, tend to push them further into (relative) poverty. Key to most of the discussions around the influence of technological innovation, however, are the opportunities it provides for long-term growth. The topic of sustainability of long-run growth is also crucially related to technological change.

The exact relation between technological change and economic growth, however, is hard to grasp with the current theoretical and empirical tools, and the data available for analysis. This chapter, nevertheless, focuses exactly on this question. The aim is to analyse the impact of technological change on long-run growth, by means of statistical analysis of the time series and cross-country data. Of course, a statistical analysis is limited by its very nature, and therefore many (crucial) aspects of the relation under investigation will not be covered. It is hoped, however, that some of the results may improve the insight into the question of what role technology played in the development of post-war Europe.

The rest of the chapter is organized as follows. In the second section, two different approaches to measuring technology (a direct one and an indirect one) will be discussed. Some technology indicators will be presented in order to provide an overview of trends in technological leadership in the European area. Section 3 will focus on some econometric exercises to assess the significance of the relationship between technology and growth. Time series analysis will be conducted for the major EU countries, and a cross-country approach will be used for a group of fourteen European countries plus the USA and Japan. Section 4 will use the results from the econometric exercises for growth accounting purposes. This section will try to quantify the contribution of technology (in the form of R&D and patenting) to labour productivity growth. The final section will summarize the arguments, and draw some conclusions.

2   Trends in technology indicators in the European area

Technology is not easily measurable. Partly, this is because of the characteristics of the phenomenon itself: technological advances occur in many different forms, each with their own field of appliance, magnitude, and diffusion speed. Economists have basically focused on two ways of measuring technology. One way is an indirect one, which (at least in its strict form) builds upon the concept of the production function. In this case, the rate of technological change is approximated by the residual of output growth after subtraction of the growth rates of labour and capital input (weighted by their shares in income).

The drawbacks of this method are well-known. It (among other things) depends heavily on the concepts of constant returns to scale (although ad hoc estimates of the residual based upon increasing returns to scale have been calculated), and equilibrium in factor markets (although more sophisticated measures of the residual are available for situations in which the quasi-fixed character of capital inputs is acknowledged). More importantly, the residual measures not only technological change, but also all other sources not taken into account by the growth rates of conventional inputs. This, as early as 1956, led Abramovitz to label the residual, also commonly known as total factor productivity growth, as the 'measure of our ignorance', rather than technological change proper.

A second method of measuring technological change also has its drawbacks. This method uses more direct indicators, such as expenditures on research and development (R&D), and patent statistics. All of these 'direct' indicators have their disadvantages. For example, R&D is only an input indicator, and does not tell us anything about the results of technological change. The R&D process is essentially a search process (Gomulka, 1990; Dosi, 1988), in which the outcomes are highly uncertain. Even abstracting from inter-firm or international differences in R&D efficiency, it is hard to imagine that 'stochastic' returns to R&D will *a priori* be constant over time.

Moreover, there are a number of aspects of the technological process which are simply not measured in official R&D statistics, even if R&D is a 'well-defined' statistical concept (by the so-called Frascati manual, published by the OECD).[1] For example, there is evidence (Kleinknecht, 1987) that 'informal' R&D activities in small firms are drastically underestimated by the official statistics. Moreover, many activities, such as design of new products and large parts of software development are not included in the formal 'Frascati' definition of R&D, but still are essential elements of the innovation process at the firm level. Recent so-called innovation surveys (see, for example, Kleinknecht *et al.* (1990)) attempt to measure more aspects of the innovation process, but the results of these exercises do not yet seem general enough to be applicable at a more aggregate level, for example by linking them to national statistics on GDP growth.

Patent statistics are the other main source for measuring technological change in a 'direct' way. Contrary to R&D, patents are a direct measure of innovation output.[2] However, they are not without other drawbacks. First, the so-called propensity to patent innovations varies greatly between sectors. For example, in pharmaceuticals, patenting is absolutely necessary, because of the threat of imitation without a patent. In computers and electronics, patenting is much less valuable, because of the short lifetime of the products involved. In general, the way in which an innovation is appropriated differs between sectors, and patenting is only one of the methods of appropriating (other methods are secrecy, lead times, continual product development, etc.).

Another difficulty with patent statistics is the fact that different national patent agencies have different novelty requirements. Thus, a patent issued in one country might be subject to more severe criteria than a patent issued in another country. Even if one uses patents issued by one agency (for example, US patents, or European patents), the novelty requirements only define a lower limit, and the quality of patented inventions differs greatly. Finally, not all patents are actually commercialized, indicating the differences in economic value between individual patents.

Summarizing, the statistical material available to the researcher wanting to investigate the economic influence of technological innovation is not very adequate. Nevertheless, the literature on the relation between, for example, R&D and productivity growth (or total factor productivity) has shown that there is a relationship between the technology indicators discussed and economic growth (see, for example, Mohnen (1992) for an overview). Before this link is investigated in the context of European economic growth, the rest of this section will summarize some of the trends in technology indicators in the European area.

R&D expenditures appeared in the official statistics of the main OECD countries from the beginning of the 1960s. Statistics broken down by R&D performer (business, (semi-)public, universities, other) are generally available from the late 1960s onwards. For some countries (the large European ones, the USA and Japan), estimates of (business) R&D go back to the 1950s.[3] The main trends in these indicators (expressed in terms of R&D intensities, defined as the ratio of R&D expenditures to GDP) are given in Table 5.1 and 5.2.

Overall, the tables show that commercial enterprises are by far the most important R&D performers in most of the countries in the tables. Commonly, they amount to more than half of the R&D expenditures. Moreover, it appears there are huge differences between countries with regard to the amount of funds spent on R&D. The USA started out as the leading nation in this respect, but during the 1970s and 1980s, some major European countries (Germany, Sweden) and Japan caught up. This was also due to US budget cuts in the field of military R&D (see below). The Japanese trend in (business) R&D intensity is quite remarkable. Starting way behind the USA in the 1960s, it had already overtaken this country in the 1970s.

In Europe, there are a couple of clear R&D leaders. Switzerland, the UK, and The Netherlands were high-R&D-investing nations in the 1960s, and Germany increased its R&D expenditures strongly during the subsequent period, in order to become a leader in the 1980s and early 1990s. The Swedish growth of business R&D is also quite strong, putting this country at the top in the 1980s. The Netherlands and (to a lesser extent) the UK could not keep up in the 'race' and fell behind in relative R&D spending.

Apart from these movements at the top of the list, the relative ranking of the follower countries remained relatively stable. There is a steady intermediate group, with Belgium, Denmark, France, The Netherlands, Norway and Finland (the latter two only recently). The other countries, such as Spain, Greece, Portugal, Italy, Ireland and Austria, lag behind considerably.

Summarizing, the conclusion of this exercise is that in a European

Table 5.1   Business R&D intensities (business R&D expenditures as a fraction of GDP), various years, Europe and its main competitors

	1967	1975	1981	1986	1990
USA	0.021	0.015	0.017	0.021	0.019
Germany	0.011	0.014	0.017	0.020	0.020
Switzerland	0.019	0.018	0.017	0.022	0.021^b
UK	0.015	0.013	0.015	0.016	0.015
Sweden	0.010	0.012	0.015	0.020^a	0.016^a
Japan	0.008	0.011	0.014	0.018	0.022
France	0.011	0.011	0.012	0.013	0.015
Belgium	0.007	0.008	0.010	0.012	0.012
Netherlands		0.011	0.010	0.013	0.011
Norway	0.004	0.006	0.007	0.011^a	0.010^a
Austria		0.005	0.007	0.007^b	0.008^b
Finland	0.003	0.005	0.006	0.010	0.012
Denmark	0.004	0.004	0.005	0.007	0.008^b
Italy	0.003	0.004	0.005	0.007	0.008
Ireland	0.002	0.002	0.003	0.005	0.006
Spain	0.001	0.002^a	0.002	0.003	0.005
Portugal	0.000	0.001^a	0.001^a	0.001	0.002
Greece			0.000	0.001	0.001^b

a Reported value is one year later than reported.
b Reported value is one year earlier than reported.

context, there appear to be some clear technological leaders (in terms of R&D spending), which form a relatively stable group. Just as in the case of per capita GDP, there is a clear distinction between the leading countries and the followers. The tendency to catch-up, however, is not so apparent in terms of R&D spending. Differences between the more advanced and less advanced countries remain large, and in some cases are even growing over time.

The aggregate statistics in the tables, however, do not reveal anything about qualitative differences in R&D spending between nations. One aspect that has caught a lot of attention relates to the amount of government spending on R&D. This government spending may have different forms and purposes. For example, it may either take the form of direct university funds (generally aimed at quite general, basic research), or firm subsidies (highly focused on projects or generic). Or government R&D spending may largely be related to military purposes, in which case the spillovers to civil applications are not always obvious.

Table 5.3 gives an overview of the degree to which different national governments finance business R&D. In the literature, it has been claimed that government-financed business R&D (for example, by means of

Table 5.2   Total R&D intensities (R&D expenditures as a fraction of GDP), various years, Europe and its main competitors

	1963	1967	1970	1975	1981	1986	1990
USA			0.027	0.023	0.025	0.029	0.028
Germany	0.014^a	0.018	0.021	0.022	0.024	0.027	0.027
UK					0.024	0.023	0.022
Japan	0.015	0.016	0.018	0.020	0.023	0.027	0.031
Sweden				0.018	0.023	0.030^a	0.025^a
Switzerland	0.025	0.024	0.023	0.024	0.023	0.029	0.029^b
France	0.016	0.021	0.019	0.018	0.020	0.022	0.024
Netherlands	0.019^a		0.020	0.020	0.019	0.022	0.021
Belgium	0.010	0.013	0.014^a	0.013	0.015^c	0.017	0.017
Norway			0.011	0.013	0.013	0.018^a	0.018^a
Finland			0.009^a	0.009	0.012	0.017	0.019
Austria		0.006	0.006	0.009	0.012	0.013	0.014
Denmark		0.008	0.010	0.010	0.011	0.013	0.016^a
Italy	0.006	0.006	0.008	0.008	0.009	0.011	0.013
Ireland	0.005	0.006	0.008^a	0.008	0.007	0.009	0.009
Spain		0.002	0.002	0.004	0.004	0.006	0.009
Portugal	0.003^a	0.002	0.004^a	0.003^a	0.004^a	0.004	0.006
Greece					0.002	0.003	0.005^b

[a] Reported value is one year later than reported.
[b] Reported value is one year earlier than reported.
[c] Reported value is average of 1979 and 1983.

subsidies) is less efficient than purely privately financed R&D (see, for example, Griliches (1979) for an early contribution). Government financing of business R&D is relatively large in the USA (although declining over the 1970s and 1980s) and the major European countries, as well as Norway, Japan and some of the less developed European countries (Greece, Spain, Portugal) have lower rates of government spending.

Next, Table 5.4 gives an impression of how important military R&D is. As could be expected, military spending (as a percentage of total government R&D spending) is relatively high in the USA, the UK, France and Sweden. Switzerland forms a somewhat intermediate case, with other countries clearly spending less on military purposes. Military spending also shows a clear trend in a number of cases (for example, the USA, France). Of course, the most recent data which are not in the table, would probably show some major differences relative to the past.

Insofar as R&D has an influence on economic growth, this influence is likely to differ between fields of economic or technological activity. Thus, the technological specialization pattern of a country determines to a

Table 5.3 Fraction of business R&D financed by direct government funds, various years

	1963	1967	1970	1975	1981	1986	1990
USA	0.58	0.51	0.43	0.36	0.32	0.32	0.29
UK	0.34	0.29^a	0.32^b	0.31	0.30	0.23	0.17
Norway			0.19	0.21	0.25	0.20^a	0.19^a
France		0.40	0.32	0.28	0.25	0.23	0.20
Germany		0.17		0.18	0.17	0.14	0.12
Ireland	0.00	0.02	0.01^a	0.05	0.14	0.14	0.05
Sweden				0.16	0.14	0.11^a	0.12^b
Denmark		0.05	0.05	0.07	0.12	0.11	0.10
Italy	0.01	0.02	0.05	0.07	0.09	0.25	0.19
Belgium					0.08	0.06	0.05
Netherlands			0.06	0.04	0.07	0.14	0.12
Austria			0.08	0.09	0.07	0.08^b	0.06^b
Greece					0.05	0.15	0.05^a
Finland			0.05^a	0.06	0.04	0.03^a	0.03^b
Portugal	0.03	0.04^a	0.02^a	0.05^a	0.04^a	0.04	0.06
Spain		0.01	0.04	0.02	0.04	0.11	0.12
Japan			0.01	0.02	0.02	0.02	0.01
Switzerland	0.01	0.02	0.02	0.03	0.01	0.02	0.01^b

[a] Reported value is one year later than reported.
[b] Reported value is one year earlier than reported.

large extent (together with pure quantitative technology efforts) its growth opportunities. The final part of this section gives an overview of differences in technological specialization between (European) countries.

Patent statistics are quite useful for measuring technological specialization, because they are relatively easily available at the sectoral level. In this case, US patents[4] are used to construct a matrix of technological specialization distances between countries. The basic input for this matrix consists of the so-called *revealed technological advantage* index, which is similar to the well-known Belassa index of revealed comparative advantage. This is defined as $(P_{ij}/P_j)/(P_i/P)$, where P is the number of patents, i and j denote a country and sector, respectively, and absence of any of the two indices points to aggregation over this index. Denote this index by I_{ij}, and define $\bar{I}_{ij} = (\bar{I}_{ij} - 1)/(\bar{I}_{ij} + 1)$.[5] The indicator $\bar{I}_{ij}$ is used to construct the matrix of technological specialization distances, where the distance between countries p and q is defined as $D_{pq} = \Sigma_j(\bar{I}_{pj} - \bar{I}_{qj})^2$.

For reasons of transparency, these distance matrices (one for each of the years 1963, 1970, 1980 and 1988) are presented by means of a multidimensional scaling exercise.[6] This technique essentially attempts to produce an n-dimensional picture, which represents all cases in the

Table 5.4   Military R&D financed by direct government funds as a fraction of total government R&D budget, various years

	1970	1975	1981	1986	1990
USA	0.52[a]	0.51	0.55	0.69	0.63
UK		0.45	0.46	0.47	0.44
France		0.30	0.38	0.34	0.40
Sweden		0.25	0.15	0.26	0.24
Switzerland	0.20	0.16	0.13	0.17	0.20
Spain		0.07[a]	0.05	0.06	0.18
Denmark	0.18	0.11	0.09	0.12	0.13
Norway			0.07	0.07	0.06
Italy	0.04	0.03	0.07	0.09	0.06
Japan					0.06[a]
Netherlands	0.05	0.03	0.03	0.03	0.03
Greece			0.02	0.03	0.02
Finland	0.03	0.02	0.02	0.02	0.01
Portugal				0.00	0.01
Denmark		0.01[a]	0.00	0.00	0.00
Belgium		0.01	0.00	0.02	0.00
Austria		0.00	0.00	0.00	0.00
Ireland	0.00	0.00	0.00	0.00	0.00

[a] Reported value is one year later than reported.
[b] Reported value is one year earlier than reported.

distance matrix in such a way that the correspondence between the original distances in the matrix and the distances in the picture is as close as possible. Naturally, if n is equal to the number of dimensions in which the distances are calculated (in this case, the number of sectors), the correspondence is perfect. However, whenever n is smaller than this number, a certain degree of mis-correspondence arises, which can be measured by a statistic called *stress* (varying between zero, for perfect correspondence, and 1, for absolute mis-correspondence).

Figure 5.1 gives the obtained constellations (with $n = 2$) for the main European countries and the USA and Japan.[7] The figures show that in the beginning of the observed period, there is a clear group of countries with similar technological specialization. This group consists of Austria, Germany, France, The Netherlands, Italy, Sweden, Switzerland, the UK, and the USA. It is remarkable to see that almost all these countries (except Austria and Italy, and arguably Sweden) were also the ones in which R&D expenditures were relatively high during the 1960s. Thus, it appears that the technological leaders in terms of R&D expenditures were also a homogeneous group (as compared to technological laggards) with regard to technological specialization.

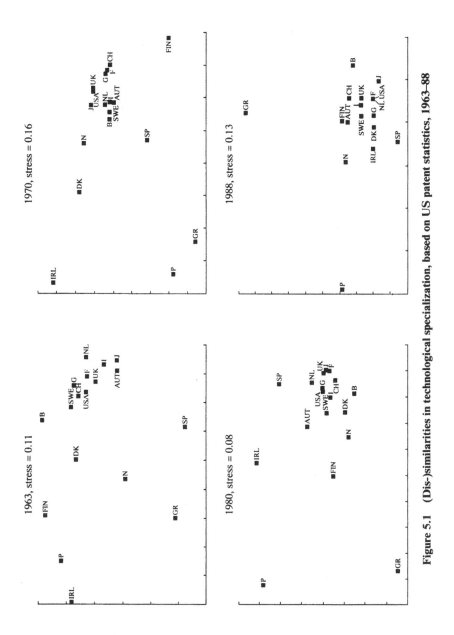

Figure 5.1 (Dis-)similarities in technological specialization, based on US patent statistics, 1963–88

223

Within this group of technological leaders, it is hard to judge whether there are significant sub-groups. It is clear, however, that the 'total' group of structural leaders is relatively stable. Over the period 1963–88, there are only a few 'entrants' into the group, such as Belgium and Denmark. Some of the other countries (Norway) do seem to be moving towards the leaders, but remain at the outskirts of the group. Relatively backward countries such as Greece, Portugal, Spain, Ireland and Finland do not seem to converge towards the leaders in a strong way.

Although in a very sketchy and incidental way, this analysis shows that there are clearly differences between the 'R&D systems' or 'national innovation systems' (Lundvall, 1992) of the different countries. Of course, these differences relate to much more than the role of the government or technological specialization alone. However, when assessing the impact of innovation on output or productivity growth, it is important to keep in mind that country differences may arise, even though the limited data that is available may not reflect these differences to any satisfactory extent.

3   Technology and growth: estimating some simple models

This section applies some simple econometric models to the data on technology and growth. The aim of this exercise is to investigate whether or not technology indicators are systematically related to growth of output and / or productivity. Two broad classes of models will be applied: time series models and cross-country models. The distinction between those two types of models is largely inspired by data availability.

The time series models are estimated for the three major European countries (Germany, France, UK), using data on capital stocks, labour input, labour productivity, R&D and patents. R&D data and data on capital stocks are not available in a broader sample of countries, so a different model is estimated for a cross-country sample of sixteen countries (fourteen European, Japan and the USA). In the latter case, data on patents, investment–output ratios and labour productivity are used.

There are many aspects of the relation between long-run growth and technology that will have to remain unassessed in the limited scope of this chapter. First, they relate to the aspects of technological change which are not captured by the R&D and patent indicators that will be used in this section. Second, there are important aspects of the relation between R&D (or patents) and growth that will not explicitly be modelled below. One of these aspects are spillovers. There is a large literature on spillovers of R&D-activity (see Griliches (1979) for an early treatment of this problem). The problem with measuring spillovers, however, is that it makes large demands on the number of degrees of freedom. Given the limited data available for the type of analysis that is the interest of this paper (a cross-country overview of some trends in the European area), these demands are clearly too high. The only way in which spillovers, along with other non-explicitly measured variables will be taken into account is therefore by means of a time trend and / or the constant in the regression.[8]

3.1 Time series models

The functional specification adopted for estimating time series models in this section, is a simple Cobb–Douglas production function. It is assumed that there are constant returns to scale with regard to capital and labour. Technological change is assumed to be neutral, and is written as a function of the knowledge stock and a time trend. The model to be estimated is, thus, as follows:

$$\ln Y_t = c + \alpha \ln k_t + \beta t + r R_t + \varepsilon_t \tag{1}$$

where Y is labour productivity, k is the capital-labour ratio, R is the knowledge stock, t is time, c is a constant, and α, β and r are elasticities. This specification is similar to Patel and Soete (1985), except that they do not use the k term (but instead approximate it by the time trend).

Long enough time series for the variables in the regression are not available for most European countries. For the three major countries (Germany, France and the UK), however, estimation is possible. A 'European' time series was also created, by simply adding the values of the variables for the three major countries (all expressed in 1985 purchasing power parities to the US$). Even with the simple Cobb–Douglas applied, there is a vast number of possible functional estimations possible. For example, R&D can be expected to turn up in the equation with various lags, as its effect will only become apparent after some time. It is unlikely that any econometric exercise of the type applied here will be able to determine the exact lag structure (which most probably is also variable across different R&D projects). Different estimations carried out, however, seem to suggest that it is not a very restricting idea to simply use the current value of the R&D stock, instead of its lagged value of some order.[9]

Different technology stock indicators are used. Both patents and business R&D expenditures are included.[10] In all cases, the technology indicators are accumulated into some stock measure. In the case of patents, this is done by a simple perpetual inventory method, assuming a fixed lifetime of patents. The difference between the two patent indicators relates to the assumed lifetime of patents. P^l uses a long lifetime of 15 years, whereas P^s uses a lifetime of 10 years. In the case of R&D, one of the methods (resulting in R^m) uses essentially a moving average (with a bell-shaped weight-structure), as in Patel and Soete (1985). The other method (resulting in R^p) uses a perpetual inventory method with a fixed rate of depreciation. The appendix lists the exact definitions of the variables.

The initial OLS estimates on these data suffered from two major problems: non-stationarity[11] of the series and autocorrelation. Most of the series appear to be $I(1)$ processes, some of them even $I(2)$ or still higher.[12] This may lead to spurious correlation while applying simple OLS methods. An Engle–Granger test for co-integration might, however, provide statistical evidence of a long-run (equilibrium) relationship between two (or more) non-stationary time series. The results for this test (not documented for space considerations) indicated that no simple OLS regression passes the co-integration test, indicating that the time series results may indeed be subject to spurious correlation. Note, however, that this conclusion even applies to regressions without technology indicators. For the moment, this result will not be explored further here. It will simply be taken as a warning against attaching too much value to the time series estimates alone, and a more thorough exploration of its robustness and implications will be left for future research.

The second problem with the simple OLS regressions was the obvious presence of autocorrelation.[13] There is a whole range of possible causes for this result. One quite general factor is probably that the applied model is to some extent mis-specified, leading to mis-fitting, rather than a true correlation between the error terms. Another possible source lies in the measurement of production, which is actual production rather than production capacity. This may lead to persistent business cycle effects turning up in the residuals.

There are a number of ways out of this problem, among which the most satisfactory ones are clearly beyond the scope of this chapter. For example, one could formulate a dynamic econometric model, in which the specific behaviour of the error term is modelled explicitly. Also, specification tests could be applied in search for a better functional form of the relationship between the variables in the model. Perhaps the most pragmatic method is to try to correct for autocorrelation by means of an adapted estimation method. This is the approach taken here. The final estimations which are used here are presented in Table 5.5, which gives Cochrane–Orcutt (CO) estimations.[14]

Table 5.5 Time series estimates of the Cobb–Douglas production function including different technology variables, Germany, France and UK, 1960–89, Cochrane–Orcutt estimations

	Estimated coefficients (t-values)				Type of R	$\bar{R}^2$	DW	CO parameter ρ (t-value)
	k	c	R	t				
Germany	0.352 (4.40)	−22.912 (3.50)	0.096 (1.89)	0.007 (2.28)	R^m	1.00	1.57	0.830 (8.91)
France	0.505 (7.05)	−12.763 (1.38)	0.077 (5.76)	0.003 (0.73)	R^m	1.00	1.70	0.747 (6.37)
UK	0.371 (6.42)	−26.353 (5.19)	0.013 (0.23)	0.010 (4.02)	R^m	1.00	1.69	0.452 (2.66)
Europe	0.389 (5.37)	−22.166 (3.37)	0.088 (2.23)	0.007 (2.34)	R^m	1.00	1.50	0.106 (7.52)
Germany	0.317 (4.01)	−17.639 (2.84)	0.157 (2.69)	0.004 (1.26)	R^p	1.00	1.74	0.105 (7.59)
France	0.494 (7.87)	−10.410 (1.29)	0.098 (7.18)	0.002 (0.45)	R^p	1.00	1.71	0.696 (5.35)
UK	0.346 (5.21)	−26.200 (5.39)	0.054 (0.75)	0.009 (3.93)	R^p	1.00	1.68	0.428 (2.46)
Europe	0.355 (4.75)	−20.459 (3.37)	0.133 (2.81)	0.006 (2.02)	R^p	1.00	1.54	0.763 (6.63)
Germany	0.304 (3.54)	−28.906 (4.58)	0.126 (2.78)	0.010 (3.61)	P^s	1.00	1.76	0.116 (6.49)
France	0.172 (2.67)	−47.113 (6.72)	0.232 (9.25)	0.018 (5.63)	P^s	1.00	1.63	0.565 (3.46)
UK	0.312 (2.79)	−31.687 (3.37)	0.037 (0.65)	0.012 (3.02)	P^s	1.00	1.70	0.535 (2.53)
Europe	0.250 (3.15)	−34.864 (5.39)	0.173 (4.81)	0.012 (4.54)	P^s	1.00	1.59	0.468 (2.75)
Germany	0.263 (3.09)	−27.361 (4.88)	0.150 (3.51)	0.009 (3.60)	P^l	1.00	1.81	0.718 (5.63)
France	0.273 (4.10)	−29.513 (3.95)	0.253 (7.43)	0.009 (2.71)	P^l	1.00	1.67	0.694 (5.32)
UK	0.340 (2.57)	−28.996 (3.00)	0.026 (0.30)	0.011 (2.80)	P^l	1.00	1.70	0.457 (2.71)
Europe	0.212 (2.51)	−33.014 (5.46)	0.210 (4.85)	0.011 (4.44)	P^l	1.00	1.61	0.510 (3.02)

The results differ between countries. In general, the coefficients on the capital–labour ratios are significant, although the values differ between countries. The estimations for the time trend, supposed to pick up all sorts of factors not explicitly in the model, such as technology spillovers, catch-up, institutional change, etc., are also mostly significant. In general, the values for the time trend seem to be somewhat higher when patents are taken as the technology indicator, suggesting that R&D is a broader concept of technology, also including aspects of spillovers. The technology indicators themselves are mostly significant, with output elasticities between 1% and 15% in the case of R&D, and (slightly) higher (3–25%) in the case of patents. The UK seems to be the exception, with low and non-significant technology parameters.

Overall, these results on time series estimation suggest a positive relationship between technology and growth. The results, however, are subject to much empirical critique, and need to be tested in a different framework before being taken too seriously.

3.2   Cross-country models

This further testing will be done in the form of a cross-country estimation. In order to do this, some changes are made relative to the previous specification. These changes are necessary because of the additional and different variables used in the regressions (data availability), and the country differences not relevant to the time series model. Because the focus of this chapter is on the complete post-war period, R&D data (which are available on a broad enough level only from the 1970s onwards) do not suffice. Therefore, patent data (available even for periods before the war) are used instead. Moreover, because of differences in initial level of per capita GDP, countries must be assumed to have realized different catch-up potentials. This is why a variable measuring initial GDP per capita relative to the USA is included in the regressions. Moreover, capital stock data is not available for the broad sample of countries used, so that the investment–output ratio is used as a proxy for the growth rate of the capital stock (see, for example Dowrick and Nguyen (1989) for a justification of this approach). The basic cross-country model used can thus be specified as follows:

$$\hat{Y}_i = c + \alpha \hat{L}_i + \beta I_i + \gamma \hat{P}_i + \delta y_i^{\text{usa}} + \varepsilon_i \tag{2}$$

where 'hats' above variables denote proportionate growth rates, I is the capital output ratio, y^{usa} denotes labour productivity relative to the USA at the beginning of the period over which growth rates are taken, and all

Table 5.6   Results for the simple cross-country model, all variables measured over the 1950–88 period[a]

Equation number	c	$\hat{L}$	I	$\hat{P}^s$	$\hat{P}^l$	y^{usa}	$\bar{R}^2$ n
1	0.035	0.701			0.118	−0.035	0.84
	(14.40)	(1.93)			(4.32)	(8.78)	16
2	0.036	0.761		0.088		−0.037	0.84
	(14.28)	(2.06)		(4.16)		(9.05)	16
3	0.040	1.170	−0.000			−0.048	0.77
	(7.19)	(2.53)	(0.46)			(8.26)	16
4	0.037	0.705	−0.000		0.121	−0.035	0.83
	(10.97)	(1.91)	(0.49)		(4.87)	(8.88)	16
5	0.039	0.766	−0.000	0.093		−0.037	0.83
	(10.64)	(2.04)	(0.64)	(5.08)		(9.21)	16

[a] Numbers in parentheses are absolute t-statistics, based upon standard errors estimated using a covariance matrix corrected for heteroscedasticity.

other variables are as defined before. This model is a simple one-period cross-country model, assuming all coefficients are equal across countries. The variable y^{usa} is put into the equation in order to catch any effects related to catch-up, which were assumed to go into the time trend above. Again, two different patent stocks are used (with varying assumptions on the lifetime of patents). The countries for which the model is estimated are Belgium, Germany, Denmark, Spain, France, UK, Greece, Ireland, Italy, The Netherlands, Portugal, Switzerland, Norway, Sweden, Japan, and the USA. The results for this model for the period 1950–88 are in Table 5.6.

In general, the results of this first cross-country estimation support the results found in the time series approach. The results for the conventional inputs (labour and capital) are mixed. Labour, which should be expected to have a negative coefficient with a value in the range 0.2–0.45, instead has fairly large positive coefficients, and the investment–output ratio is very close to zero and not significant. The patent variables are all very significant, but the output elasticities are a bit lower in general than the ones obtained in the time series approach, more in the range of the R&D variables in the previous section. The catch-up variable, as expected, has a negative sign, which is quite significant in all cases.

Thus, although the results of the simple model with respect to technological change are quite encouraging, the results for the conventional inputs are less so. This might be the result of too strict assumptions on equality of coefficients between countries. Therefore, the specification of the model might be improved by including some country-specific effects. In order to do so, a pooled sample is set up, by splitting up the 1950–88 period into three different subperiods: 1950–60, 1960–73, and 1973–88. Two different models are estimated for this pooled sample: a fixed-effect model (FE, which assumes country effects are non-stochastic), and a random-effect model (RE, which assumes the country effects go into the disturbance term). These models are formalized as follows:

$$\hat{Y}_{it} = c_{it} + \alpha \hat{L}_{it} + \beta I_{it} + \gamma \hat{P}_{it} + \delta y_i^{\text{usa}} + \varepsilon_{it} \tag{3}$$

$$\hat{Y}_{it} = c + \alpha \hat{L}_{it} + \beta I_{it} + \gamma \hat{P}_{it} + \delta y_{it}^{\text{usa}} + \phi_i + \varepsilon_{it} \tag{4}$$

Equation (3) is the FE model, and (4) is the RE model; ϕ is a normally distributed random variable, with mean zero and constant variance. These models are estimated separately, and a Hausman (χ^2) specification test of the FE model versus the RE model is applied. Note, however, that this model still makes some rather restrictive assumptions about the equality of coefficients between countries (only the intercepts are assumed to vary between countries), and over time (all the coefficients, including the country effects, are assumed to be constant over time). Estimations including time effects as well as country effects, however, showed very mixed results, probably related to the low number of degrees of freedom. The results of the estimation are given in Table 5.7.

The Hausman tests seem to indicate the RE models perform better than the FE models, something which is also evident from the significance of the estimated coefficients. Although the results for the labour variable are no longer significant, they are closer to their expected value, and in some cases the expected negative sign is found indeed. For the FE models, only the catch-up terms appears significant. For the RE models, as well as the models without any country-specific effects, the technology variable is also generally significant. Labour and capital variables are not significant in any of the specifications. With regard to the elasticities of the technology variable, they again appear between 5% and 10%. It is remarkable, however, that in most occurrences, the value of the short-lifetime patent stock is higher (although marginally in most cases) than the one for the longer lifetime. The confrontation of the results for the patent stocks with those obtained in the time series estimates suggests that in some countries (the more advanced ones), the coefficients might actually be higher than those obtained here. This refutes the implicit assumption about equality of coefficients across countries, which therefore indeed seems to be a problem in the regressions in this section. Solving this problem, without more observations in the time dimension, however, does not seem to be easy.

Table 5.7   Results for the FE versus RE cross-country model, periods 1950–60, 1960–73, 1973–88[a]

Equation number	c	$\hat{L}$	I	$\hat{P}^s$	$\hat{P}^l$	y^{usa}	$\bar{R}^2$ n
1a		0.130			0.020	−0.048	0.09
		(0.37)			(0.45)	(4.46)	48
1b	0.057	0.014			0.064	−0.052	0.18
	(9.64)	(0.05)			(1.83)	(5.51)	48
1c	0.057	0.002			0.088	−0.055	0.52
	(9.91)	(0.01)			(2.57)	(5.48)	48

Hausman χ^2 test FE v RE: 3.96 ($p = 0.27$, do not reject RE)

2a		0.091		0.026		−0.047	0.10
		(0.25)		(0.61)		(4.37)	48
2b	0.053	−0.087		0.089		−0.047	0.26
	(8.83)	(0.28)		(2.81)		(4.91)	48
2c	0.051	−0.096		0.113		−0.046	0.58
	(8.49)	(0.29)		(3.65)		(4.57)	48

Hausman χ^2 test FE v RE: 5.39 ($p = 0.15$, do not reject RE)

3a		0.135	0.000		0.019	−0.047	0.06
		(0.38)	(0.38)		(0.42)	(4.35)	48
3b	0.051	0.017	0.000		0.059	−0.052	0.16
	(4.67)	(0.05)	(0.56)		(1.62)	(5.44)	48
3c	0.053	−0.001	0.000		0.082	−0.055	0.51
	(4.75)	(0.00)	(0.45)		(2.19)	(5.44)	48

Hausman χ^2 test FE v RE: 3.81 ($p = 0.43$, do not reject RE)

4a		0.094	0.000	0.026		−0.047	0.07
		(0.26)	(0.40)	(0.59)		(4.24)	48
4b	0.046	−0.095	0.000	0.087		−0.047	0.25
	(4.32)	(0.30)	(0.74)	(2.69)		(4.84)	48
4c	0.045	−0.113	0.000	0.108		−0.046	0.57
	(4.25)	(0.34)	(0.73)	(3.40)		(4.56)	48

Hausman χ^2 test FE v RE: 4.96 ($p = 0.29$, do not reject RE)

[a] Equations 1a, 2a, 3a, and 4a are FE models (country intercepts not reported), equations 1b, 2b, 3b, and 4b are RE models, equations 1c, 2c, 3c, and 4c are models with any country-specific effects (reproduced for comparison). Numbers in parentheses are absolute t-statistics.

Concluding, the evidence from the cross-country estimates again supports the hypothesis of a long-run relationship between technological accumulation and growth of per capita GDP. As in the case of the time series estimation, the econometric results are subject to some critique, but the results on the technology variables in the two types of analyses appear strong enough to provide confident results. Output elasticities of the technology variables appear to lie in the range 5% to 15%, with possibly higher values (up to 25%) for some of the more advanced countries in the time series regressions.

3.3   Summarizing the regression evidence

The various regressions provide mixed results with regard to the assumed relation between technology and growth. Each of the models has its own shortcomings, mostly in the form of badly measured key variables, over-restricting functional specifications, or too short periods of estimation. However, given these shortcomings, the performance of the technology-related variables is still quite remarkable.

In the time series estimations, elasticities of technology related variables appeared to fall in the range 1–25%. Patents generally yielded higher elasticities than R&D variables. In the cross-country regressions, lower values (5–10%, for the most relevant regressions) for the patent elasticities were obtained (R&D variables were not in the regressions). Overall, these results seem to indicate that there is indeed a significant relationship between technology variables and economic growth. The magnitude of the output elasticities, however, varies between different technology variables (or 'ways of capturing technology'), and countries. Both aspects of variability are hard to deal with in the econometric framework used here, and the results should accordingly be taken as rough estimates.

4   The contribution of technology to growth: growth accounting

What do these results imply for the contribution of technology to growth? An answer to this question can be found by applying some growth accounting exercises using the coefficients estimated in the various regressions, along with the data in these regressions. The first case for which this will be done is the growth rate for labour productivity over the 1960–89 period for France, Germany and the UK. The contribution of technology to these growth rates is calculated by multiplying the growth rate of the technology stock variable over this period by the estimated coefficient in the time series estimation. The

Table 5.8   The contribution of technology to growth of labour productivity (average annual growth rates), percentages, based on the time series estimations for France, Germany and the UK

UK		
Growth rate of labour productivity	2.46	
	Contribution in % points	Fraction of total growth
Contribution of technology on the basis of R^p	0.21	0.09
Contribution of technology on the basis of R^m	0.05	0.02
Contribution of technology on the basis of P^s	0.01	0.00
Contribution of technology on the basis of P^l	0.01	0.00
France		
Growth rate of labour productivity	3.72	
	Contribution in % points	Fraction of total growth
Contribution of technology on the basis of R^p	0.98	0.26
Contribution of technology on the basis of R^m	0.77	0.21
Contribution of technology on the basis of P^s	0.10	0.03
Contribution of technology on the basis of P^l	0.13	0.04
Germany		
Growth rate of labour productivity	3.31	
	Contribution in % points	Fraction of total growth
Contribution of technology on the basis of R^p	1.33	0.40
Contribution of technology on the basis of R^m	0.80	0.24
Contribution of technology on the basis of P^s	0.08	0.02
Contribution of technology on the basis of P^l	0.10	0.03

outcomes of this procedure are confronted with the growth rate of output itself in Table 5.8.

As could be expected on the basis of the time series regression results for the UK, the contribution of technology to labour productivity growth in this country is not very substantial. For the other two countries, however, the contribution is quite high, at least in some cases. In general, patenting contributes less to growth than R&D does. This implies, quite in accordance with intuition, that R&D is a much broader process than patenting alone, i.e., not all results of R&D are patented, while there is a non-zero pay-off even if patenting does not take place. Of the two R&D knowledge stock measures, the perpetual inventory one has a much higher contribution than the one based upon moving averages. This is probably caused by the fact that in the moving average case, R&D expenditures vanish from the stock measure quite quickly, whereas they remain in the stock much longer in the case of the perpetual inventory. For the case of patenting, the differences between the two measures of the stock are less pronounced, but still the ones obtained with a longer lifetime are somewhat larger. Again, this indicates the long lag involved in the technology process.

Focusing on individual countries, the contribution of technology to labour productivity growth is highest in Germany. For the case of R&D measured by the perpetual inventory method, about two-fifths of total growth is explained by this variable. Even for the moving average variant, the contribution is about 0.8 percentage points a year, or roughly a quarter of total growth over the period 1970–89. For France, the contribution of R&D corresponds roughly to one-fifth or a quarter of total growth. Both for Germany and France, patents only contribute a few percentage points of total growth over the period.

To what extent do these results apply to the broader sample of countries that were analysed in the cross-country regression case? And how does the contribution of technology in the form of the R&D and patent stocks relate to technological imitation in the form of catch-up (related to initial per capita GDP levels)? These are the questions asked when analysing the results of the previous section in a broader cross-section sample.

Again, the contributions of the various factors to growth are calculated by multiplying the growth rate of the variable (in this case only patent stocks, both for long and short lifetimes) with the estimated coefficient. Growth rates and contributions too are calculated over the 1950–88 period. Because of the more plausible results (on labour) in the pooled regressions, the estimated coefficients of equations 3b and 4b in Table 5.7 are used in the calculations. This time, two factors are taken into account: first, the contribution by patents, and second, the contribution of catch-up. The latter is calculated as the sum of the constant and the coefficient estimate on y^{usa} multiplied with the value of the variable. For the USA, this variable yields a (positive) growth rate, which is assumed to be the exogenous part of the growth rate in the frontier country. Estimates for the sixteen countries in the sample are available in Table 5.9. European countries are ranked in order of decreasing overall growth rates.

Overall, the contribution of technology factors in the table varies around half a percentage point a year in the case of the short patent lifetime, and one-third of a percentage point in the case of longer patent lifetime. Japan is a positive outlier, with a contribution close to one or

Table 5.9   Contributions of technology and catch-up to labour productivity growth, estimates based upon cross-country regressions, 1950–88 (average annual growth), percentages

Country	Estimates based upon P^l				Estimates based upon P^s				
	$c-y^{usa}$	Fraction P^l of total growth		Fraction of total growth	$c-y^{usa}$	Fraction P^s of total growth		Fraction of total growth	Total growth
Greece	3.18	0.72	0.39	0.09	3.35	0.76	0.52	0.12	4.39
Italy	2.69	0.62	0.43	0.10	2.83	0.65	0.72	0.17	4.33
Portugal	3.26	0.80	0.19	0.05	3.43	0.85	0.21	0.05	4.06
Spain	2.88	0.74	0.33	0.08	3.03	0.78	0.59	0.15	3.91
Germany	2.54	0.70	0.26	0.07	2.67	0.73	0.50	0.14	3.65
France	2.32	0.71	0.30	0.09	2.44	0.75	0.51	0.16	3.27
Norway	1.98	0.67	0.24	0.08	2.08	0.70	0.42	0.14	2.95
Netherlands	1.96	0.72	0.24	0.09	2.06	0.75	0.38	0.14	2.73
Belgium	1.93	0.73	0.31	0.12	2.03	0.77	0.53	0.20	2.63
Ireland	2.66	1.05	0.27	0.11	2.80	1.11	0.49	0.19	2.53
Denmark	2.10	0.91	0.28	0.12	2.20	0.96	0.47	0.20	2.29
UK	1.84	0.83	0.13	0.06	1.93	0.87	0.19	0.09	2.21
Switzerland	1.17	0.54	0.26	0.12	1.22	0.56	0.38	0.17	2.16
Sweden	1.74	0.81	0.25	0.12	1.83	0.85	0.38	0.18	2.14
Japan	3.20	0.56	0.96	0.17	3.37	0.58	1.68	0.29	5.76
USA	0.20	0.12	0.05	0.03	0.20	0.12	0.06	0.04	1.64

even two percentage points. The USA has a contribution almost equal to zero. Based upon the shorter lifetime, technology contributes about one-fifth of total growth of labour productivity in Italy, Belgium, Denmark, Ireland, Switzerland and Sweden. The contribution is somewhat lower in Greece, Spain, Germany, France, Norway and The Netherlands, where it varies between 0.1% and 0.15%. The European countries with the lowest contribution are Portugal and the UK.

In general, the contribution of the catch-up terms is higher than the impact of the patent stock. Keeping in mind the 0.2% of the USA as a benchmark case, the additional contribution of the constant and the initial per capita GDP varies between about 3 percentage points of total growth in the case of Portugal and about 1 percentage point in the case of Switzerland. Countries such as Greece, Portugal, Spain seem to benefit somewhat more from the catch-up potential than relatively advanced countries such as Germany or The Netherlands, but even the latter countries have substantial portions of their total growth explained by the catch-up term.

4.1 Spillovers

Thus far, technology spillovers have not formed an essential part of the analysis. In the Cobb–Douglas estimates as the ones that were used in the construction of Table 5.8, it has implicitly been assumed that intranational spillovers between different firms turn up in the coefficient on the technology stock variable in the regression. The estimation of a European Cobb–Douglas function, however, provides an opportunity to look in some more detail at international technology spillovers in the European area.

In order to do so, consider first a growth accounting exercise for the European series, such as the one in Table 5.5. As in the case of the national estimates, the influence in this case implicitly internalizes spillovers between firms within each of the three countries, but also across the country borders. Thus, the estimate of the technology contribution to growth includes all (intranational as well as international) spillovers. Consider also the growth accounting exercise in which it is recognized that the output (and labour input) in this European area is a weighted sum of country outputs. Recognizing this, the growth rate of labour productivity in the European area can be calculated as the weighted (by output share) sum of the national growth rates.[15] The national growth rates are, in their turn, a function of technology accumulation, so that by weighting the national contributions of technology by their country shares in total output, one arrives at an alternative estimate of the contribution of technology to total European growth.

The latter estimate, however, does not internalize the international spillovers between firms. It should therefore be smaller than the first estimate, and the difference between the two is an approximation for the international component of technology spillovers. The results of this exercise are presented in Table 5.10. Because of the discrete representation of time that is used here, there is still the question as to which output shares of the different countries should be used. Therefore, the table gives two different estimates, one based on the shares at the beginning of the period (1960), and one based on the shares in the middle of the period (1975).

With regard to European labour productivity growth, the results in Table 5.10 suggest much the same as one would expect on the basis of Table 5.8. R&D contributes more to growth than patents do (one-fifth to one-third versus less than 5%), and the perpetual inventory variant of the R&D knowledge stock has the highest contribution (about 0.8 percentage points). Spillovers, although positive, contribute only a small

Table 5.10   The contribution of technology to growth of labour productivity in the France–Germany–UK area and the influence of spillovers, 1960–89 (average annual growth rates), percentages[a]

Time	Country shares in 1960	Country shares in 1975
Estimates on the basis of P^l		
Estimate based on European series	0.091 (0.03)	0.091 (0.03)
Sum of country contributions	0.075 (0.02)	0.082 (0.03)
Difference (spillovers)	0.016 (0.01)	0.009 (0.00)
Estimates based upon P^s		
Estimate based on European series	0.064 (0.02)	0.064 (0.02)
Sum of country contributions	0.057 (0.02)	0.062 (0.02)
Difference (spillovers)	0.008 (0.00)	0.002 (0.00)
Estimates based upon R^m		
Estimate based on European series	0.581 (0.19)	0.581 (0.19)
Sum of country contributions	0.511 (0.16)	0.550 (0.18)
Difference (spillovers)	0.070 (0.03)	0.030 (0.01)
Estimates based upon R^p		
Estimate based on European series	0.895 (0.29)	0.895 (0.29)
Sum of country contributions	0.818 (0.26)	0.861 (0.28)
Difference (spillovers)	0.077 (0.03)	0.034 (0.01)

[a] Numbers in parentheses give fraction of total labour productivity growth explained (total growth is 3.1% per year).

fraction of total growth (around 0.07 percentage points or 3% of total growth, in the most optimistic variant, based upon initial period weights). Still, this contribution is about the same size as the overall impact of patents on total growth.

4.2   Convergence

One of the crucial characteristics of post-war growth in the OECD area is the phenomenon of convergence of labour productivity levels. This trend is documented extensively in the rest of this volume, as well as in the rest of the literature on post-war growth (see, for example, Fagerberg *et al.* (1994). Figure 5.2 also illustrates this process by giving the coefficient of variation of labour productivities for the European countries included in the regressions in Section 3.2.

Technology obviously plays a role in the convergence phenomenon. The main hypothesis explaining productivity convergence is related to so-called catch-up, i.e., the idea that initially backward countries can exploit

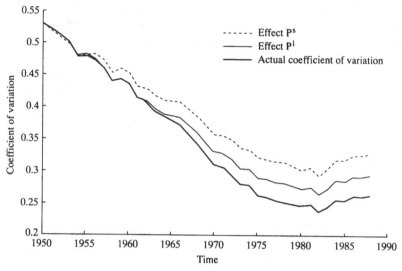

Figure 5.2   Coefficient of variation of labour productivity in fourteen European countries, actual and hypothetical constructs abstracting from the effects of patenting

a large backlog of knowledge developed in the more advanced countries, and therefore grow faster (for example, Abramovitz (1979) and Verspagen (1991a)). To what extent do technology indicators, through their relation to growth, play a role in this process?

Many aspects of technology which are related to catch-up, will probably not turn up in either R&D or patenting elasticities. The reason for this is that catch-up is crucially related to imitation. Likely mechanisms for this kind of technological imitation are imports of intermediates and investment goods, learning by doing, or import of human capital. The effects related to these processes were assumed to turn up in growth related to initial (relative) labour productivity, as in the regressions in Section 3.2, and Table 5.9 in this section. The latter table showed the crucial importance of this type of catch-up, as compared to the direct effects of patents.

However, R&D and patents must also be assumed to have an influence on convergence. As backward countries learn from the more advanced, their technology efforts in the form of R&D or patents are likely to yield higher pay-offs. In line with the arguments above, R&D is likely to have a broader influence in this respect than patents. One might therefore ask what R&D expenditures or patents contributed to convergence in the European area. With respect to R&D, this question is not easy to answer, because of the lack of data for a large enough country sample and time-period. Verspagen (1994) analysed this question for a smaller country sample and time-period, and came to the conclusion that R&D contributed both to convergence and to the slowdown in convergence since the middle of the 1970s. Here, a similar exercise can be performed for the case of patents and the period 1950–88.

Consider the hypothetical situation in which all countries would have grown along a path in which the influence of patenting was absent. This situation can be 'constructed' by calculating the actual yearly growth rates of labour productivity in each country, subtracting the assumed influence of patenting (as estimated by equations 3b and 4b in Table 5.7), and using the resulting growth rate to construct a new series for labour productivity. These new series might then be used to calculate a new coefficient of variation, which can be compared to the old one. Two such alternative scenarios are depicted in Figure 5.2 (one for each type of patenting stock). The figure clearly shows that without the influence of patenting, disparity of labour productivity in the European area (as measured by the coefficient of variation) would have been larger. In other words, patenting trends in the various countries had a net converging effect. With regard to time, it appears that the main converging effect of patenting took place in the 1960s, and slowed down (i.e., the distance between the hypothetical and actual curves remained more or less the same) in the 1970s and 1980s. This leads to the conclusion that besides imitation effects, there were also catch-up effects related to genuine convergence in technological competences.

5   Summary and conclusions

The analysis in this paper has shown that there is a clear long-run relationship between the development of technology indicators such as R&D and patents, and economic growth in the form of labour productivity trends. In general, the impact of R&D (in terms of contribution to growth in percentage points) seems to be larger than the impact of patents. Still, in a cross-section regression involving fourteen European countries, patenting was found to contribute about half a percentage point a year to the growth of labour productivity over the 1950–88 period.

Even if the econometric tests applied in this chapter are subject to much critique, only partially to be overcome by more sophisticated analysis beyond the scope of this chapter, the contribution of technological change mentioned stands out in a number of different tests, stressing different aspects of the data.

The discussion around the quality of the indicators used for technology, has shown that there are many aspects of innovations that cannot be measured in any satisfactory way. This implies that the contribution of technology to growth is probably underestimated by the indicators used here. The example of catch-up as a source of growth that was applied in Section 4 underlines this view also, stressing that international imitation was a major source of growth in Europe after World War II. Nevertheless, genuine convergence in technological competences was a factor explaining convergence of labour productivity in the post-war period in Europe.

These results underline the importance of technological change as an economic concept. They do not give any final answers to the questions posed. For example, the differential impact of technological progress on different nations was hardly captured in the methodological framework applied. Innovation deserves all the attention it can get from economists, and the only fruitful way to analyse the subject is by interaction of different methodologies. Historical, institutional, formal, and empirical analyses may all have their specific contribution to increasing knowledge about the role technology may play in stimulating long-run, sustainable, growth.

Appendix: Formal definition of variables and sources

I Investment–output ratio. Taken from the Penn World Tables (Summers and Heston, 1991). Defined as the mean value over the applicable period.

k Capital–labour ratio. Sources: the capital stock is taken from Maddison (1993), and is defined as the total of machinery and equipment and structures. For labour input, see under L.

L Labour input. Defined as hours worked in Section 3.1, and as the labour force in Section 2. Sources: hours worked are computed from series for employment from OECD, and series for average hours worked in non-agricultural activities from ILO (*Yearbook of Labour Statistics*, various issues). The series is computed as 49 times the labour force time average weekly hours. Data on the labour force used in Section 3.2 is computed from the Penn World Tables (Summers and Heston, 1991).

P^s The patent stock, using short patent lifetime. The patent stock in period t is defined as all patents granted in the USA between t and $t - 10$ (inclusive). This is essentially a perpetual inventory stock, assuming a patent lifetime of 10 years (the actual period for which a patent is granted is 18 years). Source: computations on data from the US Patent and Trademark Office.

P^l The patent stock, using a long patent lifetime. Similar definition as P^s, only with an assumed lifetime of 15 years.

R^m The R&D knowledge stock, defined as a moving average. Sources: data on R&D expenditures is taken from the OECD, the National Science Foundation in the USA, and Patel and Soete (1985), and is defined as R&D undertaken by business enterprises. The stock is defined as being equal to $0.2\,X_{t-1} + 0.3\,X_{t-2} + 0.3\,X_{t-2} + 0.2\,X_{t-4}$, where X_t is R&D expenditures in period t (as in Patel and Soete (1985)).

R^p The R&D knowledge stock, defined as a perpetual inventory. Sources: data used is the same as for R^m, but the formula used to compute the stock variable is now $R_t = 0.85\,R_{t-1} + X_t$ (R_{1956} is estimated as $5\,X_{1956}$).

Y Labour productivity. Sources: in Section 3.1, output is equal to GDP in 1985 US$ PPP, taken from Maddison (1991), and labour is defined under L. In Section 3.2, Y is taken from the Penn World Tables (Summers and Heston (1991), output measured in 1985 international prices).

y^{usa} Ratio of per capita GDP in the country and the USA at the beginning of the regression period. Source: Penn World Tables (Summers and Heston, 1991).

NOTES

My research has been made possible by a fellowship of the Royal Netherlands Academy of Arts and Sciences.

1 For a more complete discussion of the drawbacks of R&D statistics than is possible here, see Soete and Verspagen (1991).
2 For a thorough overview of patents as indicators of innovation, see Griliches (1990).
3 These 'early' data will be used in the following sections.
4 Patents are dated by year of grant and assigned to SIC classes and countries by the US Patent and Trademark Office.
5 This is done to obtain a symmetric indicator, i.e., one in which 'advantages' and 'disadvantages' are measured on an equal scale.
6 See for example Green *et al.* (1989), for an introduction to multidimensional-scaling.
7 Note that neither the axes, nor their scale, have a straightforward interpretation. Their only function is to provide degrees of freedom. This is why they are not labelled.
8 Note that since no explicit maximization restrictions are imposed, inter-firm spillovers within a country will turn up in the coefficient on the knowledge stock. The reason for this is that while these spillovers are externalities at the firm-level, there are clearly internal to the national economy. This is also the

crucial argument about increasing returns to scale in new growth theory (see Verspagen (1991b)).
9 Recall that by definition the current R&D stock includes past R&D outlays.
10 Results with total rather than business R&D are generally worse in terms of significance. See Verspagen (1994) for an application.
11 For an introduction to some of the concepts and problems in non-stationary time series-analysis, see Banerjee *et al.* (1993).
12 A process is said to be integrated of order *n*, or $I(n)$ if the time series it produces can be made stationary by differencing *n* times.
13 In fact, this problem may well be connected with the previous one, since both are dealing with the dynamic behaviour of the residuals from the regression.
14 The major difference in the results between OLS and CO estimates were the parameters obtained on *k*. These were much more plausible (taken as values for 1 minus labour's share in income) in the CO estimates. The results for the technology variables were not very different between OLS and CO.
15 There is also a structural effect, due to the changing composition by 'nationality' of output over the period 1960–90. Since this effect is not (directly) related to technology, it is not considered explicitly.

REFERENCES

Abramovitz, M.A. (1956), 'Resources and Output Trends in the United States since 1870', *American Economic Review*, **46**, 5–23.
Abramovitz, M.A. (1979), 'Rapid Growth Potential and its Realization: The Experience of Capitalist Economies in the Postwar Period', in E. Malinvaud (ed.), *Economic Growth and Resources, Vol. 1, The major Issues: Proceedings of the Fifth World Congress of the International Economic Association*, London: Macmillan, pp. 1–51.
Banerjee, A., J.G.J. Dolada, J.W. Galbraith and D.F. Hendry (1993), *Co-integration, Error-correction, and the Econometric Analysis of Non-stationary Data*, Oxford: Oxford University Press.
Dosi, G. (1988), 'Sources, Procedures and Microeconomic Effects of Innovation', *Journal of Economic Literature*, **26**, 1120–71.
Dowrick, S. and D.T. Nguyen (1989), 'OECD Comparative Economic Growth 1950–85: Catch-Up and Convergence', *American Economic Review*, **79** (5), 1010–30.
Fagerberg, J., B. Verspagen and N. von Tunzelmann (eds.) (1994), *The Dynamics of Technology, Trade and Growth*, Aldershot: Edward Elgar.
Gomulka, S. (1990), *The Theory of Technological Change and Economic Growth*, London: Routledge.
Green, P.E., F.J. Carmone and S.M. Smith (1989), *Multidimensional Scaling. Concepts and Applications*, Boston: Allyn & Bacon.
Griliches, Z. (1979), 'Issues in Assessing the Contribution of Research and Development to Productivity Growth', *The Bell Journal of Economics*, **10**, 92–116.
Griliches, Z. (1990), 'Patent Statistics as Economic Indicators: A Survey', *Journal of Economic Literature*, **XXVIII** (4), 1661–707.
Grossman, G. and E. Helpman (1991), *Innovation and Growth in the Global Economy*, Cambridge, MA: MIT Press.

Kleinknecht, A. (1987), 'Measuring R&D in Small Firms: How Much Are We Missing?', *Journal of Industrial Economics*, **XXXVI** (2), 253–6.

Kleinknecht, A.H., J.O.N. Reijnen and J.J. Verwey (1990), *Innovatie in de Nederlandse industrie en dienstverlening: een enquete-onderzoek*, The Hague: Ministerie van EZ/ATB.

Lundvall, B.A. (1992), *National Systems of Innovation: An Analytical Framework*, London: Pinter.

Maddison, A. (1991), *Dynamic Forces in Capitalist Development*, Oxford: Oxford University Press.

Maddison, A. (1993), 'Standardised Estimates of Fixed Capital Stock: A Six Country Comparison', *Innovazione e Materie Prime*, April, 1.

Mohnen, P. (1992), *The Relationship between R&D and Productivity Growth in Canada and Other Major Industrialized Countries*, Ottawa: Economic Council of Canada.

Patel, P. and L. Soete (1985), 'Recherche-Developpement, Importation de Technologie et Croissance Economique', *Revenue Economique*, **36** (5), 975–1000.

Romer, P.M. (1986), 'Increasing Returns and Long Run Growth', *Journal of Political Economy*, **94** (5), 1002–37.

Soete, L. and B. Verspagen (1991), 'Recent Comparative Trends in Technology Indicators in the OECD Area', in OECD (ed.), *Technology and Productivity. The Challenge for Economic Policy*, Paris: OECD, pp. 249–74.

Summers, R. and A. Heston (1987), 'A New Set of International Comparisons of Real Product and Price Levels Estimates for 130 Countries, 1950–1985', *Review of Income and Wealth*, **33**, 1–25.

Verspagen, B. (1991a), 'A New Empirical Approach to Catching Up or Falling Behind', *Structural Change and Economic Dynamics*, **2** (2), 359–80.

Verspagen, B. (1991b), 'Endogenous Innovation in Neo-classical Growth Models: A Survey', *Journal of Macroeconomics*, **14** (4), 631–62.

Verspagen, B. (1994), 'Technology and Growth: The Complex Dynamics of Convergence and Divergence', in G. Silverberg and L. Soete (eds.), *The Economics of Growth and Technical Change*, Aldershot: Edward Elgar.

6 Human capital and productivity in manufacturing during the twentieth century: Britain, Germany and the United States

STEPHEN N. BROADBERRY and
KARIN WAGNER

1 Introduction

Human capital is widely seen by economists as a key determinant of growth and productivity performance (Lucas, 1988; Romer, 1990). And yet surprisingly little is known about the quantitative dimensions of human capital accumulation before very recent times, beyond years of formal schooling, an indicator which suggests only minor differences between the major industrialized countries (Maddison, 1987, table A12). In this paper we present data on key aspects of human capital accumulation in the manufacturing sectors of Britain, Germany and the USA, and relate them to comparative productivity performance. We find that developments in human capital accumulation in the major industrialized countries can only be understood in relation to overall production strategies.

We emphasize competition between technological systems geared to mass production and craft/flexible production, with very different human capital requirements. We see the evolution of a mass production system in the USA in the early twentieth century, building on the American system of manufactures from the nineteenth century (Hounshell, 1984). In mass production, special-purpose machinery and resources were substituted for skilled shopfloor labour to produce standardized products. This involved heavy investment in fixed capital and the managerial aspects of human capital, but on the shopfloor involved the use of relatively unskilled labour. Over time, the investment in human capital above shopfloor level was strengthened by heavy investment in research and development. Furthermore, American R&D evolved in a 'mission-oriented' direction, concentrating on the emergence phase of new technologies (Ergas, 1987).

By contrast, European manufacturing, faced in the early twentieth century with different demand patterns and different resource and factor

244

endowments, pursued a craft production strategy, making extensive use of skilled shopfloor labour to produce customized output (Piore and Sabel, 1984; Tolliday and Zeitlin, 1991). However, since shopfloor workers retained a high degree of control over the production process, there was less need for investment in the managerial function. Although the post-war period also saw a building up of R&D in Europe, this evolved in a more 'diffusion-oriented' direction, concentrating on the consolidation phase of new technologies (Ergas, 1987).

It should be noted that labour productivity tends to be higher in mass production systems because of greater capital and resource intensity as well as economies of scale. Hence labour productivity has been substantially higher in American compared with European manufacturing (Broadberry, 1994a).

During the first two-thirds of the twentieth century there is little doubt that American mass production technology was progressive, forcing European craft producers to imitate and adapt, but not to slavishly copy, given the different endowments and demand conditions (Lazonick, 1990; Broadberry, 1994a). Since the late 1960s, however, it is equally clear that craft production has been rejuvenated by dramatic changes in information processing, and it is now American firms that are struggling to imitate and adapt to modern craft production technology, more usually known in the modern literature as 'flexible production' (Piore and Sabel, 1984; Milgrom and Roberts, 1990). These modern flexible production methods have been accompanied by a greater investment in the managerial aspects of human capital than was the case with older craft production techniques.

Within Europe, we see differing responses in the cases of Germany and Britain to the period of American technological leadership, especially after World War II. Before World War I and into the inter-war period, Britain continued to compete on the basis of a highly skilled shopfloor labour force (Harley, 1974; Pollard and Robertson, 1979). However, after World War II, an enthusiastic embrace of American methods was accompanied by a neglect of the skills of the shopfloor workforce, which left British manufacturers in a weak position to take advantage of the revival of craft production from the late 1960s. The switch to American methods was not very successful in Britain, where demand conditions and resource and factor endowments were rather different. Since British workers did not seem prepared to accept the loss of control over the production process and the erosion of the value of their human capital, the switch to American methods was a traumatic period in industrial relations, particularly during the 1970s (Lewchuk, 1987; Lorenz, 1991).

In Germany, attitudes towards American production methods were more ambivalent (Berghahn, 1991), and the post-war period saw a renewed emphasis on craft production, with the maintenance of a highly skilled shopfloor labour force. This left Germany in a strong position to take advantage of the information revolution from the late 1960s and emerge as a major force in world manufacturing. During the 1980s, British manufacturing appears to have moved back towards a skilled-labour-intensive production strategy, and indeed, the need to boost shopfloor labour qualifications seems to have become part of a new consensus in Britain (NIESR, 1991; Ryan, 1991).

It should be clear from the above analysis that to lump together Germany and the USA as a single model of modernity, as is common in the literature on British economic decline, is seriously misleading (Landes, 1969; Chandler, 1990; Elbaum and Lazonick, 1986).

2   Comparative performance in manufacturing

Before we examine the quantitative dimensions of human capital it will be helpful to establish the comparative productivity performance of Britain, Germany and the USA and relate the findings to production strategy. In this section we summarize findings reported in detail in Broadberry (1993, 1994a, 1994b).

Table 6.1 presents estimates of comparative output per worker in manufacturing for the UK, Germany and the USA over the period 1869–1989. The series are reported taking the UK as 100 in all years. The results are obtained by extrapolating with time series on output and employment from benchmark estimates indicated by asterisks. Other benchmark estimates are reported in parentheses to provide a check on the time series extrapolations. All benchmark estimates are made on a bilateral basis with the UK. Pre-1939 benchmarks are based on direct comparisons of physical output per worker following the methodology of Rostas (1948). Post-1939 benchmarks are based on comparisons of the value of net output and prices for individual products following the methodology of Paige and Bombach (1959). The use of physical quantities or price ratios obtained from production censuses means that we avoid the bias of using nominal exchange rates to compare values in different currencies (Gilbert and Kravis, 1954).

The figures in Table 6.1 suggest that US labour productivity has remained about twice the British level since at least the late nineteenth century, although there have been substantial swings in comparative productivity for sustained periods, particularly covering major wars. Furthermore, there has been a similar long-run stationarity in the relationship between British and German levels of labour productivity in

Table 6.1   Manufacturing output per person employed
(UK = 100)

	USA/UK		Germany/UK	
1869	203.8			
1875			100.0	
1879	187.8			
1889	195.4		94.7	
1899	194.8		99.0	
1907	190.0	(201.9)	106.4	
1913	212.9		119.0	
1920	222.8			
1925	234.2		95.2	
1929	249.9		104.7	
1935	207.8		*102.0	(102.0)
1937	*208.3	(208.3)	99.9	
1950	262.6	(273.4)	96.0	(99.5)
1958	250.0		111.1	
1968	242.6	(272.7)	120.0	(130.4)
1975	207.5	(224.7)	132.9	
1980	192.8		140.2	
1985	182.3		121.5	
1987	188.8	(186.6)	107.8	(112.7)
1989	177.0		105.1	

Note: * Benchmark year from which the time series are extrapolated. The figures in parentheses are actual benchmark comparisons.
Source: Broadberry (1993).

manufacturing since the late nineteenth century, although Germany built up a substantial lead during the 1970s which was eroded by rapid labour productivity growth in British manufacturing during the 1980s. We see these trends in the 1970s and 1980s as associated with changes in the bargaining environment between firms and unions, but related to changes in human capital accumulation, in particular reflecting changes in the strategy of British firms with respect to shopfloor labour (Crafts, 1991; Brown and Wadhwani, 1990; Bean and Symons, 1989).

The central finding of Table 6.1 is a persistent large labour productivity lead in the United States. In Broadberry (1994a) we relate this to the choice of technology. In particular, we see a greater reliance on mass production techniques in the USA and craft/flexible production techniques in Europe. This has resulted in higher labour productivity in the USA because of the capital intensity and resource intensity of mass production as well as economies of scale from the production of standardized products. The greater prevalence of mass production in the USA can be explained by both demand and supply factors. On the demand side, standardization in the USA was facilitated by the existence of a large, homogeneous home market in the USA compared with fragmented national markets stratified by class differences in Europe, coupled with a greater reliance on differentiated export markets (Rostas, 1948; Frankel, 1957; Chandler, 1990). On the supply side, resource-intensive American machinery could not be adopted on the same scale in Europe where resource costs were considerably higher (Ames and Rosenberg, 1968; Melman, 1956; Franko, 1976). Factor endowments reinforced these technological choices, with abundant skilled labour in Europe making continued reliance on craft production profitable (Harley, 1974). Hereafter, we shall follow Nelson and Wright (1992) in identifying national technological systems as a useful simplifying procedure.

We see the two technologies as coexisting so long as technological progress in one technology can be matched by imitation or adaptation in the other technology. Although for most of the period under considera-tion here technological leadership rested with American mass production technology, forcing European firms to adapt to survive, the period since the late 1960s has seen a revival in craft/flexible production methods, with American firms being forced to adapt to survive.

This coexistence of competing technologies, with both seen as rational in their respective environments, can be modelled along lines suggested by David (1975). Initial differences in factor proportions will be transmitted through time so long as technological progress can be seen as characterized by local learning. Although 'macro inventions' may appear to offer a country the opportunity to break free from such a technological 'lock-in', in practice decisions on whether, when or how to apply the new technology will be influenced by current factor proportions and demand conditions. In the historical literature, a useful example of the above argument is provided by Harley (1974), who explains the slow diffusion of American technology in Edwardian Britain by the existence of a large stock of skilled labour in Britain, making the continued use of craft production methods both profitable and rational.

As well as showing up in the productivity figures, the differences in technology between countries can be seen in the detailed evidence of writers who have made factory visits in different countries. These go back at least as far as the 1850s, when the British government sent a Commission to the United States to examine American machinery, with a view to improving the production of guns in Britain. The report of the

Table 6.2   Apprentices in pre-war British engineering

	Apprentices	Employment	Apprentice share of employment (%)
1914	44,917	297,680	15.1
1921	55,852	390,175	14.3
1928	38,899	416,710	9.3
1933	24,658	299,219	8.2
1938	52,840	608,897	8.7
1950	64,818	1,480,201	4.4

Notes: Blue-collar male employment from EEF data adjusted to allow for female and white-collar workers using information from Wigham (1973, appendix J) and the *Census of Production.*
Source: Engineering Employers' Federation, 'Number of Workpeople Employed'; 'Total Number of Men, Apprentices and Boys and Youths Employed' (EEF MSS.237/13/3/1–56).

Commission and the separate reports of George Wallis and Joseph Whitworth, two of the commissioners, reprinted in Rosenberg (1969), are early testimony to the development of the American system of manufactures. Nearly a century later, the Anglo-American Council of Productivity (AACP) reports confirm the continued differences in technology and organization on the two sides of the Atlantic (Hutton, 1953; AACP, 1952; Broadberry and Crafts, 1993). More recently, comparisons of matched plants in British and German manufacturing by researchers at the NIESR have highlighted the damaging implications of the decline of shopfloor skills in Britain (Daly *et al.*, 1985).

If our interpretation is correct, we should expect to see greater reliance on skilled shopfloor labour in Britain and Germany than in the USA. On the other hand, we would expect to see earlier emphasis on managerial and research capabilities in the USA. Furthermore, within Europe, differences between Britain and Germany may be useful in identifying differences in the extent of the commitment to the craft/flexible production strategy.

3   Shopfloor labour

For Britain it is possible to estimate apprentices as a share of employment in engineering, broadly defined, back to 1914. The data are presented in Table 6.2. Figures on the numbers of apprentices and male blue-collar employees are available in the Engineering Employers'

Table 6.3   Apprentices in post-war Britain

	Manufacturing	Engineering
A. Apprentices (000s)		
1964	240.4	152.5
1966	243.7	170.4
1970	218.6	151.2
1980	149.5	101.3
1989	53.6	34.1
B. Employment (000s)		
1964	8,067.9	3,461.1
1966	8,158.0	3,550.8
1970	8,033.0	3,539.2
1980	6,519.4	3,026.5
1989	4,953.1	2,130.3
C. Apprentices as a share of employment (%)		
1964	2.98	4.41
1966	2.99	4.80
1970	2.72	4.27
1980	2.29	3.35
1989	1.08	1.60

Source: Apprentices: Gospel (1993).
Employment: Business Statistics Office (1978), *Historical Record of the Census of Production*, 1907 to 1970 (London). Adjustment from census years to benchmark years using employment from Department of Employment and Productivity (1971), *British Labour Statistics Historical Abstract, 1886–1968* (London); Business Monitor (various issues), *Report of the Census of Production; Summary Tables* (London).

Federation (EEF) archive held in the Modern Records Centre at the University of Warwick. The employment data can be adjusted to allow for female employment using data from Wigham (1973) and to allow for white-collar employment using *Census of Production* data. The data show a decline in apprenticeship as a proportion of the labour force in engineering during the 1920s from about 15% to a little under 10%, and a further decline across World War II to a little less than 5%.

The data in Table 6.3 take up the story from the 1960s. A further decline in apprenticeship occurred in British engineering from the late 1960s, and has continued steadily to the present. Data here are taken from Gospel (1993) and rely on figures collected by the Department of

Employment (DE). Data are also available for total manufacturing and follow a similar downward trend but starting from a lower level. It should be noted that the DE data tend to understate the role of training in Britain, since they rely on employer reporting and adopt a stricter definition of apprenticeship than is the case in Germany. Thus, for example, trainee technicians are included in the German data but excluded from the British data.

For Germany we can track the share of apprentices in employment from the end of the nineteenth century using industrial census data. Table 6.4 presents pre-war data on apprentices and total employment for the whole economy, manufacturing, and metals and engineering, the latter category corresponding broadly to the British engineering sector of Table 6.2, since vertical integration of firms and craft organization of labour makes it very difficult to separate out engineering from metal production. The proportion of engineering employees in apprenticeships was stable before World War II. However, this is consistent with a sharp rise in the absolute number of apprentices during the 1930s which is interpreted by Gillingham (1986) as part of a 'deproletarianization' of German society in the Third Reich, although it also reflects to some extent the expansion of German territory. Table 6.5 takes the story into the post-war period. Comparing the German with the British data, there is a clear difference in trends. Whereas in Britain there has been a sharp decline in apprenticeship since World War II, in Germany there has been no clear downward trend. Indeed, although there was a small drop in apprentices as a share of employment in the engineering and manufacturing sectors, the ratio rose in the economy as a whole. Germany has retained a commitment to apprenticeships which has evaporated in post-war Britain.

Judgements concerning levels are always more hazardous than judgements about trends. Nevertheless, taken at face value, the apprenticeship data indicate a greater commitment to shopfloor training in Britain before World War I, and only a small German advantage during the inter-war period. In fact, this would be broadly in line with the existing literature (Zeitlin, 1994). Indeed, there is much favourable comment on the skills of the British labour force in the late nineteenth and early twentieth centuries. Fremdling (1986) notes the extent to which British workers were sought after by continental iron and steel producers, while Pollard and Robertson (1979) argue that Britain's success in the shipbuilding industry was based on the skill of the British workforce which allowed firms to economize on fixed capital. Harley (1974) stresses the influence of the large stock of skilled labour on the choice of technique in Edwardian Britain.

Table 6.4   Pre-war German apprenticeship data

	Metals and engineering	Manufacturing	Whole economy
A. Apprentices			
1895	158,477	519.616	701,033
1907	214,128	560,163	809,286
1925	346,441	796,999	986,567
1933	199,588	564,416	880,407
1939	483,885	740,042	1,443,447
B. Employment (000s)			
1895	1,189	6,472	23,405
1907	1,994	8,459	28,166
1925	2,858	9,972	31,033
1933	1,637	7,075	26,687
1940	4,544	12,681	39,680
C. Apprentices as a share of employment (%)			
1895	13.3	8.0	3.0
1907	10.7	6.6	2.9
1925	12.1	8.0	3.2
1933	12.2	8.0	3.3
1939/40	10.6	5.8	3.6

Source: Apprentices: 1895: Berufs- und Gewerbezählung vom 14. Juni 1895. Gewerbestatistik für das Reich im Ganzen, *Statistik des Deutschen Reichs*, Neue Folge, Band 113 (Berlin, 1898). 1907: Berufs- und Betriebszählung vom 12 Juni 1907. Gewerbliche Betriebsstatistik, *Statistik des Deutschen Reichs*, Band 213 (Berlin, 1910). 1925: Volks- Berufs- und Betriebszählung vom 16. Juni 1925, Gewerbliche B etriebszählung. Die Gewerblichen Betriebe und Unternehmungen im Deutschen Reich, Teil III, Die Technischen Betriebseinheiten im Deutschen Reiche (Berlin, 1929). 1933: Volks- Berufs- und Betriebszählung vom 1933. Das Personal der gewerblichen Niederlassungen nach der Stellung im Betrieb und die Verwendung von Kraftmaschinen (Berlin, 1935). 1940: *Statistisches Handbuch von Deutschland, 1928–1944* (Länderrat des Amerikanischen Besatzungsgebiets, München, 1949).
Employment: W.G. Hoffman, *Das Wachstum der Deutschen Wirtschaft seit der Mitte des 19. Jahrhunderts* (Berlin, 1965).

However, it may be argued that our figures give too favourable a view of British training. First it should be noted that well into the post-World War II period, British apprenticeships typically lasted five years in contrast to the three years more usual in Germany. A broadly equal proportion of the labour force being trained in both countries thus resulted in a larger stock of skilled workers in Germany.

A second and related reason for believing the figures to be too kind to

Table 6.5   Post-war German apprenticeship data

	Metals and engineering	Manufacturing	Whole economy
A. Apprentices			
1950	203,571	304,728	1,023,786
1960	339,713	553,890	1,426,389
1970	289,158	447,342	1,277,864
1980	363,245	611,734	1,674,064
1988	374,038	621,094	1,765,652
B. Employment (000s)			
1950	2,553	6,576	22,074
1960	4,739	10,016	26,247
1970	5,393	10,181	26,668
1980	5,095	9,017	27,059
1988	5,004	8,409	27,366
C. Apprentices as a share of employment(%)			
1950	8.0	4.6	4.6
1960	7.2	5.5	5.4
1970	5.4	4.4	4.8
1980	7.1	6.8	6.2
1988	7.5	7.4	6.5

Source: Apprentices: *Statistik der BRD* 45 'Die nichtlandwirtschaftlichen Arbeitsstätten' 13.9 1950 Heft 1; Fachserie C Unternehmen und Arbeitsstätten Arbeitsstättenzählung, 6 Juni 61 Heft 2; Arbeits und Sozialstatistik Hauptergebnisse 92/91/89/87/81; Unternehmen und Arbeitsstätten Fachserie 2 Heft 1. Employment: *Statistisches Jahrbuch* 1954 (Erwerbstätige 1950); Fachserie C Unternehmen und Arbeitsstätten Arbeitsstättenzählung 6 Juni 61 Heft 2; Arbeits und Sozialstatistik Hauptergebnisse 92; Zahlen für ausgewählte Wirtschaftsgruppen aus *Statistisches Jahrbuch* 1992.

Britain might be that they take no account of quality. However, studies from the 1950s and 1960s do not suggest that Britain was seriously out of step with Europe at this time (Williams, 1957, 1963; Liepmann, 1960; OEEC, 1960). This ties in with the findings of later research for the 1980s, which suggests that Britain's skills gap has more to do with the quantity rather than the quality of trained workers (NIESR, 1991). It is true that there are comments about the lack of flexibility exhibited by British craft workers, but it might be argued that this has more to do with the enforcement of strict lines of demarcation by craft unions than with the quality of training.

A third issue concerns the level of general education of British workers before training, a factor which again features in recent discussions of

Table 6.6   Proportions of the manufacturing workforce with certified qualifications in Britain and Germany (%)

	1978/79	1989
A. Britain		
Upper level	4.7	7.9
Intermediate level	24.4	35.2
No qualifications	71.0	56.8
B. Germany		
Upper level	3.6	6.6
Intermediate level	60.9	67.0
No qualifications	35.5	26.4

Source: O'Mahony and Wagner (1994).

training (NIESR, 1991). However, for the pre-war period, recent work has tended to argue that Anglo-German differences were much exaggerated in the early literature since the German centralized state-run system was being compared with the much harder to document British decentralized system, which actually underwent major reforms (Pollard, 1989; Sanderson, 1988).

Alternatively, it might be thought that our figures give too gloomy a view of British training by concentrating only on apprenticeships and neglecting other forms of training for shopfloor workers. In particular, it may be thought important to consider alternative ways of obtaining intermediate level skills, since apprenticeships have traditionally been associated with old-style craft unionism, which has been under severe attack since the late 1970s. Recent figures from the *Labour Force Survey* suggest that the decline in apprenticeships in manufacturing has been offset by a rise in City and Guilds and other similar level qualifications, so that the stock of workers with intermediate level qualifications has risen slightly between 1979 and 1989. In fact, the proportion of workers with intermediate qualifications has risen by rather more, since the reduction of employment in manufacturing during the 1980s took the form of shedding unskilled labour. However, this still leaves the stock of skilled workers in Britain far below German levels (O'Mahony and Wagner, 1994). The stock data for the manufacturing workforces in Britain and Germany from the late 1970s are given in Table 6.6. This confirms the bleak picture of the shopfloor skills of British workers that was built up through the 1980s by researchers at the National Institute of

Table 6.7   Pre-war US apprenticeship data

	Manufacturing and construction
A. Apprentices	
1880	44,170
1900	81,603
1920	140,400
1930	89,982
1940	84,080
B. Employment (000s)	
1880	4,060
1900	7,729
1920	12,595
1930	12,612
1940	13,195
C. Apprentices as a share of employment (%)	
1880	1.1
1900	1.1
1920	1.1
1930	0.7
1940	0.6

Source: Apprentices: Bolino (1989); US Bureau of the Census. Employment: US Department of Commerce (1960), *Historical Statistics of the United States: Colonial Times to 1957* (Washington, DC).

Economic and Social Research (NIESR, 1991). However, it also suggests that during the 1980s British manufacturing has begun to reverse the post-war trend towards greater use of American methods, and is returning to a more skilled-labour-intensive strategy.

For the USA, the quantitative picture is rather more difficult to establish beyond the widespread agreement that apprenticeship had virtually died out by the turn of the century as a significant form of training for industrial workers (Elbaum, 1989). This is what we would expect given the rise of mass production in the USA. As Hounshell (1984, p. 6) notes, Henry Ford believed that 'In mass production there are no fitters'. A reduction in the demand for skilled labour would seem to be a useful additional explanation for the decline of apprenticeship in addition to the problems with the enforcement of bonds which Elbaum stresses. The US apprenticeship data in Tables 6.7 and 6.8 are patchy. For the prewar period, the Bureau of the Census data have been collected together by Bolino (1989). These figures cover largely the manufacturing

Table 6.8   Post-war US apprenticeship data

	Metal working	Whole economy
A. Apprentices		
1952	14,645	172,477
1960	24,898	172,161
1970	57,406	269,626
1975		265,000
1991	57,573	255,455
B. Employment (000s)		
1952	7,026	58,918
1960	7,246	65,778
1970	7,157	78,678
1975		85,846
1991	8,303	116,877
C. Apprentices as a share of employment (%)		
1952	0.21	0.29
1960	0.34	0.26
1970	0.80	0.34
1975		0.31
1991	0.69	0.22

Source: Apprentices: Bolino (1989); US Department of Labor. Employment: US Department of Commerce (various issues), *Annual Survey of Manufactures* (Washington, DC); US Department of Commerce (various issues), *Statistical Abstract of the United States* (Washington, DC).

and construction sectors, although for some years a smaller number of apprentices in transport and mining are included. Attempts to disaggregate the figures are unreliable, but it seems likely from the evidence of later years that construction accounts for a high proportion of these apprentices (perhaps as much as a half). These low figures should thus be seen as 'upper bound' estimates for engineering, particularly since it is likely that a number of machine minders have been included due to ambiguity in the wording of Census questions. For the post-war period, data from the Department of Labor are again collected together by Bolino (1989), allowing us to distinguish metal working from the whole economy estimates. Again, the share of apprentices in employment is rather small, even in metalworking.

Our figures, then, suggest that training of shopfloor workers has been much more important in Britain and Germany compared with the USA throughout the twentieth century. They also suggest that the post-1945 period has seen a serious decline in apprenticeship in Britain, while in Germany there has been a consolidation of the industrial apprenticeship system. Recent Labour Force Survey data, however, suggests that there has been a revival in intermediate level qualifications in Britain during the 1980s, suggesting a return to a more skilled-labour-intensive strategy in British manufacturing.

4 Managerial capabilities

Although data exist on the educational qualifications of American managers in the late 1920s, comparable British and German data are only available from the early 1950s. These figures, presented in Tables 6.9 to 6.11, provide quite a range of estimates for the proportion of managers with degrees, largely because of variation in the level of management surveyed (Melrose-Woodman, 1978; Lawrence, 1980; Evers and von Landsberg, 1982; Granick, 1972). They do nevertheless appear to confirm the existence of rather different human capital strategies in Europe and America. The proportion of graduates among British and German top management in the early 1950s was at about the level of American business leaders in the late 1920s, with Britain and Germany lagging equally behind America. By the 1970s and 1980s, the proportion of top managers with degrees had risen in both Britain and Germany, although still remaining below the very high American levels.

The figures in Tables 6.9 and 6.10 may seem surprising at first sight in the light of the extensive literature on the lack of qualifications in British management (Keeble, 1992; Coleman, 1973; Gourvish, 1987; Handy *et al.*, 1988). Clearly, although some studies show a much lower proportion of graduates in British management, on the whole the impression is of similar proportions in Britain and Germany, especially if allowance is made for the different levels of management being sampled. Indeed, if membership of professional institutions is taken into account, Britain has a small advantage over Germany in higher level qualifications, as has been pointed out by researchers at the NIESR (Prais, 1993).

The importance of membership of professional institutions as a share of higher level qualifications in manufacturing has declined sharply during the 1980s according to the *Labour Force Survey*, accounting for 15.3% in 1990, down from 41.4% in 1979. This suggests that many managers now obtain a degree before taking their professional examinations. Furthermore, the fact that this is a relatively recent phenomenon suggests a way of reconciling Prais's (1981) finding of no shortfall of higher level qualifications in Britain during the 1970s with the traditional emphasis in

Table 6.9   Educational qualifications of British managers

A. Top managers

Date	Sample size	% Managers graduates	% Graduates science & eng.
1951	1,173	36	42
1954	455	30	
1970	Boards of 200 companies	52	
1974	199	46	
1975	90	57	21
1976	1,145	27	
1979	Top 50 chairmen	62	
1989	Top 50 chairmen	72	

Source: Copeman (1955); Acton Society Trust (1956); Heller (1970); Stanworth and Giddens (1974); Fidler (1981); Melrose-Woodman (1978); Hannah (1990).

B. All managers

Date	Sample size	% Managers graduates	% Graduates science & eng.
1954	3,327	19	73
1954–55	646	26	63
1964	818	35	80
1976	4,525	28	57
1980	1,058	33	56
1986	2,757	69	

Source: Acton Society Trust (1956); Clements (1958); Clark (1966); Melrose-Woodman (1978); Poole et al. (1981); Peppercorn and Skoulding (1987).

the management literature on the poor educational background of British managers, with the latter literature concentrating on degrees and ignoring the professional qualifications.

Sometimes this down playing of the positive role on professional qualifications in British management is taken one step further, with the claim that a preponderance of accountants has had significant negative effects, causing an excessive concentration on short-term financial goals (NEDO, 1987). Although the extent of the differences between Britain and Germany is sometimes exaggerated by not comparing like with like, it does seem to be the case that there are substantially more qualified accountants in Britain, where accountancy is seen as an established route into management (Handy et al., 1988). For 1992, we found a total of about 195,000 accountants in Britain and 62,000 in Germany. This reliance on large numbers of accountants in Britain appears to have long

Table 6.10   Educational qualifications of German managers

A. *Top managers*

Date	Sample size	% Managers graduates	% Graduates science & eng.
1954	6,578	31	37
1964	318	89	57
1967	217	76	46*
1970	538	58	61
1981	695	67	
1985	759	69	38*
1986	346	61	
1993	765	72	43

Notes: * Engineering only.
Source: Hartmann (1959); Zapf (1965); Brinkmann (1967); Pross and Boetticher (1971); Kienbaum Vergütungsberatung (1981, 1985, 1993) Wuppermann (1989).

B. *All managers*

Date	Sample size	% Managers graduates	% Graduates science & eng.
1964	21,707	27	36
1965	31,427	32	
1967	14,221	58	28
1981	6,670	52	
1985	5,622	58	68*
1993	4,326	59	31*

Notes: * Engineering only.
Source: Hartmann and Wienold (1967); Kruk (1967); Brinkmann (1967); Kienbaum Vergütungsberatung (1981, 1985, 1993).

historical roots (Edwards, 1989; Jones, 1981). Recent research by Matthews (1993) suggests that accountants already played a significant role in management of the quoted company sector before World War I.

The emphasis on accountancy in British management is usually contrasted with the emphasis on technology in German companies. However, it should be borne in mind that many British accountants have a background in science and engineering. Analysis of the 1992/93 entry to the Institute of Chartered Accountants in England and Wales reveals that of 4,070 entrants, 3,714 were graduates, of whom 1,091 had degrees in engineering, science or mathematics. Furthermore, the data in Tables 6.9 and 6.10 suggest a high proportion of managers with

Table 6.11   Educational qualifications of American managers

A. Top managers

Date	Sample size	% Managers graduates	% Attended college
1928	7,371	32	45
1950		62	
1952	8,300	57	76
1964		74	
1986		85	

Source: Taussig and Joslyn (1932); Newcomer (1955); Warner and Abegglen (1954); Newcomer (1965); Handy et al. (1988).

degrees in science and engineering in both Britain and Germany. This finding is consistent with the work of Prais (1981, 1989), although he recently reemphasizes the greater emphasis on pure science than on engineering in Britain (Prais, 1993). As Lawrence (1980) notes, science and engineering in Germany means mainly engineers with a few pure scientists. Thus, for example, in Table 6.10, Hartmann's (1959) figure of 37% for the proportion of graduates in science and engineering is made up of 36% in engineering and 1% in science. This discussion of the role of scientists and engineers leads us on naturally to consider research and development.

5   Research and development

In Tables 6.12 to 6.14 we assemble data on the scale of research in Britain, Germany and the USA. Tables 6.11 and 6.12 show the level of spending on R&D and the employment of researchers in Britain, the USA and Germany between 1933 and 1989, drawing on studies by Mowery (1986), Freeman (1962) and Sanderson (1972) for the period before the availability of official statistics. Figures relate as closely as possible to total R&D in manufacturing, whether carried out by private firms, public corporations or industrial research associations, and whether financed by private or public funds. Although there are obvious problems of comparability, most historians agree that the British research effort was substantially smaller than the American effort before World War II and into the 1950s, and this is indeed borne out by the figures in Tables 6.12 and 6.13. Equally clearly, there was a large increase in resources devoted to R&D in both countries after World War II, although the increase is probably overstated because of the failure of

Table 6.12 R&D expenditures in manufacturing

A. Britain

	R&D (£m)	Net output (£m)	Value added (£m)	R&D Net output (%)	R&D Value added (%)
1934	5.15	1,204		0.43	
1938	6.65	1,559		0.43	
1959	273.8	7,848		3.49	
1964	476.3	10,820		4.40	
1968	629.5	18,531		3.40	
1975	1,293.4	36,948	32,380	3.50	3.99
1983	3,869.9	80,804	65,753	4.79	5.88
1989	6,450.5	135,207	108,291	4.77	5.96

B. USA

	R&D (£m)	Net output (£m)	Value added (£m)	R&D Net output (%)	R&D Value added (%)
1937	247	25,174		0.98	
1959	9,400	161,536		5.82	
1981	49,904	837,507	649,631	5.96	7.68
1987	85,427	1,165,747	862,331	7.33	9.91

C. Germany

	R&D (Mill. DM)	Value added (Mill. DM)	R&D Value added (%)
1950	215	37,290	0.58
1959	1,413	100,660	1.40
1964	3,289	167,520	1.96
1969	7,079	229,590	3.08
1975	13,664	352,540	3.88
1983	29,733	519,420	5.72
1989	48,224	697,810	6.91

Source: Britain: R&D: 1934 from Mowery (1986); 1938 from Sanderson (1972); 1959 from Freeman (1962); 1964–89 from Business Monitor (various issues), *Industrial Research and Development Expenditure and Employment* (London). Net output and Value added: Business Statistics Office (1978), *Historical Record of the Census of Production, 1907 to 1970* (London), with adjustments from census years to benchmark years using GDP in manufacturing from Feinstein (1972); Business Monitor (various issues), *Report of the Census of Production; Summary Tables* (London).
USA: R&D: 1937 from Mowery (1986); 1959 from Freeman (1962); 1981–87 from OECD (1991), *Basic Science and Technology Statistics* (Paris). Net output and Value added: Department of Commerce (various issues), *Census of*

Manufactures (Washington, DC); OECD (1993);   *National Accounts: Detailed Tables, Vol. II* (Paris).
Germany: R&D: SV-Gemeinnützige Gesellschaft für Wissenschaftsstatistik mbH (1966), *Wissenschaftsausgaben der Wirtschaft: Ergebnisse der Registrierungen des Stifterverbandes 1948–1963* (Essen); SV-Gemeinnützige Gesellschaft für Wissenschaftsstatistik mbH (various issues), *Forschung und Entwicklung in der Wirtschaft* (Essen). Value added: Statistisches Bundesamt (1991), *Volkswirtschaftliche Gesamtrechnungen 1950 bis 1990*, Fachserie 18, Reihe S.15 (Wiesbaden).

Table 6.13   **Employment of researchers in manufacturing**

A. *Britain*

	Researchers	Employment (000s)	Researchers Employment (%)
1933	1,724	5,260	0.032
1935	2,575	5,634	0.046
1938	4,505	6,148	0.073
1945–46	5,200	7,080	0.073
1959	44,300	7,955	0.57
1968	216,000	8,033	2.69
1975	181,000	7,467	2.42
1983	186,000	5,079	3.66
1989	176,000	4,953	3.55

B. *USA*

	Researchers	Employment (000s)	Researchers Employment (%)
1933	10,900	6,558	0.17
1940	28,000	9,527	0.29
1946	45,900	14,294	0.32
1959	219,100	16,662	1.31

C. *Germany*

	Researchers	Employment (000s)	Researchers Employment (%)
1964	127,765	9,885	1.29
1969	167,752	9,883	1.70
1975	175,326	9,097	1.92
1989	285,966	8,696	3.29

Source: Britain: Researchers: 1933 to 1945–46 from Mowery (1986); 1959 from Freeman (1962); 1968 to 1989 from Business Monitor (various issues), Industrial

Research and Development Expenditure and Employment (London). Employ-ment: Business Statistics Office (1978), *Historical Record of the Census of Production, 1907 to 1970* (London). Adjustment from census years to benchmark years using employment in manufacturing from Feinstein (1972); Business Monitor (various issues), *Report of the Census of Production; Summary Tables* (London).
USA: Researchers: 1933 to 1946 from Mowery (1986); 1959 from Freeman (1962). Employment: Department of Commerce (various issues), *Census of Manufactures* (Washington, DC).
Germany: Researchers: SV-Gemeinnützige Gesellschaft für Wissenschaftsstatistik mbH (various issues), *Forschung und Entwicklung in der Wirtschaft* (Essen). Employment: Statistisches Bundesamt (1991), *Volkswirtschaftliche Gesamtrech-nungen 1950 bis 1990*, Fachserie 18, Reihe S.15 (Wiesbaden).

the pre-war statistics to adequately capture some of the research effort (Nelson and Wright, 1992, p. 1952).

The position of Britain compared with other European countries, however, is much less clear for the pre-war period, because there are no national data. However, recent research by Erker (1990) and Edgerton and Horrocks (1994) suggests that British firms did not generally lag behind European competitors in the employment of research staff in the inter-war period. The data on companies in Table 6.14 are taken from Edgerton and Horrocks (1994), and there are doubts about compar-ability between companies and over time. Nevertheless they do appear to reflect the generally larger American research effort, with Du Pont employing more researchers than ICI and GE employing more than GEC.

The exception to the large American lead in R&D appears to be chemicals, where Germany established an early strong position. In Table 6.14 this is reflected by the figures for IG Farben, which dominates both Du Pont and ICI. However, amongst the electrical producers, the British firms employed more research staff than the German firms. Edgerton and Horrocks note further that it has never been suggested that France, Italy or Japan did more R&D than Britain during the inter-war period. The above figures cast serious doubt on the claims of many writers that British industry has performed badly because of a deep-rooted bias against science and technology which permeates British society (Landes, 1969; Wiener, 1981).

Turning to the post-war period, the British research effort continues to lag behind the American effort as measured by the ratio of R&D expenditure to net output in manufacturing. Converting to a value added basis for comparison with Germany (by subtracting non-industrial services from net output), we see that the US research effort has

Table 6.14   Employment of qualified researchers in companies

	1928	1930	1933	1935	1938
IG Farben	1,050	1,100	1,000	1,020	1,150
Du Pont		687	725	847	979
ICI				464	510
GE	223	202			
GEC		125		175	
Metropolitan-Vickers		73		87	117
BTH		73		104	
Philips	48	72			
Siemens	92	68			
AEG	30		60		

Source: Edgerton and Horrocks (1994, table 6).

remained strong into the 1980s, with the ratio of R&D expenditure to value added substantially greater than in Germany or Britain.

It should be noted, however, that the German research effort looks rather better if we consider R&D expenditures as a proportion of GDP, since manufacturing accounts for a much larger share of output and employment in Germany than in Britain or the USA. Indeed, for 1989, figures from OECD, *Main Technology Indicators*, give R&D to GDP ratios of 2.88% for Germany compared with 2.82% for the USA and 2.25% for Britain. To the extent that the large German research effort has been successful in expanding the manufacturing sector, then, expressing R&D as a share of value added in manufacturing gives a misleading impression.

It is also usual to point out that in Britain and the USA a large share of R&D is in defence-related areas. In 1981, for example, defence budget R&D accounted for 54% of government financed R&D in the USA and 49% in the UK, compared with just 9% in Germany (Ergas, 1987, p. 54). In a sophisticated generalization of this observation, Ergas (1987) draws a distinction between 'mission-oriented' and 'diffusion-oriented' approaches to technology policy. In mission-oriented countries such as Britain and the USA, technology policy is geared towards radical innovations aimed at clearly set out goals of national importance. By contrast, in diffusion-oriented countries such as Germany, technology policy is aimed at the provision of innovation-related public goods, to help diffuse technological capabilities throughout industry. A similar distinction is made by Soskice (1993).

Ergas sees the appropriate technology policy as intimately bound up with overall production strategy. He sees the USA as pursuing a mission-oriented technology policy which fits in with an overall production strategy based on 'technology shifting', or concentrating on the emergence phase of new technologies. By contrast, Ergas sees Germany as following a diffusion-oriented technology policy based on 'technology deepening', or the improvement of existing technologies. It should be noted that Ergas sees the German system of vocational training as a good example of an innovation-related public good. The UK is seen as caught somewhere between the USA and Germany. Too little benefit has been reaped from a mission-oriented technology policy because of insufficient interaction between private and public researchers, which has meant relatively few spin-offs for the rest of the economy. The rest of the economy has therefore been forced to fight for competitiveness through technology deepening, but without the scale of resources devoted to the problem in Germany.

6   Concluding comments

Our analysis suggests that human capital accumulation in the three countries studied can only be understood in relation to the overall production strategy pursued by firms. In America, firms have tended to pursue a policy of standardized mass production, which has required heavy investment in managerial and research capabilities but relatively little investment in shopfloor skills. By contrast, British and German firms have pursued a policy of craft/flexible production, intensive in the use of skilled shopfloor labour.

Nevertheless, we also see some differences in the strategies pursued by British and German firms, particularly since 1945. After World War II, whereas German firms maintained their reliance on skilled shopfloor labour, British firms made a relatively unsuccessful move in the direction of standardized mass production and allowed a serious decline in the training of shopfloor workers. This has left British firms in a relatively weak position to take advantage of the information revolution which has been effectively exploited by German firms using skilled workers to produce small batches of high-quality goods within an industrial environment. This German success has been accompanied by a technology policy oriented towards diffusion of innovation-related public goods. In contrast, Britain has followed a mission-oriented technology policy, but without the success of the United States. Although Britain appears to have moved back towards a more skilled-labour-intensive production strategy during the 1980s, there is still a large skills gap to be made good after the neglect of the previous three decades.

NOTE

The collection of data for this paper has only been possible with the help of a number of people. The German data was unearthed with the research assistance of Carsten Johnson and financial support from the CEPR research initiative 'Comparative Experience of Economic Growth in Postwar Europe' funded by the Commission of the European Communities under its SPES Programme. Howard Gospel made available unpublished data on post-war British and American apprenticeships. We also thank the Engineering Employers' Federation and the Modern Records Centre at the University of Warwick for access to records. Gavin Wright and Jonathan Zeilin helped me to avoid a number of pitfalls in the data. The Chartered Institute of Accountants in England and Wales made available information on the number of accountants. The usual disclaimer applies to this chapter with particular force.

REFERENCES

AACP (Anglo-American Council on Productivity) (1952), *Final Report*, London: AACP.

Acton Society Trust (1956), *Management Succession*, London: Acton Society Trust.

Ames, E. and N. Rosenberg (1968), 'The Enfield Arsenal in Theory and History', *Economic Journal*, **78**, 827–42.

Bean, C. and J. Symons (1989), 'Ten Years of Mrs T.', Discussion Paper No. 316, Centre for Policy Research, London.

Berghahn, V.R. (1991), 'Technology and the Export of Industrial Culture: Problems of the German–American Relationship 1900–1960', in P. Mathias and J. Davis (eds.), *Innovation and Technology in Europe: From the Eighteenth Century to the Present Day*, Oxford: Blackwell, pp. 142–61.

Bolino, A.C. (1989), *A Century of Human Capital by Education and Training*, Washington, DC: Kensington.

Brinkmann, G. (1967), *Die Ausbildung von Führungskräften für die Wirtschaft*, Köln: Universitätsverlag Michael Wienand.

Broadberry, S.N. (1993), 'Manufacturing and the Convergence Hypothesis: What the Long Run Data Show', *Journal of Economic History*, **53**, 772–95.

Broadberry, S.N. (1994a), 'Technological Leadership and Productivity Leadership in Manufacturing since the Industrial Revolution: Implications for the Convergence Thesis', *Economic Journal*, **104**, 291–302.

Broadberry, S.N. (1994b), 'Comparative Productivity in British and American Manufacturing During the Nineteenth Century', *Explorations in Economic History*, **31**, 521–48.

Broadberry, S.N. and N.F.R. Crafts (1993), 'British Economic Policy and Performance in the Early Postwar Period', unpublished, University of Warwick.

Brown, W. and S. Wadhwani (1990), 'The Economic Effects of Industrial Relations Legislation since 1979', *National Institute Economic Review*, **131**, 57–69.

Chandler, A.D. Jr (1990), *Scale and Scope: The Dynamics of Industrial Capitalism*, Cambridge, MA: Harvard University Press.

Clark, D.G. (1966), *The Industrial Manager: His Background and Career Pattern*, London: Business Publications.

Clements, R.V. (1958), *Managers: A Study of their Careers in Industry*, London: Allen & Unwin.

Coleman, D.C. (1973), 'Gentlemen and Players', *Economic History Review*, 26, 92–116.

Copeman, G.H. (1955), *Leaders of British Industry*, London: Gee and Co.

Crafts, N.F.R. (1991), 'Reversing Relative Economic Decline? The 1980s in Historical Perspective', *Oxford Review of Economic Policy*, 7(3), 81–98.

Daly, A., D.M. Hitchens and K. Wagner (1985), 'Productivity, Machinery and Skills in a Sample of British and German Manufacturing Plants', *National Institute Economic Review*, 111, 48–61.

David, P.A. (1975), *Technical Choice, Innovation and Economic Growth*, Cambridge: Cambridge University Press.

Edgerton, D.E.H. and S.M. Horrocks (1994), 'British Industrial Research and Development before 1945', *Economic History Review*, 47, 213–38.

Edwards, J.R. (1989), A History of Financial Accounting, London: Routledge.

Elbaum, B. (1989), 'Why Apprenticeship Persisted in Britain but not in the United States', *Journal of Economic History*, 49, 337–49.

Elbaum, B. and W. Lazonick (1986), *The Decline of the British Economy*, Oxford: Oxford University Press.

Ergas, H. (1987), 'The Importance of Technology Policy', in P. Dasgupta and P. Stoneman (eds.), *Economic Policy and Technological Performance*, Cambridge: Cambridge University Press.

Erker, P. (1990), 'Die Verwissenschaftlichung der Industrie', *Zeitschrift für Unternehmensgeschichte*, 35, 73–94.

Evers, H. and G. von Lansberg (1982), *Qualifikation und Karriere*, Köln: Deutscher Instituts-Verlag.

Feinstein, C.H. (1972), *National Income, Expenditure and Output of the United Kingdom, 1855–1965*, Cambridge: Cambridge University Press.

Fidler, J. (1981), *The British Business Elite: Its Attitude to Class, Status and Power*, London: Routledge & Kegan Paul.

Frankel, M. (1957), *British and American Manufacturing Productivity*, Urbana: University of Illinois.

Franko, L.G. (1976), *The European Multinationals: A Renewed Challenge to American and British Big Business*, London: Harper & Row.

Freeman, C. (1962), 'Research and Development: A Comparison between British and American Industry', *National Institute Economic Review*, 20, 21–39.

Fremdling, R. (1986), *Technologischer Wandel und internationaler Handel im 18. und 19. Jahrhundert: Die Eisenindustrien in Großbritannien, Belgien, Frankreich und Deutschland*, Berlin: Duncker & Humblot.

Gilbert, M. and I.B. Kravis (1954), *An International Comparison of National Products and the Purchasing Power of Currencies*, Paris: OEEC.

Gillingham, J. (1986), 'The Deproletarianisation of German Society: Vocational Training in the Third Reich', *Journal of Social History*, 19, 423–32.

Gospel, H.F. (1993), 'Whatever Happened to Apprenticeship Training and What Has Replaced It? The British Experience', unpublished, University of Kent, Canterbury.

Gourvish, T.R. (1987), 'British Business and the Transition to the Corporate Economy: Entrepreneurship and Management Structures', *Business History*, **29**, 18–45.

Granick, D. (1972), *Managerial Comparisons of Four Developed Countries: France, Britain, United States and Russia*, Cambridge, MA: MIT Press.

Handy, C., C. Gordon, I. Gow and C. Randlesome (1988), *Making Managers*, London: Pitman.

Hannah, L. (1990), 'Business Culture and the Changing Business Environment', Discussion Paper EC8/90, Lancaster University Management School.

Harley, C.K. (1974), 'Skilled Labour and the Choice of Technique in Edwardian Industry', *Explorations in Economic History*, **2**, 391–414.

Hartmann, H. (1959), *Authority and Organisation in German Management*, Westport, CT: Greenwood.

Hartmann, H. and H. Wienold (1967), *Universität und Unternehmer*, Gütersloh: Bertelsmann.

Heller, R. (1970), 'Britain's Boardroom Anatomy', *Management Today*, September, 83–5.

Hoffmann, W.G. (1965), *Das Wachstum der deutschen Wirtschaft seit der Mitte des 19. Jahrhunderts*, Berlin: Springer-Verlag

Hounshell, D.A. (1984), *From the American System to Mass Production, 1800–1932*, Baltimore, MD: Johns Hopkins University Press.

Hutton, G. (1953), *We Too Can Prosper*, London: Allen & Unwin.

Jones, E. (1981), *Accountancy and the British Economy 1840–1980: The Evolution of Ernst & Whinney*, London: Batsford.

Keeble, S.P. (1992), *The Ability to Manage: A Study of British Management, 1890–1990*, Manchester: Manchester University Press.

Kienbaum Vergütungsberatung (1981), *Gehalts-Struktur-Untersuchung '81*, Gummersbach.

Kienbaum Vergütungsberatung (1985), *Gehalts-Struktur-Untersuchung '85*, Gummersbach.

Kienbaum Vergütungsberatung (1993), *Gehalts-Struktur-Untersuchung '93*, Gummersbach.

Kruk, M. (1967), *Die oberen 30,000*, Wiesbaden: Betriebswirtschaftlicher Verlag Gabler.

Landes, D. (1969), *The Unbound Prometheus*, Cambridge: Cambridge University Press.

Lawrence, P. (1980), *Managers and Management in West Germany*, London: Croom Helm.

Lazonick (1990), *Competitive Advantage on the Shop Floor*, Cambridge, MA: Harvard University Press.

Lewchuk, W. (1987), *American Technology and the British Vehicle Industry*, Cambridge: Cambridge University Press.

Liepmann, K. (1960), *Apprenticeship: An Enquiry into its Adequacy in Modern Conditions*, London: Routledge & Kegan Paul.

Lorenz, E.H. (1991), 'An Evolutionary Explanation for Competitive Decline: The British Shipbuilding Industry, 1890–1970', *Journal of Economic History*, **51**, 911–935.

Lucas, R.E. Jr (1988), 'On the Mechanics of Economic Development', *Journal of Monetary Economics*, **32**, 3–42.

Maddison, A. (1987), 'Growth and Slowdown in Advanced Capitalist Economies: Techniques of Quantitative Assessment', *Journal of Economic Literature*, **25**, 649–698.

Matthews, D. (1993), 'Counting the Accountants: A Trial Balance for 1911', *Accounting, Business and Financial History*, 3, 197–223.

Melman, S. (1956), *Dynamic Factors in Industrial Productivity*, Oxford: Blackwell.

Melrose-Woodman, J. (1978), 'Profile of the British Manager', British Institute of Management Foundation, Management Survey Report No. 38, London.

Milgrom, P. and J. Roberts (1990), 'The Economics of Modern Manufacturing: Technology, Strategy and Organisation', *American Economic Review*, **80**, 511–528.

Mowery, D.C. (1986), 'Industrial Research, 1900–1950', in B. Elbaum and W. Lazonick (eds.), *The Decline of the British Economy*, Oxford: Oxford University Press, pp. 189–222.

NEDO (National Economic Development Office) (1987), *The Making of Managers: A Report on Management Education, Training and Development in the USA, West Germany, France, Japan and the UK*, London: NEDO.

Nelson, R.R. and G. Wright (1992), 'The Rise and Fall of American Technological Leadership: The Postwar Era in Historical Perspective', *Journal of Economic Literature*, **30**, 1931–1964.

Newcomer, M. (1955), *The Big Business Executive*, New York: Columbia University Press.

Newcomer, M. (1965), *The Big Business Executive/1964*, New York: Scientific American.

NIESR (National Institute of Economic and Social Research) (1991), *Productivity, Education and Training: Britain and Other Countries Compared*, reprints of studies published in the National Institute Economic Review with a preface by S.J. Prais, London: NIESR.

OEEC (Organisation for European Economic Cooperation) (1960), *Vocational Training in the Footwear Industry*, Paris: OEEC.

O'Mahony, M. and K. Wagner (1994), 'Changing Fortunes: An Industry Study of Anglo-German Productivity over Three Decades', Report Series No. 7, National Institute of Economic and Social Research, London.

Paige, D. and G. Bombach (1959), *A Comparison of National Output and Productivity of the United Kingdom and the United States*, Paris: OEEC.

Peppercorn, G. and G. Skoulding (1987), *Profiles of British Industry: The Manager's View*, Corby: British Institute of Management.

Piore, M.J. and C.F. Sabel (1984), *The Second Industrial Divide: Possibilities for Prosperity*, New York: Basic Books.

Pollard, S. (1989), *Britain's Prime and Britain's Decline: The British Economy 1870–1914*, London: Edward Arnold.

Pollard, S. and P.L. Robertson (1979), *The British Shipbuilding Industry, 1880–1914*, Cambridge, MA: Harvard University Press.

Poole, M., R. Mansfield, P. Blyton and P. Frost (1981), *Managers in Focus: The British Manager in the Early 1980s*, Aldershot: Gower.

Prais, S.J. (1981), 'Vocational Qualifications of the Labour Force in Britain and Germany', *National Institute Economic Review*, **98**, 47–59.

Prais, S.J. (1989), 'Qualified Manpower in Engineering: Britain and Other Industrially Advanced Countries', *National Institute Economic Review*, **127**, 76–83.

Prais, S.J. (1993), 'Economic Performance and Education: The Nature of Britain's Deficiencies', Discussion Paper No. 52, NIESR, London.

Pross, H. and K. Boetticher (1971), *Manager des Kapitalismus*, Frankfurt: Sohrkamp.

Romer, P.M. (1990), 'Human Capital and Growth: Theory and Evidence', *Carnegie-Rochester Conference Series on Public Policy*, 32, 251–286.

Rosenberg, N. (ed.), (1969), *The American System of Manufactures*, Edinburgh: Edinburgh University Press.

Rostas, L. (1948), *Comparative Productivity in British and American Industry*, Cambridge: NIESR.

Ryan, P. (1991) (ed.), *International Comparisons of Vocational Education and Training for Intermediate Skills*, London: Falmer.

Sanderson, M. (1972), 'Research and the Firm in British Industry, 1919–1939', *Science Studies*, 2, 107–51.

Sanderson, M. (1988), 'Education and Economic Decline, 1890 to the 1980s', *Oxford Review of Economic Policy*, 4(1), 38–50.

Soskice, D. (1993), 'Product Market and Innovation Strategies of Companies and their implications for Enterprise Tenure: A Comparative Institutional Approach of Some Cross-Country Differences', unpublished, Wissenschaftszentrum, Berlin.

Stanworth, P. and A. Giddens (1974), 'An Economic Elite: A Demographic Profile of Company Chairmen', in P. Stanworth and A. Giddens (eds.), *Elites and Power in British Society*, Cambridge: Cambridge University Press.

Taussig, F.W. and C.S. Joslyn (1932), *American Business Leaders*, New York: Macmillan.

Tolliday, S. and J. Zeitlin (eds.), (1991), *The Power to Manage? Employers and Industrial Relations in Comparative Historical Perspective*, London: Routledge.

Warner, W.L. and J.C. Abegglen (1955), *Occupational Mobility in American Business and Industry, 1928–1952*, Minneapolis: University of Minnesota Press.

Wiener, M.J. (1981), *English Culture and the Decline of the Industrial Spirit 1850–1980*, Cambridge: Cambridge University Press.

Wigham, E. (1973), *The Power to Manage: A History of the Engineering Employers' Federation*, London: Macmillan.

Williams, G. (1957), *Recruitment to Skilled Trades*, London: Routledge & Kegan Paul.

Williams, G. (1963), *Apprenticeship in Europe: The Lesson for Britain*, London: Chapman & Hall.

Wuppermann, M. (1989), *Geschäftsführer in Deutschland*, Frankfurt: Campus.

Zapf, W. (1965), 'Die deutschen Manager: Sozialprofil und Karriereweg', in W. Zapf (ed.), *Beiträge zur Analyse der deutschen Oberschicht*, München: Piper.

Zeitlin, J. (1994), 'Re-forming Skills in British Engineering, 1900–1940: A Contingent Failure', unpublished, University of Wisconsin Madison.

7 Convergence and divergence in the European periphery: productivity in Eastern and Southern Europe in retrospect

BART VAN ARK

1 Introduction

Recent contributions to the literature on the catch-up and convergence performance of nation states have been either related to the growth experience of a 'maximalist' sample of countries, or they focused more narrowly on OECD countries. For the latter group the evidence on convergence of per capita income and productivity is quite strong in particular for the period 1950 to 1973. However, for larger samples of countries and other periods than the 'golden age', performance can only be explained within a catch-up and convergence framework when the model allows for a range of initial conditions for convergence, such as a minimum level of human and physical capital investment, a certain degree of openness to trade, etc.[1]

Relatively few studies have dealt with catch-up and convergence from a regional or country-specific perspective. Comparisons across a region may be useful, because one might hypothesize that geographical closeness is one of the factors strengthening convergence. Similarities in terms of technological regimes, cultural and institutional inheritance, as well as the optimal functioning of technology diffusion mechanisms through trade and investment across the region, may be forceful mechanisms driving convergence.

In this chapter regional convergence and divergence is looked into by comparing the economic performance of European countries during the post-war period with emphasis on two countries in Eastern Europe and two in Southern Europe.

Table 7.1 presents the average relative levels of per capita income compared to the United States for Northwest Europe, Southern Europe and Eastern Europe for the period 1938–92 derived from Maddison (1995).[2] The table shows clearly that, although both Eastern and Southern Europe were characterized by a greater potential for unconditional catch-

Table 7.1   Gross domestic product per capita, 1950–92, USA = 100

	Northwest Europe	Eastern Europe			Southern Europe		
		Total	Czecho-slovakia	East Germany	Total	Portugal	Spain
1938	76	30[a]	45[a]	77[b]	36	28	33
1950	58	23	36	33	24	22	25
1960	70	29	46	52	28	28	31
1970	76	32	43	53	38	40	49
1980	79	33	44	58	42	45	52
1988	78	30	40	57	42	45	52
1992	81	21	32	31	46	52	58

[a] 1937.
[b] 1936.
Note: Northwest European unweighted average: Austria, Belgium, Denmark, Finland, France, Germany (FRG), Italy, Netherlands, Norway, Sweden, Switzerland and the UK. East European unweighted average: Bulgaria, Czechoslovakia, Hungary, Poland, Romania, USSR and Yugoslavia. South European average: Greece, Ireland, Portugal, Spain and Turkey.
Source: Maddison (1995).

up than Northwest Europe, only Southern Europe caught up with the USA faster.

The table shows that the unweighted average of per capita income in Eastern and Southern Europe was very close in 1950, i.e. at 23–24% of the US level. However, the East European per capita income level reached its peak around 1980 at 33% of the US level, and has fallen since, most dramatically between 1988 and 1992.

The South European performance was one of continuous catch-up on the USA, in particular between 1960 and 1970. However, it should be noted that per capita income levels in Northwest Europe and Southern Europe diverged substantially between 1950 and 1960, and has only shown some moderate convergence since then.

This chapter concentrates on a detailed comparison of economic performance between two East European countries (former Czechoslovakia and former East Germany) and two South European countries (Portugal and Spain). Before World War II, Czechoslovakia and the eastern part of Germany were the most industrialized parts of Eastern Europe, and they both exhibited a relatively fast growth during the inter-war period. Inter-war growth in Portugal and Spain was slower and the two countries were less industrialized at the outset of the post-war period. During the 1950s the two East European countries (in particular

East Germany) exhibited a rapid growth, but the growth performance in Portugal and Spain has been much better since 1960. In terms of per capita income, the two South European countries were clearly ahead of Czechoslovakia by 1980, and probably (although the estimates in Table 7.1 suggest differently) also of East Germany.[3]

The main measure of comparison in this paper is productivity in the manufacturing sector. This measure is of specific interest, because catch-up and convergence patterns are of primary importance in manufacturing, which is characterized by a greater openness to foreign trade and investment than other sectors. Manufacturing also plays an important role in diffusing technology across countries as well as to non-manufacturing sectors of the economy.

The estimates of the comparative levels of productivity are based on the ICOP (International Comparisons of Output and Productivity) method which has been developed at the University of Groningen over the past decade. Table 7.2 summarizes ICOP estimates of comparative productivity levels for 1987 for thirteen countries. The table shows that in 1987 labour productivity levels in Czechoslovakia, East Germany and Portugal were very close, and below the levels of Korea and Brazil, and very substantially below that of Spain.[4]

This chapter essentially consists of two parts. Sections 2 and 3 are concerned with major methodological aspects of comparisons which include former centrally planned economies (CPEs). Section 2 is on the measurement of output and productivity levels for Czechoslovakia and East Germany for a benchmark year in the late 1980s. Section 3 focuses on the reconstruction of the growth rates of real output and productivity for the post-war period in these two countries. It discusses the main problems concerning the overstatement of the official growth rates of the CPEs, and the features of the 'adjusted factor cost' series of real output growth which were linked to the comparative benchmark estimates from Section 2.

The second part of the chapter begins with Section 4. A confrontation is made of the productivity results for the two East European countries with those of Portugal and Spain. It appears that although the latter two countries performed very differently among themselves, the trends in comparative productivity in Portugal and Spain are very dissimilar from those in Eastern Europe. Whereas in 1950 manufacturing productivity was highest in Czechoslovakia, followed by East Germany, Spain and Portugal, in 1989 Spain was number one among these four countries, followed by Portugal, Czechoslovakia and East Germany.

The comparison suggests a range of hypotheses on the dynamics of the catch-up and convergence process between these two European regions

Table 7.2   Comparative levels of census value added per person employed in manufacturing, as a percentage of the USA, West Germany and the UK, 1987

	United States = 100.0	West Germany = 100.0	United Kingdom = 100.0
India	7.2	*10.3*	*13.5*
East Germany	*22.5*	32.0	*41.9*
Czechoslovakia	*23.9*	34.0	*44.6*
Portugal	*24.5*	*34.9*	45.7
Korea	26.3	*37.5*	*49.1*
Brazil	30.7	*43.7*	*57.3*
Spain	*46.4*	*66.2*	86.7
United Kingdom	53.6	*76.3*	100.0
West Germany	70.2	100.0	*131.0*
France	71.2	*101.5*	*133.0*
Japan	76.4	*108.9*	*142.7*
Netherlands	83.5	*118.7*	*155.6*
United States	100.0	*142.5*	*186.7*

Note: The estimates in italics are derived inferentially from the actual binary comparisons.
Source: ICOP. See van Ark (1993, 1995a, 1995b, 1996). Portugal from Peres (1994), updated.

as well as between each region and Northwest Europe. Section 5 suggests three 'proximate' causes of explanations for the productivity gaps, i.e. differences in the intensity and productivity of physical capital, variation in the dynamics of investment in human capital and the relative openness of the economies to trade and foreign investment. In the final section, system-related factors, that is the impact of communist or autocratic political regimes on economic performance, will be dealt with more explicitly.

2   Comparing levels of output and productivity in Eastern Europe

2.1   Methodological problems in comparing CPE output and productivity[5]

Studies of comparative output and productivity levels for centrally planned economies (CPEs) raise specific problems which are of less importance for comparisons among Western market economies.

(1) Centrally planned economies (CPEs) lack meaningful prices on the

basis of which their output can be easily compared to that of market economies. Official price quotations are mostly administered prices, which are determined differently from the price formation process in a market economy. Comparisons between CPEs and market economies have therefore often been made on the basis of pricing the products at Western prices only, for example US dollars or German deutschmarks.[6] Such comparisons always imply that the output of the country for which the prices are substituted by the prices of the other country gets relatively overstated.[7] Comparisons at world prices are fraught with problems as well, because the quality of exported commodities often deviates strongly from items sold domestically.[8]

As not all products can be compared between each pair of countries, another problem (which does not exclusively relate to CPEs) is that the 'quantity relationship' for the products which are matched cannot be held representative for those products which are not matched. In the ICOP studies manufacturing output for each pair of countries is therefore converted to a common currency on the basis of so-called 'unit value ratios' (UVRs). These are the equivalent of 'purchasing power parities' by industry, and are based on ratios of the ex-factory sales value per unit of output, derived from the industrial survey in each country. Here the assumption is that not the quantity relationship but the 'price relationship' for covered products is representative for non-covered products. Although the unit values of the CPEs represent administered prices, these are the most practical for our purpose, because the output value which is 'deflated' is expressed in the same administered prices.[9]

Table 7.3 shows the average unit value ratio for manufacturing for the benchmark years, which is 1987 for the East–West German comparison and 1989 for the Czechoslovak–West German comparison. The table shows that the UVRs are in both cases less than half the commercial exchange rate, which suggests that relative price levels in both CPEs are considerably lower than in West Germany.[10] However, one should not derive too many conclusions from a comparison of UVRs and exchange rates. Firstly, as mentioned above, the domestic prices which are used here are administrative prices. Secondly, the commercial exchange rate reflects the relatively high cost of exporting goods from CPEs to market economies in order to obtain foreign currency. It is therefore not clear what the economic meaning of lower relative price levels in this respect is.

On the other hand, it needs to be emphasized that the price formation system in CPEs was not without an economic rationale. Appendix tables A.1 and A.2 shows that the UVRs by manufacturing branch and industry do not exhibit an entirely erratic pattern. Further research on the nature

Table 7.3   Unit value ratios and commercial exchange rates, Czechoslovakia/West Germany (1989) and East Germany/West Germany (1987)

	Czechoslovakia/ West Germany (Kcs./D-Mark) 1989	East Germany/ West Germany (Ost-Mark/D-Mark) 1987
Unit value ratio		
at own country weights	3.72 (3.41)[a]	1.81 (1.70)[a]
at West German weights	4.03 (3.28)[a]	1.98 (1.71)[a]
Geometric average	3.87 (3.34)[a]	1.89 (1.70)[a]
Commercial exchange rate	8.01	4.52

[a] Excluding the quality adjustment for passenger cars.
Note: See van Ark and Beintema (1993) for details on Czechoslovakia v. West Germany, and Beintema and van Ark (1994) for details on East Germany v. West Germany.
Sources: See Appendix tables A.1 and A.2.

of the administrative prices in CPEs compared to market prices in Western economies will be necessary.

(2) There are significant differences in quality between products produced in CPEs and in market economies. Although one can safely assume that on the whole average product quality in CPEs was lower than in market economies, it is not clearly documented whether such differences were equally large across the whole range of manufacturing products, including non-durable consumer goods as well as intermediate goods and investment goods. Furthermore, given the administrative nature of the pricing system in the CPEs, one cannot be sure to what extent quality differences were reflected in the prices of the products.

The present comparisons for Czechoslovakia and East Germany include only a crude quality adjustment for passenger cars. This adjustment was derived from a price valuation of a Czech-made car (a Skoda) in West Germany compared to the 'average' price of a car of West German make. At this stage I did not make any further quality adjustments, although the adjustment for cars was to some extent extrapolated to other products in machinery and transport equipment. Table 7.3 shows that the overall effect of the quality adjustment for cars on the unit value ratio for manufacturing as a whole was 16% for the Czechoslovakia–West Germany comparison and 11% for the East Germany–West Germany comparison.[11]

The handling of the quality problem is still crude and not entirely satisfactory. In a more detailed study on East and West Germany a comparison was made with the result of quality adjustment procedures from other comparative studies (van Ark, 1995b). It suggested that the effect of the quality adjustment for passenger cars may have been too small to represent the overall quality adjustment required for manufacturing as a whole. However, as will be argued below, one needs to bear in mind that a major part of the 'unmeasured' quality adjustment may be accounted for in this study by putting the comparisons on a value added basis rather than on a gross output basis.

(3) The third area of problems in comparing output and productivity performance between CPEs and market economies concerns differences in defining the output concept. Comparisons across countries can be made either on the basis of gross output or on the basis of value added. The difference between these two output measures are the intermediate inputs. In the case of CPEs, intermediate inputs only concern material inputs (raw materials, energy, packaging) and some industrial services (for example, contract labour). Non-industrial service inputs were not measured according to the traditional material product system (MPS) accounting system.

Table 7.4 shows the basic data on gross output, material inputs, value added and employment in manufacturing for the two binary comparisons including Czechoslovakia and East Germany in the benchmark year. The concepts (including those for West Germany) are all according to the MPS concept. The basic sources were the industrial surveys and censuses, though in the case of East Germany we also made use of the input–output table to obtain the estimates of value added for 1987.

The fourth row of Table 7.4 compares the ratio of material inputs to gross output in both countries, which was substantially larger in Czechoslovakia and East Germany (65–66% of gross output) than in West Germany (48–52% in West Germany).[12]

There is a range of explanations for the larger share of material inputs in gross output in CPEs compared to market economies. Firstly there may have been a greater wastage of intermediate inputs. Although in recent decades value added rather than gross output was the major performance criterion in Czechoslovakia and East Germany, there was no budget constraint on inputs. This led to an inefficient use of raw materials, energy and other intermediate inputs. Production prices were raised to allow for greater wastage and product-oriented subsidies were accorded when prices became too high.

Related to this, a second reason for the larger use of intermediate inputs

Table 7.4   Gross value of output, census value added and labour input in manufacturing, Czechoslovakia and West Germany (1989) and East and West Germany (1987)

	Czecho-slovakia (1989) (min Kcs)	West Germany (1989) (min DM)	East Germany (1987) (min OM)	West Germany (1987) (min DM)
Gross value of industrial output[a]	833.3	1,469.4	467.4	1,260.4
Material inputs[b]	542.4	758.9	307.4	605.3
Value added	290.9	710.5	160.0[d]	655.0[d]
Material inputs/gross output (%)	65.1	51.6	65.7	48.0
Number of employees[c] (1,000)	2,326.6	7,105.8	2,763.6	6,855.5
Annual hours per person	1,858	1,616	1,735	1,627

Note: Excluding units with less than 20 employees.
[a] Production of industrial goods and material services (including repair and maintenance, transport), including production for own use (in particular capital goods).
[b] Raw materials, packaging and energy inputs and contract labour.
[c] All employees in local units, including non-production employees.
[d] Including excise taxes.
Source: See Appendix tables B.1 and B.2.

is the misallocation of inputs across industries owing to the distortion in administrative prices.

Thirdly, firms tended to hold large stocks of materials and semi-finished products which they used to exchange with other firms in order to compensate for general shortages. Furthermore, much of the production for final use was kept in stock, and in many cases was never sold.

Fourthly, there may have been a trade-off between low technology and high raw material inputs for many products from CPE countries. For example, instead of producing high-performing automatic and computer-controlled machine tools as in market economies, CPEs often invested in heavy and solid machine tools which performed relatively simple functions with large margins of tolerance.[13] To the extent that productivity is compared on the basis of value added rather than gross output, the measures reflect a significant quality adjustment as the higher raw material content (and therefore lower value added) of the products from CPEs is partly an indication of their low-technology content.

A related point is that the average size of firms in East European countries was relatively large compared to capitalist countries. This is partly related to the wider extent of horizontal integration in CPEs, with each plant producing a broader range of products compared to firms in market economies (Ehrlich, 1985). In some cases horizontal integration may lead to 'economies of scope' when firms benefit from a more efficient use of overhead capital (including sales, administration, repair and maintenance, etc.). However, even for Western countries the evidence for economies of scope is slim. In Eastern Europe it is more likely that horizontal integration led to 'diseconomies of scope', leading to a greater amount of inputs per unit of output.[14]

(4) A final problem which affects output and productivity comparisons between CPEs and market economies concerns differences in their industry classification schemes. In industry classification schemes of CPEs it appears difficult to clearly separate mining and utilities from manufacturing activities. More important, employment estimates for manufacturing in CPEs often include employees from a wide range of secondary activities, such as repair and maintenance, but also social services which were provided by firms to their employees on a much wider scale than in market economies.

The West German 'Systematik für das produzierende Gewerbe' (SYPRO) is close to the European NACE classification system and the UN ISIC system. The information for East Germany on gross output and employment used for this study was based on the SYPRO classification scheme. However, for Czechoslovakia an adjustment to a Western classification scheme could not be made, although mining activities were largely excluded. Similarly as far as possible, labour input in social services, etc., was excluded from the employment data.

2.2   Output and productivity in the benchmark year

Table 7.5 shows the comparative ratios of gross output, value added and gross output and value added per employee and per hour worked which were obtained with the help of the unit value ratios from Table 7.3. The estimates shown here are the geometric averages of the original binary results at weights of each of the two countries. On average gross output in Czechoslovak and East German manufacturing (i.e. the production value of goods and industrial services) was 14.6% and 19.6% of the West German level in 1989 and 1987 respectively. Value added in Czechoslovakia and East Germany was on average only 10.6% and 12.9% of the West German level.[15] As explained above, the census value added concept is preferred for this study, as it exhibits more clearly the inefficient characteristics of East German

Table 7.5   Gross value of output, value added and labour productivity in manufacturing (Czechoslovakia and East Germany as a percentage of West Germany)

	Czechoslovakia (1989)	East Germany (1987)
Gross value of output	14.6	19.6
Value added	10.6	12.9
Gross value of output per employee	44.7	48.6
Value added per employee	32.3	32.0
Value added per hour worked	28.1	30.0

Note: Geometric average of own country and West German weights. For definitions of each of the variables see Table 7.4.
Source: For basic data, see Table 7.4; for unit value ratios, see Table 7.3. For details by manufacturing branch see Appendix tables B.1 and B.2.

manufacturing in CPEs, and takes account of a substantial part of their lower product quality.

On the basis of the geometric average of the UVRs for each binary comparison, gross output per person in manufacturing in Czechoslovakia was 45% of West Germany in 1989, and in East Germany 49% of the West German level in 1987. Value added per person as a percentage of West Germany was 32% for both Czechoslovakia and East Germany.

Finally, to obtain more precise estimates of the output per unit of labour input, labour productivity can be adjusted for differences in the number of hours worked per person. In 1987 employees in East German manufacturing worked on average 1,736 hours, which was 109 hours more than in West Germany. In 1989 production workers in the manufacturing of Czechoslovakia worked 1,858 hours which was 242 hours more than West German manufacturing workers. As a result the comparative level of value added per hour worked drops from 32.3% to 28.1% in the case of Czechoslovakia and from 32% to 30% in the case of East Germany (see Table 7.5).

3   Reconstructing output and productivity growth in Eastern Europe

To get a view of the dynamics of the comparative productivity performance in East European countries, one may construct time series of value added and employment and link these to the benchmark year estimates. This has been the usual procedure for productivity comparisons among Western countries.[16]

However, there are many problems in adequately measuring the growth of real output in Eastern Europe. Below these problems are first discussed in a general nature, after which the alternative growth estimates for Czechoslovakia and East Germany are considered in more detail.

3.1   The official growth estimates

The main problems with the official estimates of real output growth rates in CPEs are difficult to rank in order of importance. A study of the literature suggests that the following factors are the most important:[17]

(1) Firstly, the estimates of real output growth in CPEs are mostly derived by pricing physical quantities at the prices of a base year, whereas the growth rates of real income produced are obtained by deflating net material product by an official price index. The pricing of commodities at 'comparable prices' was carried out at the firm level.[18] Managers often inflated their output because they applied relatively high prices for new products. This was motivated by suggesting higher production costs for these new products or by claiming substantial quality improvements which in reality were relatively minor compared to existing products. Prices of existing products were insufficiently adjusted downwards once cost reductions had occurred or when the quality began to deteriorate. When the net material product in current prices was then deflated by the official 'constant price' deflator, insufficient account was taken of these actual pricing practices of firms.

(2) Secondly, the growth rates of real output in CPEs were often upwardly biased because of so-called 'overgrown cooperation' between firms (Lazarcik and Staller, 1968). Planning agencies in CPEs often required intensive cooperation among firms. The planning system also forced firms to subcontract part of their production to fulfil production targets. As a result the estimated growth rates of real output in CPEs were affected by the rising share of production for intermediate use.

(3) Thirdly, as the statistics of the former CPEs were set up on the basis of the material product system (MPS), they primarily reported the output of physical production and material services. However, in practice the coverage of the MPS gradually expanded over time. For example, in Czechoslovakia the concept of production during the late 1940s and early 1950s expanded from the value of 'production of goods delivered' to the value of 'productive work and services', and

finally also to the value of 'production produced and consumed' by the enterprise (Lazarcik and Staller, 1968).

(4) Fourthly, at different stages in the process there has also been deliberate overreporting of output. Managers may have overreported their gross output in order to achieve their planned target. There may also have been some overreporting at the more aggregate level to put the country in a favourable light internationally.

3.2   Alternative estimates of real output and productivity growth

The reconstruction of the growth of manufacturing real output of former CPEs can be carried out along two different routes. The first is to reestimate the current value aggregates or price indexes to eliminate the effects of hidden inflation and make to a correction for the effect of the introduction of 'new' products.[19] However, reconstructing the price series is a difficult path to pursue for long-term studies mainly because of the lack of appropriate value and price statistics.

The second option is to employ the 'adjusted factor cost' method. This method originates from the work of Abram Bergson on the reconstruction of Soviet growth performance.[20] It makes use of quantities of physical output which are weighted at 'proxy' factor cost weights, which represent the compensation for labour (i.e. the sum of wages and salaries and social security contributions) and capital (i.e. depreciation allowances and an estimate of the return on capital). This approach has advantages over the 'repricing' method, because the basic data which are needed, in particular the quantity information, is more readily available than the prices.

The adjusted factor cost approach has been extensively applied in a range of studies on real output growth in East European countries by a group of researchers headed by Thad Alton.[21] I reconstructed the Alton time series for industry by linking the series for sub-periods so that a continuous time series was obtained from 1936 (for East Germany) or 1937 (for Czechoslovakia) onwards. Table 7.6 shows that the adjusted factor cost series caused an overall downward adjustment of the annual compound growth rate of the NMP for industry in Czechoslovakia of around 1.5 percentage points for the post-war period as a whole. The adjustment for East Germany was around 2 percentage points. Given the somewhat lower growth rate of Czechoslovakia, this implies that the adjustment in percentages (rather than in percentage points) is about the same in Czechoslovakia and East Germany. The table also suggests that output and productivity growth in the former CPEs was considerably faster during the early post-war period than during the last two decades.[22]

Table 7.6 Growth rates of real output and productivity according to net material product concept and adjusted factor cost concept, Czechoslovakia and East Germany, 1936–89

	Value added				Labour productivity		
	Net material product concept. Industry (1)	Adjusted factor cost concept. Industry (2)	Difference (1)–(2) (3)	Adjusted factor cost. Manufacturing (4)	Net material product concept. Industry (5)	Adjusted factor cost. Industry (6)	Adjusted factor cost. Manufacturing (7)
(a) Czechoslovakia (1937–89)							
1937–50		2.0		1.9			
1950–60	8.9	7.4	1.5	7.2	5.3	3.8	3.5
1960–70	5.2	4.0	1.2	3.9	3.6	2.3	2.0
1970–80	5.3	3.3	2.0	3.4	4.8	2.8	2.9
1980–89	2.4	1.2	1.2	1.3	2.3	1.1	1.3
1950–89	5.5	4.0	1.5	4.0	4.0	2.5	2.4
(b) East Germany (1936–88)							
1936–50	0.5	− 1.5	2.0	− 1.8			
1950–60	10.9	9.1	1.8	9.6	8.6	6.9	7.2
1960–70	5.2	3.6	1.6	3.8	5.1	3.5	3.6
1970–80	5.4	3.2	2.2	3.3	4.2	2.0	2.2
1980–88	4.8	2.3	2.5	2.4(1.8)[a]	4.4	2.0	2.1(1.5)[a]
1950–88	6.6	4.6	2.0	4.8(4.7)[a]	5.6	3.6	3.8(3.7)[a]

[a] Alternative estimates between brackets are based on the repricing method for the period 1980–88, taken from Görzig (1991).
Source: For sources of adjusted factor cost concept and employment, see Appendix C. Net material product for Czechoslovakia for 1950–65 from Lazarcik and Staller (1968); for 1965–72 from Staller (1975), for 1972–80 from *UN National Accounts Statistics*, various issues, and for 1980–90 from Marer (1992). NMP for East Germany for 1950–70 from Sturm (1974) which was obtained on the basis of a regression of three overlapping series for sub-periods; for 1970–90 from Marer (1992).

Table 7.6 also shows the growth rates for manufacturing for the two CPE countries after removing mining and electricity from the original Alton estimates for industry. It appears that according to the adjusted factor cost estimates, the annual compound growth rate of real output in East German manufacturing (4.8% for the period 1950–88) was only slightly below that of West Germany (4.9% for 1950–89). The annual growth rate of manufacturing output in Czechoslovakia was 0.8 percentage points below the corresponding growth rate in East Germany.

Productivity growth in Czechoslovakia was even 1.4 percentage points lower than in East Germany.

3.3   The plausibility of the adjusted factor estimates of real output growth

To get a better view on the plausibility of the Alton estimates of the growth rates of real output in CPEs, one may link the series (together with the growth rates for West Germany) to the benchmark comparisons of productivity for the late 1980s, which were obtained in the previous section. Table 7.7 shows the comparative levels of value added per person employed in Czechoslovakia and East Germany as a percentage of West Germany for some years.

In the case of East Germany there have been earlier studies of comparisons with West Germany which are shown in the third column of Table 7.7.[23] It is clear that the East–West Germany estimates from this study are considerably lower than those from the other studies, but that the difference is somewhat less for the later years than for the earlier years of the post-war period.

In effect there are two, not mutually exclusive, explanations for the lower estimates of the comparative productivity levels for earlier years:

(1) A comparison of the growth rates of the CPEs (Table 7.6) with those of West Germany raises the suspicion that, despite the significant downward adjustment which has already been made compared to the official growth rates, the adjusted factor cost estimates are still

Table 7.7   Level of value added per person employed in manufacturing, West Germany = 100, 1950–89

	Czechoslovakia	East Germany		
		This study	Alternative estimates	
1950	63	39	61–69	Ritschl (1996)
1964	39	39	77	Sturm (1974)
1967	37	38	67–69	Wilkens (1970)
1970	33	34	45	Görzig and Gornig (1991)
			67	Wilkens (1981)
1976	32	30	47	Görzig and Gornig (1991)
1980	33	32	45	Görzig (1991)
1987	34	32	44	Görzig (1991)

Note: Based on extrapolation from Czechoslovakia/West Germany (1989) and East Germany/West Germany (1987).
Source: Column (1) and (2): value added per person from Appendix table C.2.

too high, in particular for East Germany. This proposition may have some validity for the following reasons. The almost exclusive reliance on physical quantities implies that the method does not take account of the lower technology and higher raw material content of products originating from CPEs compared to market economies. Furthermore, a significant part of physical output produced in former CPEs was never consumed and it is doubtful whether such production for waste should be valued at the same price as the production which is consumed.

On the other hand, some scholars have argued that the adjusted factor cost method *understated* rather than overstated real growth.[24] The main argument following this line of reasoning is that, as the method relies heavily on the output of commodities in physical quantities, it takes insufficient account of the introduction of new products in particular in the machinery and electrical equipment industries.

However, on hindsight the latter arguments seem not to have much validity. The great difficulties which the former CPEs presently face in competing with the traditional market economies, clearly show that their pace of technological change and their transformation towards producing high-quality and high-value added goods has been much slower. It is therefore hard to accept that the productivity growth rates should have been even higher than is suggested on the basis of the Alton estimates.

(2) The second, and probably more important, reason for the lower productivity level estimates for the CPEs in this study is that the earlier estimates are primarily based on gross output rather than value added comparisons and mostly make use of West German prices only. As shown in Table 7.5 gross output comparisons depict a much more favourable picture of the CPE's comparative performance, and the use of West German price weights can easily lead to an overestimation of the CPE's relative output. Van Ark (1995b) shows that after an adjustment of the comparative value added estimates according to the ICOP method to gross output using only West German prices, the comparative productivity estimates are virtually the same as those from Ritschl for 1950 and Görzig and Gornig for the 1970s and 1980s (see Table 7.7).

Summarizing, this section suggests that, if anything, the adjusted factor cost estimates still overstate the 'true' growth of real output of the CPEs. However, the most important explanation for the much lower productivity results of the CPEs obtaining in this study is the switch from comparing gross output to comparing value added. A more thorough study of the comparative productivity performance during the early post-war period will be necessary to reach more definitive conclusions. It is clear, however, that the comparative productivity performance of the CPEs was worse than was thought before, and that much of the gap already opened up at an early stage during the post-World War II period.

4   Comparing East European productivity performance with that of Southwest and Northwest Europe

As mentioned at the beginning of this chapter, comparisons of productivity across Europe are useful to test whether geographical proximity plays a role in explaining convergence trends. As has been explained in various studies, including several in this volume, there has been a significant convergence of productivity among Northwest European countries as well as a catch-up with the world economic leader, the United States, during the post-war period.

This section compares the measures of comparative productivity in two East European countries (Czechoslovakia and East Germany) with those of two Southwest European Countries (Portugal and Spain). This may help to further clarify our view on the mechanism behind regional or country-specific convergence *vis-à-vis* global convergence.

Figure 7.1 reproduces the comparative performance for Czechoslovakia, East Germany, Portugal and Spain *vis-à-vis* the USA for the period from 1950 onwards. The graph also shows the average productivity level of four 'core countries' in Northwest Europe (France, West Germany, The Netherlands and the UK), called the EURO-4. All estimates were derived on the basis of the ICOP method, which is explained in greater detail elsewhere.[25]

4.1   The legacy of the inter-war period, the Civil War and World War II

Figure 7.1 suggests that in 1950 the comparative manufacturing productivity performance of Czechoslovakia was much superior to that of the other countries, namely at approximately 24% of the USA level, compared to 15% for East Germany, 13% for Spain and 12% for Portugal. For comparison, the average productivity level of the EURO-4 was about 40% of the USA level in 1950.

To put these productivity estimates in perspective, it is useful to take a brief look at the comparative performance of these economies just before World War II. Unfortunately the estimates for the pre-war years are still

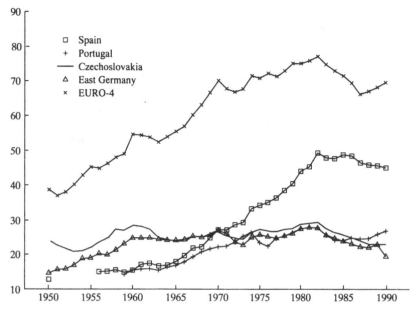

Note: See Table 7.8 for the benchmark estimates, which were linked to the USA through their original benchmark country, i.e. West Germany in case of East Germany and Czechoslovakia and the UK in case of Portugal and Spain. EURO-4 is the average productivity level of France, West Germany, The Netherlands and the UK, which was obtained by weighting each country's productivity level relative to the USA by the employment share for three subperiods (i.e. 1950–65 at 1960 weights; 1965–80 at 1975 weights; and 1980–1989 at 1985 weights).
Sources: See Appendix tables C.1 to C.4 and ICOP database.

Figure 7.1   Comparative levels of value added per person employed in manufacturing, Czechoslovakia, East Germany, Portugal and Spain as a percentage of the USA, 1950–90.

difficult to compare across countries, but it nevertheless appears possible to draw some conclusions from a comparison of pre-war and post-war estimates concerning the level of industrialization of these countries by the end of the 1930s.

During the inter-war period Czechoslovakia emerged as one of the most rapidly industrializing East European economies, a process which had started earlier in Bohemia and Moravia during the nineteenth century. Although the growth rates of manufacturing output were not significantly higher than in neighbouring countries such as Hungary or Poland, the nature of the Czechoslovak industrialization process was distinctly different. The manufacturing output structure transformed more rapidly towards a large share of investment and producer goods industries, and the productivity performance of these industries was better than in neighbouring countries.[26] Although small firms continued to account for an important share of manufacturing employment in Czechoslovakia, the rise of medium and large firms exhibiting substantial economies of scale was relatively rapid. The latter also contributed to the creation of an effective system of domestic capital formation and increased Czechoslovakia's attractiveness for foreign investment.

In 1930 over 30% of the economically active population in Czechoslovakia was employed in manufacturing, which was substantially more than in any other East European country (Mitchell, 1992). Comparative productivity estimates are not available, but estimates by the League of Nations for the 1930s suggest that manufacturing output per head of the population was just below 50% of the level in Germany.[27]

After World War II, between 1945 and 1948, Czechoslovakia moved quickly ahead with the reconstruction of the economy, with which it was helped by funds it received from the UN Relief and Rehabilitation Administration and because of its advanced industrial structure and export oriented economy, which was created during the inter-war period (Teichova, 1988). In 1948, the first five-year plan was installed, which among other things meant the expropriation of the private sector, a redirection of imports and exports from the west towards the Soviet Union and other CMEA states, and a reorientation towards heavy industrialization mainly based on accumulation instead of productivity strategies.[28] This undoubtedly is a major reason for the weak productivity performance of the Czechoslovak economy between 1950 and 1953, when the growth of employment outpaced the sluggish rise in real output in manufacturing (see also Figures 7.2 and 7.3 below).

In the eastern part of Germany, industrial performance before World War II was even better than in Czechoslovakia. Compared to West Germany, the eastern territory was relatively well-endowed with natural resources (in particular brown coal, copper and other non-ferrous metals). Although light industry was originally disproportionately represented in the east part of Germany, the Nazi economic planners had decisively moved some heavy industry to the central German area between Leipzig and Hannover, which later predominantly fell within the East German territory.[29]

A detailed production census for 1936 in combination with a post-war source which divided census estimates up between East and West German territories, provides a fairly precise estimate of comparative productivity performance in manufacturing.[30] It appeared that in 1936 sales per employee in East Germany amounted to 84% of the level in West Germany. In contrast to Czechoslovakia, East Germany had no opportunity to recover from the damage of the war on its economy. In 1945 East Germany's economic position was not significantly worse than in West Germany. East Germany had not suffered more from wartime destruction, and the structure of the East German industrial sector was not disadvantageous to that of West Germany. Ritschl (1996) argues that most of the productivity gap between East and West Germany opened up in the first five years after German capitulation, explaining its much lower productivity level compared to West Germany (and Czechoslovakia) by 1950.

Although the dismantling of the capital stock after the war was executed at a more rapid pace in East Germany than in West Germany, Ritschl argues it did not lead to a great decline in capital–labour ratios because there was an equally rapid outflux of East German employment to West Germany. As in the case of Czechoslovakia, the main reason for the productivity decline in East Germany according to Ritschl is the transformation to a command economy during the period 1945 to 1950.[31]

Unfortunately there are no precise productivity estimates available for Spain and Portugal for the pre-war period, which is mainly due to the weak estimates on employment. However, all the available evidence suggests that productivity levels in these economies during the 1930s were not higher than in 1950. Both Southwest European economies were undoubtedly less industrialized than those of Czechoslovakia and East Germany by the 1930s. Although Spain had experienced some industrialization during the late 1910s and the 1920s, Portugal effectively remained a backward agriculture-dominated country until the 1950s.[32] In 1930 the share of manufacturing employment in Spain was of the order of 20% of total employment (Carreras, 1990), and for Portugal it was even lower at around 15% (Mitchell, 1992).

Following the Civil War 1936–39, real growth in manufacturing output in Spain was slow during World War II and it did not participate in the European Reconstruction. During this period Spain was characterized by extreme isolationism and very autarkic policies. Industrial policies concentrated on state intervention to stimulate basic industry, and trade policies were highly protectionist and focused on import substitution. Spanish industry (in particular Catalan textile industries and the Basque iron industry) benefited slightly from World War II when it filled the export vacuum left by the other war-struck European economies, but soon after the war exports reversed to mainly agricultural products. As a result Spain did not benefit from intensified international trade and monetary cooperation during the first years following the war. It did not receive Marshall Aid which slowed down the much-needed construction of infrastructure following the damage of the Civil War (Ránki, 1985).

In Portugal, industrial performance during the 1930s and 1940s was not so bad as in Spain, although it started from much lower levels of industrial output than Spain. Industrial exports accounted for a very small part of overall Portuguese exports and were dominated by wine and oranges. In contrast to Spain, the Portuguese economy followed a more liberal path by the end of the 1940s, in particular concerning its foreign economic relations. Exports of textiles and other low technology products accelerated substantially during this period. Although no pre-war productivity estimates are available, one may expect that the Portuguese productivity performance relative to Spain improved between the 1930s and the 1950s.

4.2   The long-run productivity performance of the core and the periphery

The previous discussion suggests that although in 1950 the East European countries were still better placed in terms of their relative productivity performance, the preconditions for catch-up and convergence on Northwest Europe and the USA had already begun to shift to the advantage of the Southwest European countries. The increasing grip of the Soviets on the early post-war economies of Czechoslovakia and East Germany required a reorientation of trade flows and production structure which was quite different from the pre-war constellation. In contrast Portugal had become increasingly outward-looking during the 1930s and 1940s and was followed in this respect by Spain in the course of the 1950s.

Nevertheless, the two East European economies still established a respectable growth rate and caught up moderately on the USA (but not with Northwest Europe) during the 1950s. A major characteristic of the growth path in the East European countries was its extensive nature, which implied that a rise in real output was primarily driven by a rise in factor inputs. Growth of labour input was quite substantial during this period, though it was slower in East Germany than in Czechoslovakia, because of the outflux of labour from East to West Germany. The increase in employment was mainly caused by the rise in labour force participation rates (which became the highest in Europe) and the rapid transfer of labour out of agriculture.

More important than the faster rise in labour input, was the rise in physical investment and capital stock in East European industries.

Annual growth of fixed investment in East European industry, even after adjusting for a higher amount of stock creation in output, was at par with if not higher than that in Northwest Europe.[33] In the industrial sector of both countries the emphasis was strongly on the production of investment goods, which put an additional claim on high investment in physical capital. In Czechoslovakia, the employment share of the machinery and equipment branch in total industrial employment, rose from 30% in 1950 to 36% in 1960. At the same time the employment share of consumer goods, including the food industry, fell from 39% to 31% of total industrial employment.[34]

Figure 7.1 shows that, by the early 1960s, the accumulation strategies in Czechoslovakia and East Germany began to show the first signs of failure. Productivity growth rates began to decline, and both countries began to diverge significantly from the manufacturing productivity levels in Northwest Europe, and no further catch-up on the best practice in the USA was established. It was also recognized that the productive use of capital and labour had been unsatisfactory, and that more priority should be given to improving efficiency. However, the stagnant performance of the industrial sector continued into the 1970s and the 1980s, during which not only the investment rates but also the rise in labour input levelled off. At the end of the 1980s, when their political system broke down, manufacturing productivity of the two East European countries deteriorated significantly.

Although the two Southwest European countries, Spain and Portugal, experienced an acceleration of productivity during the 1950s, growth rates were still lower than in Northwest and East Europe, and as a result divergence took place when compared to these two regions. Despite signs of change towards more outward-looking policies in the course of the 1950s, the Spanish economy remained characterized by consumer shortages, rising inflation and a slow growth of real output in manufacturing until the end of the decade. When, by the end of the 1950s Spain had shaken off the remnants of isolationism, it moved into an era of liberalization of the economy, which was characterized by intensified international trade, promotion of exports and support for private investment. The annual compound growth rates of real output (11.9%) and employment (3.1%) in manufacturing were quite high between 1960 and 1973, and also higher than for the economy as a whole (i.e. 7.3% and 1.2% respectively) which is a clear indication of a significant structural change taking place.

In Portugal, the government began to stress the importance of industrialization earlier than in Spain. Because of the small size of the economy, real autarky such as in Spain was never an option, so that investment (which was in fact relatively high during the 1950s) was more in tune with Portugal's comparative advantages. International trade grew quite substantially during the 1950s. However, productivity growth remained slow and did not show any sign of catch-up on the USA until the early 1960s, although it did catch up with the level in Spain.

In 1960 still only 20% of the Portuguese labour force was employed in manufacturing. However, during the 1960s the Portuguese manufacturing growth performance was significantly better than before, although the gap with Spain again began to widen somewhat.

From the late 1960s until the mid-1980s Spain entered a growth path exhibiting very rapid catch-up on Northwest Europe and the USA. However, in Portugal productivity growth did not accelerate. By 1973 the manufacturing productivity level in Spain was already some 20% higher than in Portugal, by 1980 it was 60% higher, and by 1985 it was more than double the Portuguese level.

At face value, Figure 7.1 suggests that since the early 1970s Portugal had more in common with the two Eastern European countries than with its neighbour. However, two additional graphs need to be looked at, which depict the growth of real manufacturing output (Figure 7.2) and employment (Figure 7.3) in each of the four countries. It appears that after 1973, the Portuguese and Spanish growth performance in real output and employment dramatically diverged. Real output growth in Spain (although much slower than before 1973) was still faster than in Portugal. In 1975 the latter country even experienced a decline following its turbulent transformation to democracy in 1974–75. However, the main difference between Portugal and Spain during the period 1975–85 was that manufacturing employment in Spain declined very rapidly. This development should be interpreted not only as a sign of restructuring of the industrial sector, but also as a general underperformance of the Spanish economy during these years: the fall in manufacturing employment by almost 30% (about one million jobs) between 1975 and 1985 went in parallel with a rise in the unemployment rate from 3% to more than 20%.

During this period of 'democratic transition', which coincided with two oil crises, a range of structural problems emerged which severely affected the performance of Spain's 'new' and energy-intensive industries such as steel, shipbuilding and heavy chemicals. Oil price rises were absorbed by the state until 1980, but as a result the impact of the second oil price rise on the overstaffed, indebted and excess-capacity firms was even stronger.

The Spanish economy of the late 1970s was also characterized by some damaging remnants of the Franco period, among which were industrial rules which forbade layoffs, leading to many bankruptcies in particular

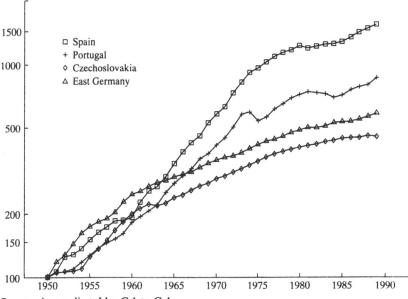

Source: Appendix tables C.1 to C.4.

Figure 7.2   Growth of real GDP in manufacturing, Czechoslovakia, East Germany, Portugal and Spain, 1950–90, 1950 = 100 (semi-log scale).

among small and medium-sized firms. The rapid productivity rise of the late 1970s was therefore essentially a process of deindustrialization, and one which resulted in stagnation during the early 1980s (Salmon, 1991; Prados and Sanz, 1996).

Another sign of the structural retrogression of the Spanish economy from the mid-1970s to the mid-1980s, was that productivity growth in manufacturing was not reflected in a rise of per capita income. Whereas manufacturing value added per person employed moved up from less than 30% of the USA level in 1973 to almost 50% in 1985 (see Figure 7.1), per capita income fell slightly from 53% of the USA level in 1973 to 49% in 1985.[35]

Since 1985 industrial restructuring in Spain has taken a positive turn, as industrial output and employment both have begun to accelerate. Of particular importance has been the rise in foreign investment and trade. However, by 1990 one still could not speak of a return to convergence in comparison to Northwest Europe nor of catch-up on the USA productivity performance.

In contrast to Spain, Portugal did not undergo a decline in manufacturing employment before the early 1980s, and the process since then was

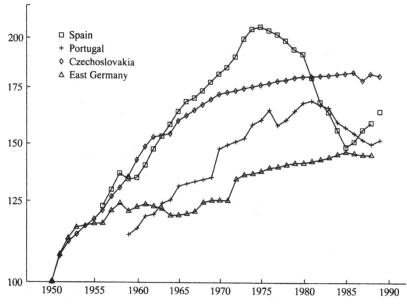

Source: Appendix tables C.1 to C.4.

Figure 7.3 Growth of number of employees in manufacturing, Czechoslovakia, East Germany, Portugal and Spain, 1950–90, 1950 = 100 (semi-log scale).

much more moderate. Given the overall lower level of per capita income, wages and productivity, Portugal continued to benefit from its long-time comparative advantage in labour-intensive industries, such as food products, textiles and non-metallic mineral products, for much longer. Nevertheless, between 1981 and 1988 manufacturing employment in Portugal declined by some 12%, and the comparative productivity performance of Portugal has shown a significant improvement compared to the USA, Northwest Europe and Spain since 1984.

4.3 Comparative performance by various indicators during the 1980s

Table 7.8 presents the productivity results for the four countries under consideration by major branch in manufacturing, expressed as a percentage of the USA productivity level for a year during the 1980s. Spain clearly had the highest level of labour productivity in all major branches. Spain did particularly well in textiles, chemicals and basic metals and metal products. Portuguese productivity levels in 1987 were only slightly above those of Czechoslovakia and East Germany. In the case of food manufacturing and basic metals and metal products Portuguese produc-

Table 7.8 Labour productivity and per capita income, Czechoslovakia, East Germany, Portugal and Spain, USA = 100

	Czecho-slovakia (1989)	East Germany (1987)	Portugal (1987)	Spain (1984)
Manufacturing (USA = 100)[a]				
Food, beverages & tobacco	16.2	30.9	25.8	38.5
Textiles, apparel & leather	22.5	30.1	31.9	56.1
Chemicals & allied products	43.7	26.2	30.9	61.9
Basic & fabr. metal products	28.0	28.0	23.6	53.4
Machinery & equipment	27.9	20.9	23.9	44.2
Other manufacturing	23.3	19.4	27.7	44.6
Total				
Value added per employee	22.7	22.5	24.5	47.6
Value added per hour worked	23.5	24.7	23.2	52.6
Total economy (USA = 100)				
Value added per hour worked[b]	37.6	n.a.	41.2	70.2
GDP per capita[c]	40.1	57.5	44.9	49.7

[a] The estimates for manufacturing in Czechoslovakia and East Germany are originally based on West Germany and are the geometric average of comparisons at own prices and West German prices. Portugal and Spain are originally based on the UK and are the geometric average of comparisons at own prices and UK prices.
[b] These estimates refer to a year near 1989 and are derived on the basis of a comparison at USA prices only.
[c] These estimates are derived on the basis of a comparison at international prices.
Source: For manufacturing estimates, see Appendix tables B.1 to B.4. The Germany/USA productivity levels were taken from van Ark and Pilat (1993) and the UK/USA levels from van Ark (1992). For productivity estimates for the total economy, see Maddison (1994). For per capita income for the total economy, see Maddison (1995).

tivity was even lower than in East Germany, and in the case of chemicals and machinery and equipment it was lower than in Czechoslovakia.

It is striking to note that despite all the emphasis of East European planners on the development of heavy and investment good industries, these branches did not show significantly higher productivity levels than the manufacturing sector as a whole, with exception of the chemicals branch in Czechoslovakia.

Table 7.8 also show that, with the exception of Portugal the adjustment from a comparison of output per employee to output per hour led to a slightly more favourable picture, reflecting the shorter working time per person in European countries compared to the USA.

It is also striking that, when comparing the manufacturing performance with that for the economy as a whole, all four countries seem to be performing relatively worse in manufacturing. The better productivity performance for the economy as a whole suggests either substantial structural differences between each country and the USA in favour of high productive activities in East and Southwest Europe, or a relatively better productivity performance in the non-manufacturing sectors of the East and Southwest European economies (i.e. mainly services) compared to the USA.

Whereas the first proposition seems implausible, the second may be more sensible. One explanation might be that technology, with which periphery countries have been less well equipped historically, plays a less crucial role in services. Another explanation is that there are important structural differences within the services sector. In advanced economies the share of social and personal services in total employment has increased more rapidly than that of producer and distributive services, and productivity levels in the former are considerably lower than in the latter.

In any case a comparison of manufacturing and total economy indicators suggest that the manufacturing productivity story may not tell the whole story of the convergence experience in Europe. On the other hand, it makes clear that in the sector (that is, manufacturing) where one might expect diffusion mechanisms to play a relatively important role at regional level the effectiveness has been quite disappointing.

5   Proximate causes of convergence and divergence

At the level of the 'proximate causes' which can be distinguished is a growth accounting framework (Maddison, 1991). The previous discussion suggests three factors of major importance in explaining the diverging trends in comparative performance, i.e. the ineffectiveness of investment in physical capital and technology, a backlog in the creation of human capital, and the lack of openness to foreign trade and investment.

5.1   Investment in physical capital and technology

Investment in physical capital is an important determinant of manufacturing output growth in any industrializing country. Unfortunately, growth accounting studies of the nature performed by Maddison in Chapter 2 of this volume, are very scarce for CPEs,[36] and even for Spain and Portugal there are major problems concerning comparability.

Table 7.9 shows the best evidence at present available from different

Table 7.9   Annual compound growth rates and contribution of labour, capital and total factor productivity to output growth, Czechoslovakia, Portugal and Spain

	Czecho-slovakia (manufac-turing)	Portugal (industry)	Portugal (total economy)	Spain (total economy)	EURO-4 (total economy)
	(1948–67)	(1952–73)	(1952–73)	(1950–73)	(1950–73)
Labour input	2.7 (18)	2.0 (13)	0.7 (6)	0.1 (1)	0.0 (0)
Capital input	6.6 (52)	8.6 (53)	5.5 (48)	6.9 (34)	5.2 (25)
TFP (residual)	2.1 (30)	2.8 (34)	2.7 (46)	3.9 (65)	3.5 (75)
Output growth	7.0 (100)	8.1 (100)	5.8 (100)	6.1 (100)	4.7 (100)
		(1974–91)	(1974–91)	(1973–89)	(1973–92)
Labour input		1.1 (36)	1.6 (31)	−0.9 (−26)	−0.4 (−1)
Capital input		4.6 (117)	3.7 (56)	5.4 (65)	3.5 (38)
TFP (residual)		−0.9 (−54)	0.3 (12)	1.5 (61)	1.4 (69)
Output growth		1.7 (100)	2.8 (100)	2.5 (100)	2.1 (100)

Note: All labour and capital inputs are not augmented for change in quality of the production factors. EURO-4 refers to an unweighted average for France, Germany, The Netherlands and the UK.
Source: Czechoslovakia from Balassa and Bertrand (1970); Portugal from Neves (1993); Spain from Hofman (1993) provided by Prados (1996). France, Germany, The Netherlands and the UK from Maddison (Chapter 2 in this volume).

studies. The figures suggest that for the first half of the post-war period, the growth rates of the capital stock were higher in Czechoslovakia, Portugal and Spain than in the four Northwest European countries (France, Germany, The Netherlands and the UK).[37] In contrast, the contribution of total factor productivity (the 'Solow residual') to growth was higher in the EURO-4, although it was also quite high for Spain. For the period since the early 1970s, a growth accounting approach was not feasible for Czechoslovakia, but it seems likely that the fall in output growth was not matched by a decline in capital input to the same degree, so that the contribution of the residual to overall growth probably declined.

The figures for Spain and Portugal for the period since 1973 show a much higher residual in Spain than in Portugal. As noted above, the process of restructuring and capital deepening in Spain went together with a decline in employment. In contrast to Spain, the Portuguese economy experienced some rise in labour input, but its TFP performance was worse than in Spain.

One may conclude that the role of capital in growth in the East and Southwest European countries was very different from that in Northwest Europe. The growth model of the former group was essentially based on 'extensive growth', that is the accumulation of factor inputs (in particular capital) was the driving force behind the growth of real output. In the 'intensive growth' model, which was predominant in West Europe during the post-war period, the greatest contribution to output growth was the rise of total factor productivity.

Recent models of growth have pointed at the possibility that growth accounting studies perhaps understate the importance of capital accumulation in market economies. This does not alter the fact that the accumulation strategies of the CPEs were not viable in the long run. According to the new growth models, greater contribution of capital derives from higher returns because of greater technology spillovers between firms and sectors in the economy.

If one interprets the residual as an indicator of technological change (as many authors have done), the growth accounting results for Table 7.9 suggest that the East European economies and Portugal (but not Spain) were unsuccessful in exploiting the possibilities for technical progress. This raises an interesting paradox because, despite the slow TFP growth, there has been quite some evidence of substantial technological progress in both East and Southwest European countries. This is supported by statistics on R&D but also by the large amount of technology-intensive imports.

There are basically three, not mutually exclusive, ways of explaining this paradox. The first is to modify the Cobb–Douglas type assumptions on which the growth accounting estimates in Table 7.9 are based, and in particular relax the assumption of constant elasticity of substitution. One may hypothesize that, despite the potential for technological progress, it could not be realized because East and Southwest European economies could not substitute capital for labour.[38]

The second way of explaining the paradox is to look at the effectiveness of investment in technology. According to Gomulka, despite substantial investment in R&D, East European countries failed to successfully absorb new technologies in the production process because of resource constraints and large-scale resource misallocation. This created a high resistance of existing firms to innovation, although this explanation seems less relevant for the case of Spain.[39]

Thirdly, it may not be justified to interpret the 'Solow residual' from Table 7.9 as an indicator of technological change. Instead this factor may include a range of explanatory variables, of which some important ones are discussed below.

Table 7.10   Students in primary, secondary and tertiary education as a percentage of the population from 5 to 24 years, Czechoslovakia, East Germany, Portugal and Spain, 1938–88

	Czechoslovakia	East Germany	Portugal	Spain
1938	47		17	27
1951	51	42	22	24
1960	56	44	35	39
1970	52	54	39	56
1980	54	49	44	65
1988	53	47	49[a]	70

[a] 1984.
Source: Numbers in primary, secondary and tertiary education from Mitchell (1992). Population from Mitchell (1992), Maddison (1995) and UN Demographic Yearbook, various issues.

5.2   Investment in human capital

The formation of human capital is an area where the former communist countries traditionally seem to have been clearly ahead of Southern Europe. By the end of the inter-war period, literacy rates and enrolment in education was much higher in Czechoslovakia and East Germany than in Spain and Portugal.

Table 7.10 shows the total number of students in primary, secondary and tertiary education as a percentage of the population from 5 to 24 years old. This broad measure is at best a proxy, but it is the most robust because of the very different characteristics of the education systems in the various countries. The figures suggest that schooling was more widely available in the East European countries until the 1960s, and in the case of Czechoslovakia even showed significant improvement.

Since the 1970s the percentage of students in the population in Eastern Europe has not shown any further increase. Another factor of concern has been the quality of the education in Eastern Europe. A recent study comparing the performance between manufacturing plants in East and West Germany shows that, despite the high rate of vocational training in East Germany, the quality of skill levels was well below that of West Germany. Training programmes in East Germany were compulsory and shorter than in West Germany, and more limited in range of competences.[40]

In Southwest Europe, the formation of human capital was neglected for much longer than in Eastern Europe. In both countries significant investments in human capital were not made before the late 1950s.[41]

Table 7.11   Annual compound growth rates of the volume of exports, Czechoslovakia, East Germany, Portugal and Spain, 1950–88

	Czechoslovakia	East Germany	Portugal	Spain
1950–60	11.3		4.6	6.7
1960–70	6.8	8.0	9.2	11.3
1970–80	7.5	6.4	1.9	10.2
1980–88	3.5	3.4	10.1	7.2

Source: 1950–70: United Nations, *International Trade Statistics Yearbook*, various issues. 1970–88: Czechoslovakia and East Germany calculated from Marer (1992); Portugal and Spain from *OECD Economic Outlook*, various issues.

However, Table 7.10 shows that in 1970, students in education accounted for a larger share of the population in Spain than in the two Eastern European countries. Since then the size of the Portuguese schooling system has caught up with that of the East European countries as well.

According to Table 7.9, the rate of total factor productivity growth in Spain was rather high during both sub-periods. However, after allowing for the effect of quality improvement of labour (and capital) inputs, the contribution of the residual to overall output growth in Spain was 62% in the period 1950–73 but fell to 28% in the period 1973–89.[42] Investment in human capital is therefore a major factor accounting for the rapid productivity growth in Spain.

5.3   Openness to trade and foreign investment

All four countries have undergone major changes in terms of the performance of their foreign sector. Table 7.11 shows that over the period under consideration the growth in export volume in Czechoslovakia and East Germany has decelerated quite substantially, whereas the corresponding rates for the Southwest European countries accelerated.

During the period under communist rule, the East European countries became locked into a self-contained and regulated trading system among the CMEA nations. Table 7.12 shows that an increasing proportion of exports from Czechoslovakia and East Germany (up to two-thirds of the export value) went to other CMEA countries. Czechoslovakia, called the 'machine shop' of Eastern Europe, quickly reached a monopoly position in the exports of various kinds of machinery. Such trends took away incentives to rationalize production and reallocate resources to the most efficient activities.[43]

Table 7.12   Composition of value of exports by major region, Czechoslovakia, East Germany, Portugal and Spain, 1950–88, in percentage

| | Czechoslovakia | | East Germany | | Portugal | | Spain | |
	CMEA[a]	Other	CMEA[b]	Other	'EC'[c]	Other	'EC'[d]	Other
1950[e]	44	56	68	32	10	90	28	72
1960	60	40	66	34	41	59	27	73
1970	62	38	66	34	31	69	33	67
1980	61	39	n.a.	n.a.	34	66	42	58
1988[f]	70	30	63	37	40	60	57	43

[a] East Germany, Hungary, Poland, Romania and USSR.
[b] Bulgaria, Czechoslovakia, Hungary, Poland and USSR.
[c] France, Spain, UK and West Germany.
[d] France, UK and West Germany.
[e] Czechoslovakia: 1949; East Germany: 1953; Spain: 1951.
[f] East Germany: 1987.
Source: Mitchell (1992).

The 'democratization' of the political systems and the restructuring of the economies in Southwest Europe during the post-war period culminating in the entry of Spain and Portugal into the EC in 1986, went together with an increasing share of exports to major EC countries. In 1988 around half of the countries' exports went to France, Germany and the UK, and obviously the EC as a whole accounts for an even bigger share. Both countries experienced significant changes in the distribution of exports across branches, away from agricultural goods to light industrial goods and lately (at least in Spain) also to investment goods.

Intensifying trade in a competitive environment often triggers off a restructuring of the economy, which in some cases leads to a painful adjustment process, in particular when combined with ineffective policies as is shown by the Spanish experience from the mid-1970s to the mid-1980s. However, the alternative experiences of heavy emphasis on import substitution, as was the case in Spain until 1950s, or a fully regulated and autarkic regional trading system as in Eastern Europe between 1950 and 1989, has contributed to stagnation in productivity growth and economic development. In these cases countries became isolated from the world market pricing mechanism and became increasingly distant from best world practice in terms of producing high-quality goods with efficient production techniques.

In addition to trade, foreign investment can also function as a major carrier of technology and innovation. In contrast to Eastern Europe, the Southwest European countries (particularly Spain) have gradually opened up to a greater amount of foreign investment over the past decades.

6   Reflections on ultimate causes of convergence and divergence

The main question posed at the outset of this paper has been whether geographical proximity plays a role in convergence of productivity levels. By expanding the sample of Northwest European countries with two East European and two Southwest European countries, this hypothesis was tested in various ways. It appears that when focusing on the manufacturing productivity performance, the latter two groups of economies have mostly shown signs of divergence from the European 'core' during the post-war period, although they showed important differences in performance among themselves. For example, the productivity performance of Czechoslovakia and East Germany has gradually worsened in comparison to the Southwest European countries. Even within Southwest Europe, the Spanish and Portuguese experience in manufacturing has been one of divergence since the 1970s.

The previous section suggested three possible sources of divergence within Europe: differences in emphasis on 'extensive' versus 'intensive' growth strategies; the variation in investment in human capital; and the openness to trade and foreign investment. In fact all three factors may be related to a fourth one, which is of a more 'ultimate' nature, namely the political–institutional system which underlies the changes in the proximate causes discussed above.

Unlike Northwest Europe, both East and Southwest Europe have been characterized by non-democratic regimes, in the case of Eastern Europe until the late 1980s and in the case of Southwest Europe up to the mid-1970s. In Eastern Europe, growth strategies based on accumulation and extensive growth led to rapid growth of real output during the first one or two decades after World War II which appeared not viable in the long run. In the second part of the post-war period East European growth slowed down substantially, as the centrally planned economies lacked the instruments to improve the quality of products and services and failed to put in motion a process of transforming the structure of output, demand and trade.[44]

Apparently the Southwest European countries have been more successful in generating growth, even during the aftermath of the days of the authoritarian regimes. The shift towards greater openness to trade led to greater complementarity in terms of comparative advantages between Northwest and Southwest Europe. Furthermore the greater volume of foreign trade and investment created more effective mechanisms for technology diffusion than in Eastern Europe. Finally, during the period under consideration the Southwest European economies shifted towards a price formation process and ownership structure which showed more resemblance to that of market economies than to that of the centrally planned economies in Eastern Europe.

This discussion of ultimate causes underlines the importance of a historical approach to the analysis of phases of convergence and divergence in the broader European region. The differences in the political–institutional constellation of Northwest, East and Southwest Europe has strong historical roots in the years, and even in the decades and centuries, before World War II. However, it is also clear from this chapter that a great deal of the present divergence has arisen during recent periods of transition from one institutional–political system to another. This seems to be true of Spain during the 1930s, East Germany between 1945 and 1950, Czechoslovakia between 1948 and 1953, Portugal in 1974–75 and (although not dealt with within the framework of this chapter) Eastern Europe as a whole around 1990. In this respect, much of the realization of the large catch-up potential in Northwest Europe by the late 1940s (which also existed in East and Southwest Europe) is explained by the smooth transition from war-struck economies to a well-functioning economic system. In this respect, there remains hope for East European countries to learn from the experiences of post-war Northwest European economies, which benefited from the political and institutional stabilization supported by major assistance programmes, such as the Marshall Plan, and the successful international attempts towards trade liberalization and monetary stability.[45]

Appendix A: Unit value ratios

For full details on the general procedures of estimating unit value ratios, see van Ark (1993, 1996) and Chapter 3 (Section 5) in this volume. For details on Czechoslovakia, see van Ark and Beintema (1993); on East Germany, see Beintema and van Ark (1994) and van Ark (1995b); on Portugal, see Peres (1994) and on Spain, see van Ark (1995a).

Basic sources on quantities and unit values:

Czechoslovakia: sales value from FSO, *The Annual Survey of Industrial Enterprises.* Quantities from *The Monthly Inquiry on Production and Sales of Selected Industrial Products.* In some cases the turnover covered some by-products as well, for which adjustments were made on the basis of information provided by FSO for individual product groups.

East Germany: Statistisches Amt der DDR, *Abrechnung der Erzeugnispositionen der Erzeugnis- und Leistungsnomenklatur* for 1987.

West Germany: Statistisches Bundesamt, *Produktion im Produzierenden Gewerbe* for 1987.

Portugal: Instituto Nacional de Estatistica, *Estatísticas Industriais* 1987.

Spain: INE, *Encuesta Industrial 1983 a 1986*.

United Kingdom: Business Statistics Office, *Quarterly Sales Inquiry*, various issues.

Appendix table A.1   Number of unit value ratios, coverage of total sales and unit value ratios (Kcs to the DM) in manufacturing, Czechoslovakia and West Germany, 1989

	Number of unit value ratios	Matched sales as % of total sales		Unit value ratios (Kcs/DM)			UVR/ commercial exchange rate
		Czecho-slovakia	West Germany	Czech weights (Kcs/DM)	German weights (Kcs/DM)	Geometric average (Kcs/DM)	
Food products, beverages and tobacco	11	44.1	34.8	3.75	3.85	3.80	47.5
Textile products	10	23.8	29.7	3.98	4.01	3.99	49.9
Wearing apparel	0	0.0	0.0	3.72	4.03	3.87	48.3
Leather and leather products	2	49.2	47.8	2.29	2.21	2.25	28.1
Wood products and furniture	2	29.2	14.5	3.48	3.47	3.47	43.4
Paper, paper products & printing	2	70.2	37.1	4.57	4.07	4.31	53.8
Chemicals, rubber, plastics and petroleum refining	8	22.4	21.4	3.29	3.28	3.28	41.0
Non-metallic minerals	3	5.8	17.2	2.83	3.52	3.16	39.4
Basic metals	16	74.1	39.3	4.25	4.72	4.48	56.0
Machinery and transport equipment	9	17.2	32.3	4.29	4.75	4.51	56.4
without adjustment for quality[a]				3.12	2.16	2.60	32.4
Electrical and metal products	6	13.1	8.2	3.55	3.70	3.63	45.3
Other manufacturing	0	0.0	0.0	3.72	4.03	3.87	48.3
Total, with adjustment for quality[a]	69	32.0	23.2	3.72	4.03	3.87	48.3
without adjustment for quality[a]	69			3.41	3.28	3.34	41.7
Commercial exchange rate				8.01	8.01	8.01	100.0

[a] Quality adjustment for passenger cars.

Appendix table A.2   Number of unit value ratios, coverage of total sales and unit value ratios (Ost-Mark to the DM) in manufacturing, East Germany and West Germany, 1987

	Number of unit value ratios	Matched output as % of branch gross value of output		Unit value ratios (OM/DM)			UVR/ commercial exchange rate
		East Germany	West Germany	East German quantity-weights	West German quantity-weights	Geometric average	
Food products	75	74.2	51.8	1.67	1.50	1.59	35.1
Beverages	11	84.8	84.0	1.71	1.39	1.54	34.1
Tobacco products	3	96.4	73.0	1.74	1.74	1.74	38.6
Textile products	35	66.6	47.1	2.17	2.46	2.31	51.1
Wearing apparel	30	64.1	59.5	1.71	2.04	1.87	41.4
Leather and leather products	7	43.6	49.7	0.97	1.10	1.03	22.8
Wood products and furniture	8	28.1	24.3	1.61	2.02	1.80	39.9
Paper, paper products & printing	8	48.9	29.1	2.13	1.86	1.99	44.1
Chemicals, rubber, and plastic products	52	20.2	18.1	1.87	2.12	1.99	44.1
Non-metallic minerals	15	33.1	34.2	1.68	1.77	1.72	38.1
Basic metals and metal products	48	56.9	53.3	1.89	1.94	1.92	42.4
Machinery and transport equipment	20	18.2	32.5	1.95	1.95	1.95	43.2
without adjustment for quality[a]				1.39	1.02	1.19	26.3
Electrical engineering	23	29.1	15.7	1.64	2.20	1.90	41.9
Other manufacturing	0	0.0	0.0	1.81	1.98	1.89	41.9
Total, with adjustment for quality[a]	355	41.4	33.7	1.81	1.98	1.89	41.9
without adjustment for quality[a]	355	41.1	33.7	1.70	1.71	1.70	37.7
Commercial exchange rate				4.52	4.52	4.52	100.0

[a] Quality adjustment for passenger cars.

Appendix table A.3   Number of unit value ratios, coverage of total sales and unit value ratios (escudos to the pound sterling) in manufacturing, Portugal and UK, 1987

	Number of unit value ratios	Matched output as % of branch gross value of output		Unit value ratios (PTE/pound)			UVR/ exchange rate
		Portugal	UK	Portuguese quantity-weights	UK quantity-weights	Geometric average	
Food products	18	31.1	18.2	209.22	212.65	210.93	98.9
Beverages	2	49.6	45.0	105.09	109.73	107.38	50.4
Tobacco products	3	88.9	100.0	129.28	145.89	137.34	64.4
Textile products	22	28.5	26.8	194.97	175.57	185.02	86.8
Wearing apparel	12	60.8	63.3	198.31	191.19	194.72	91.3
Leather and leather products	10	79.9	35.5	174.05	181.33	177.65	83.3
Wood products and furniture	2	29.9	8.3	114.16	113.36	113.76	53.4
Paper, paper products & printing	3	16.8	7.2	154.71	147.39	151.01	70.8
Chemicals	27	30.6	15.6	195.41	204.95	200.12	93.9
Rubber, and plastic products	11	44.3	21.1	189.75	204.58	197.03	92.4
Non-metallic minerals	3	33.7	10.6	231.47	247.47	239.34	112.3
Basic metals and metal products	8	29.9	35.1	242.20	206.30	223.53	104.8
Machinery and transport equipment	2	4.1	17.2	208.41	209.52	208.96	98.0
Electrical engineering	7	15.6	5.3	212.54	200.52	206.45	96.8
Other manufacturing	0	0.0	0.0	184.82	195.36	190.02	89.1
Total manufacturing	130	29.7	14.4	184.82	195.36	190.02	89.1
Commercial exchange rate						213.20	100.0

Appendix table A.4   Number of unit value ratios, coverage of total sales and unit value ratios (pesetas to the pound sterling) in manufacturing, Spain and UK, 1984

	Number of unit value ratios	Matched output as % of branch gross value of output		Unit value ratios (Ps/£)			UVR/ commercial exchange rate
		Spain	UK	Spanish quantity-weights	UK quantity-weights	Geometric average	
Food products and beverages	21	42.1	35.2	175.65	178.80	177.22	82.9
Tobacco products	1	93.2	90.2	185.58	185.58	185.58	86.8
Textiles	10	28.8	18.6	225.06	207.92	216.32	101.2
Wearing apparel	19	60.0	43.4	239.78	273.41	256.04	119.8
Leather products	9	66.8	56.7	210.79	213.63	212.21	99.3
Wood products	4	14.5	15.0	169.08	189.68	179.09	83.8
Paper products	3	32.9	20.2	139.50	139.80	139.65	65.3
Printing and publishing	0	0.0	0.0	189.64	203.73	196.56	91.9
Chemicals	19	27.7	15.9	184.54	184.36	184.45	86.3
Rubber, and plastic products	6	33.5	17.6	213.36	209.46	211.40	98.9
Stone, clay and glass products	3	24.5	10.1	128.50	135.33	131.87	61.7
Basic metals and metal products	10	18.5	15.7	217.32	224.00	220.63	103.2
Electric engineering	4	13.4	4.8	258.03	258.50	258.27	120.8
Machinery and transport equipment	6	41.2	6.5	202.79	207.59	205.18	96.0
Instruments and other industries	0	0.0	0.0	189.64	203.73	196.56	91.9
Total manufacturing	115	30.7	16.8	189.64	203.73	196.56	91.9
Exchange rate				213.78	213.78	213.78	100.0

Appendix B: Value added, employment, hours worked and labour productivity

Basic sources on gross output, value added and labour input:

Czechoslovakia: FSO, *The Annual Survey of Industrial Enterprises*.

East Germany: Gemeinsames Statistisches Amt, *Ergebnisse der Erfassung der Arbeitsstätten der Betriebe des Wirtschaftsbereiches Industrie*. For food products the ratio of 'Nettoprodukt' to 'Bruttoprodukt' was obtained from Staatliche Zentralverwaltung für Statistik, *Verflechtungsbilanz des gesellschaftlichen Gesamtproduktes 1987*.

West Germany: Statistisches Bundesamt, *Kostenstruktur der Unternehmen 1987*.

Portugal: Instituto Nacional de Estatistica, *Estatísticas Industriais 1987*.

Spain: INE, *Encuesta Industrial 1983 a 1986*.

United Kingdom: Business Statistics Office, *Report on the Census of Production*, various issues.

Appendix table B.1   Gross value of output, census value added, number of employees, hours worked and comparative levels of labour productivity, Czechoslovakia and West Germany, 1989

	Czechoslovakia				West Germany				Czechoslovakia/West Germany(%)		
	Gross value of industrial output (mln Kcs) (1)	Value added ('material concept') (mln Kcs) (2)	Number of persons employed (000s) (3)	Annual hours per worker (4)	Gross value of industrial output (mln DM) (5)	Value added ('material concept') (mln DM) (6)	Number of persons employed (000s) (7)	Annual hours per worker (8)	Gross value of industrial output per employee (9)	Value added per employee (10)	Value added per hour employee (11)
Food products, beverages and tobacco	137,965	20,735	211.7	1,967	164,885	52,706	485.7	1,784	50.5	23.7	21.5
Textile products	41,004	16,851	198.2	1,771	35,496	16,172	213.5	1,600	31.2	28.1	25.4
Wearing apparel	10,380	4,431	56.9	1,751	21,855	9,431	167.4	1,483	36.1	35.7	30.3
Leather and leather products	18,269	3,961	79.8	1,789	6,693	2,898	50.1	1,567	76.2	38.1	33.4
Wood products and furniture	23,390	6,873	92.4	1,864	38,882	19,387	232.8	1,697	43.6	25.7	23.4
Paper, paper products and printing	24,117	9,022	67.0	1,873	62,746	31,064	312.7	1,621	41.6	31.4	27.2
Chemicals, rubber, plastics and petroleum refining	138,003	54,502	172.2	1,816	278,258	128,502	984.4	1,628	86.4	73.9	66.2
Non-metallic minerals	35,579	18,543	159.7	1,881	42,605	25,798	243.3	1,747	40.3	34.7	32.2
Basic metals	108,612	32,928	191.4	1,838	125,522	56,623	526.5	1,637	53.1	35.7	31.8
Machinery and transport equipment[a]	198,446	79,478	769.3	1,910	397,931	198,105	2,030.1	1,596	29.2	23.5	19.6
without quality adjustment[a]									50.7	40.8	34.1
Electrical and metal products[b]	86,736	39,345	303.0	1,847	271,051	155,037	1,668.6	1,556	48.6	38.5	32.5
Other manufacturing[c]	10,785	4,272	25.0	1,847	23,509	14,761	190.7	1,576	90.3	57.1	48.7
Total, with adjustment for quality[d]	833,285	290,940	2,326.6	1,858	1,469,432	710,484	7,105.9	1,616	44.7	32.3	28.1
without quality adjustment[d]									51.3	37.4	32.6

[a] Watches are included with machinery and transport equipment; excluding bicycles.   [c] Excluding watches.   [d] Quality adjustment for passenger cars.
[b] Computing machinery and bicycles are included with electrical products.

Appendix table B.2 Gross value of output, census value added, number of employees, hours worked and comparative levels of labour productivity, East Germany and West Germany, 1987

	East Germany				West Germany				East Germany/West Germany (%)		
	Gross value of industrial output (mln OM)	Value added ('material concept') (mln OM)	Number of persons employed (000s)	Annual hours per worker	Gross value of industrial output (mln DM)	Value added ('material concept') (mln DM)	Number of persons employed (000s)	Annual hours per worker	Gross value of industrial output per employee	Value added per employee	Value added per hour employee
	(1)	(2)	(3)	(4)	(5)	(6)	(7)	(8)	(9)	(10)	(11)
Food products	60,622	15,198	197.6	1,806	107,331	32,753	363.8	1,817	64.6	53.8	46.6
Beverages	13,003	6,388	44.6		23,286	14,023	87.3		69.8	57.9	
Tobacco products	4,633	3,604	5.3		20,089	16,875	16.8		42.1	39.0	
Textile products	30,834	12,121	198.4	1,644	32,560	15,381	222.0	1,617	45.7	38.1	
Wearing apparel	10,344	4,200	107.0		20,223	8,960	171.7		43.8	40.2	40.4
Leather and leather products	7,114	2,082	64.7		6,806	3,044	54.6		85.5	55.9	b
Wood products and furniture	12,901	4,630	106.5	b	32,973	16,489	214.3	b	43.4	31.3	b
Paper, paper products and printing	10,499	3,199	57.0	b	53,758	27,982	293.4	b	50.2	29.6	b
Chemicals, rubber and plastics	99,135	35,090	290.4	1,712	239,022	129,855	949.2	1,644	68.3	44.4	42.6
Non-metallic minerals	16,471	6,903	149.6	b	37,132	22,507	239.4	b	41.3	28.5	b
Basic metals and metal products	70,912	20,742	324.9	1,784	159,307	80,189	965.3	1,620	66.7	40.1	36.4
Machinery and transport equipment	84,066	28,658	764.1	1,753	358,172	184,493	2,031.2	1,586	32.1	21.2	
without adjustment for quality[a]									53.5	34.8	20.3
Electrical engineering	40,165	14,343	360.9		147,491	88,409	1,054.2		41.7	25.0	27.3[a]
Other manufacturing	6,718	2,859	92.5	1,713	22,210	14,080	192.3	1,641	33.2	22.3	26.5
Total, with adjustment for quality[a]	467,418	160,017	2,763.6	1,735	1,260,359	655,041	6,855.5	1,627	48.6	32.0	30.0
without adjustment for quality[a]									54.2	35.6	33.4

[a] Quality adjustment for passenger cars.
[b] Included in other manufacturing.

Appendix table B.3 Gross value added, number of employees, hours worked and comparative levels of labour productivity, Portugal and UK, 1987

	Portugal			UK			Portugal/UK (%)	
	Gross value added (mln PTE)	Number of persons employed (000s)	Annual hours per worker	Gross value added (mln pnd)	Number of persons employed (000s)	Annual hours per worker	Gross value added per employee	Gross value added per hour
	(1)	(2)	(3)	(4)	(5)	(6)	(7)	(8)
Food products	115,490	69.0	2,043	7,863	464.6	1,703	46.9	49.6
Beverages	30,265	8.4	2,043	2,434	68.7	1,703	94.4	
Tobacco products	21,332	1.9	2,043	837	18.5	1,703	179.5	
Textile products	166,502	139.7	2,051	2,672	211.4	1,569	51.0	42.3
Wearing apparel	46,207	51.1	2,051	1,607	192.4	1,569	55.6	
Leather and leather products	32,373	30.9	2,051	794	70.5	1,569	52.4	
Wood products and furniture	45,663	48.6	2,060	2,277	151.1	1,851	54.9	49.3
Paper, paper products and printing	120,520	39.3	2,000	7,825	367.3	1,642	95.2	78.2
Chemicals	109,233	34.2	1,903	9,897	285.3	1,743	46.1	42.2
Rubber and plastic products	33,207	20.0	1,940	3,558	195.1	1,714	46.1	40.7
Non-metallic minerals	91,200	49.8	2,031	4,032	185.5	1,859	35.2	32.3
Basic metals and metal products	80,652	50.2	2,072	7,316	399.0	1,789	39.2	33.8
Machinery and transport equipment	75,027	52.3	2,025	20,147	1,061.6	1,818	36.2	32.5
Electrical engineering	59,937	28.2	1,924	8,441	512.3	1,749	62.5	56.8
Other manufacturing	5,918	5.1	2,011	1,876	127.9	1,706	41.4	35.1
Total manufacturing	1,033,526	628.7	2,021	81,574	4,311.2	1,770	45.7	40.0

Appendix table B.4 Gross value added, number of employees, hours worked and comparative levels of labour productivity, Spain and UK, 1984

	Spain			UK			Spain/UK	
	Gross value added at (mln Pst)	Persons employed (000s)	Annual hours per person employed	Gross value added (mln £)	Persons employed (000s)	Annual hours per person employed	Gross value added per person employed	Gross value added per hour worked
	(1)	(2)	(3)	(4)	(5)	(6)	(7)	(8)
Food products and beverages	865,623	332.3	1,794	8,431.0	542.6	1,705	94.6	89.9
Tobacco products	74,596	10.6	1,608	780.2	26.7	1,705	129.7	137.6
Textiles	239,274	124.2	1,764	1,995.8	217.0	1,711	96.9	94.0
Wearing apparel	149,019	101.2	1,763	1,467.5	207.9	1,599	81.5	73.9
Leather products	114,264	60.4	1,786	593.0	63.5	1,658	95.5	88.6
Wood products	214,344	155.1	1,757	1,533.9	142.4	1,829	71.7	74.6
Paper products	151,683	41.8	1,796	1,941.3	147.5	1,732	197.3	190.3
Printing and publishing	170,392	68.5	1,747	3,782.9	227.6	1,615	76.1	70.4
Chemicals	509,359	117.8	1,747	7,298.1	285.8	1,738	91.8	91.4
Rubber and plastic products	220,017	84.9	1,750	2,379.1	183.1	1,747	94.3	94.2
Stone, clay and glass products	370,540	131.9	1,793	3,117.1	187.4	1,870	128.1	133.6
Basic metals and metal products	769,249	293.8	1,742	6,481.4	488.8	1,800	89.5	92.5
Electric engineering	350,242	121.7	1,700	7,360.0	523.0	1,723	79.2	80.2
Machinery and transport equipment	710,244	322.1	1,554	15,486.8	1,103.1	1,812	76.5	89.2
Instruments and other industries	70,090	32.1	1,767	1,452.5	120.8	1,672	92.4	87.4
Total manufacturing	4,978,936	1,998.3	1,728	64,100.6	4,467.2	1,749	88.3	89.4

Appendix C: Real output and employment growth in manufacturing

Basic sources:

Czechoslovakia: output (1937–65) is from Lazarcik and Staller (1968). Manufacturing part of industry included 249 products which were largely weighted at 1948 wholesale prices for Czechoslovakia. The indices for industries in machinery were weighted at the gross value of output in 1956 and for the other industries at the wages and salaries for 1947. The indices for the 18 branches were weighted at 1956 factor cost weights which represented the sum of wages and salaries, social security contribution, depreciation allowances and the return on capital. The index excludes output from military production. Output (1965–75) is from Alton *et al.* (1980), which is an update from Staller (1975) including 272 industrial products mostly weighted at gross value of production for 1967: industries were weighted at their employment for 1967. The indexes for the fifteen branches were weighted at 1967 factor cost weights from the 1967 input–output table for Czechoslovakia. This index also appears to be corrected for the output of military end-products, but it is not clear how it was done. Some intermediate years (1966, 1968 and 1969) were interpolated on the basis of Staller (1975), but could not be adjusted to exclude mining and electricity generation. Output (1975–84) is from Alton *et al.* (1986), including about 350 industrial products which were mostly weighted at 1977 employment weights, except for about 50 items which were weighted at 1977 wholesale prices for West Germany. The twelve manufacturing branches were weighted at 1977 adjusted factor cost weights. Output (1984–90) is from Alton *et al.* (1992) including the same sample of products as for the period 1975–84, but from 1985 onwards the branch series were weighted at 1987 adjusted factor weights.

Employment (1948–65) from Lazarcik (1969) including all employees in manufacturing, i.e. manual workers, engineers, white collar workers, and on employees in auxiliary units. Employment (1970–90) is from Federal Statistical Office of Czechoslovakia (1991), *Prepocty casovych rad zakladnich ukazatelu v prumyslu za roky 1948–1990*, Prague, including all manual and non-manual workers. 1970–80 interpolated by estimates from ILO, *Labour Statistics Yearbook*.

East Germany: output (1936–65) is from Czirjak and Dusek (1972). The estimates for manufacturing included physical quantities for 308 products (mining and electricity production were excluded from the original index) which were mostly weighted at 1958 producer price weights for Hungary. The indexes for the 58 industries were weighted at 1958 East

German labour costs, and the 18 branches were weighted at factor cost weights based on 1958 labour costs plus a 10% mark-up for the average return on the gross fixed capital to represent depreciation as well as the net return. The index excludes output from military production and establishments with fewer than ten employees. Output (1965–75) is from Alton *et al.* (1980). The industry and branch weights were replaced by 1968 adjusted factor cost weights. Some intermediate years (1966, 1967 and 1969) were interpolated on the basis of Alton *et al.* (1975). Output (1975–84) from Alton *et al.* (1986). The indexes from 1965 onwards include an unknown number of industrial products, which were mostly weighted at 1967 employment weights, although some items were weighted at 1975 wholesale prices for West Germany. The eight manufacturing branches were weighted at 1975 adjusted factor cost weights. Output (1984–90) is from Görzig (1991), whose estimates were based on a unit value index for East German exports to West Germany which was used to deflate value added in current prices. Employment from *Statistisches Jahrbuch der DDR*, various issues.

Portugal: output (1950–58) is from Instituto Nacional de Estatistica (1960), *O rendimento Nacional Portugues*, table 4. Output (1958–62) is from Instituto Nacional de Estatistica, *As Contas Nacionais Portuguesas, 1958–71*. Output (1962–90) from OECD, *National Accounts, Volume II*, various issues. There is a break in 1976–77, for which a link is constructed by taking the geometric average of the 1975–76 and 1977–78 movements.

Employment (1950–77) is from OECD, *Labour Force Statistics*, various issues. Employment (1977–90) is from OECD, *National Accounts, Volume II*, various issues.

Spain: manufacturing GDP (1950–64) is from Prados (1995) and manufacturing GDP (1964–81) from Gandoy Juste (1988). Gandoy's estimates were based on reconstructed and reconciled estimates of gross output, value added and labour input from input–output tables, production indices and production censuses for 22 manufacturing branches. Value added at constant prices was obtained by double deflation of gross output and intermediate consumption. Manufacturing GDP (1981–90) from OECD, *National Accounts, Volume II*, various issues.

Employment (1965–90) as for GDP series. Employment (1960–64) is from OECD, *Labour Force Statistics*; 1950 and 1960 are labour force estimates from population censuses from Carreras (1990).

Germany and USA: see van Ark and Pilat (1993).

UK and USA: see van Ark (1992).

Appendix tables C.1 and C.2   Real output, number of employees and comparative levels of labour productivity in manufacturing, Czechoslovakia and East Germany, 1950–90

	Czechoslovakia			East Germany		
	Real output (1950 = 100)	Employment (1950 = 100)	Value added per employee (USA = 100)	Real output (1950 = 100)	Employment (1950 = 100)	Value added per employee (USA = 100)
1950	100.0	100.0	23.95	100.0	100.0	14.89
1951	105.2	107.5	22.58	119.7	108.3	15.86
1952	106.8	112.1	21.68	128.7	113.6	16.03
1953	107.0	114.5	20.78	144.7	117.0	17.09
1954	110.2	117.2	21.04	162.6	118.3	19.14
1955	125.4	119.6	21.89	175.3	118.2	19.26
1956	136.5	122.5	23.56	184.7	118.5	20.50
1957	150.2	127.5	24.62	189.9	122.7	20.12
1958	167.8	130.7	27.22	204.4	125.3	21.51
1959	182.8	134.9	26.94	229.4	122.4	23.17
1960	199.9	141.3	28.29	248.8	124.1	24.94
1961	212.1	146.7	28.10	256.9	124.9	24.88
1962	221.9	150.9	27.22	270.0	124.2	25.04
1963	218.0	151.6	24.83	281.1	123.5	24.46
1964	224.2	152.4	24.11	288.8	121.0	24.33
1965	238.4	158.0	23.73	299.4	121.2	24.17
1966	244.8	160.5	23.75	307.7	121.6	24.48
1967	257.5	162.9	24.95	316.6	122.4	25.39
1968	270.3	165.4	25.95	332.3	125.6	25.11
1969	277.3	167.9	25.02	346.9	126.3	25.88
1970	292.5	170.5	26.43	359.6	126.3	27.27
1971	300.2	171.2	25.38	369.2	126.3	26.33
1972	313.5	172.1	24.79	376.1	134.2	23.72
1973	325.7	173.3	24.38	386.5	135.8	22.97
1974	337.7	174.1	26.42	405.2	136.3	25.19
1975	353.7	175.1	27.23	424.6	137.2	25.96
1976	369.4	175.7	26.79	442.2	138.5	25.31
1977	382.2	176.9	26.60	451.9	139.2	24.86
1978	392.5	177.5	27.20	465.5	139.7	25.48
1979	400.2	178.7	27.56	481.2	140.5	26.21
1980	409.7	179.2	28.71	496.1	140.5	27.58
1981	418.7	179.4	28.96	511.6	141.2	27.96
1982	424.4	179.7	29.24	511.6	142.0	27.74
1983	434.1	179.9	27.57	517.6	142.8	25.74
1984	440.7	180.5	26.26	535.3	144.1	24.85
1985	450.1	181.0	25.59	543.9	145.0	24.00
1986	453.7	181.4	24.66	546.0	144.4	23.18
1987	454.9	177.3	23.90	557.3	143.7	22.46
1988	462.7	180.6	23.04	571.2	143.7	22.24
1989	459.0	179.5	22.69	593.3	142.1	23.04
1990	448.7	174.1	22.93	436.5	122.6	19.71

Appendix tables C.3 and C.4 Real output, number of employees and comparative levels of labour productivity in manufacturing, Portugal and Spain, 1950–90

	Portugal			Spain		
	Real output (1950 = 100)	Employ-ment (1950 = 100)	Value added per employee (USA = 100)	Real output (1950 = 100)	Employ-ment (1950 = 100)	Value added per employee (USA = 100)
1950	100.0	100.0	12.05	100.0	100.0	12.94
1951	100.0			106.5		
1952	105.8			125.4		
1953	109.3			128.1		
1954	117.8			137.0		
1955	127.1			151.2		
1956	137.5			163.1	124.1	15.02
1957	145.1			173.0	130.0	15.04
1958	151.8			184.7	135.9	15.58
1959	160.9	114.4	14.07	186.5	133.9	14.98
1960	181.8	116.5	15.69	192.0	134.3	15.45
1961	193.8	120.5	15.73	226.4	139.3	17.08
1962	206.0	121.2	15.83	254.8	146.0	17.47
1963	220.6	125.1	15.33	269.3	151.2	16.62
1964	252.2	126.3	16.47	298.0	156.5	16.87
1965	277.6	131.3	16.74	343.5	162.3	18.00
1966	301.0	132.1	17.83	389.6	166.9	19.62
1967	323.9	133.0	19.35	429.6	168.5	21.76
1968	361.2	133.7	20.75	461.4	171.9	22.15
1969	382.6	134.6	21.66	533.5	176.4	24.77
1970	418.4	146.0	22.20	587.0	180.6	27.06
1971	453.8	147.7	22.39	635.2	184.0	27.02
1972	508.6	149.2	23.35	736.6	189.7	28.57
1973	583.2	150.5	25.30	829.0	199.2	29.17
1974	601.1	156.5	26.32	925.7	204.9	33.26
1975	542.7	158.5	23.22	966.4	206.2	34.16
1976	567.1	163.1	22.29	1038.7	204.1	35.05
1977	620.8	156.3	24.60	1102.1	201.8	36.34
1978	653.7	158.7	25.49	1150.5	198.3	38.57
1979	697.5	162.5	26.57	1179.7	193.7	40.51
1980	722.9	166.4	27.44	1238.0	191.1	43.98
1981	745.6	167.5	27.80	1207.5	178.7	45.32
1982	737.8	165.1	27.84	1228.7	166.6	49.34
1983	728.1	164.0	25.51	1257.8	162.1	47.90
1984	699.7	157.7	24.01	1264.9	154.4	47.63
1985	717.1	155.5	23.88	1288.4	146.8	48.80
1986	761.9	152.7	24.75	1354.1	149.1	48.40
1987	783.8	150.0	24.50	1423.9	154.3	46.47
1988	803.5	147.9	25.58	1485.2	157.3	45.90
1989	868.3	149.8	25.88	1544.2	162.3	45.64
1990	908.2	152.0	26.75	1566.6	167.6	44.95

NOTES

I am grateful to Nienke Beintema who assisted in obtaining the output productivity benchmark estimates for Czechoslovakia/Germany in 1989 (Van Ark and Beintema, 1993) and for East Germany/West Germany (Beintema and van Ark, 1994). The comments on earlier drafts of this paper (including van Ark, 1994) from participants in the following seminars are appreciated: a CEPR workshop on 'Interpreting Postwar Growth' (Berlin, 4–5 June 1993), the 23rd General Conference of International Association for Research in Income and Wealth (Canada, 21–26 August 1994) and the 3rd Conference of the European Association for Comparative Economics (Budapest, 8–10 September 1994). Nick Crafts, Angus Maddison, Remco Kouwenhoven, Luis Perez Lopes, Albrecht Ritschl and Gyorgi Szilagyi kindly commented on an earlier draft. I would also like to acknowledge the CEPR for financing part of the research, i.e. the comparison of productivity between East and West Germany. Only I remain responsible for the way the data are represented and discussed in this paper.

1 For a comprehensive review on recent contributions to this topic, see Baumol *et al.* (1994). For tests on 'maximalist' samples, see, for example, Baumol (1986), De Long (1988), Baumol and Wolff (1988), Barro (1991) and Mankiw *et al.* (1992). For studies of OECD countries see Abramovitz (1986, 1994), Maddison (1987, 1991), Dowrick and Nguyen (1989), Englander and Mittelstadt (1988) and Englander and Gurney (1994).

2 Following Maddison, Italy is included in the sample for Northwest Europe, and Ireland in the sample for Southern Europe, because the per capita income levels of both countries are closer to the average of their group than to the average of the region to which they belong in geographical terms. Clearly, this in itself is a sign that regional convergence cannot be seen as an all-inclusive event.

3 It is noted that Maddison argues that the East German per capita income estimates appear implausibly high. The estimates show that by benchmarking the relative East–West German growth performance on a 1936 estimate of per capita income in Reichsmark for both territories, per capita income in East Germany was 73% of the West German level in 1950, falling to 69% in 1989 and then suddenly dropping to 30% in 1990 (Maddison, 1995, table B.7). Maddison argues that this is an implausibly large fall for a single year, which suggests that the East German growth performance has probably been slower, and as a consequence the per capita income estimates for the latter part of the post-war period should have been lower. See also the discussion on growth rates in Section 3 of this chapter.

4 In fact Korea would come out just below Czechoslovakia and East Germany, when the estimates are adjusted from a 'per employee' to a 'per hour' basis. For details on the ICOP procedures see Section 5 of Chapter 3 in this volume. See also Maddison and van Ark (1988, 1994) and van Ark (1993) for a general overview of the ICOP project, the methodology and results.

5 This section and Section 3 concentrate on the main problems of comparisons including former CPEs. For a more detailed account of the specific methods and procedures for each binary comparison as well as more detailed estimates, see van Ark and Beintema (1993) for the comparison of Czechoslovakia and West Germany, and Beintema and van Ark (1994) for East Germany *vis-à-vis* West Germany. See also van Ark (1994, 1995b).

6 Van Ark (1995b) extensively describes earlier comparisons of East and West German output, including Sturm (1974), Wilkens (1970) and Görzig and Gornig (1991). There has also been one study comparing Czechoslovakia and France in the framework of a four-country comparison (Austria, Czechoslovakia, France and Hungary) by the UN Conference of European Statisticians at the end of the 1960s (Conference of European Statisticians, 1971, 1972). All these studies, to a considerable extent at least, make use of the method by which quantities were valued at Western prices. In fact, most comparisons for former CPEs have been among themselves and were mostly carried out by the CMEA Standing Statistical Commission. These estimates were based on detailed repricing of individual commodities usually with the former USSR as the numeraire country. For a detailed description of earlier estimates for these countries, see Drechsler and Kux (1972). Until the dissolution of the CMEA, these estimates were mostly not disclosed, although recently estimates for 1988 were provided by COMECON (1990).

7 This phenomenon is caused by the negative relationship between prices and quantities. An item with a relatively high price in the denominator country (say, West Germany) is associated with relatively small quantities in that country. The quantity for that item in the numerator country (say, East Germany) is therefore relatively large compared to that of the denominator country. As a result, relatively abundant items receive relatively higher prices than scarce items. This index number phenomenon is sometimes called the 'Gerschenkron effect', as Alexander Gerschenkron (1962) described it in detail explaining the relatively backwardness of Russian industry during the inter-war period.

8 See Hare and Hughes (1991) for a study of the competitiveness of three former centrally planned economies in Eastern Europe (Czechoslovakia, Hungary and Poland) making use of ratios of border prices to domestic prices. See also Hughes and Hare (1994).

9 See Appendix Tables A.1 and A.3 for details on unit value ratios by manufacturing branch, the number of product matches on which the unit value ratios are based and the coverage percentage of output from which the UVRs are derived. Here we abstain from the distorting effect which administrative prices may have on the weighting system, which may affect the interpretation of the aggregate results. See, for example, Marer (1985).

10 In East Germany, there have been annual calculations of a so-called 'Valuta Gegenwert', which is defined as the cost in Ost-Mark to earn one Deutsch-Mark of exports. The Valuta Gegenwert for 1989 was published in the Statistisches Jahrbuch der DDR, 1990 (Statistisches Amt der DDR), and came to 4.4 Ost-Marks to the D-Mark. Akerlof and others (1991, table 6) estimated the actual domestic resource cost of exports from East Germany to non-CMEA countries per Deutsch-Mark earned at 3.73 Mark for total industry in 1989. For a detailed discussion of Ost-Mark/D-Mark conversion factors, see also Schwarzer (1994).

11 The larger effect of the quality adjustment on the UVR at West German weights compared to the UVR at own country weights in Table 7.3 reflects the greater share of cars in West German manufacturing output. Table 7.3 also shows that in the case of the Czechoslovakia–West Germany comparison, the UVRs at Czechoslovak and West German weights before the adjustments for quality are, according to the Gerschenkron thesis, even in the

wrong order (see also endnote 7). The Skoda price was around one-third of the price of the West German-made car. As the East German market was dominated at the time by Trabants, which had a lower quality than Skodas, the East German quality level for cars was put at a quarter of the West German level.

12 The basic information from Table 7.4 slightly differs from what was used in earlier working papers. The original Czechoslovakia–West Germany comparison (van Ark and Beintema, 1993) included the activity in the non-industrial part of manufacturing. The original East Germany–West Germany comparison (Beintema and van Ark, 1994) excluded the deduction of contract labour as a material input. See also van Ark (1995b). For the sake of comparison, I put all countries here on the same MPS output concept.

13 This difference between firms in former CPEs and market economies comes out clearly in a range of comparisons between manufacturing plants in East and West European countries. See, for example, Hitchens *et al.* (1993), chapter 5.

14 At the same time there has also been a tendency of manufacturing firms in planned economies to integrate along vertical lines. This may decrease the overall ratio of intermediate inputs to gross output, because a larger share of intermediate inputs are used up within the firm. However, it seems that the industrial censuses have divided large firms up into smaller units. For example, the East German source is a census of local units rather than firms, so that the effect of vertical integration on the input–output ratio is quite small.

15 For the comparisons of census value added the same unit value ratios were used as for gross output, assuming that the price ratios for gross output were also representative for the intermediate inputs. Although this assumption (which can be contrasted with double deflation in case intermediate inputs were converted with an independent UVR for intermediate inputs) could not be cross-checked with other evidence, there is no immediate reason to expect a systematic difference between UVRs at gross output level and UVRs for intermediate inputs. One method to make further advance on this issue is to compare the estimates within an input–output framework. For a discussion of an input–output table for East Germany on West German standards for 1987, see Ludwig and Stäglin (1993).

16 See Van Ark (1993 and 1996) for a discussion of procedures to update or backdate benchmark results.

17 See, for example, Bureau of Labor Statistics/Eurostat (1991) and Marer (1985, 1991, 1992).

18 It is important to distinguish 'comparable' prices from 'constant' prices, as the former does not necessarily mean that prices always refer to one and the same base year. This was in particular so when new products were introduced for which no price was available in the base year (Bergson, 1991).

19 For East Germany, a variant of this method was applied for the 1980s in a study by the Deutsches Institut für Wirtschaftsforschung, which used a unit value index for East German exports to West Germany (including a correction for devaluation) instead of the original 'constant' price index for the deflation of value added in East Germany. See Görzig (1991).

20 See Bergson (1961, 1991) and Marer (1985, 1992).

21 For details see Appendix C. For East Germany this method was in effect first

applied by Stolper (1960) for the period 1936 to 1958, who used physical quantity series which were weighted at West German prices for 1936 and 1950 alternatively. Stolper adjusted the gross production series to value added making use of value added weights derived from 1936 input–output relationships.

22 However, Czirjak and Dusek (1972) admit that their estimates for the earlier years may contain some overestimation because they are to some extent based on the official data publication policies concerning the introduction of 'new products'.

23 See van Ark (1994, 1995b) for a more detailed discussion of the alternative estimates. Ritschl's estimate is one for gross output per person derived from the German production census for 1936, which was updated to 1950 on the basis of time series from Stolper (1960) and Barthel (1979). Sturm (1974) and Wilkens (1970, 1981) are based on quantity comparisons of physical output weighted at West German prices. The branch estimates in these studies are only weighted at value added, which differs from a genuine value added comparison. Görzig and Gornig (1991) are partly based on quantity comparisons and partly on unit value ratios without an adjustment to value added. Görzig (1991) is based on a comparison of value added for 1990 using value added/gross output ratios for West Germany.

24 See, for example, Sturm (1974) and Boretzky (1987).

25 See endnote 4 for references to general ICOP studies as well as Chapter 3 in this volume. The measures for all countries in Figure 7.1 are expressed as a percentage of the USA, although the estimates for Czechoslovakia and East Germany were originally compared on a binary basis to West Germany, and those for Portugal and Spain were originally compared to the UK. These were linked to the USA making use of the ICOP binary comparisons for Germany/USA (van Ark and Pilat, 1993) and UK/USA (van Ark, 1992). The estimates may therefore suffer from intransitivity, i.e. a direct comparison between Spain and the USA may give a somewhat different result from an indirect comparison through the UK. This problem can be tackled by multilateral comparisons (such as are applied in ICP studies by Eurostat, OECD and the UN), making use of the weights of all countries in the sample. See, for example, Pilat and Prasada Rao (1991) for an application of multilateral techniques to industry of origin comparisons.

26 See, for example, Teichova (1985), tables 5.14 and 5.15, which suggest that in 1935, 37.8% of manufacturing output in Czechoslovakia was in metallurgy, engineering and chemicals compared to 32.9% in Hungary (1937) and 31.7% in Poland (1937). In contrast, employment in these branches accounted for 33% of total manufacturing employment in Czechoslovakia, 35.6% in Hungary (1937) and 43.3% in Poland (1937).

27 See Moore (1972), table 11.

28 See Section 5 for more details on accumulation versus productivity strategies.

29 See, Ritschl, 1996. The major exceptions were the iron and steel plants in central Germany which fell just within the post-war West German territory.

30 See, *Die Deutsche Industrie. Gesamtergebnisse der amtlichen Produktionsstatistik*, Schriftenreihe des Reichsamtes für wertschaftliche Planung, Berlin, 1939, and Länderrat des Amerikanischen Besatzungsgebiets (1949), *Statisches Handbuch von Deutschland 1928–1944*. Total sales (in Reichsmark) and employment in manufacturing industries on German territory which was

occupied by the Soviet Union in 1945 (Soviet Zone and half of Berlin) was compared to sales and employment in the area occupied by western allies (American, British and French zones and half of Berlin).

31 However, as shown in Table 7.1, Ritschl still estimates the productivity level in East German industry in 1950 at 61% of West Germany at the lowest, which seems too high in relation to the figure of 63% for Czechoslovakia (compared to West Germany) in 1950.

32 See Prados and Sanz (1996) on Spain, and Neves (1996) on Portugal.

33 See, for example, Watts (1982), who quotes figures from various sources on gross investment–GDP ratios for East European countries between 25 and 35% and for West European countries below 25%. Czirjak (1970) estimates the annual compound growth rate of capital input in Czechoslovak industry, using the adjusted factor cost method, at 6.7% between 1950 and 1967, whereas for the same period Maddison (1993) estimates it at 6.6% for the West German economy as a whole. See also Section 5 of the present chapter.

34 See, Czirjak (1970). See also Teichova (1988), in particular chapters 9 and 10.

35 See, Maddison (1995). That the industrial restructuring did not have a significant positive effect on productivity growth for the economy as a whole, can also be seen from the estimates on the contribution of structural change to overall productivity growth in Chapter 3 of this volume. Whereas 1.1 percentage points out of the 5.4% annual average productivity growth between 1950 and 1973 was explained by structural change (i.e. the 'net shift effect' plus the 'interaction effect') the corresponding figures for the period 1973 to 1990 were 0.5 percentage points out of 3.6 percentage points (see Table 3.1, Chapter 3). Much of the slowdown in structural change after 1973 was due to a negative interaction effect which confirms that employment shares declined exceptionally rapidly in sectors with relatively rapid productivity growth (i.e. agriculture and manufacturing) whereas the productivity rises were much more moderate in those sectors with rising employment shares (i.e. services).

36 See, for example, Balassa and Bertrand (1970) and Czirjak (1970). More extensive and very informative studies of this kind have been carried for the former Soviet Union by Ofer (1987) and Pitzer and Baukol (1992).

37 There are no reliable estimates available for East Germany.

38 For a detailed discussion of this issue for East European countries, see Ofer (1987). For a recent study strongly favouring this explanation, see Easterly and Fischer (1994).

39 See Gomulka (1986), in particular chapter 3 where he explains that static efficiency may be low because of the low rate of diffusion of a new technology, whereas dynamic efficiency may still be high because of the fast rate of physical investment which raises the overall flow of new products and processes.

40 See Hitchens et al. (1993). After reunification a larger number of previously skilled workers from East Germany were demoted to realign with the West German hierarchy of skills. In general East German workers were seen as not well trained in using hydraulics, new materials or electronics.

41 For example, in 1930, 69% of the Spanish population was literate and only 41% in Portugal. In 1960, literacy rates were 86% and 62% in Spain and Portugal, respectively. See Tortella (1994).

42 Hofman (1993), quoted in Prados and Sanz (1996).

43 For an extensive discussion of the relation between productivity, trade and competitiveness in socialist countries, see Ofer (1992).

44 A study by Bergson (1987), comparing four socialist economies (Hungary, Poland, USSR and Yugoslavia) with seven western market economies (France, Germany, Italy, Japan, Spain, the UK and the USA), estimates that the communist planning systems of the East European countries accounts for a decline in efficiency by some 25% to 30%.

45 See, for example, Eichengreen and Uzan (1992) and Dornbusch *et al.* (1993).

REFERENCES

Abramovitz, M. (1986), 'Catching Up, Forging Ahead and Falling Behind', *Journal of Economic History*, **46** (2), 385–406.

Abramovitz, M. (1994), 'Catch-up and Convergence in the Postwar Growth Boom and After', in W.J. Baumol, R.R. Nelson and E.N. Wolff (eds.), *Convergence of Productivity*, Oxford: Oxford University Press.

Akerlof, G.A. and others (1991), 'East Germany in from the Cold: The Economic Aftermath of Currency Union', *Brookings Papers on Economic Activity*, no. 1, pp. 1–87.

Alton, Th., E.M. Bass, L. Czirjak and G. Lazarcik (1975), 'Statistics on East European Structure and Growth', Research Project on National Income in East Central Europe, Occasional Paper No. 48, New York: L.W. International Financial Research, Inc.

Alton, Th., G. Lazarcik, E.M. Bass, G.J. Staller and W. Znayenko (1980), 'Economic Growth in Eastern Europe 1965–1979', Research Project on National Income in East Central Europe, Occasional Paper No. 59, New York: L.W. International Financial Research, Inc.

Alton, Th., K. Badach, E.M. Bass, G. Lazarcik and G.J. Staller (1983), 'Economic Growth in Eastern Europe 1965, 1970 and 1975–1982', Research Project on National Income in East Central Europe, Occasional Paper No. 75, New York: L.W. International Financial Research, Inc.

Alton, Th., K. Badach, E.M. Bass, G. Lazarcik and G.J. Staller (1986), 'Economic Growth in Eastern Europe, 1970 and 1975–1985', Research Project on National Income in East Central Europe, Occasional Paper No. 90, New York: L.W. International Financial Research, Inc.

Alton, Th., K. Badach, E.M. Bass, R. Bakondi, A. Brumaru, J.T. Bombelles, G. Lazarcik and G.J. Staller (1990), 'Economic Growth in Eastern Europe 1975–1989', Research Project on National Income in East Central Europe, Occasional Paper No. 110, New York: L.W. International Financial Research, Inc.

Alton, Th., K. Badach, E.M. Bass, R. Bakondi, A. Brumaru, J.T. Bombelles, G. Lazarcik and G.J. Staller (1992), 'Economic Growth in Eastern Europe, 1975–1991', Research Project on National Income in East Central Europe, Occasional Paper No. 120, New York: L.W. International Financial Research, Inc.

Ark, B. van (1992), 'Comparative Productivity in British and American Manufacturing', *National Institute Economic Review*, November.

Ark, B. van (1993), *International Comparisons of Output and Productivity*, Monograph Series No. 1, Groningen: Groningen Growth and Development Centre.

Ark, B. van (1994), 'Reassessing Growth and Comparative Levels of Performance in Eastern Europe: The Experience of Manufacturing in Czechoslovakia and East Germany', paper presented at 3rd EACES Conference, Budapest.

Ark, B. van (1995a), 'Producción y Productividad en el Sector Manufacturero Español. Un analisis comparativo 1950–1992', *La Actividad Empresarial en España*, Madrid: ICE, no. 746, 67–77.

Ark, B. van (1995b), 'The Manufacturing Sector in East Germany: A Reassessment of Comparative Productivity Performance', *Jahrbuch für Wirtschaftsgeschichte*, no. 2, 75–100.

Ark, B. van and N.M. Beintema (1993), 'Output and Productivity Levels in Czechoslovak and German (FR) Manufacturing', University of Groningen, mimeographed.

Ark, B. van and D. Pilat (1993), 'Productivity Levels in Germany, Japan and the United States: Differences and Causes', *Brookings Papers on Economic Activity*, Microeconomics 2, Washington, DC, December.

Balassa, B. and T.J. Bertrand (1970), 'Growth Performance of Eastern European Economies and Comparable Western European Countries', *American Economic Review*, May.

Barro, R.J. (1991), 'Economic Growth in a Cross Section of Countries', *Quarterly Journal of Economics*, May, 407–43.

Barthel, H. (1979), *Die wirtschaftlichen Ausgangsbedingungen der DDR*, Akademie-Verlag: East Berlin.

Baumol, W.J. (1986), 'Productivity Growth, Convergence and Welfare: What the Long Run Data Show', *American Economic Review*, **76**.

Baumol, W.J. and E.N. Wolff (1988), 'Productivity, Convergence and Welfare: Reply', *American Economic Review*, **78**.

Baumol, W.J., R.R. Nelson and E.N. Wolff (eds.) (1994), *Convergence of Productivity*, Oxford: Oxford University Press.

Beintema, N.M. and B. van Ark (1994), 'Comparative Productivity in East and West German Manufacturing before Reunification', CEPR Discussion Paper Series, No. 895, London: Centre for Economic Policy Research.

Bergson, A. (1961), *The National Income of Soviet Russia Since 1928*, Rand Corporation.

Bergson, A. (1987), 'Comparative Productivity: The USSR, Eastern Europe, and the West', *American Economic Review*, **77** (3), 342–57.

Bergson, A. (1991), 'Real National Income Measurement: In Soviet Perspective', in *Economic Statistics for Economies in Transition: Eastern Europe in the 1990s*, Washington, DC: Bureau of Labor Statistics/Eurostat.

Boretzky, M. (1987), 'The Tenability of the CIA Estimates of Soviet Economic Growth', *Journal of Comparative Economic Studies*, **11**, 517–42.

Bureau of Labor Statistics/Eurostat (1991), *Economic Statistics for Economies in Transition: Eastern Europe in the 1990s*, Washington, DC.

Carreras, A. (1990), *Estadisticas Historicas de España, Siglos XIX–XX*, Fundacion Banco Exterior.

Collier, I.L. (1985), 'The Estimation of Gross Domestic Product and its Growth Rate for the German Democratic Republic', World Bank Staff Working Papers, No. 773, Washington, DC: World Bank.

COMECON (1990), 'Results of International Comparisons of the Most Important Cost Indices of Economic Growth of the CMEA Member

Countries and the Socialist Federated Republic of Yugoslavia for 1988', Moscow, mimeographed.

Conference of European Statisticians (1971), 'Methodological Problems of International Comparison of Levels of Labour Productivity in Industry', *Statistical Standards and Studies No. 21*, New York: United Nations.

Conference of European Statisticians (1972), 'Comparison of Labour Productivity in Industry in Austria, Czechoslovakia, France and Hungary', *Statistical Standards and Studies No. 24*, New York: United Nations.

Cornelsen, D. and W. Kirner (1990), 'Zum Produktivitätsvergleich Bundesrepublik – DDR', *DIW Wochenbericht*, No. 14, Berlin.

Czirjak, L. (1970), 'Industrial Structure, Growth and Productivity in Eastern Europe', in Joint Economic Committee, *Economic Developments in Countries of Eastern Europe*, Subcommittee on Foreign Economic Policy, Washington, DC: US Government Printing Office.

Czirjak, L. and J. Dusek (1972), 'Growth of East German Industrial Output, 1936, 1946 and 1950–1967', Occasional Papers of the Research Project on National Income in East Central Europe, No. 35, New York: International Financial Research Inc.

De Long, B. (1988), 'Productivity, Convergence and Welfare: Comment', *American Economic Review*, 78.

Deutscher Bundestag (1987), *Materialien zum Bericht zur Lage der Nation im geteilten Deutschland 1987*, Drucksache 11/11, Bonn.

Dornbusch, R., W. Nölling and R. Layerd (eds.) (1993), *Postwar Economic Reconstruction and Lessons for the East Today*, Cambridge, MA: MIT Press.

Dowrick, S. and D. Nguyen (1989), 'OECD Comparative Economic Growth 1950–85: Catch-Up and Convergence', *American Economic Review*, 79 (5). 1010–30.

Drechsler, L. and J. Kux (1972), *International Comparisons of Labour Productivity* (in Czech), Prague: SEVT.

Easterly, W. and S. Fischer (1994), 'The Soviet Economic Decline: Historical and Republican Data', NBER Working Paper No. 4735, Cambridge, MA: NBER, May.

Ehrlich, E. (1985), 'The Size Structure of Manufacturing Establishments and Enterprises: An International Comparison', *Journal of Comparative Economics*, 9, 267–295.

Eichengreen, B. and M. Uzan (1992), 'The Marshall Plan: Economic Effects and Implications for Eastern Europe and the Former USSR', *Economic Policy*, no. 14, 14–75.

Englander, A.S. and A. Gurney (1994), 'Medium-Term Determinants of OECD Productivity', *OECD Economic Studies*, no. 22, Spring, pp. 49–110.

Englander, A.S. and A. Mittelstadt (1988), 'Total Factor Productivity: Macroeconomic and Structural Aspects of the Slowdown', *OECD Economic Studies*, No. 10, Spring, pp. 8–56.

European Commission for Europe (1994), *International Comparison of Gross Domestic Product in Europe*, Geneva.

Gandoy Juste, R. (1988), 'Evolucion de la Productividad global en la Industria Española. Un Analisis Desagregado para el Periodo 1964–1981. Editorial de la Universidad Complutense de Madrid.

Gerschenkron, A. (1962), *Economic Backwardness in Historical Perspective*, Cambridge, MA: Harvard University Press.

Görzig, B. (1991), 'Produktion und Produktionsfaktoren in Ostdeutschland', *Dokumentation*, Berlin: DIW.

Görzig, B. and M. Gornig (1991), *Produktivität und Wettbewerbsfähigkeit der Wirtschaft der DDR*, Beiträge zur Strukturforschung, Heft 121, Berlin.

Gomulka, S. (1986), *Growth, Innovation and Reform in Eastern Europe*, Brighton: Wheatsheaf Books.

Hare, P. and G. Hughes (1991), 'Competitiveness and Industrial Restructuring in Czechoslovakia, Hungary and Poland', CEPR Discussion Paper Series, No. 543, London: CEPR.

Hitchens, D.M.W.N., K. Wagner and J.E. Birnie (1993), *East German Productivity and the Transition to the Market Economy*, Aldershot: Avebury.

Hofman, A. (1993), 'Long Run Growth in Spain and Smaller Latin American Countries. A Comparative Perspective', SPES/EHES Conference on Long-Run Economic Growth in the European Periphery, Coruña.

Hughes, G. and P. Hare (1994), 'The International Competitiveness of Industries in Bulgaria, Czechoslovakia, Hungary and Poland', *Oxford Economic Papers*, no. 46, 200–221.

Lazarcik, G. (1969), 'Czechoslovak National Product by Sector of Origin and by Final Use, 1937 and 1948–1965', in Th. Alton (ed.), Research Project on National Income in East Central Europe, Occasional Paper No. 26, New York: Columbia University.

Lazarcik, G. and G.J. Staller (1968), 'A New Index of Czechoslovak Industrial Output, 1937 and 1947–1965', in Th. Alton (ed.), Research Project on National Income in East Central Europe, Occasional Paper No. 24, New York: Columbia University.

Ludwig, U. and R. Stäglin (1993), 'Problems in Comparing Input–Output Tables for East and West Germany', *Economic Systems Research*, **5** (2).

Maddison, A. (1987), 'Growth and Slowdown in Advanced Capitalist Countries: Techniques of Quantitative Assessment', *Journal of Economic Literature*, **25** (2), 649–58.

Maddison, A. (1991), *Dynamic Forces in Capitalist Development*, Oxford: Oxford University Press.

Maddison, A. (1993), 'Standardised Estimates of Fixed Capital Stock: A Six-Country Comparison', *Innovazione e Materie Prime*, April.

Maddison, A. (1994), 'Explaining the Economic Performance of Nations, 1820–1989', in W.J. Baumol, R.R. Nelson and E.N. Wolff (eds.), *Convergence and Productivity*, Oxford: Oxford University Press.

Maddison, A. (1995), *Monitoring the World Economy, 1820–1992*, Paris: OECD Development Centre.

Maddison, A. and B. van Ark (1988), 'Comparison of Real Output in Manufacturing', World Bank Working Papers WPS5, Washington DC.

Maddison, A. and B. van Ark (1994), 'The International Comparison of Real Product and Productivity', Research Memorandum, no. 567 (GD-6), Groningen Growth and Development Centre.

Mankiw, F., D. Romer and D. Weil (1992), 'A Contribution to the Empirics of Economic Growth', *Quarterly Journal of Economics*, **107**, 407–438.

Marer, P. (1985), *Dollar GNPs of the USSR and Eastern Europe*, London/Baltimore: World Bank, Johns Hopkins University Press.

Marer, P. (1991), 'Conceptual and Practical Problems of Comparative Measurement of Economic Performance: The East European Economies in Transition', in *Economic Statistics for Economies in Transition: Eastern Europe in the 1990s*, Washington, DC: Bureau of Labor Statistics/Eurostat.

Marer, P. (1992), *Historically Planned Economies, A Guide to the Data*, Washington, DC: World Bank.

Melzer, M. (1989), 'Price Formation', in DIW, *GDR and Eastern Europe – A Handbook*, Aldershot: Avebury.

Mitchell, B.R. (1992), *International Historical Statistics, Europe 1760–1988*, 3rd edn, New York: Stockton Press.

Moore, W.E. (1972), *Economic Demography of Eastern and Southern Europe*, New York: Arno Press.

Neves, J.L.C. das (1993), 'Portuguese Postwar Growth: A Global Approach', paper presented at CEPR Workshop on Comparative Economic Growth in Postwar Europe, 11–12 June, Lund.

Neves, J.L.C. das (1996), 'Portuguese Postwar Growth: A Global Approach', in N.F.R. Crafts and G. Toniolo, eds., *Economic Growth in Europe since 1945*, Cambridge: CEPR, Cambridge University Press.

Ofer, G. (1987), 'Soviet Economic Growth: 1928–1985', *Journal of Economic Literature*, **25**, 1767–1833.

Ofer, G. (1992), 'Productivity, Competitiveness and the Socialist System', in B.G. Hickman (ed.), *International Productivity and Competitiveness*, New York: Oxford University Press.

Peres Lopes, L.M. (1994), 'Manufacturing Productivity in Portugal in a Comparative Perspective', *Notas Economicas*, no. 4, Universidade de Coimbra, pp. 57–76.

Pilat, D. and D.S. Prasada Rao (1991), 'A Multilateral Approach to International Comparisons of Real Output, Productivity and Purchasing Power Parities in Manufacturing', Research Memorandum, no. 440, Institute of Economic Research, Groningen.

Pitzer, J.S. and A.P. Baukol (1992), 'Recent GNP and Productivity Trends', *Soviet Economy*, 46–82.

Prados de la Escosura, L. (1995), 'Spain's Gross Domestic Product, 1850–1993: Quantitative Conjectures', Universidad Carlos III de Madrid, mimeographed.

Prados de la Escosura, L. and J.C. Sanz (1996), 'Growth and Macroeconomic Performance in Spain, 1939–1993', in N.F.R. Crafts and G. Toniolo (eds.), *Economic Growth in Europe since 1945*, Cambridge: CEPR, Cambridge University Press.

Ránki, G. (1985), 'Problems of Southern European Economic Development', in G. Arrighi (ed.), *Semiperipheral Development. The Politics of Southern Europe in the Twentieth Century*, Beverly Hills, CA: Sage Publications.

Ritschl, A. (1996), 'An Exercise in Futility: East German Economic Growth and Decline, 1945–1989', in N.F.R. Crafts and G. Toniolo (eds.), *Economic Growth in Europe since 1945*, Cambridge: CEPR, Cambridge University Press.

Salmon, K.G. (1991), *The Modern Spanish Economy*, London: Pinter Publishers.

Schwarzer, O. (1994), 'Kaufkraft-paritäten-Koeffizienten zwischen Mark der DDR und DM', in J. Schneider and W. Harbrecht (eds.), *Wirtschaftsordnung und Wirtschaftspolitik in Deutschland, 1933–1993*, Stuttgart: Franz Steiner Verlag.

Staller, G.J. (1975), 'Czechoslovak Industrial Production, 1948–72', Research

Project on National Income in East Central Europe, Occasional Paper No. 45, New York: L.W. International Financial Research, Inc.

Stolper, W. (1960), *The Structure of the East German Economy*, Cambridge, MA: Harvard University Press.

Sturm, P. (1974), 'A Comparison of Aggregate Production Relationships in East and West Germany', Ph.D. thesis, Yale University.

Teichova, A. (1985), 'Industry', in M.C. Kaser (ed.), *The Economic History of Eastern Europe, 1919–1975*, Vol. I, Oxford: Clarendon Press, pp. 222–322.

Teichova, A. (1988), *The Czechoslovak Economy, 1918–1980*, London: Routledge.

Tortella, G. (1994), 'Patterns of Economic Retardation and Recovery in the Nineteenth and Twentieth Centuries', *Economic History Review*, XLVII (1), 1–21.

Watts, N. (1982), 'Eastern and Western Europe', in A. Boltho (ed.), *The European Economy. Growth and Crisis*, Oxford: Oxford University Press, pp. 259–286.

Wilkens, H. (1970), 'Arbeitsproduktivität in der Industrie der DDR und der Bundesrepublik – ein Vergleich', DIW Wochenbericht, 14 May, Berlin.

Wilkens, H. (1981), *The Two German Economies. A Comparison between the National Product of the German Democratic Republic and the Federal Republic of Germany*, Aldershot: Gower.

8 Convergence: what the historical record shows

STEPHEN N. BROADBERRY

1 Introduction

In this chapter we provide a survey of the long-run evidence for convergence of productivity levels among the advanced industrialized countries. In addition to work based on Maddison's (1991) well-known national income data we also survey evidence from two other sets of data. Broadberry (1994c) examines labour productivity in manufacturing for twelve countries while Williamson (1991) provides evidence on real wages of unskilled workers for fifteen countries. We argue that the evidence is best seen as consistent with a process of local rather than global convergence, with more than one 'convergence club', even amongst the advanced industrial economies. Furthermore, the convergence process has not been smooth or continuous. In short, both geography and history matter.

2 Definitions

2.1 Exogenous and endogenous growth

Underlying the convergence debate is a conflict over the vision of the growth process. The standard neoclassical growth model predicts global convervence of productivity and living standards (Lucas, 1988). Rejection of global convergence thus implies a move away from the model which has dominated economists' thinking about growth in recent decades. Rather than seeing growth as exogenously given by population growth and technical progress and independent of savings and investment as in the standard neoclassical model, in the more recent literature the rate of growth has been endogenized and can be influenced by the accumulation strategy of individuals and governments. The new growth literature has placed a new emphasis on the accumulation of human

327

capital (Lucas, 1988, 1993; Romer, 1990). Learning effects and externalities mean that there is no guarantee of convergence in a world of competitive economies since social and private returns often differ. In models with more than one sector, specialization according to comparative advantage can have persistent growth effects (Lucas, 1988; Young, 1991; Grossman and Helpman, 1991).

2.2   Conditional and unconditional convergence

Before we turn to the evidence it is important to set out some definitions since there are a number of conceptions of convergence in the literature. The most important distinction is between conditional and unconditional convergence. Unconditional convergence is simply the straightforward notion that countries actually move towards the same standard of living or level of productivity. Conditional convergence is more subtle, allowing for the possibility that there are forces propelling an economy towards the steady-state level of productivity and steady-state growth rate, but that the steady state may differ between economies. In other words, there may be catch-up forces at work, but they may be offset by other effects keeping economies apart. Conditional convergence regressions, then, may actually be more useful in establishing factors making for divergence than in establishing convergence.

We can check for unconditional convergency by looking at the relationship between the initial level of labour productivity (Y/L_0) and the subsequent labour productivity growth rate ($g_{Y/L}$):

$$g_{Y/L} = \alpha - \beta(Y/L_0) \tag{1}$$

For unconditional convergence, there is a negative relationship between productivity growth and the initial level of productivity. The parameter β tells us about the speed of the convergence process.

For conditional convergence, allowance needs to be made for additional factors which may explain differences in steady states between countries:

$$g_{Y/L} = \alpha - \beta(Y/L_0) + \gamma Z \tag{2}$$

where Z represents a variable (or group of variables) that could affect the steady state. For example, Barro and Sala-i-Martin (1991) use education and government spending as additional variables in their conditional convergence regressions. Again, the coefficient β provides information on the speed of convergence.

2.3   β-convergence and σ-convergence

In fact the above analysis is restricted to forms of what is known in the literature as β-convergence. Barro and Sala-i-Martin (1991) also consider an alternative conception of convergence, which they call σ-convergence. This refers to a narrowing dispersion of productivity levels over time, as measured by the standard deviation or coefficient of variation. In fact, perhaps surprisingly at first sight, σ-convergence is not guaranteed by β-convergence. First, in a stochastic world, shocks which affect only some countries or all countries differentially (for example, wars or famines) may increase dispersion to offset any catching-up effects that are present. Second, Chatterji (1992) notes that the absolute difference in income levels between two countries can grow, even as the poorer country catches up proportionately. Third, Barro and Sala-i-Martin (1991) note the example of the ordinal rankings of teams in a sports league. Since the number of teams is fixed the dispersion remains constant, i.e. there is no σ-convergence. However, we can still discuss β-convergence in terms of how quickly the champions return to mediocrity. This is an example of Galton's fallacy: the observation that heights of people in a family regress to the mean across generations does not imply that the dispersion of heights across the population diminishes over time.

2.4   Global and local convergence

A recent paper by Durlauf and Johnson (1992) makes a useful distinction between local and global convergence. For global convergence we require that all economies are converging to a single productivity path, i.e. in the limit productivity levels are equalized between all countries. For local convergence, however, we can have a group of economies converging on a productivity path which remains below the path of another group.

3   National income data

Data on national income and labour inputs for sixteen advanced industrialized countries over the period since 1870 have been collected by Maddison (1964, 1982, 1991). The basic data are set out in Tables 8.1 and 8.2, which can be used to illustrate the way in which the convergence hypothesis has altered our perceptions of the growth process. From Table 8.1, we see that during the period 1950–73 productivity growth in the UK and the USA was relatively slow, while Japan, Germany and a number of other European economies achieved very rapid productivity

Table 8.1   Growth of GDP per hour worked (% per annum)

	1870–1913	1913–1950	1950–1973	1973–1987	1870–1987
Australia	1.1	1.5	2.7	1.8	1.6
Austria	1.8	0.9	5.9	2.7	2.4
Belgium	1.2	1.4	4.4	3.0	2.1
Canada	2.3	2.4	2.9	1.8	2.4
Denmark	1.9	1.6	4.1	1.6	2.2
Finland	1.8	2.3	5.2	2.2	2.7
France	1.6	1.9	5.0	3.2	2.6
Germany	1.9	1.0	5.9	2.6	2.5
Italy	1.7	2.0	5.8	2.6	2.7
Japan	1.9	1.8	7.6	3.5	3.2
Netherlands	1.3	1.3	4.8	2.4	2.1
Norway	1.6	2.5	4.2	3.5	2.6
Sweden	1.7	2.8	4.4	1.6	2.6
Switzerland	1.5	2.7	3.3	1.2	2.2
UK	1.2	1.6	3.2	2.3	1.0
USA	1.9	2.4	2.5	1.0	2.1

Source: Maddison (1991, p. 51).

Table 8.2   Comparative levels of labour productivity (US GDP per hour worked = 100)

	1870	1913	1950	1973	1987
Australia	132	93	67	70	78
Austria	51	48	27	59	74
Belgium	82	61	42	64	86
Canada	64	75	75	83	92
Denmark	59	58	43	63	68
Finland	34	33	31	57	67
France	56	48	40	70	94
Germany	50	50	30	64	80
Italy	41	37	31	64	79
Japan	19	18	15	46	61
Netherlands	88	69	46	77	92
Norway	48	43	43	64	90
Sweden	47	44	49	76	82
Switzerland	62	51	56	67	68
UK	104	78	57	67	80
USA	100	100	100	100	100
Average of 15	62	54	43	66	79
CV	0.44	0.35	0.35	0.13	0.13

Source: Maddison (1991, p. 53).

growth rates. This disparity in economic performance has been widely used to make inferences about the superiority of economic institutions and policy in the more corporatist Japanese and European countries over the more liberal Anglo-Saxon economies (Peaker, 1974; Stafford, 1981; Rowthorn, 1986; Cowling, 1989). However, once we examine levels of productivity in Table 8.2, this conclusion is seen to be much less secure. The rapid post-war growth in Japan and Europe was from a much lower base and can be seen as catch-up growth.

An important figure in the development of the convergence hypothesis was Abramovitz (1979, 1986) who saw the period since 1945 as an important phase of catch-up growth. In fact the idea that economic backwardness may lead to a spurt of catch-up growth was not new in economic history, going back at least to Veblen's (1915) study of Imperial Germany and Gerschenkron's (1962) analysis of European and especially Russian industrialization. However, the modern debate really began with Baumol's (1986) classic paper. Baymol ran a regression relating the productivity growth rate to the level of productivity in 1870:

$$g_{Y/L} = 5.25 - 0.75(Y/L_0) \qquad R^2 = 0.88 \qquad (3)$$

where $g_{Y/L}$ is the growth rate of labour productivity over the period 1870–1979 and Y/L_0 is the level of labour productivity in 1870 relative to the USA. This regression can be taken as strong evidence in favour of unconditional β-convergence.

The strong negative relationship between the initial level of labour productivity and its subsequent growth over this long period can be seen clearly in the data plotted as Figure 8.1. Baumol argues that a striking conclusion follows from the fact that the level of productivity in 1870 is a good predictor of subsequent productivity growth, with other variables having only a peripheral influence. It appears to have mattered little 'whether or not a particular country had free markets, a high propensity to invest, or used policy to stimulate growth' (1986, p. 1077). In fact, this conclusion is a little too strong, as Baumol recognizes, since it is still possible that policy and investments affect growth, but the efforts of one country spill over to all countries through imitation. Furthermore, Baumol appears to accept Abramovitz's (1986) qualification to the catch-up process, that a nation must have attained a threshold level of social capabilities. Thus, using the larger Summers and Heston (1984) data set for the post-1950 period, Baumol identifies three separate 'convergence clubs' of the advanced industrialized nations, the centrally planned economies and the other countries. For the twentieth century as a whole,

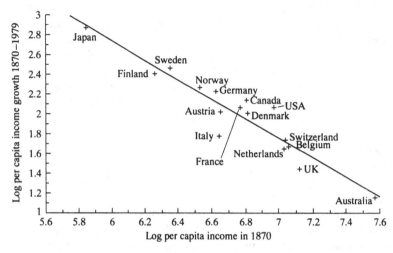

Figure 8.1   Per capita GDP regression for Maddison's sixteen

Maddison (1989) uses data on GDP per head of population to identify separate convergence clubs for the OECD and Latin American countries, but finds divergence among Asian economies. The idea of separate convergence clubs has been formalized by Durlauf and Johnson (1992) with their distinction between local and global convergence.

For the advanced industrialized countries, then, Baumol appears to offer strong evidence in favour of convergence. However, a paper by De Long (1988) apears to cast doubt even on this. The first point that De Long makes is that Baumol's sample is biased. Baumol reports results for an *ex post* sample of countries that are now rich and have developed successfully. Maddison's sample deliberately excludes nations that were relatively rich in 1870 but which have not developed successfully since and are now relatively poor. Hence convergence is all but guaranteed in Baumol's sample, but this tells us little about the forces making for convergence among the nations that in 1870 seemed likely to converge. We need an *ex ante* sample of countries that in 1870 seemed likely to converge. It is then possible to ask an *ex ante* question of the data: 'Have those nations that a century ago appeared well placed to appropriate and utilize industrial technology converged?' (De Long, 1988, p. 1139).

The problem in implementing a test of this question is that if Japan is to be included, as it is in the Maddison sample, about half of the countries in the world should also be included, because Japan was a very poor country in 1870. However, the second poorest country in 1870 in the Maddison sample is Finland, and if this is regarded as the cut-off level of

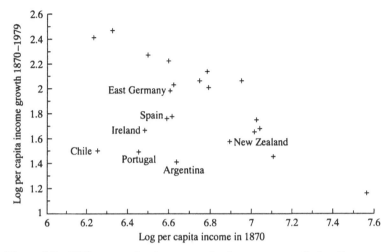

Figure 8.2 1870 per capita income and subsequent growth for the once-rich twenty-two

productivity then only seven more countries of equal or higher productivity need to be included: East Germany, Spain, Portugal, Ireland, Chile, Argentina and New Zealand. If these countries are added to the Maddison sample and Japan excluded, we arrive at a sample of twenty-two 'once-rich' nations. Comparing Figure 8.2 with Figure 8.1 it is clear that the neat convergence relationship breaks down for the twenty-two countries.

It is worth considering the choice of period as well as the choice of countries. Initially, Abramovitz (1979, 1986) stressed the role of catch-up growth during the post-war period and was much more equivocal about earlier periods. The reasons for this caution are apparent in Table 8.2. The arithmetic average of fifteen countries excluding the USA falls from 1870 to 1913 and again to 1950. Furthermore, the coefficient of variation (CV) falls only slightly between 1870 and 1913 and then remains constant to 1950. Although there is a substantial fall in the CV between 1950 and 1973, there is no further fall after 1973. Given these findings, it is not surprising that Abramovitz chose to concentrate on the period 1950–73. However, in understanding the convergence during this period it is as well to keep in mind the effects of World War II. Using the data appendices in Maddison (1991) it is possible to calculate the figures for 1938. These figures indicate a fall in the dispersion between 1913 and 1938, followed by an increase in dispersion between 1938 and 1950. Thus much of the catching-up in the early post-war period can be seen as post-war reconstruction. Indeed, Dumke (1990) argues that much of the European 'supergrowth' of the post-war period can be explained in this way. Using regression analysis, he finds that the ratio of GDP in 1948 to GDP in 1938, his measure of a war-induced disturbance, continues to exert an influence over growth into the 1960s.

De Long makes a further criticism of Baumol's (1986) work, pointing out that there is a problem due to measurement error. The problem is that in the Maddison sample the level of productivity in 1870 is obtained by extrapolating back from an estimate of the productivity level in 1970 in US dollars. This means that if the growth rate is too high because of measurement error, then the 1870 level of productivity is too low, or if the growth rate is too low, then the 1870 level of productivity is too high. Either way, this will tend to create the appearance of a negative relationship between the initial level of productivity and the subsequent growth rate. In other words, measurement error in either direction tends to create the appearance of β-convergence. However, there is no reason to expect measurement error to affect σ-convergence, since errors could be in either direction.

So far, we have considered unconditional convergence, but there is a large literature on conditional convergence. Using both OECD data for the advanced industrialized countries and the Summers and Heston data for a larger sample of countries, Dowrick and Nguyen (1989) find a strong catch-up effect even when allowance is made for capital deepening and greater labour force participation. This suggests that convergence of per capita incomes occurs not simply through greater investment and longer hours but also through catching-up of total factor productivity (TFP). However, Wolff (1991) notes that investment and TFP growth are related; there is correspondence by period between the degree of capital intensity catch-up and the degree of TFP convergence, there is correspondence by period between TFP convergence and average growth in capital intensity, and countries with higher capital/labour growth generally had higher TFP growth.

Barro and Sala-i-Martin (1991, 1992) report conditional convergence results based on a variety of income-based data sets, including US regions since 1840 and European regions since 1950 as well as the Summers and Heston post-war sample. Their results suggest an 'iron law' of convergence. Using the conditional convergence equation, they find a speed of convergence of around 2% per year in all cases. However, it should be noted that this finding is conditional on a large number of dummy variables for outliers as well as variables such as education and government spending. A recent investigation of the robustness of the relationship between growth and economic policy, political and institutional indicators by Levine and Renelt (1992) found that the conditional convergence result received only qualified support in the Summers and Heston data set, requiring the inclusion of a measure of the initial level of human capital and even then, not holding in the 1974–89 period. Our discussion above of the choice of period suggests that it would be difficult to conceive of the whole period 1870–1979 as a single era with a constant rate of convergence.

Our survey of the national income literature above suggests that the long-run evidence in favour of the convergence hypothesis is rather less clear than might be thought from a first reading of Baumol (1986). Nevertheless, if we limit ourselves to the *ex post* sample of countries studied by Maddison, it seems clear that convergence has occurred over the long period since 1870, although not as rapidly as might be thought from a consideration of the period 1950–73 alone.

4   The role of manufacturing

To the extent that convergence in levels of GDP per hour worked has occurred between the advanced industrial economies, it is usually attributed to the transfer of technology in manufacturing (Nelson and Wright, 1992; Gomulka, 1971; Cornwall, 1977). In this section we investigate this issue by examining directly data on labour productivity in manufacturing. We show that amongst the advanced industrial economies over the long run, levels and trends of productivity have often differed greatly between manufacturing and the whole economy. Productivity patterns in manufacturing can most usefully be characterized as local rather than global convergence. Even within the sample of advanced industrialized countries we find more than one convergence club.

The data on comparative levels of labour productivity in manufacturing are presented in Table 8.3, drawing on the sample of countries in Broadberry (1994c). For a number of key countries the estimates are described in detail in Broadberry (1993, 1994a). The basic methodology is to obtain benchmark estimates of productivity levels from production census material and extrapolate to other years using time series of real output and employment. In this respect, the methodology is very similar to that of Maddison (1991), and used for a recent study of productivity in manufacturing since 1950 by van Ark (1993). However, we are able to provide independent checks on the accuracy of the time series extrapolations because of the existence of a number of historical studies of comparative productivity levels in manufacturing. For the pre-World War II period the benchmark checks are based on the methodology of

Table 8.3   Comparative levels of labour productivity in manufacturing
(UK output per employee = 100)

	1870	1913	1929	1938	1950	1973	1989
UK	100	100	100	100	100	100	100
USA	204	213	250	192	263	215	177
Canada	88	153	170	145	151	153	123
Australia		138	102	101	96	86	81
Germany	100	119	105	107	96	119	105
Netherlands			102	117	88	133	128
Norway		90	109	95	103	104	85
Sweden		102	94	100	118	128	121
Denmark			115	98	88	89	93
France		79	82	76	84	114	115
Italy		59	59	49	68	96	111
Japan		24	32	42	20	95	143

Source: Broadberry (1994c).

Rostas (1948) using physical indicators, while for the post-1945 period benchmark estimates are based on comparisons of value added converted to a common currency using relative factory gate prices, following the approach of Paige and Bombach (1959).

It should be noted that most historical studies of comparative productivity in manufacturing have compared Britain bilaterally with other countries. Hence we report Table 8.3 with the UK as the numeraire country rather than the USA, since bilateral comparisons are not strictly transitive. To facilitate comparisons between productivity levels in manufacturing and the whole economy we also report in Table 8.4 figures for productivity in the whole economy with the UK as numeraire. In fact, Table 8.4 is not quite the same as a rebased Table 8.2 for two reasons. First, Table 8.4 uses the number of employees as the labour input rather than the number of hours worked, since there is little reliable information on hours worked by sector before World War II. The figures of van Ark (1993) for the post-1950 period suggest that hours remain substantially longer in Japan than in all other countries, which makes Japanese productivity performance less impressive on a per hour basis, while there has been a sizeable fall in annual hours worked in Continental Europe during the 1980s, bringing productivity on a per hour basis closer to US levels. Second, US productivity is rather higher in Table 8.4 than in Table 8.2. This results from the fact that Maddison compares GDP between countries in US prices only, whereas we report results using the geometric mean of US and own country prices. The use of only US prices

Table 8.4 Comparative labour productivity for the whole economy (UK GDP per employee = 100)

	1870	1913	1929	1938	1950	1973	1989
UK	100	100	100	100	100	100	100
USA	106	142	171	159	186	169	148
Canada	65	102	110	96	139	139	135
Australia	130	123	113	115	115	110	106
Germany	49	64	64	75	63	105	111
Netherlands	85	90	112	102	92	121	109
Norway	46	55	69	75	82	99	119
Sweden	43	54	55	64	84	102	95
Denmark	55	73	88	85	88	96	90
France	53	61	72	70	69	110	121
Italy	38	46	51	54	56	92	103
Japan	18	24	34	39	29	85	105

Source: Calculated from Maddison (1991).

has the advantage of transitivity, but it also biases productivity comparisons against the USA. This is because if, say, the USA is relatively good at producing cars and the UK relatively bad, the relative price of cars will tend to be low in the USA and high in the UK. Thus, if output is valued at US prices the high volume of US cars has a low value, but if output is valued at UK prices the high volume of US cars will have a high value. Hence it is usual in bilateral comparisons to calculate results in prices of both countries and take the geometric mean. Reporting results in the prices of one country inevitably biases productivity comparisons against that country. It should be noted that allowing for this factor is enough to change the productivity position of the USA in 1870 from 4% behind the UK to 6% above (with the USA overtaking Britain in the 1860s rather than the 1890s).

Now comparing Tables 8.3 and 8.4 we see some striking differences in levels and trends. First, as noted in Broadberry (1993) we see that in manufacturing there has been no clear trend over the last 130 years in comparative labour productivity performance between the three major exporting nations of Britain, Germany and the USA. Over this long period, labour productivity in US manufacturing has fluctuated around a level of about twice the British level, while German manufacturing labour productivity has fluctuated around a level broadly equal to the British level. This contrasts strikingly with the position at the whole economy level, where the USA has pulled substantially ahead of Britain from a position of broad equality in 1870, and Germany has come from a productivity level less than half the British level to a small productivity advantage over Britain. Clearly, then, the USA forging ahead between 1870 and 1950 at the whole economy level cannot be explained in terms of productivity growth in manufacturing, although given the scale of the productivity gap in this sector, there is clearly some role for the expansion of the share of the labour force in US manufacturing. Similarly, Germany's catching up of Britain at the whole economy level cannot be explained by trends in manufacturing productivity, but must be attributed to trends in other sectors and sectoral reallocation of labour, particularly the reduction of the labour force in low productivity agriculture.

Second, whereas the whole economy data in Table 8.4 (and *a fortiori* in Table 8.2) are generally interpreted as consistent with global convergence, it is rather easier to identify a number of separate convergence clubs in the manufacturing data of Table 8.3 and hence to see a process of local convergence. The countries have been ordered in Table 8.3 to identify these separate convergence clubs by informal means, since we have insufficient observations to use the formal methods proposed by Durlauf and Johnson (1992). We think it is useful to distinguish in our sample between the New World, Northern Europe, Southern Europe and Asia.

For the New World, the figures in Table 8.3 suggest a high level of labour productivity in manufacturing relative to Britain in the USA throughout the period since 1870. For the other New World countries, although there are periods of high labour productivity relative to the UK, the trends are rather different. Although there does appear to be local convergence in North America for much of the twentieth century, this follows a dramatic period of catching-up by Canada in the first decade of the twentieth century. We thus agree with Altman's (1987) recent characterization of the period 1900–1910 as a significant discontinuity in the Canadian growth process. However, to really capture the local convergence process in North America it is necessary to consider performance across US states. Barro and Sala-i-Martin (1991) find unconditional convergence as well as conditional convergence across US states, albeit in overall economic activity rather than in manufacturing alone. Despite initially high levels of labour productivity, Australian manufacturing has suffered a serious decline in its relative productivity position. This relative decline in Australian manufacturing has been worse than the relative decline at the whole economy level. Long-run trends in the manufacturing sector of the New World, then, caution against simple claims of global convergence.

Within Europe we see local convergence along two paths in the North and the South. In Germany, The Netherlands, Norway, Sweden and

Denmark, labour productivity in manufacturing has fluctuated around the British level throughout the twentieth century. Hence the expansion of the industrial sector, and particularly the reduction in the size of low productivity agriculture, have been important factors in explaining the catching-up on Britain which occurred at the whole economy level, particularly in Scandinavia and Germany. The picture is somewhat different in Southern Europe, however, with labour productivity levels substantially lower than in Britain in the pre-World War II period. The figures for the post-1945 period, however, suggest that in France and Italy convergence to average European productivity levels has been achieved both in manufacturing and at the whole economy level.

Turning to Asia, we see the remarkable catching-up by Japan, particularly in the post-1945 period. In contrast to the North European situation, where catching-up at the whole economy level has occurred without any substantial catching-up in manufacturing, in Japan the improvement in manufacturing has been much greater than at the whole economy level. Although Japan has now substantially overtaken European manufacturers on an output per worker basis and is continuing to catch-up with the USA, it should be noted that on a per hour worked basis German and Japanese labour productivity levels in manufacturing are now broadly similar, as Japanese hours are substantially longer.

We would suggest on the basis of these trends that convergence at the whole economy level should not be seen primarily as a result of technology transfer in manufacturing. It seems clear that there are still substantial international differences in labour productivity levels in manufacturing, particularly between North America and Europe, and there is a large literature linking these productivity differences to choice of technology. It is not possible to survey fully this literature here and the interested reader is referred to Broadberry (1994a). Nevertheless, we can provide a brief summary of the key ideas.

Underlying the global convergence perspective is the notion that in a fully integrated world, productivity would be the same in all countries since they would all be using the same techniques. By contrast, our perspective suggests that countries with different endowments and demand conditions will produce with different techniques and hence with different levels of labour productivity, an idea that draws on the famous Habakkuk (1962) thesis and in particular on the modified versions of Ames and Rosenberg (1968) and David (1975).

We see the higher labour productivity in North America as a result of a greater reliance on mass production techniques in the USA and craft/ flexible production techniques in Europe. The higher labour productivity in the USA results from the greater capital intensity and resource intensity of production as well as from economies of scale associated with the production of standardized products. The greater prevalence of mass production in the USA can be explained by both demand and supply factors. On the demand side, standardization in the USA was facilitated by the existence of a large, homogeneous home market in the USA compared with fragmented national markets stratified by class differences in Europe, coupled with greater reliance on differentiated export markets (Rostas, 1948; Frankel, 1957; Chandler, 1990). On the supply side, resource-intensive American machinery could not be adopted on the same scale in Europe, where resource costs were considerably higher (Ames and Rosenberg, 1968; Melman, 1956; Franko, 1976). Factor endowments reinforced these technological choices, with abundant skilled labour in Europe making continued reliance on craft production profitable (Harley, 1974).

We see the two technologies as coexisting so long as progress in one technology can be matched by imitation or adaptation in the other technology. Although for most of the period under consideration in this paper technological leadership rested with American mass production technology, forcing European firms to adapt to survive, in the first half of the nineteenth century technological leadership rested with British craft production technology (Broadberry, 1994a, 1994b). Furthermore, since the late 1960s there has been a revival in craft production methods, with technological leadership shifting to Germany and Japan, and American firms being forced to adapt to survive. Note, however, that these changes in technological leadership have not been accompanied by changes in labour productivity leadership. Throughout the period since 1820, at least, factor proportions and demand conditions have given the USA a labour productivity advantage.

This coexistence of competing technologies, with both seen as rational in their respective environments, can be modelled along lines suggested by David (1975). Initial differences in factor proportions will be transmitted through time so long as technological progress can be characterized by local learning. Although 'macro inventions' may appear to offer a country the opportunity to break free from such a technological 'lock-in', in practice decisions on when or how to apply the new technology will be influenced by current factor proportions and demand conditions. This can be seen as an endogenous growth model in a stochastic environment with learning effects, and is consistent with the absence of global convergence. As well as showing up in the productivity figures, the differences in technology between countries can be seen in the detailed evidence of writers making factory visits in different countries, going back at least to the 1850s (Rosenberg, 1969; Anglo-American Council on Productivity, 1952; Daly *et al.*, 1985).

Our survey of the evidence from manufacturing suggests that even amongst the advanced industrial economies the long-run evidence is best viewed as supporting local rather than global convergence. In particular, we note the continued existence of a substantial labour productivity gap between Europe and North America.

5 Real wages and convergence

Williamson (1991) has constructed an alternative data set which offers a perspective on long-run convergence. He presents annual estimates of real wage levels for fifteen countries, going back to 1830 in some cases. We present the data at benchmark years in Table 8.5 for ease of comparison with earlier tables.

The first stage in the construction of the data is to obtain time series for the nominal wages of urban, unskilled labourers, usually based on the hourly, daily or weekly wages of building labourers. The nominal wage series are then deflated by cost of living indices, usually for urban areas with weights based on budget studies of unskilled labourers. The resulting real wage series are then used to extrapolate from benchmark estimates of comparative real wage levels obtained by comparing nominal wages in each country with nominal wages in Britain and converting to a common currency using a purchasing power parity (PPP). Williamson establishes three benchmarks at 1905, 1938 and 1975, which means that the time series have discontinuities at 1913 and 1945.

Williamson's results paint a plausible picture, which points towards local rather than global convergence. Williamson identifies three groups: the English-speaking New World (USA, Canada and Australia); Latin New and Old World (Argentina, Italy and Spain); Other Old World. These groups correspond to our New World, South European and North European groups apart from the linking together of the Latin New and Old Worlds via the inclusion of Argentina in the sample.

Williamson argues that Baumol's (1986) concentration on the end points gives a misleading impression of a continuous, smooth process of convergence. In addition to pointing to the strength of forces for convergence after World War II, he also argues that there was an earlier period of relatively strong convergence between the 1850s and World War I, followed by a period of divergence between 1914 and 1945. He links the periods of convergence to the integration of global product and factor markets. He sees barriers to trade and the free migration of capital and labour as halting the process of convergence during the inter-war period.

Table 8.5   Comparative levels of real wages (UK = 100)

	1870	1913	1929	1938	1950	1973	1989
UK	100	100	100	100	100	100	100
USA	167	154	129	171	230	180	126
Canada	143	199	139	136	112	176	139
Australia	187	117	138	132	85	78	56
Argentina	104	98	109	95	81	48	30
Germany	84	83	85	72	74	115	113
Netherlands	60	74	120	111	104	119	101
Norway	44	63	105	104	117	114	112
Sweden	40	89	102	103	127	163	133
Denmark	52	93	151	148	123	154	138
Ireland	71	83	116	109	81	98	117
France	72	60	87	83	52	84	85
Belgium	72	73	62	66	97	118	105
Italy	34	50	46	47	90	102	108
Spain	42	44	56	58	61	72	99

Source: Williamson (1991, table A2.1).

These are important issues and Williamson's work is useful in focusing our attention on them, although they have not been entirely neglected before. Thus, for example, Baumol and Wolff (1988) discuss the period of convergence before World War I, while Maddison (1989) notes the importance of a liberal world order. However, there are a number of practical and conceptual problems with Williamson's paper. First, since he does not attempt to reconcile the time series and benchmark evidence, Williamson has a number of large discontinuities in his series. Thus, for example, between 1913 and 1914 real wages relative to Britain fall from 154 to 108 in the USA, while in France they rise from 60 to 93. Between 1945 and 1946, real wages relative to Britain rise dramatically in the USA, The Netherlands and Italy while falling spectacularly in Canada, Australia and Argentina. Clearly there are some big index number problems here which Williamson simply ignores. Second, the real wages of unskilled labourers have rather different significance in different economies, particularly as we have argued above that European economies have relied more heavily than New World countries on a rather more skill-intensive craft production process in manufacturing. Third, we cannot necessarily infer what is happening to the average product of labour from the marginal product of labour.

Fourth, and perhaps more importantly, if we are to relate these results to Maddison's GDP data we need to know what is happening to profits and rents as well as wages. This could be very important during the

1850–1913 period when European countries responded in various ways to the availability of cheap food supplies from the New World. Thus, for example, the consequences for rents and profits must have been rather different in free trade Britain than in protectionist Germany. Finally, we must ask the question whether global integration should be expected to lead to convergence or divergence To a large extent the answer depends on whether you consider the issue from the consumption or the production side. From the consumption side the answer must be that increased integration leads to convergence. However, if the gains from trade come from increased specialization, viewed from the production side economies may actually diverge. The choice of consumer prices over producer prices may not be so innocuous, then.

Despite these caveats, however, the Williamson real wage data set is broadly consistent with the findings for manufacturing and can be seen as suggestive of a process of local convergence.

6 Concluding comments

Our survey of three data sets has revealed a pattern of local rather than global convergence, with a number of clearly identifiable separate convergence clubs, even amongst the advanced industrialized countries. In particular, we see persistently higher productivity levels in North America than in Europe, and a slower convergence to average European productivity levels in Latin countries. Further, it is clear that convergence has not been a continuous, smooth process. In particular, there was an interruption to the process of convergence between 1914 and 1945. Williamson's (1991) suggestion of a link between the integration of factor and product markets and convergence seems an important lead to follow here.

NOTE

The financial support of the Research and Innovations Fund of the University of Warwick is gratefully acknowledged. I thank without implicating Nick Crafts and Mary O'Mahony for helpful discussions and advice. Helpful comments were also received from seminar/conference participants in Lisbon and Oxford.

REFERENCES

Abramovitz, M. (1979), 'Rapid Growth Potential and its Realisation: The Experience of the Capitalist Economies in the Postwar Period', in E. Malinvaud (ed.), *Economic Growth and Resources, Proceedings of the Fifth World*

Congress of the International Economic Association, Vol. I, London: Macmillan.

Abramovitz, M. (1986), 'Catching-Up, Forging Ahead and Falling Behind', *Journal of Economic History*, **46**, 385–406.

Altman, M. (1987), 'A Revision of Canadian Economic Growth: 1870–1910 (A Challenge to the Gradualist Interpretation), *Canadian Journal of Economics*, **20**, 86–113.

Ames, E. and N. Rosenberg (1986), 'The Enfield Arsenal in Theory and History', *Economic Journal*, **78**, 827–942.

Anglo-American Council on Productivity (1952), *Final Report*, London: AACP.

van Ark, B. (1993), 'International Comparisons of Output and Productivity: Manufacturing Productivity Performance of Ten Countries from 1950 to 1990', Groningen Growth and Development Centre Monograph Series, No. 1.

Barro, R.J. and X. Sala-i-Martin (1991), 'Convergence Across States and Regions', *Brookings Papers on Economic Activity*, 107–82.

Barro, R.J. and X. Sala-i-Martin (1992), 'Convergence' *Journal of Political Economy*, **100**, 223–51.

Baumol, W.J. (1986), 'Productivity Growth, Convergence and Welfare: What the Long Run Data Show', *American Economic Review*, **76**, 1072–159.

Baumol, W.J. and E.N. Wolff (1988), 'Productivity Growth, Convergence and Welfare: Reply', *American Economic Review*, **78**, 1155–9.

Broadberry, S.N. (1993), 'Manufacturing and the Convergence Hypothesis: What the Long Run Data Show', *Journal of Economic History*, **53**, 772–95.

Broadberry, S.N. (1994a), 'Technological Leadership and Productivity Leadership in Manufacturing since the Industrial Revolution: Implications for the Convergence Debate', *Economic Journal*, **104**, 291–302.

Broadberry, S.N. (1994b), 'Comparative Productivity in British and American Manufacturing During the Nineteenth Century', *Explorations in Economic History*, **31**, 521–48.

Broadberry, S.N. (1994c), 'Historical patterns of Comparative Productivity in Manufacturing', unpublished, University of Warwick.

Chandler, A.D. Jr. (1990), *Scale and Scope: The Dynamics of Industrial Capitalism*, Cambridge, MA: Harvard University Press.

Chatterji, M. (1992), 'Convergence Clubs and Endogenous Growth', *Oxford Review of Economic Policy*, **8**(4), 57–69.

Cornwall, J. (1977), *Modern Capitalism: its Growth and Transformation*, London: Martin Robertson.

Cowling, K. (1989), 'The Strategic Approach', in Industrial Strategy Group (ed.), *Beyond the Review: Perspectives on Labour's Economic and Industrial Strategy*, Edinburgh: University of Edinburgh.

Daly, A., D.M. Hitchens and K. Wagner (1985), 'Productivity, Machinery and Skills in a Sample of British and German Manufacturing Plants', *National Institute Economic Review*, **111**, 48–61.

David, P.A. (1975), *Technical Choice, Innovation and Economic Growth*, Cambridge: Cambridge University Press.

De Long, J.B. (1988), Productivity Growth, Convergence and Welfare: Comment', *American Economic Review*, **78**, 1138–54.

Dowrick, S. and D.-T. Nguyen (1989), 'OECD Comparative Economic Growth 1950–85: Catch-Up and Convergence', *American Economic Review*, **79**, 1010–30.

Dumke, R. (1990), 'Reassessing the Wirtschaftswunder: Reconstruction and Postwar Growth in West Germany in an International Context', *Oxford Bulletin of Economics and Statistics*, **52**, 451–91.

Durlauf, S.N. and P.A. Johnson (1992), 'Local versus Global Convergence Across National Economies', Working Paper No. 3996, National Bureau of Economic Research, Cambridge, MA.

Frankel, M. (1957), *British and American Manufacturing Productivity*, Urbana: University of Illinois.

Franko, L.G. (1976), *The European Multinationals: A Renewed Challenge to American and British Big Business*, London: Harper & Row.

Gerschenkron, A. (1962), *Economic Backwardness in Historical Perspective*, Cambridge, MA: Harvard University Press.

Gomulka, S. (1971), *Inventive Activity, Diffusion and the Stages of Economic Growth*, Aarhus: Institute of Economics.

Grossman, G.M. and E. Helpman (1991), *Innovation and Growth in the Global Economy*, Cambridge, MA: MIT Press.

Habakkuk, H.J. (1962), *American and British Technology in the Nineteenth Century*, Cambridge: Cambridge University Press.

Harley, C.K. (1974), 'Skilled Labour and Choice of Technique in Edwardian Industry', *Explorations in Economic History*, **2**, 391–414.

Levine, R. and D. Renelt (1992), 'A Sensitivity Analysis of Cross-Country Growth Regressions', *American Economic Review*, **82**, 942–63.

Lucas, R.E. Jr (1988), 'The Mechanics of Economic Development', *Journal of Monetary Economics*, **22**, 3–42.

Lucas, R.E. Jr (1993), 'Making a Miracle', *Econometrica*, **61**, 251–72.

Maddison, A. (1964), *Economic Growth in the West*, London: Allen & Unwin.

Maddison, A. (1982), *Phases of Capitalist Development*, Oxford: Oxford University Press.

Maddison, A. (1989), *The World Economy in the 20th Century*, Paris: Organisation for Economic Cooperation and Development.

Maddison, A. (1991), *Dynamic Forces in Capitalist Development*, Oxford: Oxford University Press.

Melman, S. (1956), *Dynamic Factors in Industrial Productivity*, Oxford: Blackwell.

Nelson, R.R. and G. Wright (1992), 'The Rise and Fall of American Technological Leadership: The Postwar Era in Historical Perspective', *Journal of Economic Literature*, **30**, 1931–64.

Paige, D. and G. Bombach (1959), *A Comparison of National Output and Productivity of the United Kingdom and the United States*, Paris: Organisation for European Economic Cooperation.

Peaker, A. (19740, *Economic Growth in Modern Britain*, London: Macmillan.

Romer, P.M. (1990), 'Human Capital and Growth: Theory and Evidence', *Carnegie-Rochester Conference Series on Public Policy*, **32**, 251–86.

Rosenberg, N. (1969) (ed.), *The American System of Manufactures*, Edinburgh: Edinburgh University Press.

Rostas, L. (1948), *Comparative Productivity in British and American Industry*, Cambridge: National Institute of Economic and Social Research.

Rowthorn, R. (1986), 'The Passivity of the State', in D. Coates and J. Hillard, (eds.), *The Economic Decline of Modern Britain: The Debate Between Left and Right*, Brighton: Wheatsheaf.

Stafford, G.B. (1981), *The End of Economic Growth? Growth and Decline in the UK since 1945*, Oxford: Martin Robertson.

Summers, R. and A. Heston (1984), 'Improved International Comparisons of Real Product and its Composition: 1950–80', *Review of Income and Wealth*, **30**, 207–62.

Veblen, T. (1915), *Imperial Germany and the Industrial Revolution*, New York: Macmillan.

Williamson, J.G. (1991), 'The Evolution of Global Labour Markets in the First and Second World since 1830: Background Evidence and Hypotheses', Discussion Paper No. 1571, Harvard Institute of Economic Research.

Wolff, E.N. (1991), 'Capital Formation and Productivity Convergence Over the Long Term', *American Economic Review*, **81**, 565–79.

Young, A. (1991), 'Learning by Doing and the Dynamic Effects of International Trade', *Quarterly Journal of Economics*, **106**, 369–406.

9 Growth and convergence in OECD countries: a closer look

JAVIER ANDRÉS, RAFAEL DOMÉNECH
and CÉSAR MOLINAS

1 Introduction

Economic integration among European countries is expected to bring about faster average growth. Less advanced countries hope to narrow the gap with the richer ones in terms of per capita income. However, whether or not this distributional effect will work is still an open question. From a theoretical viewpoint, growth theory is the appropriate framework to deal with these issues. In the long run, two basic features determine a country's economic achievements. One is the preferences of households, firms and governments for current consumption as opposed to future consumption. The other is the technological capability (in a broad sense) of the society to use the resources not devoted to current consumption.

In this chapter we carry out an empirical analysis of convergence patterns among the OECD countries, which satisfy reasonably well the traditional hypothesis of neoclassical growth models: they present a sustained growth of income per capita from the 1950s onwards, well-developed markets for production factors and relatively constant saving rates. We check the robustness of the main parameters in the constant returns to the scale Solow model under alternative specifications and estimation procedures. We also analyse the stability of the model (in particular the convergence rate) over time and across country groups.

Convergence regressions are carried out in the way popularized by Barro and Sala-i-Martin (1991) and Mankiw *et al.* (1992), MRW hereafter, among others.[1] Our interest is not merely to assess whether or not convergence has taken place, but also to see whether the long-run evolution of these economies can be explained in the theoretical framework of the Solow (1956) model. We provide estimates of the basic technological parameters and the convergence rate in a cross-section of the average values of variables over the twenty-four OECD countries for

347

the sample period 1960–90. This procedure imposes though, too many restrictions; in particular, the aggregate analysis assumed that technological parameters (and hence the convergence rate) are stable across countries and along the sample period. To assess to what extent this can be maintained, we split the sample in more homogeneous country groups to find that the estimation results are non-robust to the exclusion of some countries. We have also estimated the model, using six shorter period (5 years) averages of the variables to take the advantage of the time series dimension of the information set. Pooling model estimates reveal some differences in the relevant parameters and, most important, display a clear pattern of convergence which breaks down between 1975 and 1985.

The model and the theoretical arguments are sketched in Section 2. According to MRW's findings, the Solow model augmented to account for the accumulation of human capital can explain much of the variance of growth rates in OECD countries. We follow their suggestion and develop our empirical analysis in the context of this model. In Section 3 we introduce a first descriptive look at the most relevant variables is also carried out in this section. Unlike most previous work, generally based on the Summers–Heston data set, most data in our sample are taken from OECD statistics and are expressed in 1990 international dollars. In particular, we have used the 1990 OECD purchasing power parities and the national accounts rates of growth. Sections 4 and 5 present the estimation results for the cross-section and the pooled sample.

Section 6 concludes with the main findings and their interpretation, as well as with suggestions for further research. The overall picture that can be drawn from this exercise can be summarized as follows. The human capital augmented Solow model explains growth and convergence among the OECD economies reasonably well over the 1960–90 period; however, a closer look reveals many features that remain to be explained. Convergence occurs at different speeds among different groups of countries, depending on their income levels. Convergence seems a feature of times of fast growth. During recessions, convergence is much slower or non-existent. The model does not fit very well in shorter time periods of macroeconomic turbulence.

None of the existing theoretical models can account for all the features of economic growth, as summarized among others by Romer (1989) and Parente and Prescott (1993). Nevertheless the convergence proposition, built in the constant returns to scale technology, has made the Solow model the most popular analytical framework in this field, despite the fact that the constant returns to scale technology does not necessarily imply convergence, and that observed convergence does not rule out the possibility of stochastic increasing returns (Kelly, 1992). The basic exogenous growth model is a suitable framework to organize our knowledge about the long-run performance of advanced market economies. However, the failure of some parameter restrictions to hold across time and across countries suggests that this framework is far from complete, and that richer models may be necessary.

2 The 'augmented' Solow model

According to the augmented Solow model (Mankiw *et al.*, 1992; Durlauf and Johnson, 1992) the economy produces one good Y using a constant returns to scale technology and three productive factors, in efficiency units labour (AL), and physical (K) and human (H) capital,

$$Y_t = K_t^\alpha H_t^\gamma (A_t L_t)^\beta \qquad \alpha + \beta + \gamma = 1 \tag{1}$$

the evolution of different inputs follow the accumulation equations (2) to (5):

$$A_t = A_0 e^{\phi t} \tag{2}$$

$$L_t = L_0 e^{nt} \tag{3}$$

$$\frac{dK_t}{dt} = s_k Y_t - \delta^k K_t \tag{4}$$

$$\frac{dH_t}{dt} = s_h Y_t - \delta^h K_t \tag{5}$$

where n and ϕ are the exogenous rates of growth of population and labour augmenting technical progress respectively. The parameters s_k and s_h represent the share of output devoted to the accumulation of physical and human capital respectively. Finally we shall assume that both types of capital depreciate at the same rate so that $\delta^k = \delta^h = \delta$. Solving the model, the unique steady-state input combinations can be shown to be:

$$\left[\frac{K}{AL}\right]^* = \left[\frac{s_k^{1-\gamma} s_h^\gamma}{n + \phi + \delta}\right]^{\beta-1} \tag{6}$$

$$\left[\frac{H}{AL}\right]^* = \left[\frac{s_h^{1-\alpha} s_k^\alpha}{n + \phi + \delta}\right]^{\beta-1} \tag{7}$$

Plugging (6) and (7) into (1) we can write the expression for the steady state per capita income as follows:

$$\left[\frac{Y}{L}\right]^* = A^* \left[\frac{s_k^{1-\gamma}\, s_h^{\gamma}}{n+\phi+\delta}\right]^{(\alpha/\beta)} \left[\frac{s_h^{1-\alpha}\, s_k^{\alpha}}{n+\phi+\delta}\right]^{(\gamma/\beta)} \tag{8}$$

The main implication of this model is the so-called *conditional convergence proposition*, which means that in an economy of this kind, per capita growth between two periods of time (T and $T+\tau$) can be expressed as a fraction of its distance to the steady state at period T. In particular, it may be shown that this growth can be expressed as

$$\ln\left[\frac{Y_{T+\tau}}{(AL)_{T+\tau}}\right] - \ln\left[\frac{Y_T}{(AL)_T}\right] = \left(1-e^{-\lambda\tau}\right)\left[\ln\left[\frac{Y}{AL}\right]^* - \ln\left[\frac{Y_T}{(AL)_T}\right]\right] \tag{9}$$

where λ is the rate of convergence that can be written as: $\lambda = \beta(n^* + \phi + \delta)$ (for a detailed discussion of this proposition see Sala-i-Martin (1990a, 1990b). For a given τ, the larger is λ the closer the economy gets to its steady state. Similarly, for a given λ the economy approaches its steady state as τ increases. Equations (8) and (9) fully characterize the long run and the medium-term evolution of the economy. As long as they can be written in terms of observable variables they constitute the basic exogenous growth model that has been the focus of a great amount of empirical research in recent years. For the ith country, the empirical counterpart of (8) and (9) are the following expressions:

$$\ln y^i_{T+t^*} = B_{i1} + \phi_i T + \beta_i^{-1}\left[\alpha \ln\left(s_k^{i*}\right) + \gamma \ln\left(s_h^{i*}\right) - (\alpha_i + \gamma_i)\ln\left(n^{i*} + \phi_i + \delta_i\right)\right] \tag{10}$$

$$\ln y^i_{T+\tau} - \ln y^i_T = \phi_i \tau + \left(1 - \exp\{-\lambda_i\tau\}\right)$$
$$\left(B_{i2} + \phi_i T + \beta_i^{-1}\left[\alpha_i \ln\left(s_k^{i*}\right) + \gamma \ln\left(s_h^{i*}\right) - (\alpha_i + \gamma_i)\ln\left(n^{i*} + \phi_i + \delta_i\right)\right] - \ln y^i_T\right) \tag{11}$$

where starred variables represent their steady-state values, and

$$y = \left[\frac{Y}{L}\right]$$
$$B_1 = \ln A_0 + \phi t^*$$
$$B_2 = \ln A_0$$

The main purpose of this chapter is to investigate the size of the parameter λ. This can be done in several ways according to data availability. A natural approach is to estimate the parameter set $\{B_1, B_2, \alpha, \gamma, \phi, \lambda\}$ using time series for a single country; nevertheless the expressions (10) and (11) focus on long-run issues that can hardly be tackled with annual data. The usual procedure in the literature consists in taking some sort of time average of variables, letting τ be large enough (30, 10 or even 5 years) as to remove the contamination of short-run fluctuations in the economy. In such case we can suffer severe degrees-of-freedom limitations. The alternative way to increase the number of observations is to enlarge the data set to consider several countries (or regions) simultaneously. In this case we must further assume that all countries in the data set share the same parameter values in the production function $\{\alpha_i = \alpha, \beta_i = \beta, \gamma_i = \gamma, \phi_i = \gamma, \phi_i = \phi, \theta_i = \theta, A_{0i} = A_0, \forall i\}$, so that the empirical model becomes:[2]

$$\ln y^i_{T+t^*} = B_1 + \phi T + \beta^{-1}\left[\alpha\ln\left(s^{i^*}_k\right) + \gamma\ln\left(s^{i^*}_h\right) - (\alpha+\gamma)\ln\left(n^{i^*} + \phi + \delta\right)\right] + \nu_i \quad (12)$$

$$\ln y^i_{T+\tau} - \ln y^i_T = \phi\tau + \left(1 - \exp\{-\lambda\tau\}\right)$$

$$\left(B_2 + \phi T + \beta^{-1}\left[\alpha\ln\left(s^{i^*}_k\right) + \gamma\ln\left(s^{i^*}_h\right) - (\alpha+\gamma)\ln\left(n^{i^*} + \phi + \delta\right)\right] - \ln y^i_Y\right) + \eta_i$$
$$(13)$$

where λ can be either directly estimated or computed out from the estimated parameter values.[3] Most previous work has proceeded to estimate a linear version of (13) as the so-called *convergence equation*. It should be noticed that the parameter λ can be recovered from the parameter π_1 in the following equation:

$$\ln y^i_{T+\tau} - \ln y^i_T = \pi_0 + \pi_1 \ln y^i_T + \pi_2 \ln\left(s^{i^*}_k\right) + \pi_3 \ln\left(s^{i^*}_h\right) + \pi_4 \ln\left(n^{i^*} + \phi + \delta\right) + \epsilon_i$$
$$(14)$$

Our aim is not only to test the convergence hypothesis but also to assess the relevance of the augmented Solow model to describe the long-run behaviour of the OECD economies. The estimation of the relevant parameters of the production function can shed some light on the legitimacy of the technological restrictions imposed. We will proceed to estimate directly the technological parameters, imposing as many theoretical restrictions as possible. In particular we shall estimate jointly (12) and (13) and compare the fit with the unrestricted linear model (14). The overall loss of explanatory power of the more restricted model will be taken as a measure of the adequacy of the Solow model for the OECD countries during the sample period.

Finally we shall also compare the model with and without controlling for the steady state. The *absolute*, or *unconditional*, *convergence* hypothesis implies that all countries move towards the same steady state or at least that there is no correlation among the steady state and the initial conditions. In this case, λ can be consistently estimated in the convergence equation (13′) or in its linear version (14′):

$$\ln y^i_{T+\tau} - \ln y^i_T = \phi\tau + \left(1 - e^{-\lambda\tau}\right)\left[B'_2 + \phi T - \ln y^i_T\right] + \eta'_i \qquad (13')$$

$$\ln y^i_{T+\tau} - \ln y^i_T = \pi'_0 + \pi_1 \ln y^i_T + \epsilon'_i \qquad (14')$$

Absolute convergence does not take place in a model with factors, such as human capital, that are less than perfectly mobile across borders. If physical capital can move across countries but human capital cannot do so, the homogenization of marginal returns can be achieved without convergence in per capita income over the long run (Lucas, 1993), unless these countries have identical behavioural and technological parameters (as well as initial conditions). Hence 'homogeneous' country groups, such as the OECD, that share a great deal of *steady-state* properties (in terms of technology, saving rates and population growth) are the appropriate empirical framework to compare the conditional and unconditional rate of convergence. For that purpose we shall estimate also the model in (13′) and (14′) to compute the rate of absolute convergence and to analyse to what extent the steady state varies across countries and how it is related to the initial conditions at T.

3   The data

Empirical growth studies have traditionally used the Summers and Heston (1991) data set, known as *Penn World Table Mark 5 (PWT5)*, recently updated and revised in a new version called *PWT5.5*. These data cover a wide range of countries from 1950 to 1990 in *PWT5.5*. However, there are several reasons that justify the use of data taken from OECD statistics.[4] First, we are interested in using all recent OECD information, including the 1990 purchasing power parities (PPP) for all OECD members. Both *PWT5* and *PWT5.5* provide PPPs for Iceland and Switzerland estimated by an indirect method. Second, *PWT5* variables for countries with more than one benchmark have slightly modified national accounts data, which are obtained using what Summers and Heston call a *consistentization* procedure which does not maintain national accounts rates of growth. This makes it more difficult to assemble the series from different sources. In fact, this procedure is not used in *PWT5.5*, where adjustments factors are applied only to benchmark estimates. Third, *PWT5* and *PWT5.5* do not maintain the *fixity* convention in PPP adopted by OECD, which allows the original results of OECD multilateral comparisons to remain unchanged when these countries are included in a larger group. The Geary–Khamis aggregation method, used in the elaboration of *PWT5* and *PWT5.5*, is affected by inclusion of countries with different GDP composition. In general, the larger the number and heterogeneity of the included countries, the larger the divergence in comparisons within the initial group with respect to the original results. Finally, *PWT5* and *PWT5.5* do not give data for all variables we could be interested in, such as exports and imports.[5] Consistency with other variables of National Accounts recommends the use of a unique source of data.

In this chapter we use the *EKS* PPP published by OECD for 1990 as benchmark year. These data include all twenty-four OECD members.[6] The *EKS* method has the advantage of not suffering from the Gerschenkron effect. All nominal variables have been transformed to real terms using their price index from national accounts, and expressed in *international dollars* of 1990 using estimated OECD PPPs from 1990 for each aggregate (for exports and imports, the exchange rate to US dollars) and the USA as numeraire. In contrast with the Geary–Khamis method, the *EKS* is not additive, i.e., real private consumption, C, public consumption, C, investment, I, exports, X, imports, M, and variation of stocks, VS, do not add up to real GDP. Although differences are small, we have readjusted the GDP composition, but not the GDP level, to ensure additivity as it is determined by the following expression:

$$
re_{ij}^{*t,90} = \frac{e_{ij}^{t,90}}{(PPP_j^{90})_i} \frac{GDP_j^{t,90}}{PPP_j^{90}} \frac{1}{\sum_i \dfrac{e_{ij}^{t,90}}{(PPP_j^{90})_i}}
\tag{15}
$$

$$
e_i = C, G, I, X, M, VS; \qquad j = 1, \ldots, 24
$$

where $e_{ij}^{t,90}$ is the expenditure level in category i in year t for country j at 1990 national prices and national currency, $(PPP_j^{90})_i$ its corresponding OECD parity, and $re_{ij}^{*t,90}$ the adjusted magnitude in international prices.

Figure 9.1 shows the dispersion of $\ln y_{it}$, the log of GDP per capita, in OECD from 1960 to 1991. This figure is a representation of σ-convergence, following the terminology proposed by Barro and Sala-i-Martin (1991). The reduction in the dispersion was very significant from 1960 to the mid-1970s, but convergence seems to be slower from those years until the mid-1980s. The figure also shows the different behaviour of σ-convergence when we exclude the poorest countries at the end of the period.[7] As we can see, convergence seems not to be constant across countries and across time.

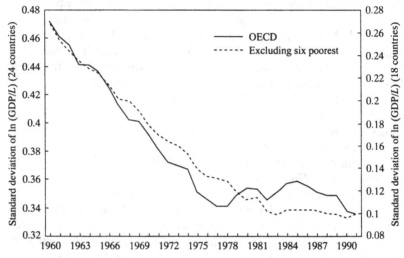

Figure 9.1   σ-convergence in the OECD. Different GDP per capita comparisons

Table 9.1 shows the 1960 to 1990 averages of the main variables used in the following sections. Comparing each country's GDP per capita in 1960 and 1990, expressed as a percentage of that of the USA, most OECD members have narrowed their gap with the richest country in the sample. Table 9.1 also shows these variables for two different subperiods. The whole sample has been divided into a period of high growth from 1960 to 1975 and from 1986 to 1990, and a period of slow growth from 1976 to 1985. Combining the information of this table with Figure 9.1, we may point out that convergence is a feature of high growth periods.

In Figure 9.2 we represent the scatter of average rates of growth for 1960–90 against the initial level of per capita income in 1960. The strong negative relationship is the basic representation of what is called *unconditional β-convergence*: poor countries have higher rates of growth than rich ones. Again this result for the whole period does not hold for different subperiods. For all variables we have obtained 5-year averages for 1960–65, and so on, until 1990. Figure 9.3 represents the scatter of average rates of growth against the initial level of per capita income in 1960, but now for periods 1960–75 and 1985–90—panel (a)—and 1975–85—panel (b). As panel (b) confirms, convergence does not hold for the whole sample. However, excluding the countries that were poorest in 1975 (Turkey, Portugal, Greece, Ireland and Spain), there is again a negative correlation between initial GDP per capita and its rate of growth.

Table 9.1 Growth performance of OECD countries, 1960–90

Country	1960–90: GDP/L gr.(%)	1960–90: L gr.(%)	GDP/L 1960 (USA=100)	GDP/L 1990	Real I/GDP	Nominal I/GDP	Human capital[a]	1961–75 & 1986–90: GDP/L gr.(%)	L gr.(%)	Real I/GDP	Nominal I/GDP	Human capital[a]	1976–85: GDP/L gr.(%)	L gr.(%)	GDP/L 1975 (USA=100)	GDP/L 1985	Real I/GDP	Nominal I/GDP
Australia	2.22	1.62	67.25	73.07	28.78	24.00	7.82	2.47	1.88	23.37	24.60	7.67	1.71	1.29	75.78	75.21	21.60	22.84
Austria	3.21	0.30	52.03	75.63	21.65	24.67	7.61	3.63	0.49	22.06	25.11	7.47	2.37	−0.03	68.09	72.15	21.08	24.06
Belgium	3.08	0.29	53.27	74.59	16.47	19.53	8.48	3.70	0.43	17.22	20.38	8.33	1.85	0.06	69.87	70.36	14.93	17.82
Canada	2.84	1.33	66.59	86.86	18.72	18.14	9.17	3.07	1.56	18.62	18.03	9.01	2.39	1.03	82.01	86.91	19.05	18.46
Switzerland	1.89	0.80	97.20	95.85	21.57	23.28	6.24	2.16	1.15	22.59	23.55	6.45	1.35	0.20	96.39	94.34	19.67	21.37
Germany	2.65	0.44	67.73	83.61	18.75	22.61	9.36	2.81	0.77	19.57	24.30	9.48	2.32	−0.13	76.39	80.52	16.84	20.45
Denmark	2.56	0.39	63.17	75.73	18.79	20.91	7.41	2.59	0.55	20.02	22.11	6.89	2.49	0.11	71.52	76.62	16.43	18.65
Spain	3.75	0.81	31.76	53.66	17.50	21.85	6.87	5.25	0.85	18.34	22.81	6.25	0.75	0.81	52.37	47.36	16.18	20.37
Finland	3.45	0.40	48.57	75.53	27.18	27.70	7.77	3.90	0.42	28.29	28.57	7.41	2.56	0.40	65.32	70.48	24.65	25.65
France	2.94	0.73	58.81	79.13	18.55	21.37	9.40	3.48	0.89	19.15	22.00	9.07	1.86	0.48	75.53	76.17	17.60	20.38
UK	2.16	0.31	67.85	72.56	12.02	17.74	7.71	2.30	0.45	12.48	18.36	7.76	1.87	0.07	67.74	68.35	11.26	16.73
Greece	3.96	0.66	18.97	33.83	15.49	21.81	7.52	4.99	0.55	16.19	22.69	7.31	1.90	0.94	34.11	34.51	14.14	20.08
Ireland	3.49	0.71	31.22	49.14	16.93	20.62	7.79	4.01	0.55	16.19	19.72	7.44	2.46	1.09	39.09	41.74	19.02	23.17
Iceland	3.44	1.24	50.05	76.22	23.40	23.17	7.56	3.40	1.43	23.91	23.58	7.41	3.52	1.01	63.73	75.24	22.22	22.12
Italy	3.44	0.46	47.23	73.20	18.39	22.86	7.92	3.77	0.57	19.29	23.91	7.70	2.78	0.30	62.60	68.99	16.31	20.43
Japan	5.39	0.94	29.91	80.63	25.21	27.48	8.32	6.42	1.07	25.55	27.77	8.13	3.34	0.80	61.46	71.64	25.33	27.72
Luxemburg	2.62	0.64	75.18	91.16	21.10	26.75	6.10	2.83	0.89	22.53	28.42	5.50	2.18	0.22	78.54	81.67	18.20	23.36
Netherlands	2.40	0.88	63.50	72.77	18.35	23.19	8.41	2.99	1.09	19.53	24.61	8.29	1.23	0.59	74.99	71.00	15.92	20.29
Norway	3.23	0.56	50.10	73.27	29.66	28.59	8.82	2.98	0.70	29.59	28.38	8.75	3.73	0.36	62.07	75.06	30.02	29.25
New Zealand	1.31	1.18	75.13	61.86	14.24	17.19	8.46	1.44	1.56	14.58	17.55	8.39	1.03	0.58	73.49	68.17	13.68	16.61
Portugal	4.08	0.57	20.77	38.24	18.23	27.40	6.20	5.15	0.34	18.86	28.17	5.23	1.93	1.05	33.32	33.78	16.90	25.78
Sweden	2.40	0.45	67.26	77.16	17.46	19.66	8.09	2.90	0.61	18.32	20.51	7.86	1.39	0.19	80.42	77.45	15.68	17.98
Turkey	2.96	2.40	17.43	23.36	18.22	25.32	4.43	3.69	2.57	18.02	24.94	4.03	1.48	2.30	21.86	21.17	18.83	26.37
USA	1.94	1.09	100.00	100.00	17.25	17.25	11.26	2.01	1.18	17.51	17.51	10.77	1.79	1.03	100.00	100.00	16.73	16.73

Note: [a] Estimated average years of schooling in the labour force.
Source: OECD (various publications); Human capital from Kyriacou (1991) and own calculations.

355

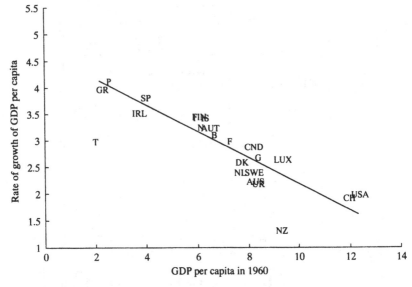

Figure 9.2   Convergence in OECD countries, 1960–90

As has been noted by several authors, the ratio of investment to GDP (I/Y) is a measure of *nominal* efforts in investment. However, according to the growth literature what is required is a measure of *real* investment. The reason for the discrepancies between the two measures is that two countries with the same nominal ratio I/Y can face different price levels for investment goods. In general, and OECD countries are no exception, an empirically robust finding is that poor countries have higher investment prices in relative terms than rich ones. In what follows, every country's ratio of investment to its GDP is expressed in real terms, i.e., we use different PPPs for investment and GDP.

Using standard results of the partitioned matrix estimation we can display the partial correlation of two variables in the presence of other explanatory variables. Figure 9.4 is similar to Figure 9.2 but it takes into account the basic differences in steady states. Both initial per capita income and its rate of growth are regressed on I/Y and population growth. The scatter of their residuals shows a strong negative correlation that can be interpreted as a first approximation to conditional convergence.

Figure 9.5 shows the positive correlation between real investment share as a percentage of GDP and the per capita income rate of growth, after controlling for initial income and population growth, while Figure 9.6 represents the correlation between growth in per capita income and

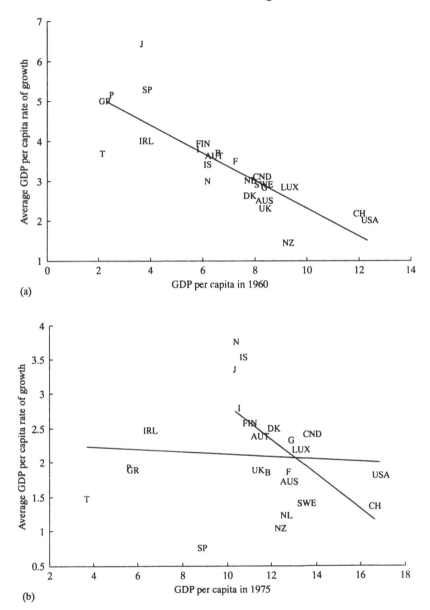

Figure 9.3   Convergence in OECD countries, 1960–75, 1986–90 and 1976–85

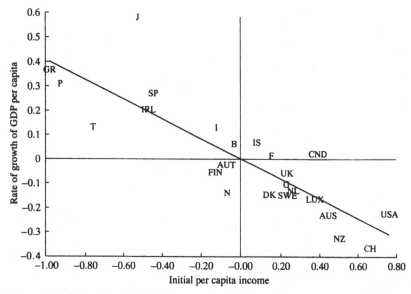

Figure 9.4   Convergence in OECD countries. Orthogonal components to I/GDP, n

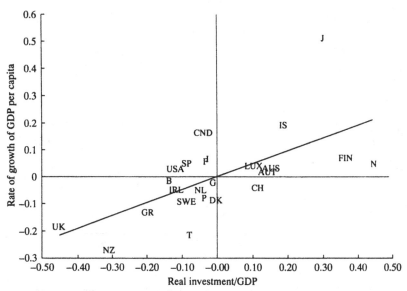

Figure 9.5   Real investment and growth. Orthogonal components to GDP/L, n

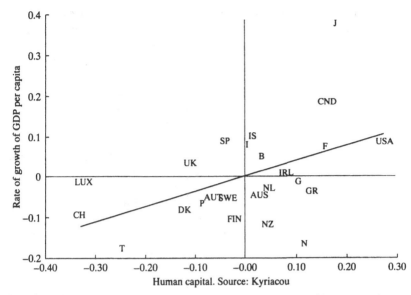

Figure 9.6   Human capital and growth. Orthogonal components $I/$GDP, GDP$/L$, n

human capital, including in this case the ratio I/Y as a regressor. Human capital corresponds to estimated average years of schooling in the labour force (Kyriacou, 1991).[8] As Table 9.1 displays, there is a strong correlation between this measure of human capital and initial per capita income in 1960. However, even taking this into account, Figure 9.6 exhibits a positive correlation between human capital and growth in per capita income.

4   Basic model results

4.1   Cross-section estimation

In this section we estimate the model in (12), (13), (14), (13′) and (14′), setting T to 1960 and τ equal to 30. We consider only cross-section variability to analyse the convergence hypothesis over the very long run. Steady-state values of the variables are then approximated by their 30-year averages. This procedure (common to much of the work in this field) also makes less relevant the endogeneity problem in estimating the convergence equation, which would otherwise make it pretty difficult to obtain consistent estimates, given the difficulty of finding suitable instruments. Alternatively we could find lagged values as instruments cutting the sample at some intermediate date. The reasons for not proceeding in this way will become clear in the next section, when we analyse the sample taking shorter period averages. As we shall see, the differences across subperiods are large, so that splitting the sample is not a trivial decision.

In Table 9.2 we present different versions of the linear model in (14) and (14′). In column 1 a first test of unconditional convergence displays a strongly significant negative parameter for per capita income in 1960. Both the parameter size and the equation fit are similar to the results reported by Mankiw et al. (1992). As in their case, the poor fit suggests the convenience of controlling for steady-state variation across countries. In columns 2 and 3 the model includes the ratio of investment to GDP (I/Y) as well as the 'augmented rate of population growth' $(n + \phi + \delta)$. Following the convention in many studies of this kind we impose, at this stage,[9] the values of 0.02 and 0.03 for ϕ and δ respectively. The inclusion of these variables improves the fit substantially, producing a 25% fall in the standard error and a substantial increase in the R^2. The coefficients $\hat{\pi}_2$ and $\hat{\pi}_3$ have the expected sign and the imposition of theoretical restrictions $(\hat{\pi}_2 = \hat{\pi}_3)$ is not rejected by the data $(\rho = 14.1)$. Most important, though, is that the negative coefficient of initial per capita income remains consistently negative and becomes even more significant in the conditional model. In fact, $\hat{\pi}_1$ increases, suggesting that conditional convergence has taken place at a faster rate than in the unconditional case.[10] This implies that steady states are different across countries and positively correlated with the initial per capita income levels. Richer countries in 1960 still approach higher steady-state per capita income. The omission of these variables biases the convergence parameter downwards. Comparing these results with Mankiw et al.'s, we get a better fit as well as faster convergence speed. This could be explained by the different homogenization method (as explained in Section 3) as well as by the enlarged time span in our sample, that includes the period 1985–90 in which faster growth has brought about faster convergence than in 1975–80 and 1980–85.

In columns 4 and 5 the convergence equation is augmented to include a proxy for the share of output devoted to the accumulation of human capital (s_h). Many of the criticisms of the Solow model focus on the extremely simple technological structure incorporated in the two inputs, constant returns to scale production function. What these results show is in accordance with the suggestion of Mankiw et al. that isolating human capital as an accumulable factor in the production function can greatly improve the explanatory power of the basic model of exogenous growth (Lucas, 1988, 1993). The augmented model improves the fit with a

Table 9.2 Linear models of convergence. Cross-section estimation

	1	2	3	4	5
constant	1.56	−2.57	−1.38	−2.69	−2.70
	(7.73)	(2.22)	(1.66)	(3.03)	(3.03)
$\log(Y_{60}^i)$	−0.38	−0.41	−0.44	−0.48	−0.47
	(3.82)	(7.60)	(8.92)	(7.91)	(10.0)
$\log(I/Y)^i$	—	0.48	0.53	0.49	0.47
		(3.48)	(3.49)	(3.04)	(3.61)
$\log(n+\phi+\delta)^i$	—	−0.97	−0.53*	−0.59	−0.82*
		(2.89)		(3.40)	
$\log(s_h^i)$	—	—	—	0.37	0.35
				(2.51)	(3.98)
$\bar{R}^2$	0.517	0.733	0.704	0.782	0.792
σ	0.172	0.128	0.135	0.116	0.113
χ_1^2			2.16		0.037
ρ			14.1%		84.8%

Notes: * Restricted parameter.
Dependent variable $\log(Y_{90}^i/Y_{60}^i)$. Sample i: 1, ..., 24. Estimation method: OLS.

further 10% reduction in the standard error and with an increase in the R^2; the human capital proxy is highly significant and both the size and the sign of the estimated parameters are as expected. The theoretical restrictions on the linear model are much more easily accepted by the data with a very high probability value ($\rho = 84.8$). The estimated parameters are also in the range of values reported by Mankiw et al. (1992) and Durlauf and Johnson (1992) among others. The conditional convergence parameter is also higher (in absolute value) in the fully specified model than in the ones we have previously discussed. This is consistent with the idea that there is enough variation in human capital formation across OECD countries and that richer countries in 1960 have devoted more resources to investment in schooling, which in turn has contributed to an increase in their welfare prospects in the long run.

So far we have discussed signs. A more detailed analysis of the data set is needed to assess the validity of the augmented Solow model, in order to explain growth and convergence processes in the OECD countries. Several econometric studies have recently suggested that the direction of causality runs from growth to savings rather than in the opposite way, which casts some doubts on the conventional interpretation of the empirical correlation among savings and growth.[11] On the hand, convergence does not necessarily imply the validity of the Solow model.[12]

Equations (12) and (13) contain information about restrictions that we can exploit in order to obtain direct estimates of the parameters of interest, and to test to what extent the data are compatible with the Solow model. We do not claim that we are testing it against a well-defined alternative. Rather, we test whether convergence equations keep their explanatory power when we explicitly derive them from a well-specified theoretical framework. We have taken three different approaches to estimate the technological and convergence parameters. First, we estimate α and γ through the joint estimation of the convergence and the steady-state equations,[13] both with and without the corresponding cross-equation restrictions. Second, we run non-linear regressions of the fully restricted convergence equation both with and without steady-state variables (equations (13) and (13′)) in order to compare the unconditional and the conditional convergence hypotheses; in this case we have also removed the restriction on ϕ. Finally, we have also tried the partially restricted convergence equation in which λ is directly estimated. In some specifications, there is a non-negligible difference among these two estimation procedures as far as the estimated λ is concerned.

MRW provide a reason for performing the joint estimation of convergence and steady-state equations. If the initial level of technology varies across countries according to a white noise perturbance, which is not correlated with other regressors in the steady-state equation, the initial level of income will be correlated with the error term in the convergence equation, given that there is not any other perturbation in this equation that cancels this correlation. Following MRW, countries with a higher initial level of technology will have higher initial incomes, that would be uncorrelated with subsequent growth rates, biasing the coefficient of initial income toward zero and allowing more comfortably acceptance of the hypothesis of non-convergence. Theoretically, the joint estimation of the steady-state and convergence equations can partially solve this problem when we impose full restrictions across equations, and when λ is restricted to be equal to $\beta(n^* + \phi + \delta)$. In practice, the difficulties of obtaining a good proxy for the dependent variable in the steady-state equation are an obstacle in the implementation of this procedure.

The results of all these estimation methods are presented in Table 9.3. In column 1, the estimation imposes all parameter restrictions across equations. The model does not reject the restrictions imposed by theory and the convergence equation fits better than its linear version with a moderate fall in the standard error and an increase in the R^2. Similarly the cross-equation restrictions are not rejected at the 5% level. The estimated parameter set has also sensible values with a balanced share of

Table 9.3 Non-linear estimation of steady-state and convergence equations. Cross-section

	1^j	2^{ss}	3	4	$5^\dagger$	6
B_2	-5.84 (5.26)		-6.81 (5.16)	-7.91 (5.02)	2.56 (16.7)	-7.12 (4.28)
B_1	-6.45 (5.26)	-4.40 (2.35)				
α	0.27 (4.32)	0.10 (0.88)	0.35 (5.05)	0.36 (5.18)		0.37 (4.84)
γ	0.33 (6.08)	0.45 (4.63)	0.28 (4.80)	0.30 (4.41)		0.27 (3.74)
λ						0.022 (6.02)
$(\alpha + \gamma)$					0.75 (10.6)	
ϕ	0.02^*	0.02^*	0.02^*	0.025 (2.19)	0.02^*	0.02^*
$\bar{R}^2$	0.818		0.833	0.805	0.425	0.793
$\bar{R}^2_{ss}$	0.384	0.440				
σ	0.106		0.101	0.110	0.248	0.113
σ_{ss}	0.294	0.280				
β_{imp}	0.39	0.45	0.37	0.34	0.25	0.36
λ_{imp}	0.023	0.026	0.021	0.020	0.014	0.021
$\lambda_{imp}(\phi)$	0.023	0.026	0.021	0.021	0.014	0.021

Notes: * Restricted parameter.
^{j} Joint estimation, full restrictions: $\chi_1(\alpha) = 3.96$ (4.67%); $\chi_1(\gamma) = 2.60$ (10.97%; $\chi_2(\alpha, \gamma) = 3.95$ (13.84).
Cols. 2, 3: joint estimation without cross-equation restrictions.
^{ss} Steady-state equation.
† This equation does not include steady-state variables.
Dependent variable log (Y^i_{90}/Y^i_{60}). Sample i: 1, ..., 24. Estimation method: non-linear least squares.

physical capital, human capital and labour in national income ($\hat{\alpha} \approx \hat{\beta} \approx \hat{\gamma} \approx 1/3$). The convergence rate that can be drawn from these estimates is also in the range of values found in previous work (Barro and Sala-i-Martin, 1991) – about 2.1%. The joint estimation without imposing cross-equation restrictions (columns 2 and 3) uncovers some interesting differences. The point estimates in the convergence equation are closer to the {1/3, 1/3, 1/3} set than those in the steady-state one, with a slightly higher capital share and lower human capital share. Again the fit improves somewhat, and the implicit convergence rate is around 2%. This seems a promising line of research which suggests, at least, that there is weak evidence in favour of the technological restrictions implied by the Solow model. However, the fit of the steady-state equation is very poor and the point estimates of α and γ take some rather implausible values (close to zero in the case of $\hat{\alpha}$). This has two possible explanations. On the one hand, the steady-state equation is static in nature and suffers the problems of these equations (for instance, production functions) in modelling aggregate macroeconomic relations. On the other hand, the sample average may not be a good proxy for $(Y/L)^*$. This may affect the parameter estimates to the extent that the accumulation rates are correlated with the measurement error. We shall return to this later, in the pooled sample model, but in what follows we abandon the joint estimation of the complete model to focus on the convergence equation.

In columns 4 to 6 we present different versions of the convergence equation. In columns 4 and 6 we estimate all the parameters in (13) with and without imposing the restrictions implied in the definition of λ. In both cases the implicit labour share $(\hat{\beta})$ is about 0.33; estimated α are slightly higher than expected; nevertheless, values around 0.40 are in the range of those reported for the richer countries in Durlauf and Johnson's paper, who report values between 0.34 and 0.55 for samples containing most OECD countries. On the other hand, $\hat{\gamma}$ is slightly lower than expected, but again this result is not at odds with Durlauf and Johnson's findings who report many estimations ranging from 0.0 to 0.4. Similarly, in Holtz-Eakin (1992) the estimated γ is around 0.20. The convergence rate (γ_{imp}) is fairly robust to alternative specifications. In column 4, the parameter ϕ is estimated to be 0.025, slightly higher than the value usually imposed at 0.02. The convergence rate lies also in the range of values obtained so far, and is also similar to the estimated value obtained in column 6 (0.022). It is worth noting that the data seem to accept the restrictions in the definition of λ fairly well. Actually, the restricted model (in columns 3 or 4) displays better standard error and $\bar{R}^2$ than the partially restricted one (column 6).

Finally, in column 5 we estimate the model in (13′) without controlling for the steady-state. The unconditional convergence rate is much lower than the conditional one, and this shows that the unconditional model suffers from mis-specification problems due to the correlation between initial conditions and steady-state variables. There is one additional insight we can get from the explanatory power of the unconditional convergence model. In this case the fully restricted non-linear version fits significantly worse than its linear counterpart.[14] The parameter restrictions implied by the augmented Solow model are rejected in the unconditional case but not in the conditional one. This suggests that controlling for the steady state is crucial in order to test the adequacy of the basic growth model. Ad hoc convergence regressions without a fully specified steady state are uninformative about the structural features of long-run economic performance.

4.2 Subsample estimates

The results we have discussed so far seem robust to alternative econometric specifications. However, the descriptive analysis in Section 3 has revealed large economic differences among OECD countries both in their long-run and in their short-run achievement. It is interesting to know to what extent differences in the accumulation rates (mainly savings and human capital accumulation) can account for the variance in growth rates, or, alternatively, whether the aggregate results fail to hold when we look at the OECD at a more disaggregate level. In order to draw the implications of the Solow model for the cross-country distribution of income we must assume a common technology within the sample. However, if some countries do not have access to the common technology, there might be long-lasting or permanent differences in wealth even under a constant returns technology. Several studies report sizeable differences in the most relevant parameters as well as in the convergence speed across countries.

These technological differences can be justified in several ways. Durlauf and Johnson (1992) put forward an explanation for these differences in terms of technological non-convexities. Some technologies may require a given amount of accumulated factors so that they only become available at a given stage of the growth process. Andrés and Boscá (1993) argue that differences in initial conditions may lead to permanent differences in productivity even among otherwise identical economies. Finally, it might also be the case that some advanced OECD countries have access to an increasing returns to scale technology that is hidden under the maintained assumption of a common technology. At any point in time there might be several available technologies distributed across countries according to some economic or institutional features; if we can identify homogeneous groups among the twenty-four countries in our sample, it is worth testing whether convergence has taken place at the widespread accepted 2% rate inside each group.

Given our degrees of freedom limitation we have proceeded to control for differences in technological parameters in two ways. First, we have run the linear version of the model (14) for each of the twenty-four subsamples of twenty-three countries, and selected those countries whose exclusion produces a 5% change in some of the parameters $\hat{\pi}_1, \hat{\pi}_2, \hat{\pi}_3$. At the same time we have tested the significance of country dummies in the full sample regression. To our surprise this procedure revealed little change in the relevant parameters with the exception of Turkey, Greece and, to a lesser extent, Japan. For this reason we kept the subsample of the twenty-two OECD countries having excluded Turkey and Greece. Additionally, following Durlauf and Johnson's (1992) suggestion (see also Helliwell and Chung (1992)), we took the level of income at different points in time as an alternative splitting method. We did not try an endogenous splitting procedure, but we chose groups of countries large enough to be able to estimate the parameters of interest. Unlike Durlauf and Johnson we did not choose a single year based split, but rather we tried to identify groups of countries according to their position in 1960 and in 1990. As discussed in Andrés and Boscá (1993), the choice of subsamples according to the observed variables (in particular the dependent variable) at a particular point in time can be very misleading. However, even in this case, it seems wise to focus on the observed value of per capita income at the end of the sample period, since we are trying to identify groups of countries with a similar technology, that must have produced a similar long-run performance.[15]

Before describing the results in Tables 9.4 and 9.5 it is worth making a short comment about the unreported linear estimates. Some of the most important differences among subsamples can only be seen in a non-restricted setting; otherwise, restricted estimation hides some changes in relative parameters. Excluding Turkey and (to a lesser extent) Greece, the Solow model no longer holds; the parameter values are significantly different from those found for the OECD as a whole; in particular, the augmented rate of population growth $(n + \phi + \delta)$ turns out to be non-significant. Turkey presents the highest rate of population growth and one of the lowest rates of per capita growth in the OECD controlling by its initial income (see Figure 9.4); the negative correlation between these two variables is strong enough only because of this outlier. Similarly, the positive correlation between growth and savings is sharply weakened when we exclude Japan. The coincidence of a high savings rate and growth rates in Japan explains a large proportion of what is considered evidence in favour of the Solow model.

In Tables 9.4 and 9.5 we present estimates of the model (13) and (13′) for the five subsamples chosen. The exclusion of Turkey and Greece (column 1) generates a substantial increase in the convergence rate to 2.6, which is 30% higher than for the OECD as a whole. Notice that these two countries have been permanently at the bottom in the OECD

Table 9.4   Subsamples: models of conditional convergence

	1	2	3	4	5
B_2	−4.16	−7.36	−3.37	−7.13	1.85
	(1.95)	(3.87)	(1.16)	(5.53)	(1.13)
α	0.36	0.27	0.33	0.29	0.06
	(4.19)	(2.43)	(3.65)	(4.11)	(0.41)
γ	0.19	0.38	0.20	0.35	0.05
	(1.93)	(3.86)	(1.95)	(5.58)	(0.36)
ϕ	0.017	0.023	0.013	0.023	0.01
	(1.90)	(1.93)	(1.82)	(2.77)	(1.66)
$\bar{R}_2$	0.831	0.673	0.771	0.832	0.876
σ	0.104	0.121	0.083	0.087	0.081
β_{imp}	0.453	0.35	0.477	0.36	0.89
$\lambda_{imp}(\phi = 0.02)$	0.026	0.021	0.027	0.022	0.051
$\lambda_{imp}(\phi)$	0.025	0.022	0.024	0.021	0.046

Notes: * Restricted parameter.
Col. 1:   excluding Turkey and Greece.
Col. 2:   excluding the seven richest countries in 1960.
Col. 3:   excluding the seven poorest countries in 1960.
Col. 4:   excluding the seven richest countries in 1990.
Col. 5:   excluding the seven poorest countries in 1990.
Dependent variable log (Y_{90}^i / Y_{60}^i). Sample i: 1, ..., 24. Estimation method: non-linear least squares.

ranking for per capita income. Hence, an alternative way of looking at this issue is to split the sample in the way we do in columns 2 and 3. We first exclude[16] from the sample the seven richest countries[17] in 1960 (column 2) and then the seven poorest[18] (column 3). A careful look at the estimates reveals some striking differences. First, the parameter estimates are rather different, in particular B_2, γ and, to a lesser extent, ϕ. Differences in B_2 and γ are consistent with the technological non-convexity argument discussed earlier. In particular the sharp difference in the constant term B_2 among the poorest and the richest countries is largely consistent with the notion that the latter have enjoyed a higher level of efficiency per worker (A_0):[19]

$$B_2^P = \ln A_0^P < B_2^R = \ln A_0^R$$

Surprisingly, though, the rest of the model seems rather stable to this particular sample split. In particular, the estimated factor share for

Table 9.5   Subsamples: models of absolute convergence

	1	2	3	4	5
B_2	2.55	3.52	2.46	2.97	2.47
	(25.6)	(4.07)	(34.5)	(6.65)	(52.6)
$(\alpha + \gamma)$	0.52	0.84	0.29	0.80	0.14
	(5.17)	(10.2)	(1.28)	(10.5)	(0.820)
ϕ	0.02^*	0.02^*	0.02^*	0.02^*	0.02^*
$\bar{R}^2$	0.711	0.093	0.657	0.272	0.890
σ	0.136	0.201	0.101	0.182	0.077
β_{imp}	0.48	0.160	0.71	0.20	0.86
λ_{imp}	0.028	0.009	0.041	0.011	0.049

Notes: * Restricted parameter.
Col. 1:   excluding Turkey and Greece.
Col. 2:   excluding the seven richest countries in 1960.
Col. 3:   excluding the seven poorest countries in 1960.
Col. 4:   excluding the seven richest countries in 1990.
Col. 5:   excluding the seven poorest countries in 1990.
Dependent variable log $(\hat{y}_{90}/Y_{60}^i)$. Sample i: 1, ..., 24. Estimation method: non-linear least squares.

physical capital is similar in columns 2 and 3, and close to the point estimates obtained for the OECD as a whole. However, there is a significant difference in the human capital parameter, which affects the implicit convergence rate. Finally, the overall fit of the convergence equation is consistently better for the group of more advanced countries; this is a common feature which we shall find in alternative specifications and which we shall discuss later.

Some of these results carry over to the split based on 1990 relative wealth.[20] Comparisons between the rankings in 1960 and 1990 suggest that there is some mobility between countries (which is the case for Japan, UK and New Zealand) but also some signs of persistence (some of the richest countries in 1960 are also the richest ones in 1990 and the same for some of the poorest countries). In this case, columns (4) and (5), both the parameter set and the overall fit, are very different across subsamples. The high rate of convergence among the rich countries is not surprising and may be criticized on the basis of sample selection. If homogeneity is measured as the final achievement (per capita income in 1990) we find faster intragroup convergence, whereas if homogeneity is measured at the starting point this is no longer the case. The split based on initial per capita income is not free of criticism. Similar per capita